Mike Holt's Illustrated Guide to

Understanding NEC® Requirements for GROUNDING vs. BONDING

Based on the 2011 NEC®

Mike Holt Enterprises, Inc.
888.NEC.CODE (632.2633) • www.MikeHolt.com • Info@MikeHolt.com

NOTICE TO THE READER

Mike Holt's Illustrated Guide to Understanding NEC® Requirements for Grounding vs. Bonding

First Printing: December 2010

Technical Illustrator: Mike Culbreath
Cover Design: Madalina Iordache-Levay
Layout Design and Typesetting: Cathleen Kwas

ISBN 978-1-932685-83-1

For more information, call 888.NEC.CODE (632.2633), or E-mail Info@MikeHolt.com.

I dedicate this book to the
Lord Jesus Christ,
my mentor and teacher.
Proverbs 16:3

One Team

To Our Instructors and Students:

We're committed to providing you the finest product with the fewest errors, but we're realistic and know that there'll be errors found and reported after the printing of this book. The last thing we want is for you to have problems finding, communicating, or accessing this information. It's unacceptable to us for there to be even one error in our textbooks or answer keys. For this reason, we're asking you to work together with us as One Team.

Students: Please report any errors you may find to your instructor.
Instructors: Please communicate these errors to us by sending an email to corrections@mikeholt.com.

Our Commitment:

We'll continue to list all of the corrections that come through for all of our textbooks and answer keys on our Website. The most up-to-date answer keys will always be available to instructors to download from our instructor Website. We don't want you to have problems finding this updated information, so we're outlining where to go for all of this below:

To view textbook and answer key corrections: Students and instructors go to our Website, www.MikeHolt.com, click on "Books" in the sidebar of links, and then click on "Corrections."

To download the most up-to-date answer keys: Instructors go to our Website, www.MikeHolt.com, click on "Instructors" in the sidebar of links and then click on "Answer Keys." On this page you'll find instructions for accessing and downloading these answer keys.

If you're not registered as an instructor you'll need to register. Your registration will be sent to our educational director who in turn will review and approve your registration. In your approval E-mail will be the login and password so you can have access to all of the answer keys. If you have a situation that needs immediate attention, please contact the office directly at 888.NEC.CODE (632.2633).

Call 888.NEC.CODE (632.2633) or visit us online at www.MikeHolt.com

Table of Contents

Introduction

Mike Holt's Illustrated Guide to Understanding NEC Requirements for Grounding vs. Bonding

This textbook covers the Grounding and Bonding requirements contained in the *National Electrical Code*. Grounding is the most important and least understood article in the *NEC*, and surveys have repeatedly shown that the majority of electrical shocks and power quality problems are due to improper grounding or bonding. The writing style of this textbook, and in all of Mike Holt's products, is meant to be informative, practical, useful, informal, easy to read, and applicable for today's electrical professional. Also, just like all of Mike Holt's textbooks, it contains hundreds of full-color illustrations to help you see the safety requirements of the *National Electrical Code* in practical use, as they apply to today's electrical installations.

This illustrated textbook contains cautions regarding possible conflicts or confusing *NEC* requirements, tips on proper electrical installations, and warnings of dangers related to improper electrical installations. In spite of this effort, some rules may seem to be unclear or need additional editorial improvement.

We can't eliminate confusing, conflicting, or controversial *Code* requirements, but we do try to put them into sharper focus to help you understand their intended purpose. Sometimes a requirement is so confusing nobody really understands its actual application. When this occurs, this textbook will point the situation out in an upfront and straightforward manner. We apologize in advance if that ever seems disrespectful, but our intention is to help the industry understand the current *NEC* as best as possible, point out areas that need refinement, and encourage *Code* users to be a part of the change process that creates a better *NEC* for the future.

The *Code* is updated every three years to accommodate new electrical products and materials, changing technologies, and improved installation techniques, and to make editorial refinements to improve readability and application. While the uniform adoption of each new edition of the *NEC* is the best approach for all involved in the electrical industry, many inspection jurisdictions modify the *Code* when it's adopted. In addition, the *NEC* allows the authority having jurisdiction, typically the "Electrical Inspector," the flexibility to waive specific *Code* requirements, and to permit alternative wiring methods contrary to the *NEC* requirements. This is only allowed when he or she is assured the completed electrical installation is equivalent in establishing and maintaining effective safety [90.4].

Keeping up with the *Code* should be the goal of everyone involved in the safety of electrical installations. This includes electrical installers, contractors, owners, inspectors, engineers, instructors, and others concerned with electrical installations.

About the 2011 *NEC*

The actual process of changing the *Code* takes about two years, and it involves thousands of individuals making an effort to have the *NEC* as current and accurate as possible. Let's review how this process works:

Step 1. Proposals—November, 2008. Anybody can submit a proposal to change the *Code* before the proposal closing date. Over 5,000 proposals were submitted to modify the 2011 *NEC*. Of these proposals, over 300 rules were revised that significantly effect the electrical industry. Some changes were editorial revisions, while others were more significant, such as new articles, sections, exceptions, and Informational Notes.

Step 2. *Code*-Making Panel(s) Review Proposals—January, 2009. All *Code* proposals were reviewed by *Code*-Making Panels. There were 19 panels in the 2011 *Code* process who voted to accept, reject, or modify them.

Step 3. Report on Proposals (ROP)—July, 2009. The voting of the *Code*-Making Panels on the proposals was published for public review in a document called the "Report on Proposals," frequently referred to as the "ROP."

Step 4. Public Comments—October, 2009. Once the ROP was available, public comments were submitted asking the *Code*-Making Panel members to revise their earlier actions on change proposals, based on new information. The closing date for "Comments" was October, 2009.

Step 5. Comments Reviewed by *Code* Panels—December, 2009. The *Code*-Making Panels met again to review, discuss, and vote on public comments.

Step 6. Report on Comments (ROC)—April, 2010. The voting on the "Comments" was published for public review in a document called the "Report on Comments," frequently referred to as the "ROC."

Step 7. Electrical Section—June, 2010. The NFPA Electrical Section discussed and reviewed the work of the *Code*-Making Panels. The Electrical Section developed recommendations on last-minute motions to revise the proposed *NEC* draft that would be presented at the NFPA annual meeting.

Step 8. NFPA Annual Meeting—June, 2010. The 2011 *NEC* was voted by the NFPA members to approve the action of the *Code*-Making Panels at the annual meeting, after a number of motions (often called "floor actions") were voted on.

Step 9. Standards Council Review Appeals and Approves the 2011 *NEC*—July, 2010. The NFPA Standards Council reviewed the record of the *Code*-making process and approved publication of the 2011 *NEC*.

Step 10. 2011 *NEC* Published—September, 2010. The 2011 *National Electrical Code* was published, following the NFPA Board of Directors review of appeals.

> **Author's Comment:** Proposals and comments can be submitted online at the NFPA Website (www.nfpa.org). From the homepage, click on "Codes and Standards" at the top of the page, then from the Codes and Standards page click on "Proposals and Comments" in the box on the right-hand side of the page. The deadline for proposals to create the 2014 *National Electrical Code* is November 5, 2011. If you would like to see something changed in the *Code*, you're encouraged to participate in the process.

The Scope of this Textbook

This textbook, Mike Holt's *Illustrated Guide to Understanding NEC Requirements for Grounding vs. Bonding*, covers the general installation requirements contained in the *NEC* from Article 90 through 820 that Mike considers to be of critical importance, and is based on the following conditions:

1. Power Systems and Voltage. All power-supply systems are assumed to be one of the following, unless identified otherwise:

2-wire, single-phase, 120V
3-wire, single-phase, 120/240V
4-wire, three-phase, 120/240V Delta
4-wire, three-phase, 120/208V or 277/480V Wye

2. Electrical Calculations. Unless the question or example specifies three-phase, they're based on a single-phase power supply. In addition, all amperage calculations are rounded to the nearest ampere in accordance with Section 220.5(B).

3. Conductor Material. Conductors are considered copper, unless aluminum is identified or specified.

4. Conductor Sizing. Conductors are sized based on a THHN/THWN copper conductor terminating on a 75°C terminal in accordance with 110.14(C), unless the question or example identifies otherwise.

5. Overcurrent Device. The term "overcurrent device" refers to a molded-case circuit breaker, unless specified otherwise. Where a fuse is specified, it's a single-element type fuse, also known as a "one-time fuse," unless the text specifies otherwise.

Grounding versus Bonding Library

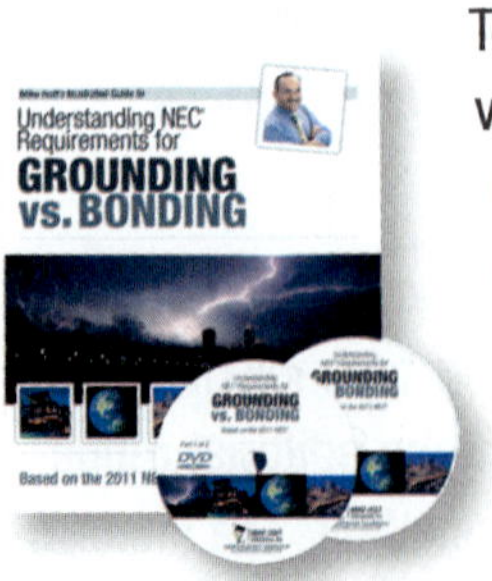

To get a better understanding of grounding versus bonding, order the DVDs and watch Mike and his Video Team explain this difficult to understand article. Order the 2011 ***Grounding versus Bonding*** DVDs by calling 888.NEC.CODE (632.2633).

About This Textbook

This textbook is to be used along with the *NEC*, not as a replacement for it, so be sure to have a copy of the 2011 *National Electrical Code* handy. Compare what Mike is explaining in this book to what the *Code* book says, and discuss any topics that you find difficult to understand with others.

You'll notice that in this book, a great deal of the *NEC* wording has been paraphrased, and some of the article and section titles appear different from the wording in the actual *Code*. Mike believes doing so makes it easier to understand the content of the rule, so keep this in mind when comparing this textbook against the actual *NEC*.

We hope that as you read through this textbook, you'll allow sufficient time to review the text along with the outstanding graphics and examples, which are invaluable to your understanding.

Textbook Format

This textbook follows the *NEC* format, but it doesn't cover every Code requirement. For example, it doesn't include every article, section, subsection, exception, or Informational Note. So don't be concerned if you see the textbook contain Exception 1 and Exception 3, but not Exception 2.

Important Changes for the 2011 Edition of This Textbook

In order to better meet the needs of our customers, we have improved the layout of this textbook. These changes include:

- Examples or practical application questions with their answer and solution have a light yellow background.
- Special Sections which contain additional information to better help you understand a concept are identified with a colored frame.
- Graphics that contain a 2011 *Code* change will have a green border with a green 2011 CC icon 2011 CC next to the heading.
- Any *NEC* changes in graphics will be in green underlined text. If you see a green bordered graphic with no green underlined text, it most likely indicates that the *Code* change is the removal of some text. Graphics without a color border support the concept being discussed, but nothing in the graphic was affected by a change for 2011.
- Any 2011 *Code* change is denoted by underlined text and in the corresponding chapter color. For example, in Chapter 1 the change text will be red and underlined; in Chapter 2 the change text will be cyan and underlined, and so on.

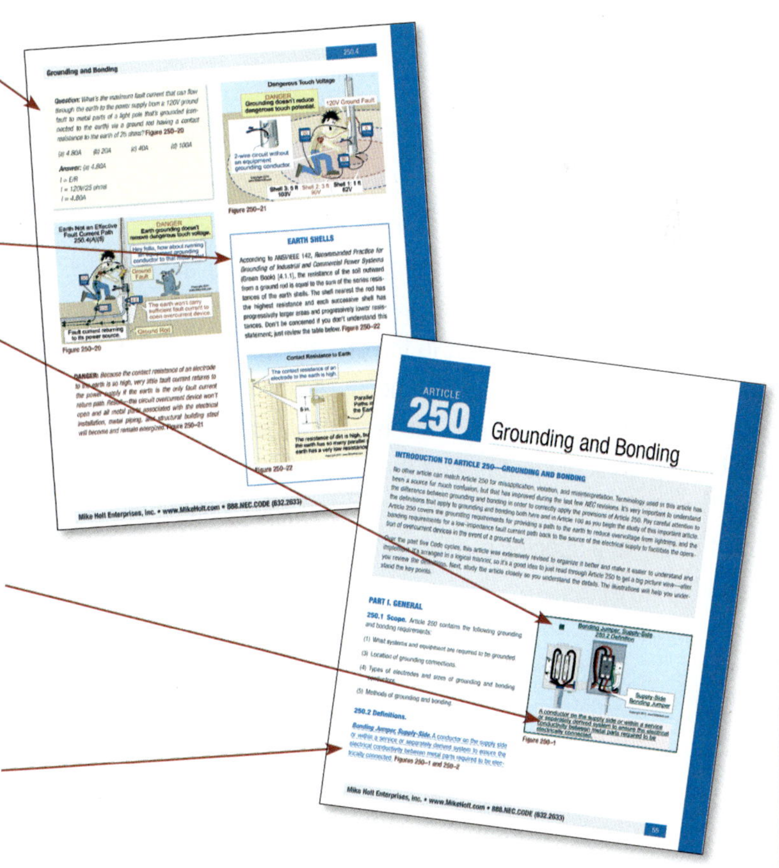

Cross-References and Author's Comments

Cross-References. This textbook contains several *NEC* cross-references to other related *Code* requirements to help you develop a better understanding of how the *NEC* rules relate to one another. These cross-references are indicated by *Code* section numbers in brackets, an example of which is "[90.4]."

Author's Comments. "Author's Comments," written by Mike, are intended to help you understand the *NEC* material, and to bring to your attention things of which you should be aware.

Difficult Concepts

As you progress through this textbook, you might find that you don't understand every explanation, example, calculation, or comment. Don't become frustrated, and don't get down on yourself. Remember, this is the *National Electrical Code* and sometimes the best attempt to explain a concept isn't enough to make it perfectly clear. If you're still confused, visit www.MikeHolt.com, and post your question on the *Code* Forum for help.

Different Interpretations

Some electricians, contractors, instructors, inspectors, engineers, and others enjoy the challenge of discussing the *NEC* requirements, hopefully in a positive and productive manner. This give-and-take is important to the process of better understanding the *Code* requirements and application. However, if you're going to get into an *NEC* discussion, please don't spout out what you think without having the actual *Code* book in your hand. The professional way of discussing an *NEC* requirement is by referring to a specific section, rather than talking in vague generalities.

Textbook Errors and Corrections

Humans develop the text, graphics, and layout of this textbook, and since currently none of us are perfect, there may be a few errors. This can occur because the *NEC* is dramatically changed each *Code* cycle; new articles are added, some are deleted, some are relocated, and many are renumbered. We take great care in researching the *NEC* requirements to ensure this textbook is correct. If you believe there's an error of any kind in this textbook (typographical, grammatical, technical, or anything else), no matter how insignificant, please let us know.

Any errors found after printing are listed on our Website, so if you find an error, first check to see if it's already been corrected. Go to www.MikeHolt.com, click on the "Books" link, and then the "Corrections" link (www.MikeHolt.com/bookcorrections.htm).

If you don't find the error listed on the Website, contact us by sending an E-mail to Corrections@MikeHolt.com. Be sure to include the book title, page number, and any other pertinent information.

How to Use the *National Electrical Code*

The *National Electrical Code* is written for persons who understand electrical terms, theory, safety procedures, and electrical trade practices. These individuals include electricians, electrical contractors, electrical inspectors, electrical engineers, designers, and other qualified persons. The *Code* isn't written to serve as an instructive or teaching manual for untrained individuals [90.1(C)].

Learning to use the *NEC* is like learning to play the game of chess; it's a great game if you enjoy mental warfare. When learning to play chess, you must first learn the names of the game pieces, how the pieces are placed on the board, and how each piece moves.

Once you understand the fundamentals, you're ready to start playing the game. Unfortunately, at this point all you can do is make crude moves, because you really don't understand how all the information works together. To play chess well, you'll need to learn how to use your knowledge by working on subtle strategies before you can work your way up to the more intriguing and complicated moves.

Not a Game

Electrical work isn't a game, and it must be taken very seriously. Learning the basics of electricity, important terms and concepts, as well as the basic layout of the *NEC* gives you just enough knowledge to be dangerous. There are thousands of specific and unique applications of electrical installations, and the *Code* doesn't cover every one of them. To safely apply the *NEC*, you must understand the purpose of a rule and how it affects the safety aspects of the installation.

NEC Terms and Concepts

The *NEC* contains many technical terms, so it's crucial for *Code* users to understand their meanings and their applications. If you don't understand a term used in a *Code* rule, it will be impossible to properly apply the *NEC* requirement. Be sure you understand that Article 100 defines the terms that apply to two or more *Code* articles. For example, the term "Dwelling Unit" is found in many articles; if you don't know what a dwelling unit is, how can you apply the requirements for it?

In addition, many articles have terms unique for that specific article and definitions of those terms are only applicable for that given article. For example, Section 250.2 contains the definitions of terms that only apply to Article 250—Grounding and Bonding.

Small Words, Grammar, and Punctuation

It's not only the technical words that require close attention, because even the simplest of words can make a big difference to the application of a rule. The word "or" can imply alternate choices for equipment wiring methods, while "and" can mean an additional requirement. Let's not forget about grammar and punctuation. The location of a comma (",") can dramatically change the requirement of a rule.

Slang Terms or Technical Jargon

Electricians, engineers, and other trade-related professionals use slang terms or technical jargon that isn't shared by all. This makes it very difficult to communicate because not everybody understands the intent or application of those slang terms. So where possible, be sure you use the proper word, and don't use a word if you don't understand its definition and application. For example, lots of electricians use the term "pigtail" when describing the short conductor for the connection of a receptacle, switch, luminaire, or equipment. Although they may understand it, not everyone does.

NEC Style and Layout

Before we get into the details of the *NEC*, we need to take a few moments to understand its style and layout. Understanding the structure and writing style of the *Code* is very important before it can be used and applied effectively. The *National Electrical Code* is organized into ten major components.

1. Table of Contents
2. Article 90 (Introduction to the *Code*)
3. Chapters 1 through 9 (major categories)
4. Articles 90 through 840 (individual subjects)
5. Parts (divisions of an article)
6. Sections and Tables (*Code* requirements)
7. Exceptions (*Code* permissions)
8. Informational Notes (explanatory material)
9. Annexes (information)
10. Index

1. Table of Contents. The Table of Contents displays the layout of the chapters, articles, and parts as well as the page numbers. It's an excellent resource and should be referred to periodically to observe the interrelationship of the various *NEC* components. When attempting to locate the rules for a particular situation, knowledgeable *Code* users often go first to the Table of Contents to quickly find the specific *NEC* Part that applies.

2. Introduction. The *NEC* begins with Article 90, the introduction to the *Code*. It contains the purpose of the *NEC*, what's covered and what isn't covered along with how the *Code* is arranged. It also gives information on enforcement and how mandatory and permissive rules are written as well as how explanatory material is included. Article 90 also includes information on formal interpretations, examination of equipment for safety, wiring planning, and information about formatting units of measurement.

3. Chapters. There are nine chapters, each of which is divided into articles. The articles fall into one of four groupings: General Requirements (Chapters 1 through 4), Specific Requirements (Chapters 5 through 7), Communications Systems (Chapter 8), and Tables (Chapter 9).

Chapter 1 General
Chapter 2 Wiring and Protection
Chapter 3 Wiring Methods and Materials
Chapter 4 Equipment for General Use
Chapter 5 Special Occupancies
Chapter 6 Special Equipment
Chapter 7 Special Conditions
Chapter 8 Communications Systems (Telephone, Data, Satellite, Cable TV and Broadband)
Chapter 9 Tables–Conductor and Raceway Specifications

4. Articles. The *NEC* contains approximately 140 articles, each of which covers a specific subject. For example:

Article 110 General Requirements
Article 250 Grounding and Bonding
Article 300 Wiring Methods
Article 430 Motors and Motor Controllers
Article 500 Hazardous (Classified) Locations
Article 680 Swimming Pools, Fountains, and Similar Installations
Article 725 Remote-Control, Signaling, and Power-Limited Circuits
Article 800 Communications Circuits

5. Parts. Larger articles are subdivided into parts.

Because the parts of a *Code* article aren't included in the section numbers, we have a tendency to forget what "part" the *NEC* rule is relating to. For example, Table 110.34(A) contains working space clearances for electrical equipment. If we aren't careful, we might think this table applies to all electrical installations, but Table 110.34(A) is located in Part III, which only contains requirements for "Over 600 Volts, Nominal installations." The rules for working clearances for electrical equipment for systems 600V, nominal, or less are contained in Table 110.26(A)(1), which is located in Part II—600 Volts, Nominal, or Less.

6. Sections and Tables.

Sections. Each *NEC* rule is called a "*Code* Section." A *Code* section may be broken down into subsections by letters in parentheses (A), (B), and so on. Numbers in parentheses (1), (2), and so forth, may further break down a subsection, and lowercase letters (a), (b), and so on, further break the rule down to the third level. For example, the rule requiring all receptacles in a dwelling unit bathroom to be GFCI protected is contained in Section 210.8(A)(1). Section 210.8(A)(1) is located in Chapter 2, Article 210, Section 8, Subsection (A), Sub-subsection (1).

Many in the industry incorrectly use the term "Article" when referring to a *Code* section. For example, they say "Article 210.8," when they should say "Section 210.8." Section numbers in this book are shown without the word "Section," unless they begin a sentence. For example, Section 210.8(A) is shown as simply 210.8(A).

Tables. Many *Code* requirements are contained within tables, which are lists of *NEC* requirements placed in a systematic arrangement. The titles of the tables are extremely important; you must read them carefully in order to understand the contents, applications, limitations, and so forth, of each table in the *Code.* Many times notes are provided in or below a table; be sure to read them as well since they're also part of the requirement. For example, Note 1 for Table 300.5 explains how to measure the cover when burying cables and raceways, and Note 5 explains what to do if solid rock is encountered.

7. Exceptions. Exceptions are *Code* requirements or permissions that provide an alternative method to a specific requirement. There are two types of exceptions—mandatory and permissive. When a rule has several exceptions, those exceptions with mandatory requirements are listed before the permissive exceptions.

Mandatory Exceptions. A mandatory exception uses the words "shall" or "shall not." The word "shall" in an exception means that if you're using the exception, you're required to do it in a particular way. The phrase "shall not" means it isn't permitted.

Permissive Exceptions. A permissive exception uses words such as "shall be permitted," which means it's acceptable (but not mandatory) to do it in this way.

8. Informational Notes. An Informational Note contains explanatory material intended to clarify a rule or give assistance, but it isn't a *Code* requirement.

9. Annexes. Annexes aren't a part of the *NEC* requirements, and are included in the *Code* for informational purposes only.

Annex A. Product Safety Standards
Annex B. Application Information for Ampacity Calculation
Annex C. Raceway Fill Tables for Conductors and Fixture Wires of the Same Size
Annex D. Examples
Annex E. Types of Construction
Annex F. Critical Operations Power Systems (COPS)
Annex G. Supervisory Control and Data Acquisition (SCADA)
Annex H. Administration and Enforcement
Annex I. Recommended Tightening Torques

10. Index. The Index at the back of the *NEC* is helpful in locating a specific rule.

Changes to the *NEC* since the previous edition(s), are identified by shading, but rules that have been relocated aren't identified as a change. A bullet symbol "•" is located on the margin to indicate the location of a rule that was deleted from a previous edition. New articles contain a vertical line in the margin of the page.

How to Locate a Specific Requirement

How to go about finding what you're looking for in the *Code* depends, to some degree, on your experience with the *NEC. Code* experts typically know the requirements so well they just go to the correct rule without any outside assistance. The Table of Contents might be the only thing very experienced *NEC* users need to locate the requirement they're looking for. On the other hand, average *Code* users should use all of the tools at their disposal, including the Table of Contents and the Index.

Table of Contents. Let's work out a simple example: What *NEC* rule specifies the maximum number of disconnects permitted for a service? If you're an experienced *Code* user, you'll know Article 230 applies to "Services," and because this article is so large, it's divided up into multiple parts (actually eight parts). With this knowledge, you can quickly go to the Table of Contents and see it lists the Service Equipment Disconnecting Means requirements in Part VI.

Author's Comment: The number 70 precedes all page numbers because the *NEC* is NFPA Standard Number 70.

Index. If you use the Index, which lists subjects in alphabetical order, to look up the term "service disconnect," you'll see there's no listing. If you try "disconnecting means," then "services," you'll find that the Index specifies that the rule is located in Article 230, Part VI. Because the *NEC* doesn't give a page number in the Index, you'll need to use the Table of Contents to find the page number, or flip through the *Code* to Article 230, then continue to flip through pages until you find Part VI.

Many people complain that the *NEC* only confuses them by taking them in circles. As you gain experience in using the *Code* and deepen your understanding of words, terms, principles, and practices, you'll find the *NEC* much easier to understand and use than you originally thought.

Customizing Your *Code* Book

One way to increase your comfort level with the *Code* is to customize it to meet your needs. You can do this by highlighting and underlining important *NEC* requirements, and by attaching tabs to important pages. Be aware that if you're using your *Code* book to take an exam, some exam centers don't allow markings of any type.

Highlighting. As you read through this textbook, be sure you highlight those requirements in the *Code* that are the most important or relevant to you. Use yellow for general interest and orange for important requirements you want to find quickly. Be sure to highlight terms in the Index and the Table of Contents as you use them.

Underlining. Underline or circle key words and phrases in the *NEC* with a red pen (not a lead pencil) and use a 6-inch ruler to keep lines straight and neat. This is a very handy way to make important requirements stand out. A small 6-inch ruler also comes in handy for locating specific information in the many *Code* tables.

Tabbing the *NEC*. By placing tabs on *Code* articles, sections, and tables, it will make it easier for you to use the *NEC*. However, too many tabs will defeat the purpose. You can order a set of *Code* tabs designed by Mike Holt online at www.MikeHolt.com, or by calling 888.NEC.CODE (888.632.5633).

About the Author

Mike Holt

Mike Holt worked his way up through the electrical trade from an apprentice electrician to become one of the most recognized experts in the world as it relates to electrical power installations. He has worked as a journeyman electrician, master electrician, and electrical contractor. Mike's experience in the real world gives him a unique understanding of how the *NEC* relates to electrical installations from a practical standpoint. You'll find his writing style to be direct, nontechnical, and practical.

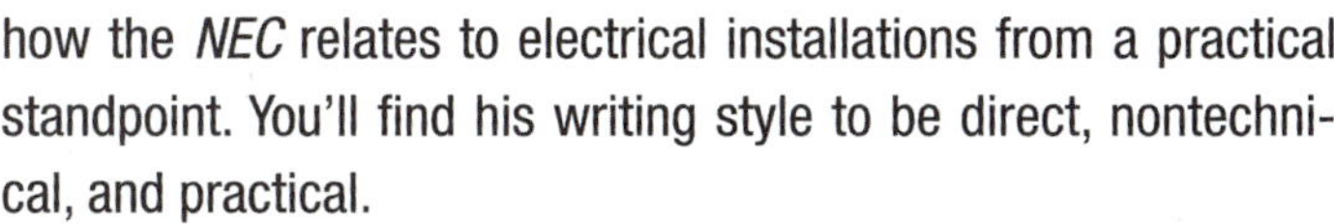

Did you know that he didn't finish high school? So if you struggled in high school or if you didn't finish it at all, don't let this get you down, you're in good company. As a matter of fact, Mike Culbreath, master electrician, who produces the finest electrical graphics in the history of the electrical industry, didn't finish high school either. So two high school dropouts produced the text and graphics in this textbook! However, realizing success depends on one's continuing pursuit of education. Mike immediately attained his GED (as did Mike Culbreath) and ultimately attended the University of Miami's Graduate School for a Master's degree in Business Administration (MBA).

Mike Holt resides in Central Florida, is the father of seven children, and has many outside interests and activities. He's a six-time National Barefoot Water-Ski Champion (1988, 1999, 2005, 2006, 2007, and 2008), has set many national records, has competed in three World Championships (2006, 2008, and 2010) and continues to train and work out year-round so that he can qualify to ski in the 2012 World Barefoot Championships at the age of 61!

What sets him apart from some, is his commitment to living a balanced lifestyle; placing God first, family, career, then self.

Special Acknowledgments

First, I want to thank God for my godly wife who's always by my side and my children, Belynda, Melissa, Autumn, Steven, Michael, Meghan, and Brittney.

A special thank you must be sent to the staff at the National Fire Protection Association (NFPA), publishers of the *NEC*—in particular Jeff Sargent for his assistance in answering my many *Code* questions over the years. Jeff, you're a "first class" guy, and I admire your dedication and commitment to helping others understand the *NEC*. Other former NFPA staff members I would like to thank include John Caloggero, Joe Ross, and Dick Murray for their help in the past.

A personal thank you goes to Sarina, my long-time friend and office manager. It's been wonderful working side-by-side with you for over 25 years nurturing this company's growth from its small beginnings.

About the Graphic Illustrator

Mike Culbreath

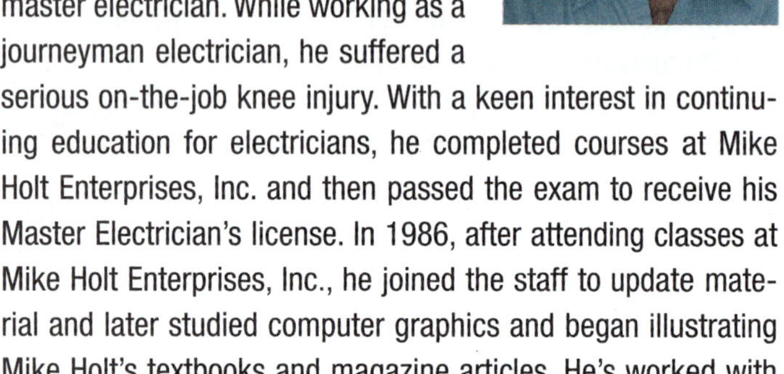

Mike Culbreath devoted his career to the electrical industry and worked his way up from an apprentice electrician to master electrician. While working as a journeyman electrician, he suffered a serious on-the-job knee injury. With a keen interest in continuing education for electricians, he completed courses at Mike Holt Enterprises, Inc. and then passed the exam to receive his Master Electrician's license. In 1986, after attending classes at Mike Holt Enterprises, Inc., he joined the staff to update material and later studied computer graphics and began illustrating Mike Holt's textbooks and magazine articles. He's worked with the company for almost 25 years and, as Mike Holt has proudly acknowledged, has helped to transform his words and visions into lifelike graphics.

Special Acknowledgments

I want to thank my wonderful children, Dawn and Mac, who have had to put up with me during the *Code* revision seasons.

I would like to thank Steve Arne, our amazing technical editorial director, Eric Stromberg, an electrical engineer and super geek (and I mean that in the most complimentary manner, this guy is brilliant), and Ryan Jackson, an outstanding and very knowledgeable code guy, for helping me keep our graphics as technically correct as possible.

I would like to give a special thank you to Cathleen Kwas for making me look good with her outstanding layout design and typesetting skills. I would also like to acknowledge Belynda Holt Pinto, our Chief Operations Officer and the rest of the outstanding staff at Mike Holt Enterprises, for all the hard work they do to help produce and distribute these outstanding products.

And last but not least, I need to give a special thank you to Mike Holt for not firing me about 25 years ago when I "borrowed" one of his computers and took it home to begin the process of learning how to do computer illustrations. He gave me the opportunity and time needed to develop my computer graphic skills. He has been an amazing friend and mentor since I met him as a student many years ago. Thanks for believing in me and allowing me to be part of the Mike Holt Enterprises family.

Mike Holt Enterprises Team

Editorial Team

I want to thank **Toni Culbreath** and **Barbara Parks** who worked tirelessly to proofread and edit the final stages of this publication. Their attention to detail and dedication to this project is greatly appreciated.

Production Team

I want to thank **Cathleen Kwas** who did the layout and production of this book. Her desire to create the best possible product for our customers is greatly appreciated.

Video Team Members

The following special persons provided assistance in the development of this textbook; particularly in ensuring that the technical content is accurate. In addition, they all provided outstanding technical advice as they served on the video team along with author Mike Holt and a guest appearance by graphic illustrator Mike Culbreath.

Steve Arne
Technical Training Consultant
Arne Electro Tech
Rapid City, SD
ElectricalMaster.com

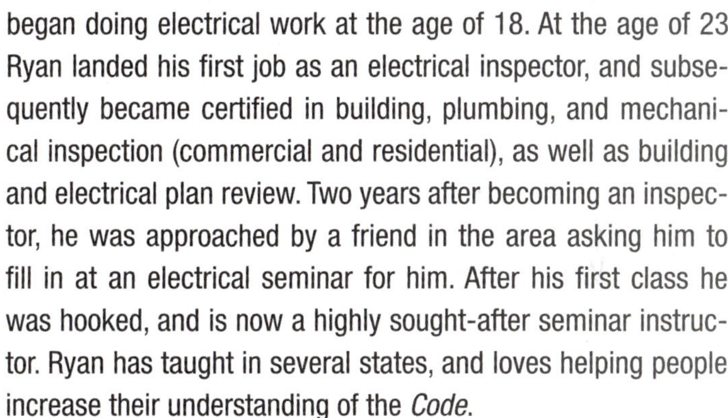

Steve Arne has been involved in the electrical industry since 1974 working in various positions from electrician to full-time instructor and department chair in technical postsecondary education. Steve has developed curriculum for many electrical training courses and has developed university business and leadership courses. Currently, Steve offers occasional exam prep and continuing education *Code* classes. Steve enjoys helping others as they learn and experience new insights. His goal is to help others understand more of the technological marvels that surround us. Steve thanks God for the wonders of His creation and for the opportunity to share it with others.

Steve and his lovely wife Deb live in Rapid City, South Dakota where they're both active in their church and community. They have two grown children and five grandchildren.

Ryan Jackson
Electrical Inspector
Draper City, Ut
West Valley City, UT

Ryan Jackson is a combination inspector in the Salt Lake City, Utah, area. He began doing electrical work at the age of 18. At the age of 23 Ryan landed his first job as an electrical inspector, and subsequently became certified in building, plumbing, and mechanical inspection (commercial and residential), as well as building and electrical plan review. Two years after becoming an inspector, he was approached by a friend in the area asking him to fill in at an electrical seminar for him. After his first class he was hooked, and is now a highly sought-after seminar instructor. Ryan has taught in several states, and loves helping people increase their understanding of the *Code*.

In 2005, Ryan met Mike Holt in Salt Lake City, and they became friends immediately. He helped Mike with his *Understanding the NEC, Volume 2* videos and began editing his books as well. Ryan believes that there are only a small handful of opportunities that change a person's life and career, and meeting Mike was one of them.

Ryan can often be found in his garage turning wood on his lathe, and in the autumn you'll find him at as many University of Utah football games as he can attend, which is typically all of them. Ryan married his high school sweetheart, Sharie, and they have two beautiful children together: Kaitlynn and Aaron.

Scott Harding
Electrical Contractor,
F.B. Harding, Inc.
Rockville, MD
http://fbharding.com

Scott Harding began his electrical career as an electrician's helper working part time in the family business. After graduating with an Electrical Engineering degree from Clemson University, he worked as an electrical engineer for RTKL Associates, a large design firm located in Baltimore, MD.

After leaving RTKL, Scott went to work at F.B. Harding, Inc. an electrical contractor located in Rockville, MD where he's been for the last 19 years. He's a licensed master electrician in multiple jurisdictions and is the current President and CEO of F.B. Harding, Inc., making the family business a third generation company.

Scott also serves on the *NEC Code*-Making Panel Number 5 (Grounding and Bonding) and worked on the 2005 and 2008 cycles.

Eric Stromberg
Electrical Engineer/Instructor
Stromberg Engineering, Inc.
Lake Jackson, TX
www.strombergengineering.com

Eric Stromberg started in the Electrical field by working as a journeyman electrician for a small contractor in the Houston area while going to college pursuing a degree in Electrical Engineering. After graduation, in 1982, Eric worked as an electronic technician where he installed and maintained life safety control systems in high rise buildings. In 1989, Eric went to work for Dow Chemical where he designed power distribution systems for major industrial complexes in the U.S., Spain, Brazil, and Germany. Eric was very involved in both creating Electrical standards and procedures as well as checking existing standards and procedures for alignment with national standards.

He also worked as a Construction Manager where he ensured *Code* compliancy of installations as well as provided field engineering support. Eric currently has his own business and spends a good deal of time teaching classes in both the *National Electrical Code* and electrical circuits. He is also a member of the Electrical Safety and Licensing Advisory Board for the State of Texas.

Eric lives in Lake Jackson, Texas, with his wife Jane. They have three children: Ainsley, Austin, and Brieanna. Ainsley is a teacher in Boston who will be getting married in the summer of 2011. Austin will be enlisting in the Air Force, and Brieanna will be starting college in the Fall of 2010.

Introduction to the *National Electrical Code*

INTRODUCTION TO ARTICLE 90—INTRODUCTION TO THE *NATIONAL ELECTRICAL CODE*

Many *NEC* violations and misunderstandings wouldn't occur if people doing the work simply understood Article 90. For example, many people see *Code* requirements as performance standards. In fact, the *NEC* requirements are bare minimums for safety. This is exactly the stance electrical inspectors, insurance companies, and courts take when making a decision regarding electrical design or installation.

Article 90 opens by saying the *NEC* isn't intended as a design specification or instruction manual. The *National Electrical Code* has one purpose only, and that's the "practical safeguarding of persons and property from hazards arising from the use of electricity." It goes on to indicate that the *Code* isn't intended as a design specification or instruction manual. The necessity to carefully study the *NEC* rules can't be overemphasized, and the role of textbooks such as this one are to help in that undertaking. Understanding where to find the rules in the *Code* that apply to the installation is invaluable. Rules in several different articles often apply to even a simple installation.

Article 90 then describes the scope and arrangement of the *NEC*. A person who says, "I can't find anything in the *Code*," is really saying, "I never took the time to review Article 90." The balance of Article 90 provides the reader with information essential to understanding those items you do find in the *NEC*.

Typically, electrical work requires you to understand the first four chapters of the *Code* which apply generally, plus have a working knowledge of the Chapter 9 tables. That knowledge begins with Article 90. Chapters 5, 6, and 7 make up a large portion of the *NEC*, but they apply to special occupancies, special equipment, or other special conditions. They build on, modify, or amend the rules in the first four chapters. Chapter 8 contains the requirements for communications systems, such as telephone systems, antenna wiring, CATV, and network-powered broadband systems. Communications systems aren't subject to the general requirements of Chapters 1 through 4, or the special requirements of Chapters 5 through 7, unless there's a specific reference in Chapter 8 to a rule in Chapters 1 through 7.

90.1 Purpose of the *NEC*.

(A) Practical Safeguarding. The purpose of the *NEC* is to ensure that electrical systems are installed in a manner that protects people and property by minimizing the risks associated with the use of electricity.

(B) Adequacy. The *Code* contains requirements considered necessary for a safe electrical installation. If an electrical installation is installed in compliance with the *NEC*, it will be essentially free from electrical hazards. The *Code* is a safety standard, not a design guide.

NEC requirements aren't intended to ensure the electrical installation will be efficient, convenient, adequate for good service, or suitable for future expansion. Specific items of concern, such as electrical energy management, maintenance, and power quality issues aren't within the scope of the *Code*. Figure 90-1

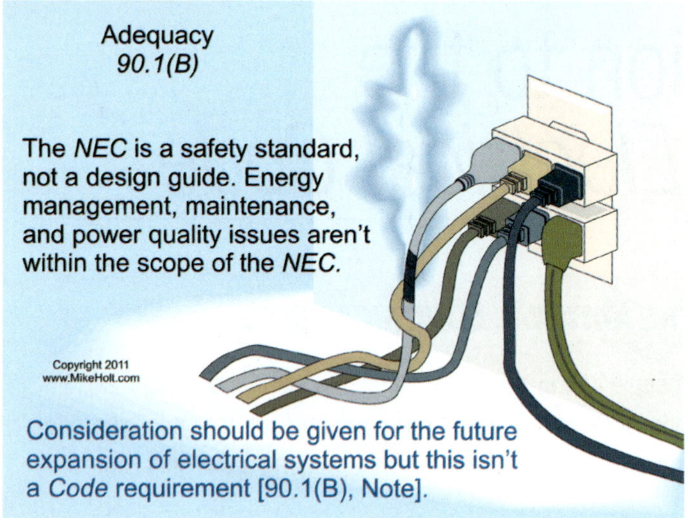

Figure 90-1

Note: Hazards in electrical systems often occur because circuits are overloaded or not properly installed in accordance with the *NEC.* These often occur if the initial wiring didn't provide reasonable provisions for system changes or for the increase in the use of electricity.

Author's Comments:

- See the definition of "Overload" in Article 100.
- The *Code* doesn't require electrical systems to be designed or installed to accommodate future loads. However, the electrical designer, typically an electrical engineer, is concerned with not only ensuring electrical safety (*NEC* compliance), but also with ensuring the system meets the customers' needs, both of today and in the near future. To satisfy customers' needs, electrical systems are often designed and installed above the minimum requirements contained in the *Code.* But just remember, if you're taking an exam, licensing exams are based on your understanding of the minimum *NEC* requirements.

(C) Intention. The *Code* is intended to be used by those skilled and knowledgeable in electrical theory, electrical systems, construction, and the installation and operation of electrical equipment. It isn't a design specification standard or instruction manual for the untrained and unqualified.

(D) Relation to International Standards. The requirements of the *NEC* address the fundamental safety principles contained in the International Electrotechnical Commission (IEC) standards, including protection against electric shock, adverse thermal effects, overcurrent, fault currents, and overvoltage. **Figure 90-2**

Figure 90-2

Author's Comments:

- See the definition of "Overcurrent" in Article 100.
- The *NEC* is used in Chile, Ecuador, Peru, and the Philippines. It's also the electrical code for Colombia, Costa Rica, Mexico, Panama, Puerto Rico, and Venezuela. Because of these adoptions, the *NEC* is available in Spanish from the National Fire Protection Association, 617.770.3000, or www.NFPA.Org.

90.2 Scope of the *NEC.*

(A) What is Covered. The *NEC* contains requirements necessary for the proper installation of electrical conductors, equipment, and raceways; signaling and communications conductors, equipment, and raceways; as well as optical fiber cables and raceways for the following locations: **Figure 90-3**

(1) Public and private premises, including buildings or structures, mobile homes, recreational vehicles, and floating buildings.

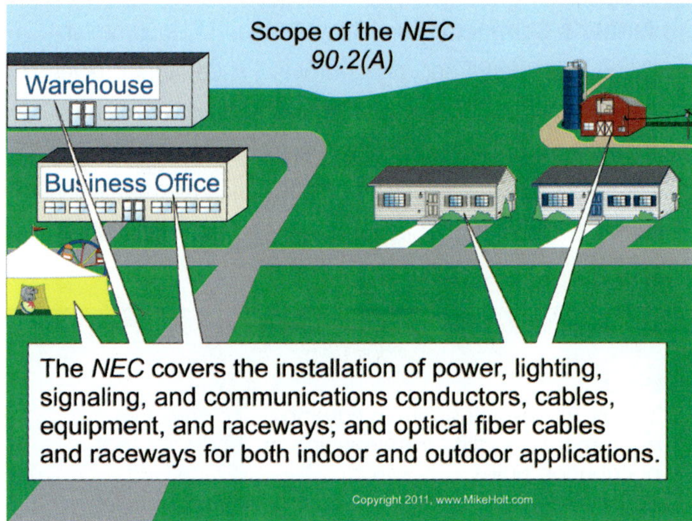

Figure 90-3

(2) Yards, lots, parking lots, carnivals, and industrial substations.

(3) Conductors and equipment connected to the utility supply.

(4) Installations used by an electric utility, such as office buildings, warehouses, garages, machine shops, recreational buildings, and other electric utility buildings that aren't an integral part of a utility's generating plant, substation, or control center. **Figure 90-4**

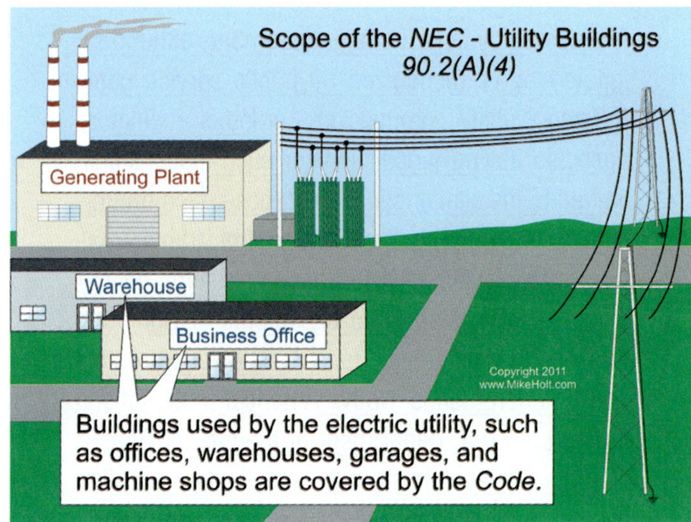

Figure 90-4

(B) What Isn't Covered. The *NEC* doesn't apply to:

(4) Communications Utilities. The installation requirements of the *Code* don't apply to communications (telephone), Community Antenna Television (CATV), or network-powered broadband utility equipment located in building spaces used exclusively for these purposes, or outdoors if the installation is under the exclusive control of the communications utility. **Figures 90-5 and 90-6**

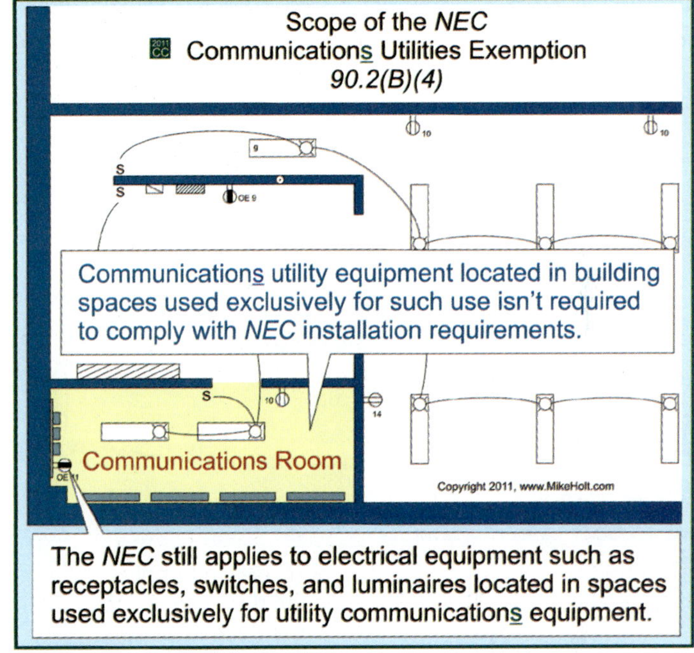

Figure 90-5

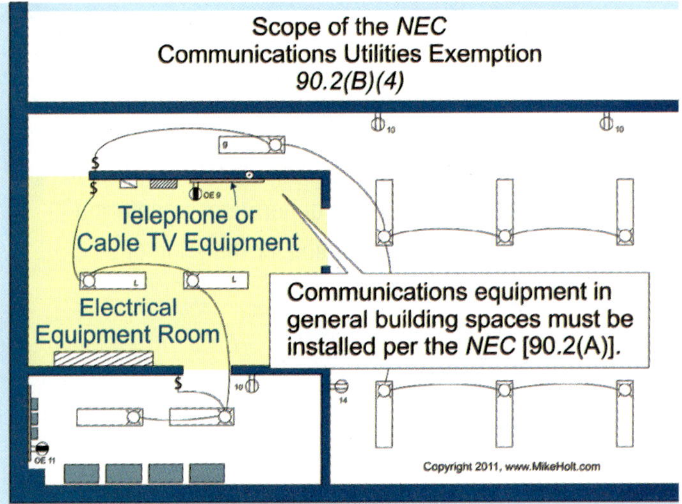

Figure 90-6

Author's Comment: Interior wiring for communications systems, not in building spaces used exclusively for these purposes, must be installed in accordance the the following Chapter 8 Articles:

- Telephone and Data, Article 800
- CATV, Article 820
- Network-Powered Broadband, Article 830

(5) Electric Utilities. The *NEC* doesn't apply to installations under the exclusive control of an electric utility where such installations:

a. Consist of service drops or service laterals and associated metering. **Figure 90-7**

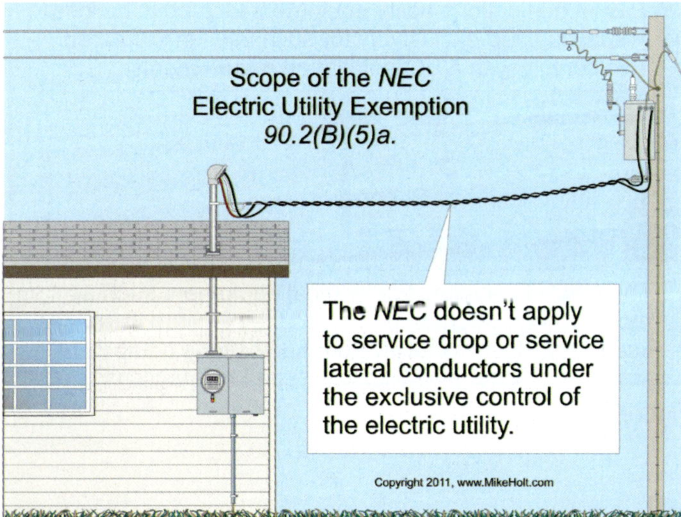

Figure 90-7

b. Are on property owned or leased by the electric utility for the purpose of generation, transformation, transmission, distribution, or metering of electric energy. **Figure 90-8**

Author's Comment: Luminaires located in legally established easements, or rights-of-way, such as at poles supporting transmission or distribution lines, are exempt from the *NEC*. However, if the electric utility provides site and public lighting on private property, then the installation must comply with the *Code* [90.2(A)(4)]. See **Figure 90–8**

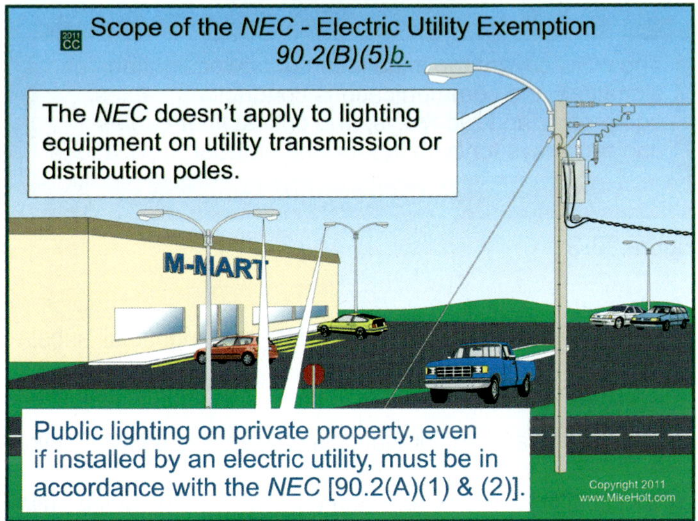

Figure 90-8

c. Are located on legally established easements, or rights-of-way. **Figure 90-9**

d. Are located by other written agreements either designated by or recognized by public service commissions, utility commissions, or other regulatory agencies having jurisdiction for such installations; limited to installations for the purpose of communications, metering, generation, control, transformation, transmission, or distribution of electric energy where legally established easements or rights-of-way can't be obtained. These installations are limited to federal lands, Native American reservations through the U.S. Department of the Interior Bureau of Indian Affairs, military bases, lands controlled by port authorities and state agencies and departments, and lands owned by railroads.

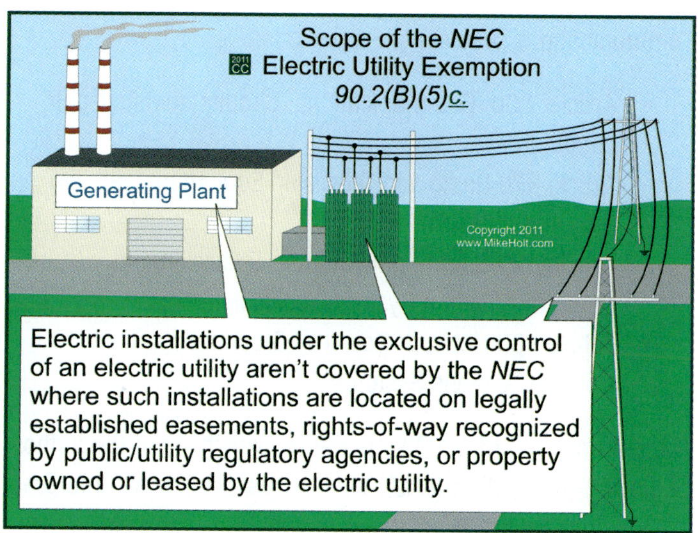

Figure 90-9

Note to 90.2(B)(4) and (5): Utilities include entities that install, operate, and maintain communications systems (telephone, CATV, Internet, satellite, or data services) or electric supply (generation, transmission, or distribution systems) and are designated or recognized by governmental law or regulation by public service/utility commissions. Utilities may be subject to compliance with codes and standards covering their regulated activities as adopted under governmental law or regulation.

90.3 *Code* Arrangement.

The *Code* is divided into an introduction and nine chapters. Figure 90-10

General Requirements. The requirements contained in Chapters 1, 2, 3, and 4 apply to all installations.

Author's Comment: These first four chapters may be thought of as the foundation for the rest of the *Code*, and are the main focus of this textbook.

Special Requirements. The requirements contained in Chapters 5, 6, and 7 apply to special occupancies, special equipment, or other special conditions. These chapters can supplement or modify the requirements in Chapters 1 through 4.

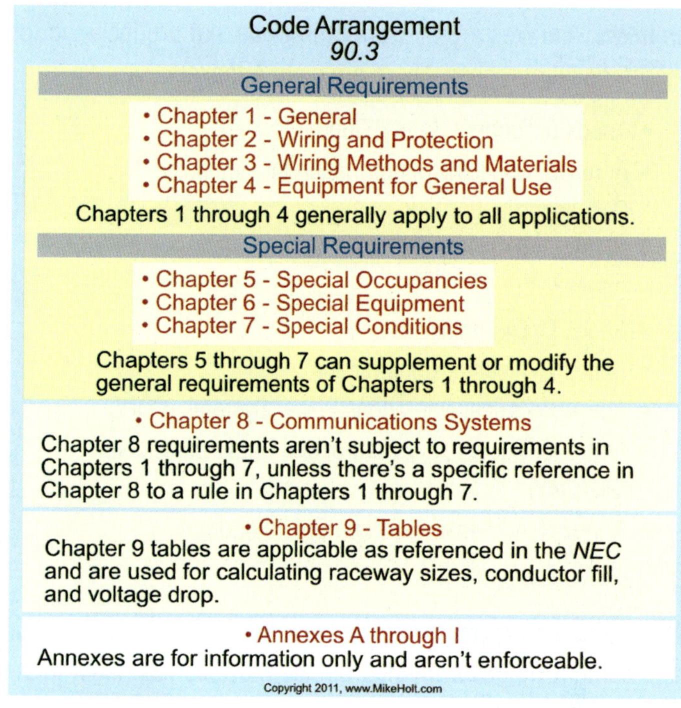

Figure 90–10

Communications Systems. Chapter 8 contains the requirements for communications systems, such as telephone systems, antenna wiring, CATV, and network-powered broadband systems. Communications systems aren't subject to the general requirements of Chapters 1 through 4, or the special requirements of Chapters 5 through 7, unless there's a specific reference in Chapter 8 to a rule in Chapters 1 through 7.

Author's Comment: An example of how Chapter 8 works is in the rules for working space about equipment. The typical 3 ft working space isn't required in front of communications equipment, because Table 110.26(A)(1) isn't referenced in Chapter 8.

Tables. Chapter 9 consists of tables applicable as referenced in the *NEC*. The tables are used to calculate raceway sizing, conductor fill, the radius of raceway bends, and conductor voltage drop.

Annexes. Annexes aren't part of the *Code*, but are included for informational purposes. There are eight Annexes:

- Annex A. Product Safety Standards
- Annex B. Application Information for Ampacity Calculation
- Annex C. Raceway Fill Tables for Conductors and Fixture Wires of the Same Size
- Annex D. Examples
- Annex E. Types of Construction
- Annex F. Critical Operations Power Systems (COPS)
- Annex G. Supervisory Control and Data Acquisition (SCADA)
- Annex H. Administration and Enforcement

90.4 Enforcement. The *Code* is intended to be suitable for enforcement by governmental bodies that exercise legal jurisdiction over electrical installations for power, lighting, signaling circuits, and communications systems, such as: Figure 90-11

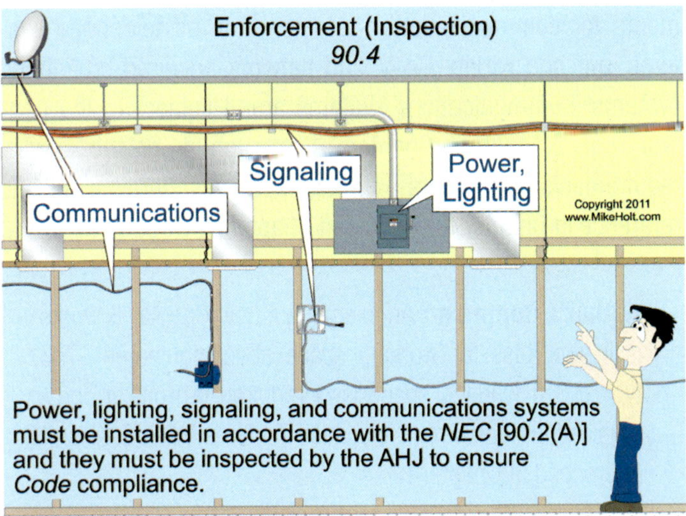

Figure 90–11

Signaling circuits which include:

- Article 725 Class 1, Class 2, and Class 3 Remote-Control, Signaling, and Power-Limited Circuits
- Article 760 Fire Alarm Systems
- Article 770 Optical Fiber Cables and Raceways

Communications systems which include:

- Article 800 Communications Circuits (twisted-pair conductors)
- Article 810 Radio and Television Equipment (satellite dish and antenna)
- Article 820 Community Antenna Television and Radio Distribution Systems (coaxial cable)
- Article 830 Network-Powered Broadband Communications Systems

The enforcement of the *NEC* is the responsibility of the authority having jurisdiction (AHJ), who is responsible for interpreting requirements, approving equipment and materials, waiving *Code* requirements, and ensuring equipment is installed in accordance with listing instructions.

> **Author's Comment:** See the definition of "Authority Having Jurisdiction" in Article 100.

Interpretation of the Requirements. The authority having jurisdiction is responsible for interpreting the *NEC*, but his or her decisions must be based on a specific *Code* requirement. If an installation is rejected, the authority having jurisdiction is legally responsible for informing the installer of which specific *NEC* rule was violated.

> **Author's Comment:** The art of getting along with the authority having jurisdiction consists of doing good work and knowing what the *Code* actually says (as opposed to what you only think it says). It's also useful to know how to choose your battles when the inevitable disagreement does occur.

Approval of Equipment and Materials. Only the authority having jurisdiction has authority to approve the installation of equipment and materials. Typically, the authority having jurisdiction will approve equipment listed by a product testing organization, such as Underwriters Laboratories, Inc. (UL). The *NEC* doesn't require all equipment to be listed, but many state and local AHJs do. See 90.7, 110.2, 110.3, and the definitions for "Approved," "Identified," "Labeled," and "Listed" in Article 100. Figure 90-12

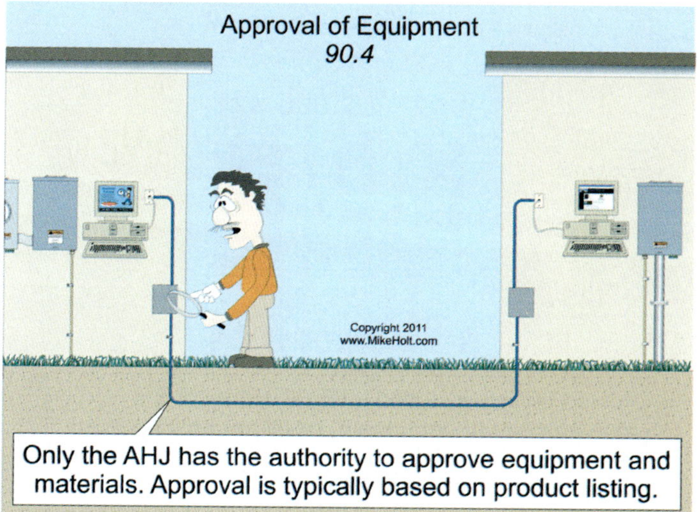

Figure 90–12

Author's Comment: According to the *NEC*, the authority having jurisdiction determines the approval of equipment. This means he or she can reject an installation of listed equipment and can approve the use of unlisted equipment. Given our highly litigious society, approval of unlisted equipment is becoming increasingly difficult to obtain.

Waiver of Requirements. By special permission, the authority having jurisdiction can waive specific requirements in the *Code* or permit alternative methods where it's assured equivalent safety can be achieved and maintained.

Author's Comment: Special permission is defined in Article 100 as the written consent of the authority having jurisdiction.

Waiver of New Product Requirements. If the 2011 *NEC* requires products that aren't yet available at the time the *Code* is adopted, the authority having jurisdiction can allow products that were acceptable in the previous *Code* to continue to be used.

Author's Comment: Sometimes it takes years before testing laboratories establish product standards for new *NEC* requirements, and then it takes time before manufacturers can design, manufacture, and distribute these products to the marketplace.

Compliance with Listing Instructions. It's the authority having jurisdiction's responsibility to ensure electrical equipment is installed in accordance with equipment listing and/or labeling instructions [110.3(B)]. In addition, the authority having jurisdiction can reject the installation of equipment modified in the field [90.7].

Author's Comment: The *NEC* doesn't address the maintenance of electrical equipment because the *Code* is an installation standard, not a maintenance standard. See NFPA 70B—*Recommended Practice for Electrical Equipment Maintenance.*

90.5 Mandatory Requirements and Explanatory Material.

(A) Mandatory Requirements. In the *NEC* the words "shall" or "shall not," indicate a mandatory requirement.

Author's Comment: For the ease of reading this textbook, the word "shall" has been replaced with the word "must," and the words "shall not" have been replaced with "must not." Remember that in many places, we'll paraphrase the *Code* instead of providing exact quotes, to make it easier to read and understand.

(B) Permissive Requirements. When the *Code* uses "shall be permitted" it means the identified actions are permitted but not required, and the authority having jurisdiction isn't permitted to restrict an installation from being done in that manner. A permissive rule is often an exception to the general requirement.

Author's Comment: For ease of reading, the phrase "shall be permitted," as used in the *Code*, has been replaced in this textbook with the phrase "is permitted" or "are permitted."

(C) Explanatory Material. References to other standards or sections of the *NEC*, or information related to a *Code* rule, are included in the form of Informational Notes. Such notes are for information only and aren't enforceable as a requirement of the *NEC*.

For example, Informational Note 4 in 210.19(A)(1) recommends that the voltage drop of a circuit not exceed 3 percent. This isn't a requirement; it's just a recommendation.

Author's Comment: For convenience and ease of reading, in this textbook, I will identify Informational Notes simply as "Note."

(D) Informative Annexes. Nonmandatory informative annexes contained in the back of the *Code* book are for information only and aren't enforceable as a requirement of the *NEC*.

90.6 Formal Interpretations. To promote uniformity of interpretation and application of the provisions of the *NEC*, formal interpretation procedures have been established and are found in the NFPA *Regulations Governing Committee Projects*.

Author's Comment: This is rarely done because it's a very time-consuming process, and formal interpretations from the NFPA aren't binding on the authority having jurisdiction.

90.7 Examination of Equipment for Product Safety. Product evaluation for safety is typically performed by a testing laboratory, which publishes a list of equipment that meets a nationally recognized test standard. Products and materials that are listed, labeled, or identified by a testing laboratory are generally approved by the authority having jurisdiction.

Author's Comment: See Article 100 for the definition of "Approved."

Listed, factory-installed, internal wiring and construction of equipment need not be inspected at the time of installation, except to detect alterations or damage [300.1(B)]. Figure 90-13

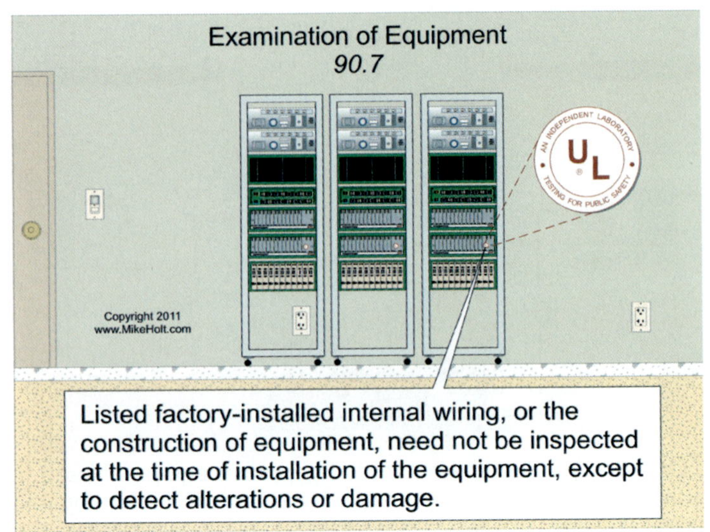

Figure 90–13

90.9 Units of Measurement.

(B) Dual Systems of Units. Both the metric and inch-pound measurement systems are shown in the *NEC*, with the metric units appearing first and the inch-pound system immediately following in parentheses.

Author's Comment: This is the standard practice in all NFPA standards, even though the U.S. construction industry uses inch-pound units of measurement. You will need to be cautious when using the tables in the *Code* because the additional units can make the tables more complex and more difficult to read.

(D) Compliance. Installing electrical systems in accordance with the metric system or the inch-pound system is considered to comply with the *Code*.

Author's Comment: Since compliance with either the metric or the inch-pound system of measurement constitutes compliance with the *NEC*, this textbook uses only inch-pound units.

ARTICLE

90 Practice Questions

ARTICLE 90. INTRODUCTION—PRACTICE QUESTIONS

1. *The NEC* is ______.

   (a) intended to be a design manual
   (b) meant to be used as an instruction guide for untrained persons
   (c) for the practical safeguarding of persons and property
   (d) published by the Bureau of Standards

2. Compliance with the provisions of the *NEC* will result in ______.

   (a) good electrical service
   (b) an efficient electrical system
   (c) an electrical system essentially free from hazard
   (d) all of these

3. The *Code* contains provisions considered necessary for safety, which will not necessarily result in ______.

   (a) efficient use
   (b) convenience
   (c) good service or future expansion of electrical use
   (d) all of these

4. Hazards often occur because of ______.

   (a) overloading of wiring systems by methods or usage not in conformity with the *NEC*
   (b) initial wiring not providing for increases in the use of electricity
   (c) a and b
   (d) none of these

5. The *Code* isn't a design specification standard or instruction manual for the untrained and unqualified.

   (a) True
   (b) False

6. The following system(s) shall be installed in accordance with the following *NEC* requirements: ______.

   (a) signaling
   (b) communications
   (c) electrical conductors, equipment, and raceways
   (d) all of these

7. The *NEC* applies to the installation of ______.

   (a) electrical conductors and equipment within or on public and private buildings
   (b) outside conductors and equipment on the premises
   (c) optical fiber cables
   (d) all of these

8. This *Code* covers the installation of ______ for public and private premises, including buildings, structures, mobile homes, recreational vehicles, and floating buildings.

   (a) optical fiber cables
   (b) electrical equipment
   (c) raceways
   (d) all of these

9. Installations of communications equipment that are under the exclusive control of communications utilities, and located outdoors or in building spaces used exclusively for such installations ______ covered by the *NEC*.

(a) are
(b) are sometimes
(c) are not
(d) may be

10. Electric utilities may include entities that install, operate, and maintain ______.

(a) communications systems (telephone, CATV, Internet, satellite, or data services)
(b) electric supply systems (generation, transmission, or distribution systems)
(c) local area network wiring on the premises
(d) a or b

11. Utilities may be subject to compliance with codes and standards covering their regulated activities as adopted under governmental law or regulation.

(a) True
(b) False

12. Utilities may include entities that are designated or recognized by governmental law or regulation by public service/utility commissions.

(a) True
(b) False

13. The *NEC* does not apply to electric utility-owned wiring and equipment ______.

(a) installed by an electrical contractor
(b) installed on public property
(c) consisting of service drops installed by a utility
(d) in a utility office building

14. Chapters 1 through 4 of the *NEC* apply ______.

(a) generally to all electrical installations
(b) only to special occupancies and conditions
(c) only to special equipment and material
(d) all of these

15. Communications wiring such as telephone, antenna, and CATV wiring within a building shall not be required to comply with the installation requirements of Chapters 1 through 7, except where it is specifically referenced in Chapter 8.

(a) True
(b) False

16. The material located in the *NEC* Annexes is part of the *Code* and shall be complied with.

(a) True
(b) False

17. The authority having jurisdiction shall not be required to enforce any requirements of Chapter 7 (Special Conditions) or Chapter 8 (Communications Systems).

(a) True
(b) False

18. The ______ has the responsibility for deciding on the approval of equipment and materials.

(a) manufacturer
(b) authority having jurisdiction
(c) testing agency
(d) none of these

19. By special permission, the authority having jurisdiction may waive specific requirements in this *Code* where it is assured that equivalent objectives can be achieved by establishing and maintaining effective safety.

(a) True
(b) False'

20. The authority having jurisdiction has the responsibility ______.

(a) for making interpretations of rules
(b) for deciding upon the approval of equipment and materials
(c) for waiving specific requirements in the *Code* and permitting alternate methods and material if safety is maintained
(d) all of these

21. If the *NEC* requires new products that are not yet available at the time a new edition is adopted, the ______ may permit the use of the products that comply with the previous edition of the *Code* adopted by that jurisdiction.

(a) electrical engineer
(b) master electrician
(c) authority having jurisdiction
(d) permit holder

22. In the *NEC*, the word(s) "______" indicate a mandatory requirement.

(a) shall
(b) shall not
(c) shall be permitted
(d) a or b

23. When the *Code* uses the word(s) "_____," it means the identified actions are allowed but not required, and they may be options or alternative methods.

(a) shall
(b) shall not
(c) shall be permitted
(d) a or b

24. Explanatory material, such as references to other standards, references to related sections of the *NEC*, or information related to a *Code* rule, are included in the form of Informational Notes.

(a) True
(b) False

25. Nonmandatory informative annexes contained in the back of the *Code* book ______.

(a) are for information only
(b) aren't enforceable as a requirement of the *Code*
(c) are enforceable as a requirement of the *Code*
(d) a and b

26. Factory-installed ______ wiring of equipment need not be inspected at the time of installation of the equipment, except to detect alterations or damage.

(a) external
(b) associated
(c) internal
(d) all of these

27. Compliance with either the metric or the inch-pound unit of measurement system shall be permitted.

(a) True
(b) False

Notes

GENERAL

INTRODUCTION TO CHAPTER 1—GENERAL

Chapter 1 consists of two topics. Article 100 provides definitions so people can understand one another when trying to communicate about *Code*-related matters and Article 110 provides the general requirements needed to correctly apply the rest of the *NEC*.

Time spent learning this general material is a great investment. After understanding Chapter 1, some of the *Code* requirements that seem confusing to other people—those who don't understand Chapter 1—will become increasingly clear to you. The requirements will strike you as being "common sense," because you'll have the foundation from which to understand and apply them. When you read the *NEC* requirements in later chapters, you'll understand the principles upon which many of them are based, and not be surprised at all. You'll read them and feel like you already know them.

- **Article 100—Definitions.** Part I of Article 100 contains the definitions of terms used throughout the *Code* for systems that operate at 600V, nominal, or less. The definitions of terms in Part II apply to systems that operate at over 600V, nominal.

Author's Comment: This textbook covers the requirements for systems that operate at 600V, nominal, or less.

Definitions of standard terms, such as "volt," "voltage drop," "ampere," "impedance," and "resistance," aren't listed in Article 100. If the *NEC* doesn't define a term, then a dictionary suitable to the authority having jurisdiction should be consulted. A building code glossary might provide better definitions than a dictionary found at your home or school.

Definitions located at the beginning of an article apply only to that specific article. For example, the definition of a "Swimming Pool" is contained in 680.2, because this term applies only to the requirements contained in Article 680—Swimming Pools, Fountains, and Similar Installations. As soon as a defined term is used in two or more articles, its definition is included in Article 100.

- **Article 110—Requirements for Electrical Installations.** This article contains general requirements for electrical installations for the following:
    - Part I. General
    - Part II. 600V, Nominal, Or Less

Notes

Definitions

INTRODUCTION TO ARTICLE 100—DEFINITIONS

Have you ever had a conversation with someone, only to discover that what you said and what he or she heard were completely different? This often happens when people in a conversation don't understand the definitions of the words being used, and that's why the definitions of key terms are located right at the beginning of the *NEC* (Article 100), or at the beginning of each article.

If we can all agree on important definitions, then we speak the same language and avoid misunderstandings. Because the *Code* exists to protect people and property, it's very important to know the definitions presented in Article 100. Now, here are a couple of things you may not know about Article 100:

Article 100 contains many, but not all, of the terms defined by the *NEC*. In general, only those terms used in two or more articles are defined in Article 100. Those terms used only within one article are located within that article, often near the beginning of the article.

- Part I of Article 100 contains the definitions of terms used throughout the *Code* for systems that operate at 600V, nominal, or less.
- Part II of Article 100 contains only terms that apply to systems that operate at over 600V, nominal.

How can you possibly learn all of these definitions? There seem to be so many. Here are a few tips:

- Break the task down. Study a few words at a time, rather than trying to learn them all at one sitting.
- Review the graphics in the textbook. These will help you see how a term is applied.
- Relate them to your work. As you read a word, think about how it applies to the work you're doing. This will provide a natural reinforcement to the learning process.

DEFINITIONS

Accessible *(as it applies to equipment).* Admitting close approach and not guarded by locked doors, elevation, or other effective means.

Accessible *(as it applies to wiring methods).* Not permanently closed in by the building structure or finish and capable of being removed or exposed without damaging the building structure or finish. Figure 100–1

Author's Comments:

- Conductors in a concealed raceway are considered concealed, even though they may become accessible by withdrawing them from the raceway. See the definition of "Concealed" in this article.
- Raceways, cables, and enclosures installed above a suspended ceiling or within a raised floor are considered accessible, because the wiring methods can be accessed without damaging the building structure. See the definitions of "Concealed" and "Exposed" in this article.

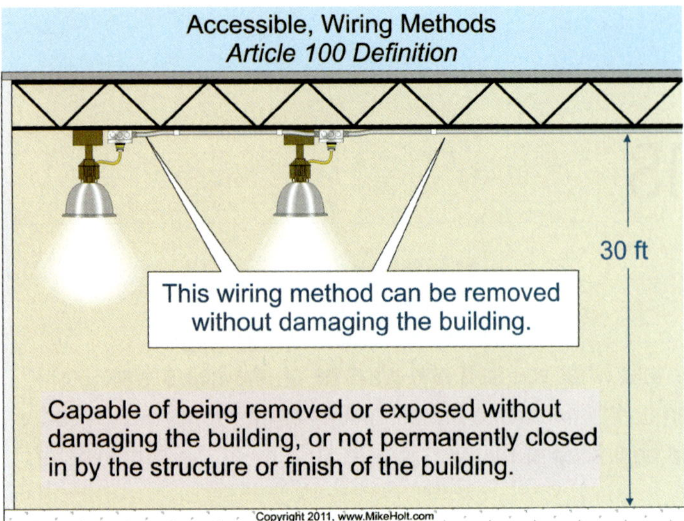

Figure 100–1

Approved. Acceptable to the authority having jurisdiction, usually the electrical inspector.

> **Author's Comment:** Product listing doesn't mean the product is approved, but it's a basis for approval. See 90.4, 90.7, 110.2, and the definitions in this article for "Authority Having Jurisdiction," "Identified," "Labeled," and "Listed."

Authority Having Jurisdiction (AHJ). The organization, office, or individual responsible for approving equipment, materials, an installation, or a procedure. See 90.4 and 90.7 for more information.

> **Note:** The authority having jurisdiction may be a federal, state, or local governmental department or an individual, such as a fire chief, fire marshal, chief of a fire prevention bureau or labor department or health department, a building official or electrical inspector, or others having statutory authority. In some circumstances, the property owner or his/her agent assumes the role, and at government installations, the commanding officer, or departmental official may be the authority having jurisdiction.

Author's Comments:

- Typically, the authority having jurisdiction is the electrical inspector who has legal statutory authority. In the absence of federal, state, or local regulations, the operator of the facility or his or her agent, such as an architect or engineer of the facility, can assume the role.
- Some believe the authority having jurisdiction should have a strong background in the electrical field, such as having studied electrical engineering or having obtained an electrical contractor's license, and in a few states this is a legal requirement. Memberships, certifications, and active participation in electrical organizations, such as the International Association of Electrical Inspectors (IAEI), speak to an individual's qualifications. Visit www.IAEI.org for more information about that organization.

Bonded (Bonding). Connected to establish electrical continuity and conductivity. Figure 100–2

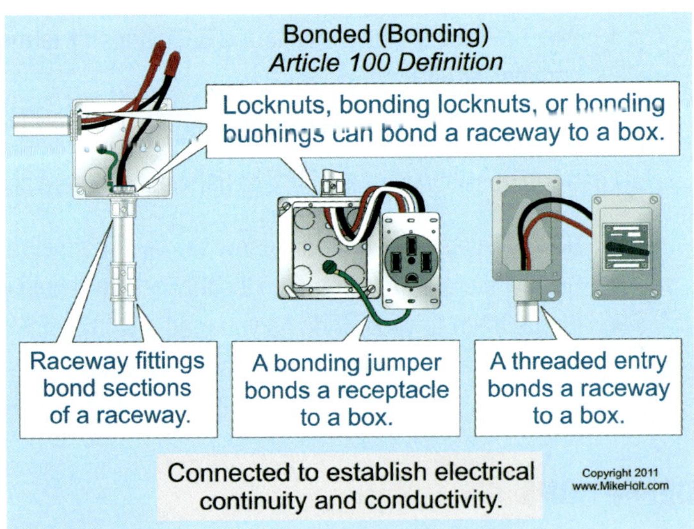

Figure 100–2

> **Author's Comment:** The purpose of bonding is to connect two or more conductive objects together to ensure the electrical continuity of the fault current path, provide the capacity and ability to conduct safely any fault current likely to be imposed, and to minimize potential differences (voltage) between conductive components. Figure 100–3

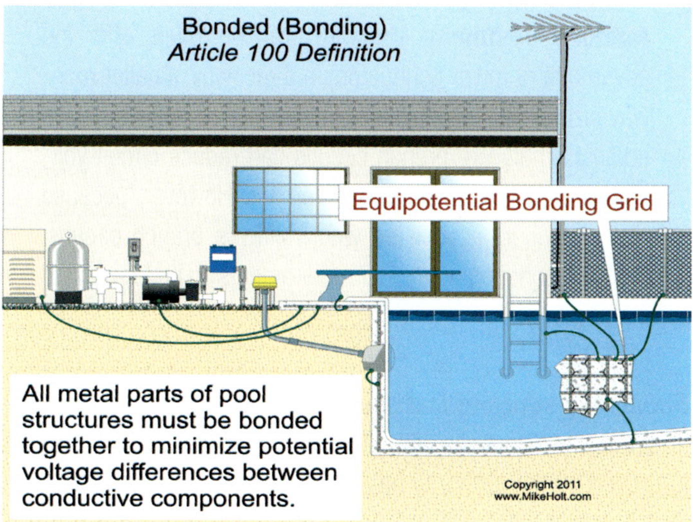

Figure 100–3

Bonding Conductor or Jumper. A conductor that ensures electrical conductivity between metal parts of the electrical installation. **Figure 100–4**

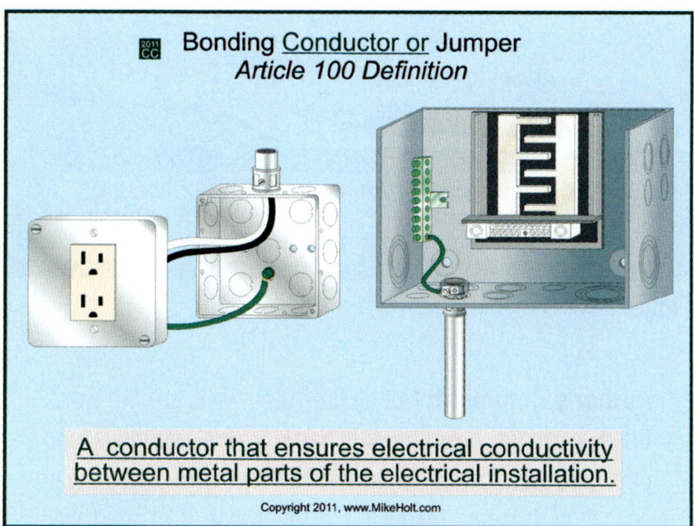

Figure 100–4

Bonding Jumper, Main. A conductor, screw, or strap that connects the circuit equipment grounding conductor to the neutral conductor at service equipment in accordance with 250.24(B) [250.24(A)(4), 250.28, and 408.3(C)]. **Figure 100–5**

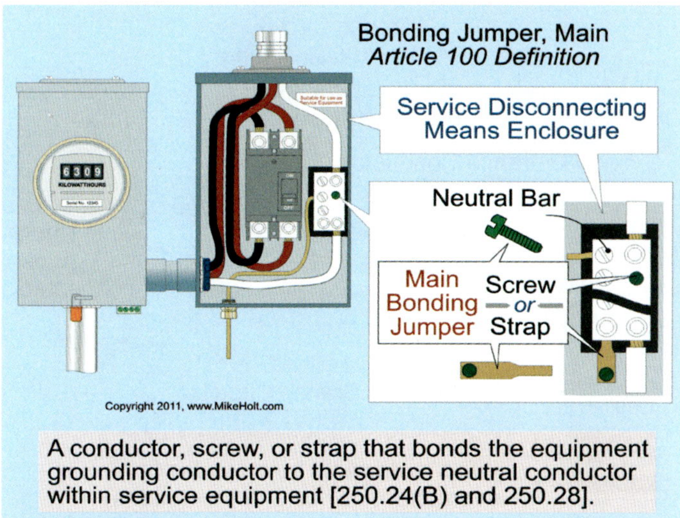

Figure 100–5

Bonding Jumper, System. The connection between the neutral conductor and the supply-side bonding jumper or equipment grounding conductor, or both at a separately derived system. **Figure 100–6**

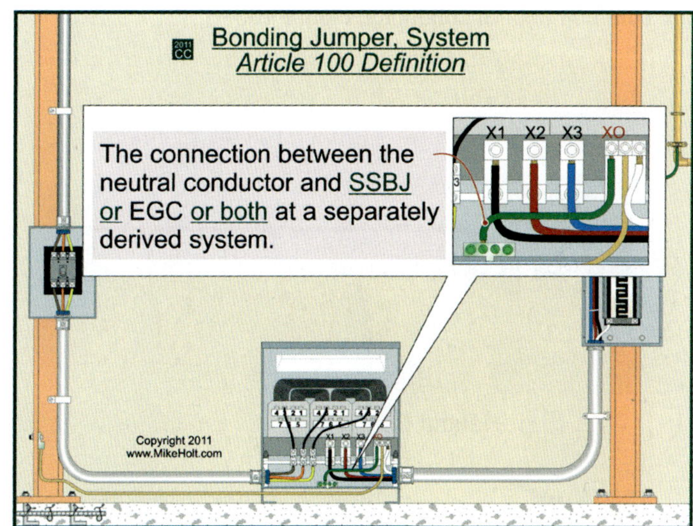

Figure 100–6

Branch Circuit *[Article 210].* The conductors between the final overcurrent device and the receptacle outlets, lighting outlets, or other outlets as defined in this article. **Figure 100–7**

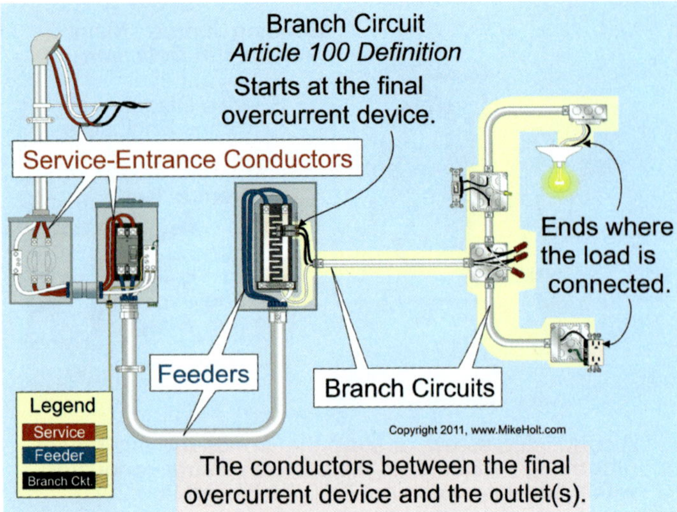

Figure 100–7

Branch Circuit, Multiwire. A branch circuit that consists of two or more ungrounded circuit conductors with a common neutral conductor. There must be a difference of potential (voltage) between the ungrounded conductors and an equal difference of potential (voltage) from each ungrounded conductor to the common neutral conductor. **Figure 100–8**

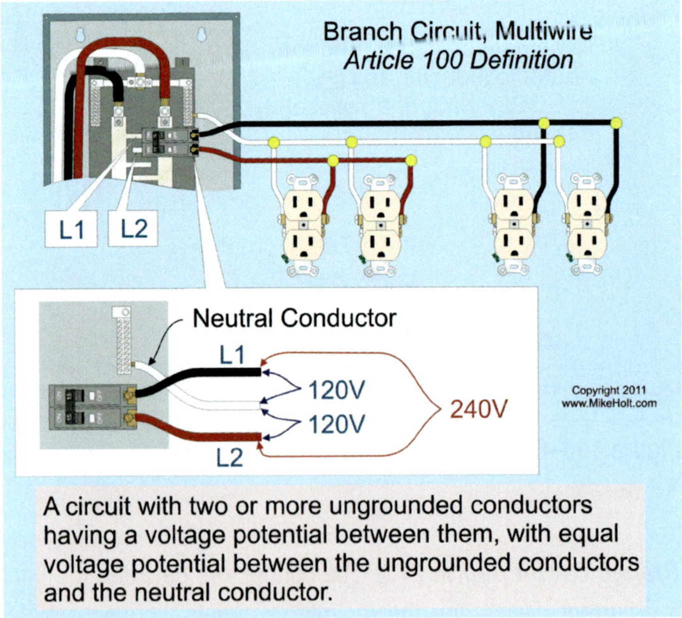

Figure 100–8

Author's Comment: Multiwire branch circuits offer the advantage of fewer conductors in a raceway, smaller raceway sizing, and a reduction of material and labor costs. In addition, multiwire branch circuits can reduce circuit voltage drop by as much as 50 percent. However, because of the dangers associated with multiwire branch circuits, the *NEC* contains additional requirements to ensure a safe installation.

Building. A structure that stands alone or is cut off from other structures by fire walls with all openings protected by fire doors approved by the authority having jurisdiction. **Figure 100–9**

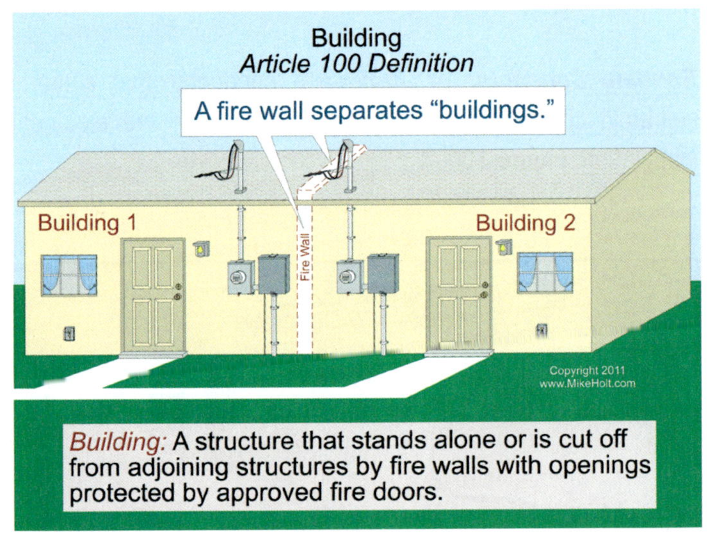

Figure 100–9

Author's Comment: Not all fire-rated walls are fire walls. Building codes describe fire barriers, fire partitions and other fire-rated walls, in addition to fire walls. Check with your local building inspector to determine if a rated wall creates a separate building (fire wall).

***Cabinet** [Article 312].* An enclosure for either surface mounting or flush mounting provided with a frame in which a door can be hung. **Figure 100–10**

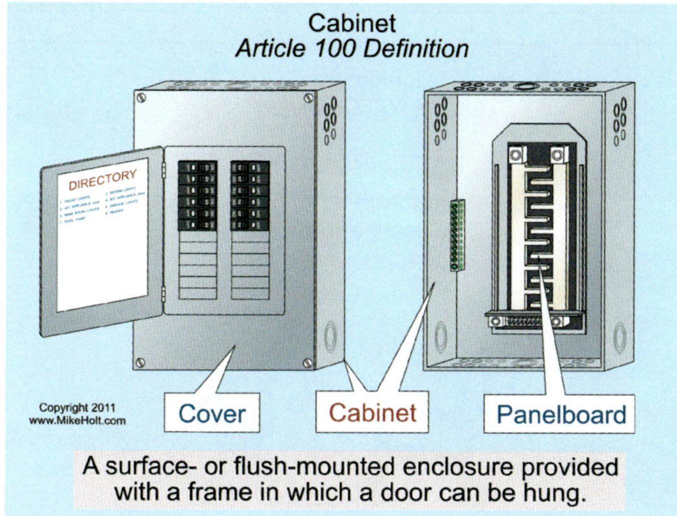

Figure 100–10

Author's Comment: Cabinets are used to enclose panelboards. See the definition of "Panelboard" in this article.

Communications Equipment. Electronic telecommunications equipment used for the transmission of audio, video, and data, including support equipment such as computers. Figure 100–11

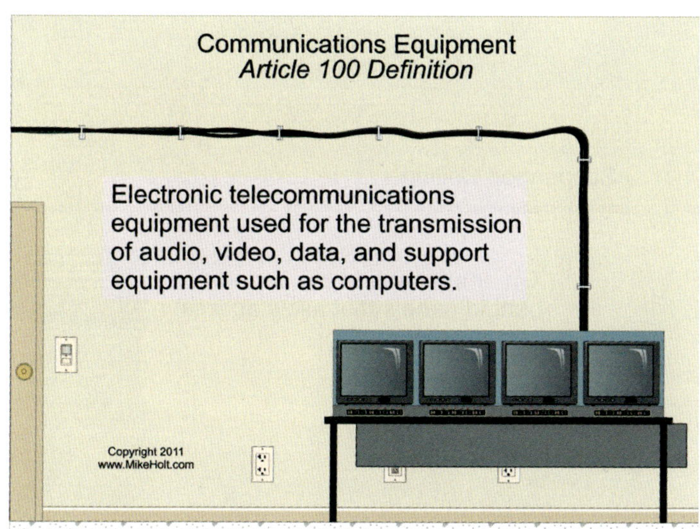

Figure 100–11

Connector, Pressure (Solderless). A device that establishes a conductive connection between conductors or between a conductor and a terminal by the means of mechanical pressure.

Device. A component of an electrical installation intended to carry or control electric energy as its principal function. Figure 100–12

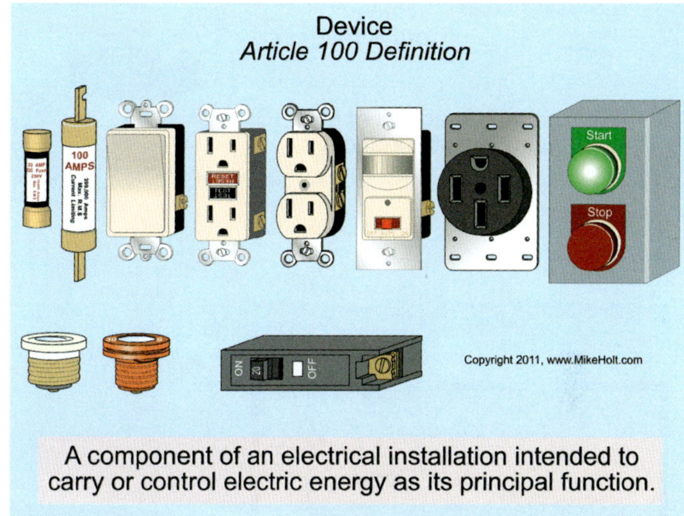

Figure 100–12

Author's Comment: Devices include wires and busbars, receptacles, switches, illuminated switches, circuit breakers, fuses, time clocks, controllers, and so forth, but not locknuts or other mechanical fittings. A device may consume very small amounts of energy, such as an illuminated switch, but still be classified as a device based on its principal function.

Disconnecting Means. A device that opens all of the ungrounded circuit conductors from their power source. This includes devices such as switches, attachment plugs and receptacles, and circuit breakers. Figure 100–13

Dwelling Unit. A space that provides independent living facilities, with space for eating, living, and sleeping; as well as permanent facilities for cooking and sanitation. Figure 100–14

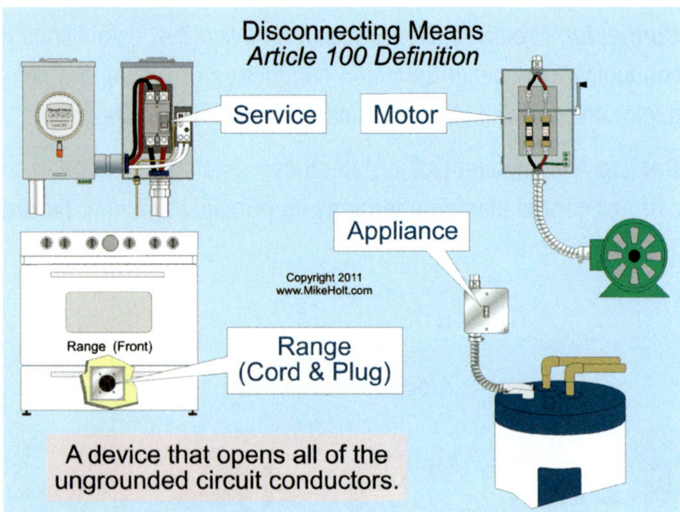

Figure 100–13

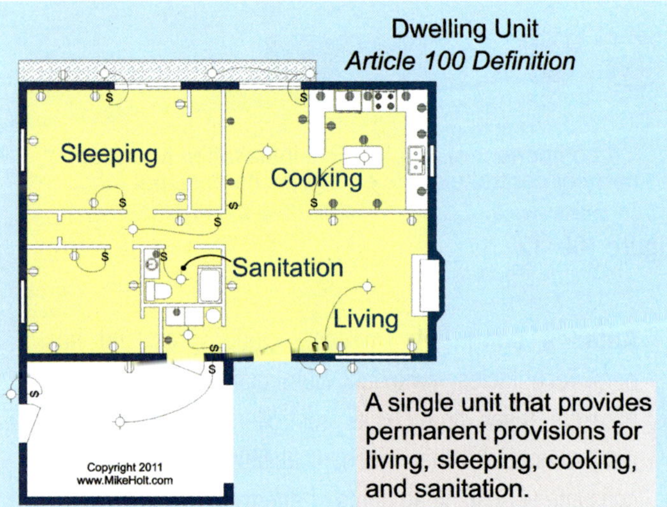

Figure 100–14

Electric Sign *[Article 600].* A fixed, stationary, or portable self-contained, electrically illuminated piece of equipment with words or symbols designed to convey information or attract attention.

Energized. Electrically connected to a source of voltage.

Equipment. A general term including fittings, devices, appliances, luminaires, machinery, and the like. **Figure 100–15**

Exposed *(as applied to live parts).* Capable of being touched if not suitably guarded, isolated, or insulated.

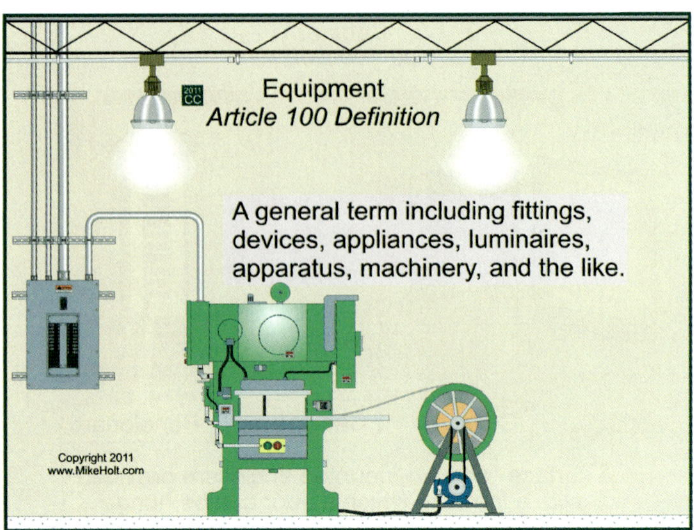

Figure 100–15

Exposed *(as applied to wiring methods).* On or attached to the surface of a building, or behind panels designed to allow access.

Author's Comment: An example is wiring located in the space above a suspended ceiling or below a raised floor. **Figure 100–16**

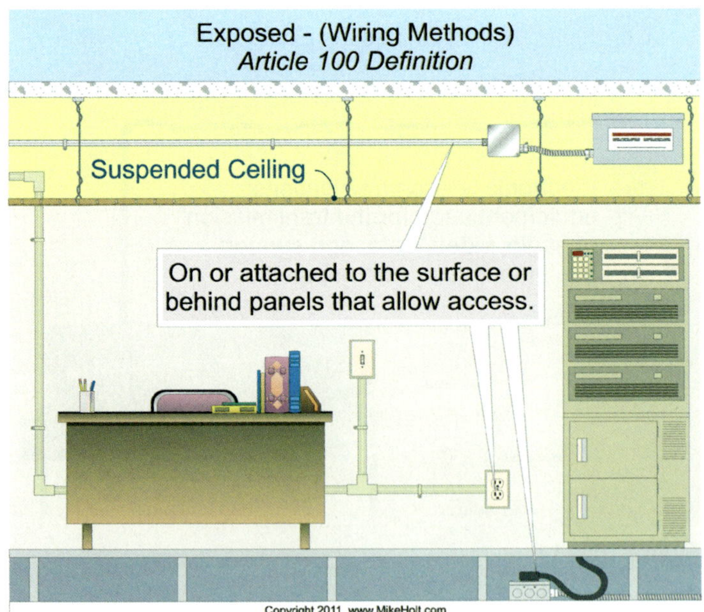

Figure 100–16

Feeder *[Article 215].* The conductors between the service equipment, a separately derived system, or other power supply and the final branch-circuit overcurrent device. Figure 100–17

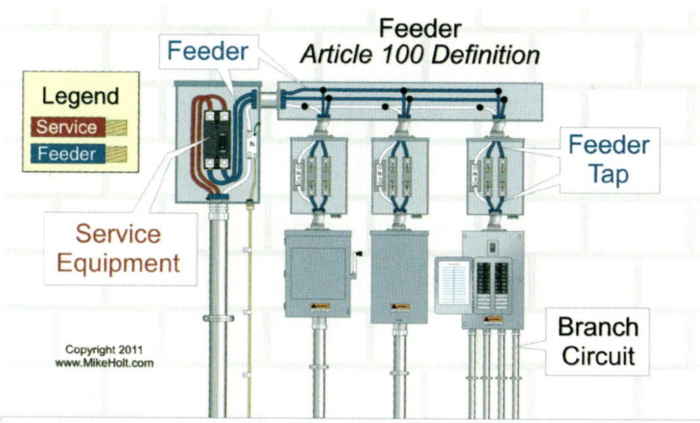

Figure 100–17

Author's Comments:

- An "other power source" includes a solar energy (photovoltaic) system.
- To have a better understanding of what a feeder is, be sure to review the definitions of "Service Equipment" and "Separately Derived System."

Fitting. An accessory, such as a locknut, intended to perform a mechanical function.

Ground. The earth. Figure 100–18

Ground Fault. An unintentional electrical connection between an ungrounded conductor and the metal parts of enclosures, raceways, or equipment. Figure 100–19

Grounded (Grounding). Connected to ground or to a conductive body that extends the ground connection.

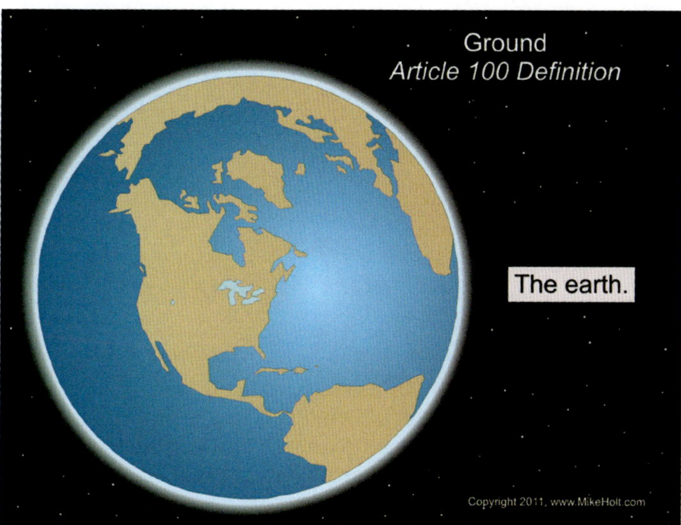

Figure 100–18

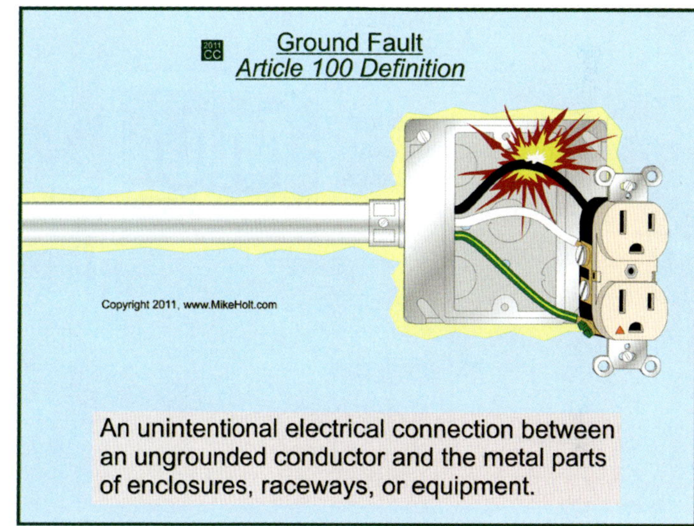

Figure 100–19

Author's Comment: An example of a "body that extends the ground (earth) connection" is the termination to structural steel that's connected to the earth either directly or by the termination to another grounding electrode in accordance with 250.52. Figure 100–20

Grounded, Solidly. Connected to ground without inserting any resistor or impedance device. Figure 100–21

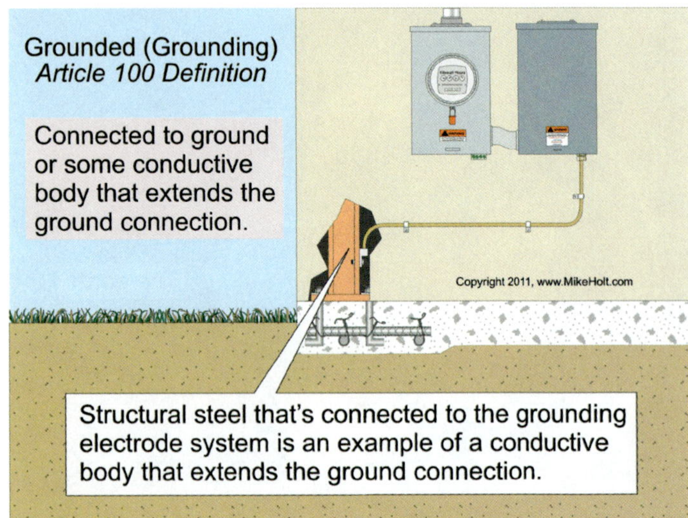

Figure 100–20

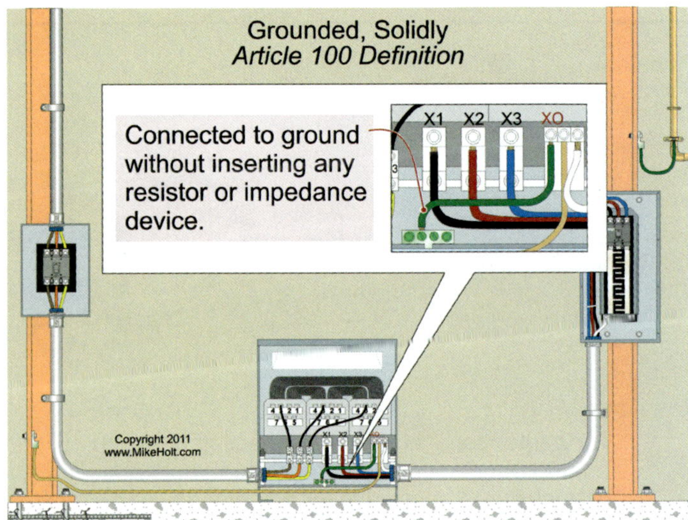

Figure 100–21

Grounded Conductor *[Article 200].* The system or circuit conductor that's intentionally grounded (connected to the earth). Figure 100–22

Author's Comment: Because the neutral conductor of a solidly grounded system is always grounded (connected to the earth), it's both a "grounded" conductor and a "neutral" conductor. To make it easier for the reader of this textbook, we'll refer to the "grounded" conductor of a solidly grounded system as the "neutral" conductor, except for the applications contained in Article 690—Solar Photovoltaic Systems.

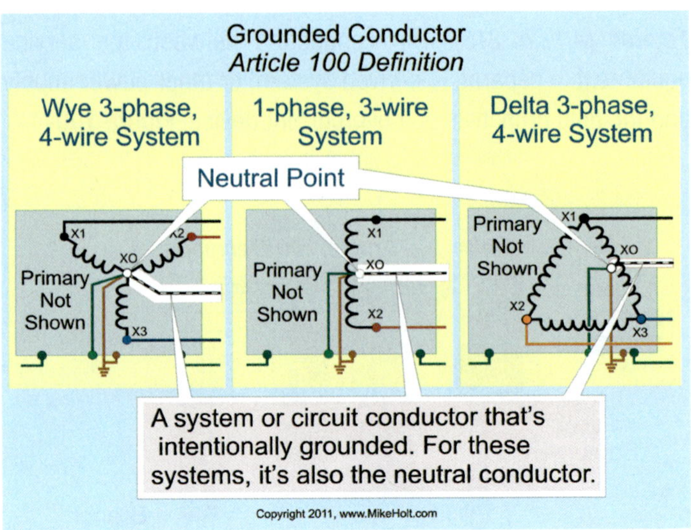

Figure 100–22

Ground-Fault Circuit Interrupter (GFCI). A device intended to protect people by de-energizing a circuit when the current to ground exceeds the value established for a "Class A" device.

Note: A "Class A" ground-fault circuit interrupter opens the circuit when the current to ground has a value of 6 mA or higher and doesn't trip when the current to ground is less than 4 mA. Figure 100–23

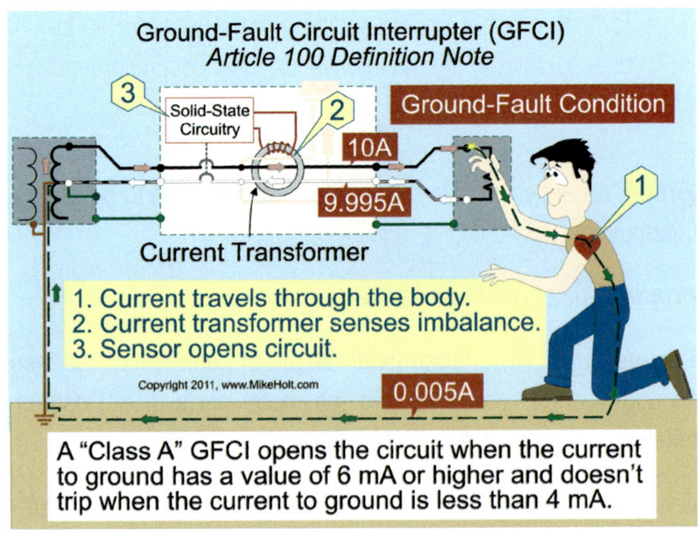

Figure 100–23

Author's Comment: A GFCI operates on the principle of monitoring the unbalanced current between the current-carrying circuit conductors. On a 120V circuit, the GFCI will monitor the unbalanced current between the ungrounded and neutral conductors; on 240V GFCIs, this monitoring is between ungrounded conductors. GFCI-protective devices are commercially available in receptacles, circuit breakers, cord sets, and other types of devices. **Figure 100–24**

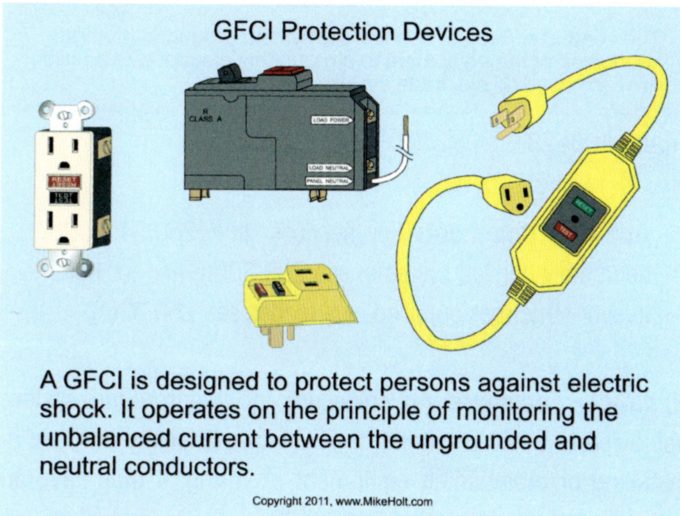

Figure 100–24

Grounding Conductor, Equipment (EGC). The conductive path(s) that connect metal parts of equipment to the system neutral conductor, to the grounding electrode conductor, or both [250.110 through 250.126]. **Figure 100–25**

Note 1: The circuit equipment grounding conductor also performs bonding.

Author's Comment: To quickly remove dangerous touch voltage on metal parts from a ground fault, the equipment grounding conductor must be connected to the system neutral conductor at the source, and have low enough impedance so that fault current will quickly rise to a level that will open the branch-circuit overcurrent device [250.2 and 250.4(A)(3)].

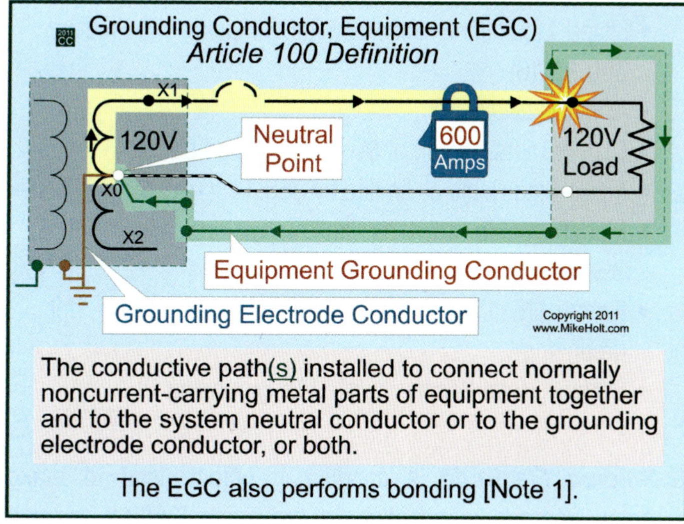

Figure 100–25

Note 2: An equipment grounding conductor can be any one or a combination of the types listed in 250.118. **Figure 100–26**

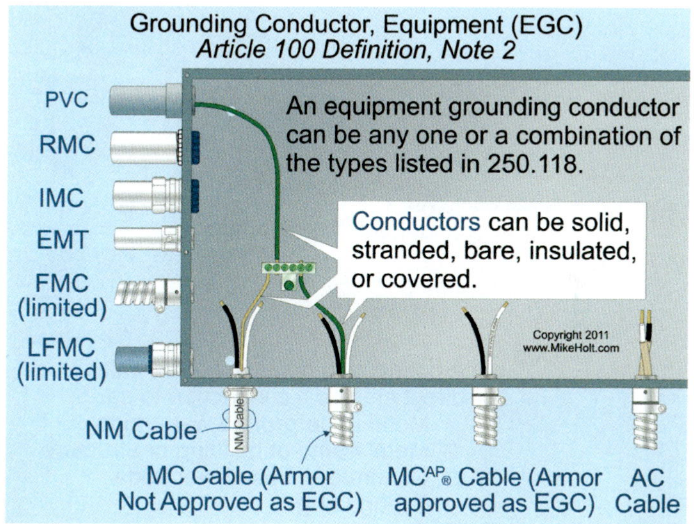

Figure 100–26

Author's Comment: Equipment grounding conductors include:

- A bare or insulated conductor
- Rigid Metal Conduit
- Intermediate Metal Conduit
- Electrical Metallic Tubing
- Listed Flexible Metal Conduit as limited by 250.118(5)

- Listed Liquidtight Flexible Metal Conduit as limited by 250.118(6)
- Armored Cable
- Copper metal sheath of Mineral Insulated Cable
- Metal-Clad Cable as limited by 250.118(10)
- Metallic cable trays as limited by 250.118(11) and 392.60
- Electrically continuous metal raceways listed for grounding
- Surface Metal Raceways listed for grounding

Grounding Electrode. A conducting object used to make a direct electrical connection to the earth [250.50 through 250.70]. **Figure 100–27**

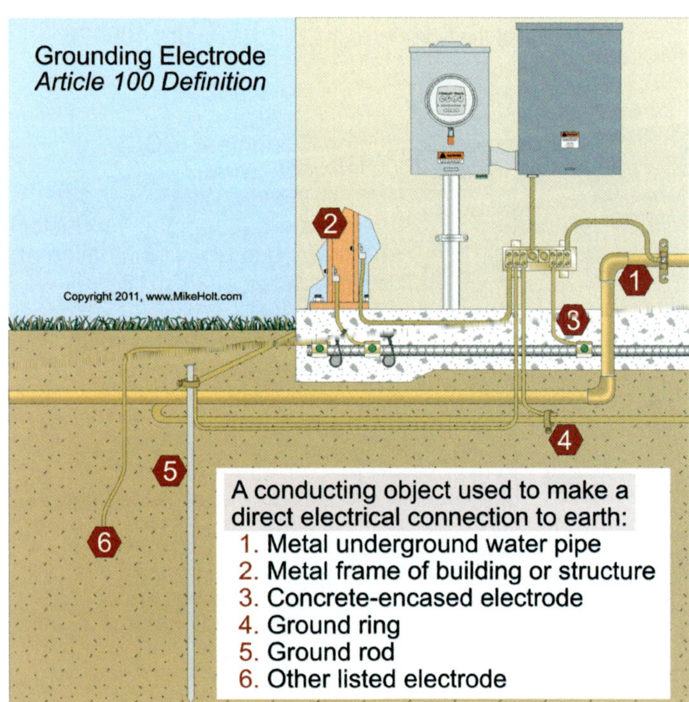

Figure 100–27

Grounding Electrode Conductor (GEC). The conductor used to connect the system grounded conductor (neutral) to a grounding electrode or to a point on the grounding electrode system. **Figure 100–28**

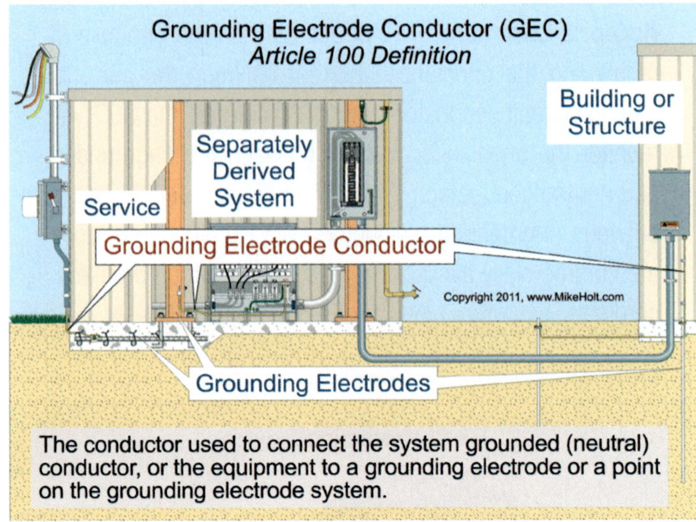

Figure 100–28

Author's Comment: For services, see 250.24(A); for separately derived systems, see 250.30(A); and for buildings or structures supplied by a feeder, see 250.32(A).

Handhole Enclosure. An enclosure for underground system use sized to allow personnel to reach into it for the purpose of installing or maintaining equipment or wiring. It may have an open or closed bottom. **Figure 100–29**

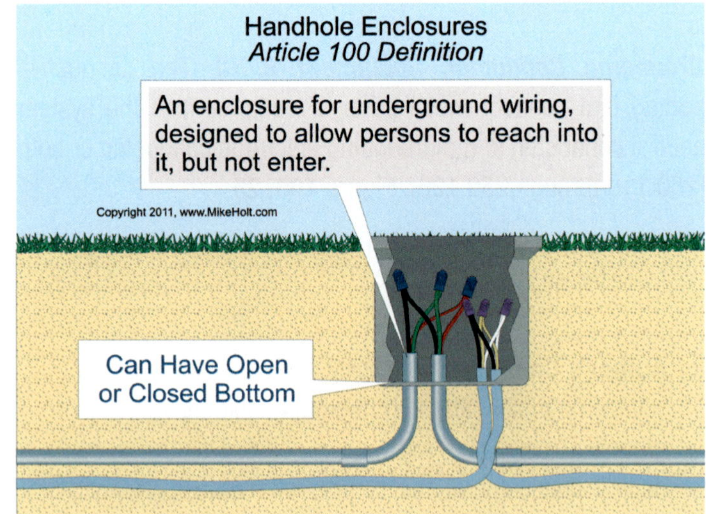

Figure 100–29

Author's Comment: See 314.30 for the installation requirements for handhole enclosures.

Identified Equipment. Recognized as suitable for a specific purpose, function, or environment by listing, labeling, or other means approved by the authority having jurisdiction.

Author's Comment: See 90.4, 90.7, 110.3(A)(1), and the definitions for "Approved," "Labeled," and "Listed" in this article.

Intersystem Bonding Termination. A device that provides a means to connect bonding conductors for communications systems to the grounding electrode system, in accordance with 250.94. **Figure 100–30**

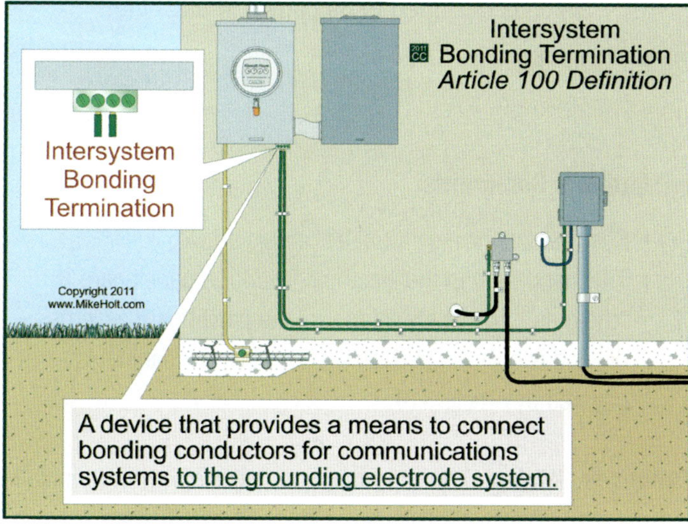

Figure 100–30

Labeled. Equipment or materials that have a label, symbol, or other identifying mark in the form of a sticker, decal, printed label, or molded or stamped into the product by a testing laboratory acceptable to the authority having jurisdiction.

Author's Comment: Labeling and listing of equipment typically provides the basis for equipment approval by the authority having jurisdiction [90.4, 90.7, 110.2, and 110.3].

Listed. Equipment or materials included in a list published by a testing laboratory acceptable to the authority having jurisdiction. The listing organization must periodically inspect the production of listed equipment or material to ensure the equipment or material meets appropriate designated standards and is suitable for a specified purpose.

Author's Comment: The *NEC* doesn't require all electrical equipment to be listed, but some *Code* requirements do specifically require product listing. Organizations such as OSHA increasingly require that listed equipment be used when such equipment is available [90.7, 110.2, and 110.3].

Luminaire *[Article 410].* A complete lighting unit consisting of a light source with the parts designed to position the light source and connect it to the power supply and distribute the light. A lampholder by itself isn't a luminaire. **Figure 100–31**

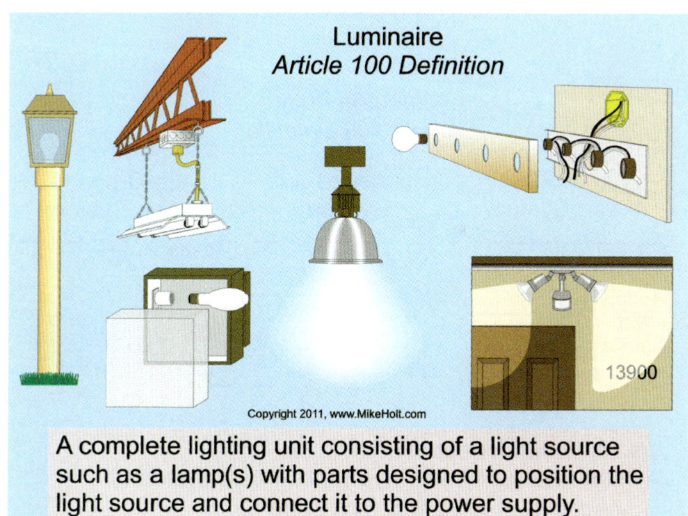

Figure 100–31

Neutral Conductor. The conductor connected to the neutral point of a system that's intended to carry current under normal conditions. **Figure 100–32**

Author's Comment: The neutral conductor of a solidly grounded system is required to be grounded (connected to the earth), therefore this conductor is also called a "grounded conductor."

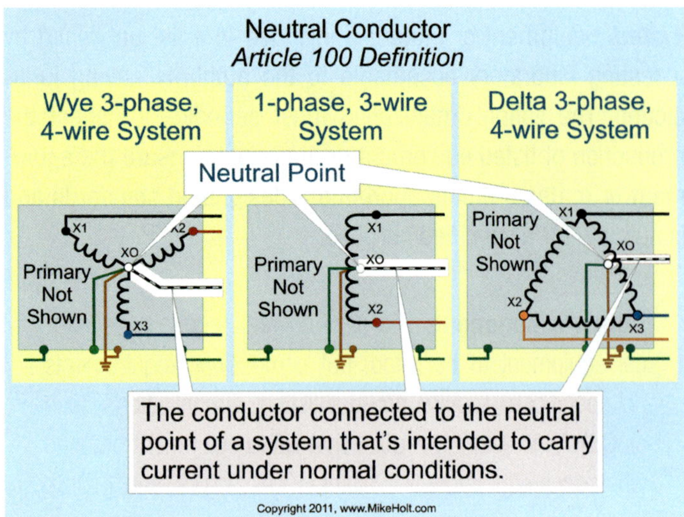

Figure 100–32

Neutral Point. The common point of a 4-wire, three-phase, wye-connected system; the midpoint of a 3-wire, single-phase system; or the midpoint of the single-phase portion of a three-phase, delta-connected system. Figure 100–33

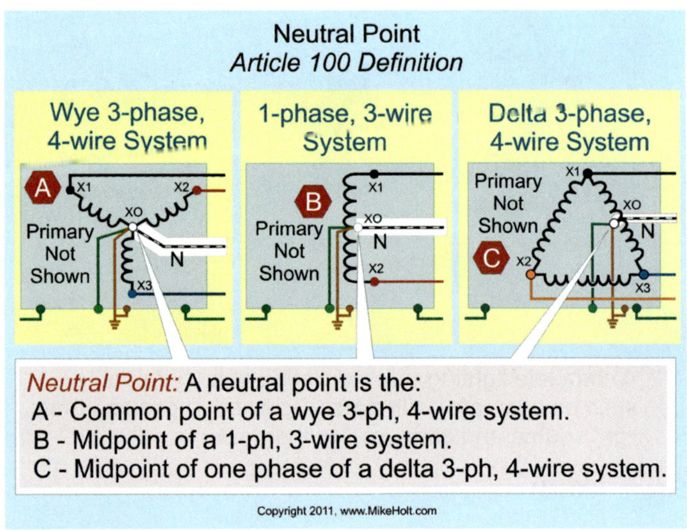

Figure 100–33

Outline Lighting *[Article 600].* An arrangement of incandescent lamps, electric-discharge lighting, or other electrically powered light sources to outline or call attention to certain features such as the shape of a building or the decoration of a window.

Panelboard *[Article 408].* A distribution point containing overcurrent devices and designed to be installed in a cabinet. Figure 100–34

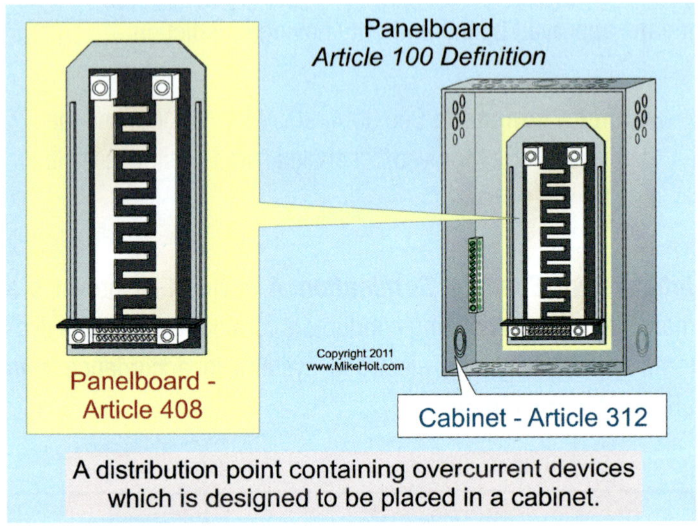

Figure 100–34

Author's Comments:

- See the definition of "Cabinet" in this article.
- The slang term in the electrical field for a panelboard is "the guts." This is the interior of the panelboard assembly and is covered by Article 408, while the cabinet is covered by Article 314.

Premises Wiring. The interior and exterior wiring, including power, lighting, control, and signal circuits, and all associated hardware, fittings, and wiring devices. This includes both permanently and temporarily installed wiring from the service point to the outlets, or where there's no service point, wiring from and including the power source to the outlets.

Premises wiring doesn't include the internal wiring of electrical equipment and appliances, such as luminaires, dishwashers, water heaters, motors, controllers, motor control centers, air-conditioning equipment, and so on [90.7 and 300.1(B)].

Raceway. An enclosure designed for the installation of conductors, cables, or busbars. Raceways in the *NEC* include:

Raceway Type	Article
Busways	368
Electrical Metallic Tubing	358
Electrical Nonmetallic Tubing	362
Flexible Metal Conduit	348
Intermediate Metal Conduit	342
Liquidtight Flexible Metal Conduit	350
Liquidtight Flexible Nonmetallic Conduit	356
Metal Wireways	376
Multioutlet Assemblies	380
Rigid Metal Conduit	344
PVC Conduit	352
Strut-Type Channel Raceways	384
Surface Metal Raceways	386
Surface Nonmetallic Raceways	388

Author's Comments: A cable tray system isn't a raceway; it's a support system for cables and raceways [392.2].

Receptacle *[Article 406].* A contact device installed at an outlet for the connection of an attachment plug. A single receptacle contains one device on a strap (mounting yoke), and a multiple receptacle contains more than one device on a common yoke. **Figure 100–35**

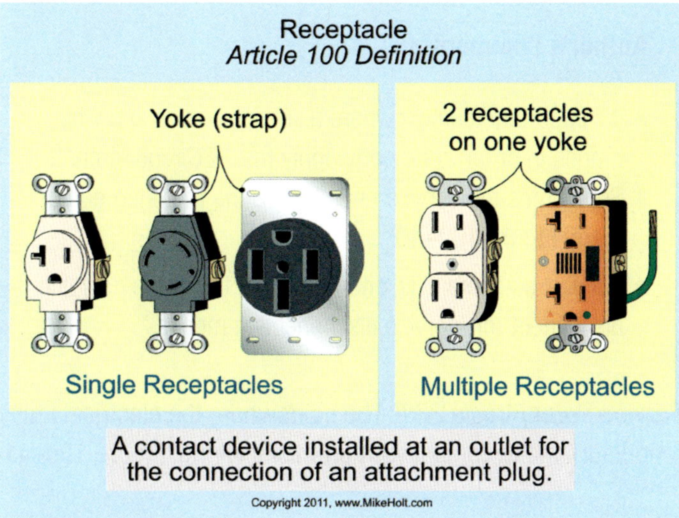

Figure 100–35

Separately Derived System. A wiring system whose power is derived from a source of electric energy or equipment other than the electric utility service. This includes a generator, a battery, a solar photovoltaic system, a transformer, or a converter winding, where there's no direct electrical connection from circuit conductors of one system to circuit conductors of another system, other than connections through the earth, metal raceways, or equipment grounding conductors. **Figures 100–36 and 100–37**

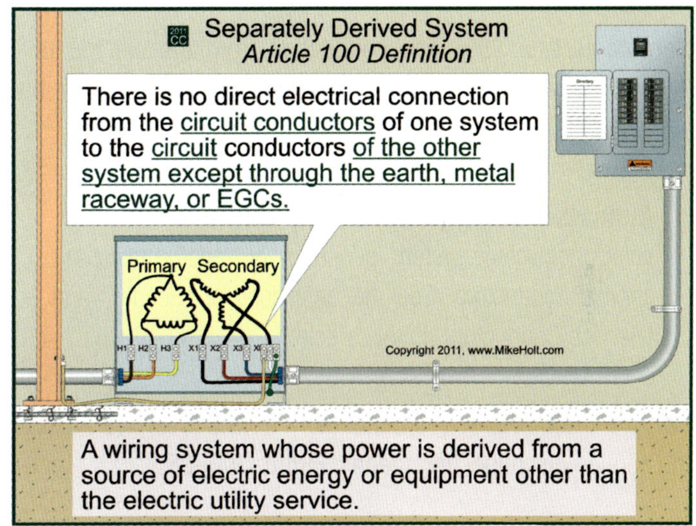

Figure 100–36

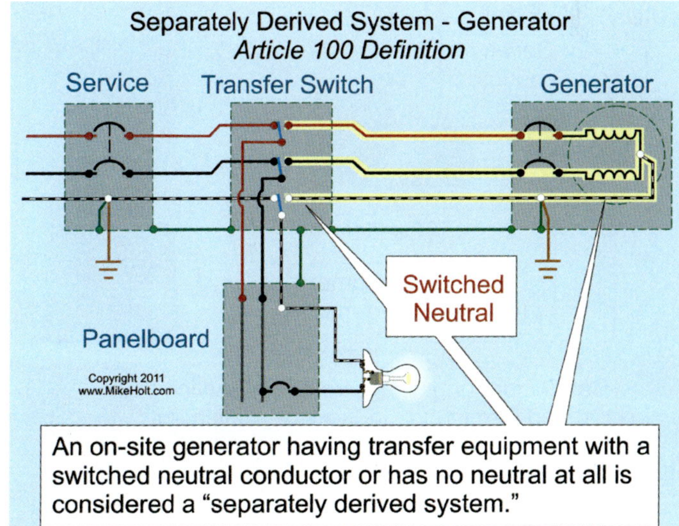

Figure 100–37

Author's Comments:

- This definition clarifies that separately derived systems also include equipment such as transformers, converters, and inverters, which might not be considered sources of energy.
- Separately derived systems are actually a lot more complicated than the above definition suggests, and understanding them requires additional study. For more information, see 250.30.

Service *[Article 230].* The conductors from the electric utility that deliver electric energy to the wiring system of the premises.

Author's Comment: Conductors from a UPS system, solar photovoltaic system, generator, or transformer aren't service conductors. See the definitions of "Feeder" and "Service Conductors" in this article.

Service Conductors. The conductors from the service point to the service disconnecting means. **Figure 100–38**

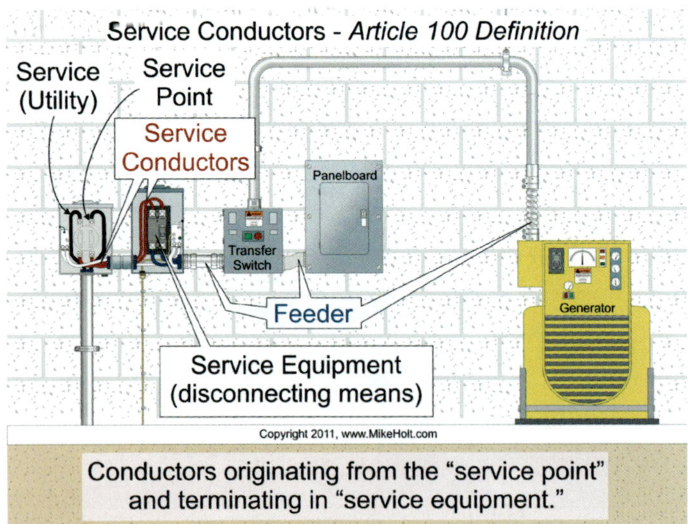

Figure 100–38

Author's Comments:

- These conductors fall within the requirements of Article 230, since they aren't under the exclusive control of the electric utility.
- "Service Conductors" is a term that can include service drop, service lateral, and service-entrance conductors.

Service Equipment *[Article 230].* The one to six disconnects connected to the load end of service conductors intended to control and cut off the supply to the building/structure. **Figure 100–39**

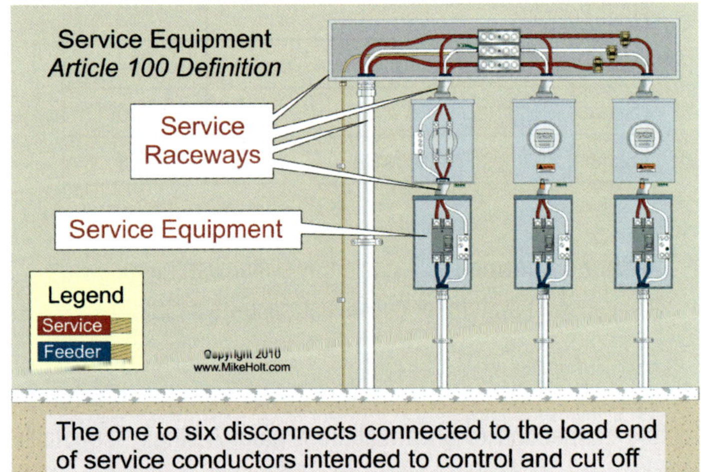

Figure 100–39

Author's Comments:

- It's important to know where a service begins and where it ends in order to properly apply the *NEC* requirements. Sometimes the service ends before the metering equipment. **Figure 100–40**
- Service equipment is often referred to as the "service disconnect" or "service disconnecting means."

Service Point *[Article 230].* The point where the electrical utility conductors make contact with premises wiring. **Figure 100–41**

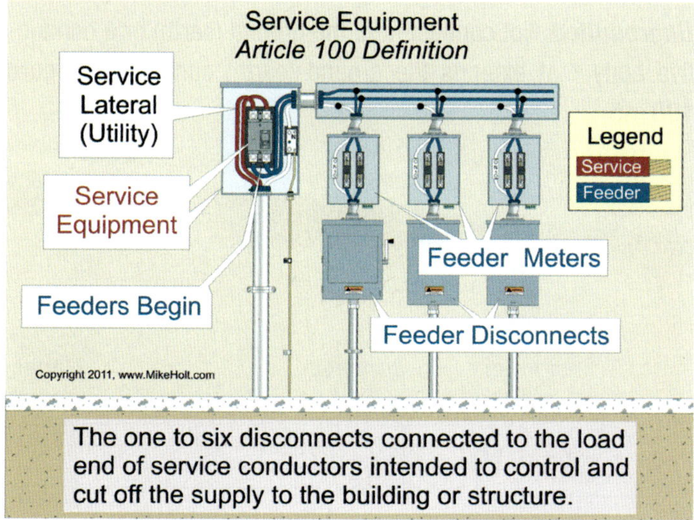

Figure 100–40

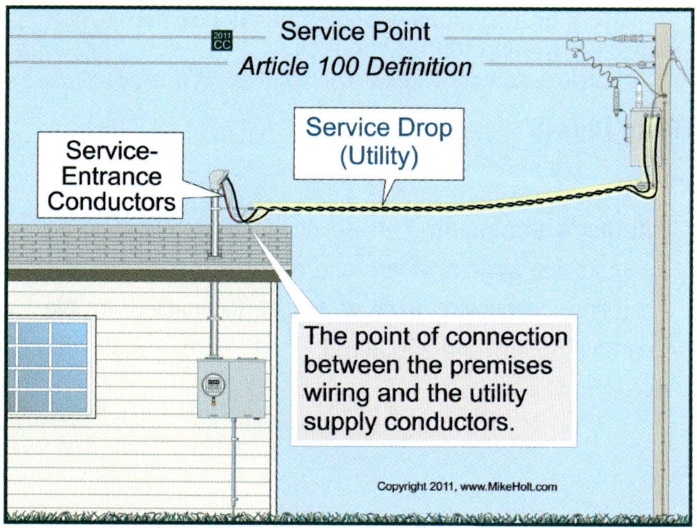

Figure 100–41

Note: The service point is the point where the serving utility ends and the premises wiring begins.

Author's Comments:

- See the definition of "Premises Wiring" in this article.
- The service point can be at the utility transformer, at the service weatherhead, or at the meter socket enclosure, depending on where the utility conductors terminate. **Figure 100–42**

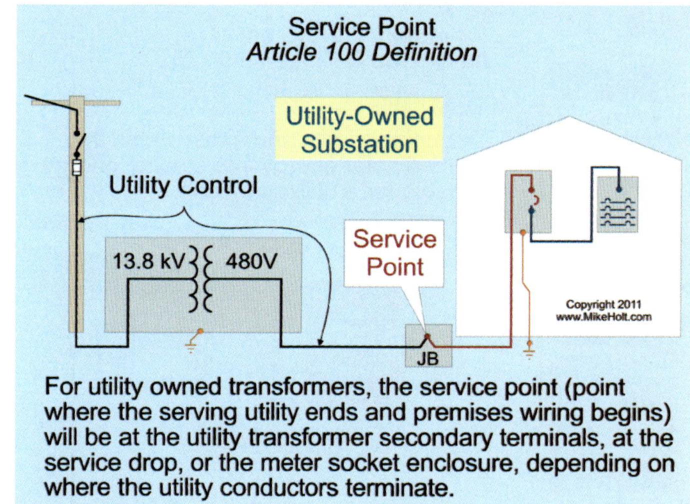

Figure 100–42

- For customer owned transformers, the service point (point where the serving utility ends and premises wiring begins) will be at the termination of the utility conductors, often at the utility pole. **Figure 100–43**

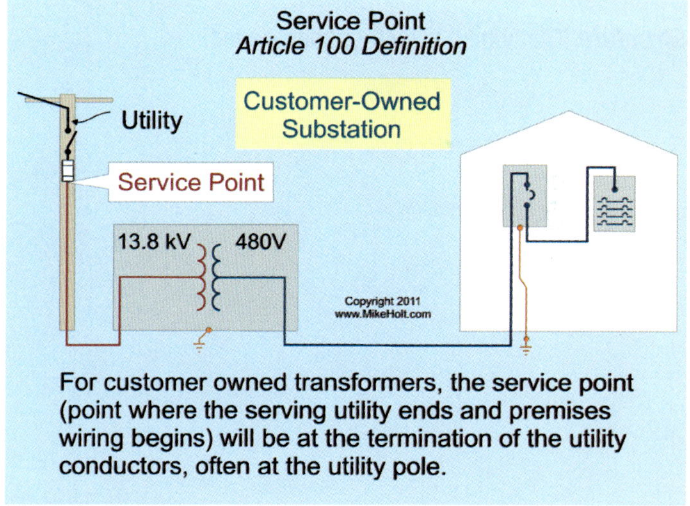

Figure 100–43

Solar Photovoltaic System. The combination of all components and subsystems that convert solar energy into electrical energy suitable for connection to a utilization load. **Figure 100-44**

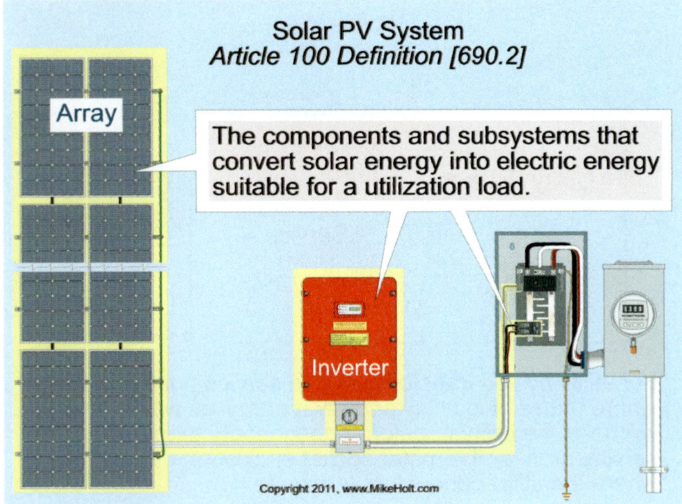

Figure 100–44

Special Permission. Written consent from the authority having jurisdiction.

> **Author's Comment:** See the definition of "Authority Having Jurisdiction" in this article.

Structure. That which is built or constructed.

Ungrounded. Not connected to the ground (earth) or a conductive body that extends the ground (earth) connection. **Figure 100–45**

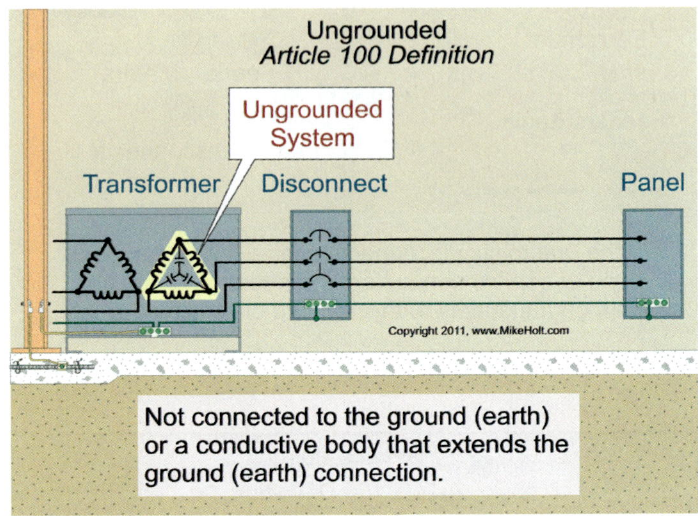

Figure 100–45

> **Author's Comment:** The use of this term relates to an ungrounded system, where one of the system's current-carrying conductors isn't grounded (connected to the earth) [250.4(B) and 250.30(B)].

Requirements for Electrical Installations

INTRODUCTION TO ARTICLE 110—REQUIREMENTS FOR ELECTRICAL INSTALLATIONS

Article 110 sets the stage for how you'll implement the rest of the *NEC*. This article contains a few of the most important and yet neglected parts of the *Code*. For example:

- How should you terminate conductors?
- What kinds of warnings, markings, and identification does a given installation require?
- What's the right working clearance for a given installation?
- What do the temperature limitations at terminals mean?
- What are the *NEC* requirements for dealing with flash protection?

It's critical that you master Article 110, and that's exactly what Mike Holt's *Illustrated Guide to Understanding the 2011 NEC Requirements for Grounding versus Bonding* is designed for. As you read this article, you're building your foundation for correctly applying the *NEC*. In fact, this article itself is a foundation for much of the *Code*. The purpose for the *National Electrical Code* is to provide a safe installation, but Article 110 is perhaps focused a little more on providing an installation that is safe for the installer and maintenance electrician, so time spent in this article is time well spent

PART I. GENERAL REQUIREMENTS

110.1 Scope. Article 110 covers the general requirements for the examination and approval, installation and use, access to and spaces about electrical equipment; as well as general requirements for enclosures intended for personnel entry (manholes, vaults, and tunnels).

110.2 Approval of Conductors and Equipment. The authority having jurisdiction must approve all electrical conductors and equipment. Figure 110–1

Author's Comment: For a better understanding of product approval, review 90.4, 90.7, 110.3 and the definitions for "Approved," "Identified," "Labeled," and "Listed" in Article 100.

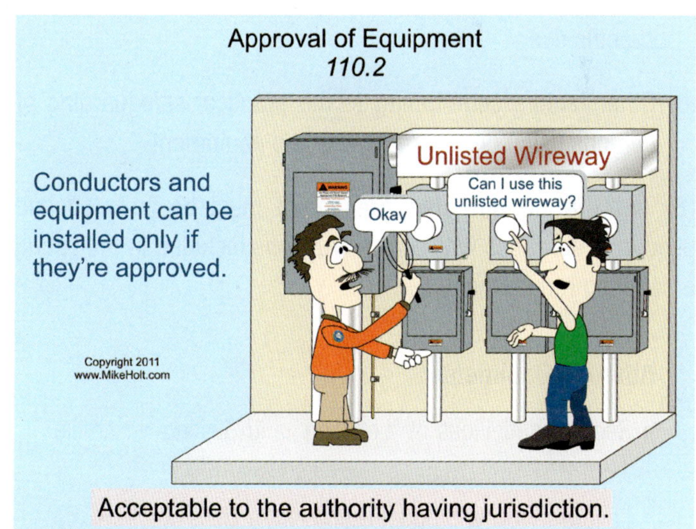

Figure 110–1

110.3 Examination, Identification, Installation, and Use of Equipment.

(A) Guidelines for Approval. The authority having jurisdiction must approve equipment. In doing so, consideration must be given to the following:

(1) Suitability for installation and use in accordance with the *NEC*

Note: Suitability of equipment use may be identified by a description marked on or provided with a product to identify the suitability of the product for a specific purpose, environment, or application. Special conditions of use or other limitations may be marked on the equipment, in the product instructions, or appropriate listing and labeling information. Suitability of equipment may be evidenced by listing or labeling.

(2) Mechanical strength and durability

(3) Wire-bending and connection space

(4) Electrical insulation

(5) Heating effects under all conditions of use

(6) Arcing effects

(7) Classification by type, size, voltage, current capacity, and specific use

(8) Other factors contributing to the practical safeguarding of persons using or in contact with the equipment

(B) Installation and Use. Equipment must be installed and used in accordance with any instructions included in the listing or labeling requirements.

Author's Comments:

- See the definitions of "Labeling" and "Listing" in Article 100.
- Failure to follow product listing instructions, such as the torquing of terminals and the sizing of conductors, is a violation of this *Code* rule. **Figure 110–2**

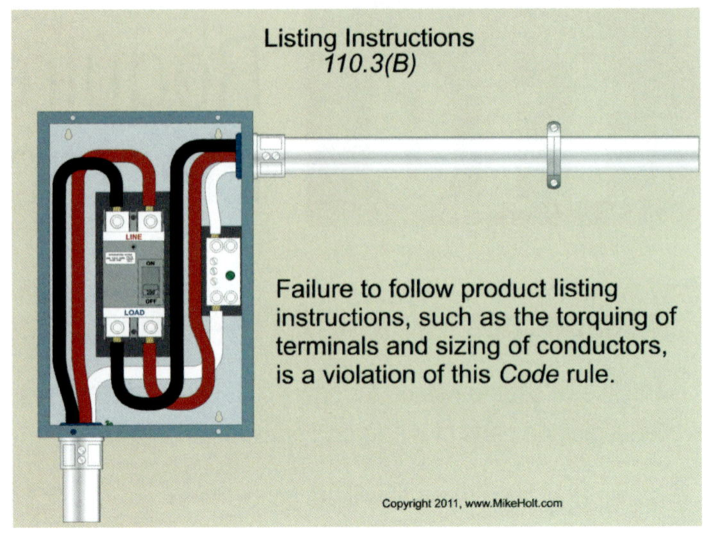

Figure 110–2

110.5 Copper Conductors. If the conductor material isn't specified in a rule, the material and the sizes given in the *Code* (and this textbook) are based on copper.

110.6 Conductor Sizes. Conductor sizes are expressed in American Wire Gage (AWG), typically from 18 AWG up to 4/0 AWG. Conductor sizes larger than 4/0 AWG are expressed in kcmil (thousand circular mils). **Figure 110–3**

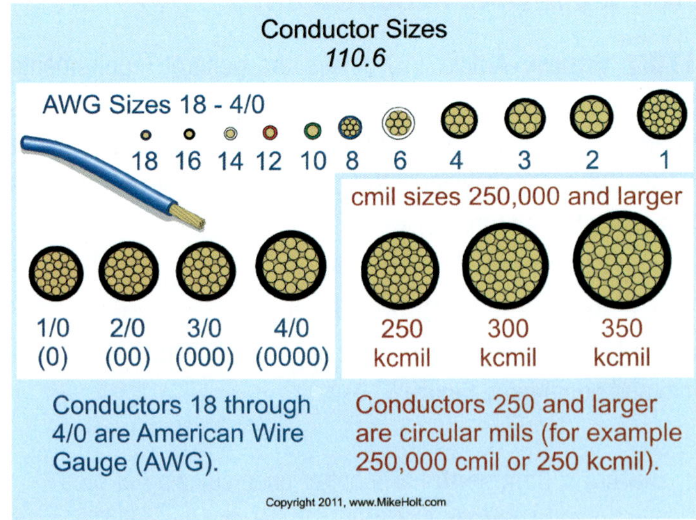

Figure 110–3

110.12 Mechanical Execution of Work. Electrical equipment must be installed in a neat and workmanlike manner.

> **Note:** Accepted industry practices are described in ANSI/NECA 1, *Standard Practices for Good Workmanship in Electrical Contracting.*

> **Author's Comment:** The National Electrical Contractors Association (NECA) created a series of *National Electrical Installation Standards* (NEIS®) that established the industry's first quality guidelines for electrical installations. These standards define a benchmark or baseline of quality and workmanship for installing electrical products and systems. They explain what installing electrical products and systems in a "neat and workmanlike manner" means. For more information about these standards, visit www.neca-neis.org/.

110.14 Conductor Termination and Splicing. Conductor terminal and splicing devices must be identified for the conductor material and they must be properly installed and used. Figure 110–4

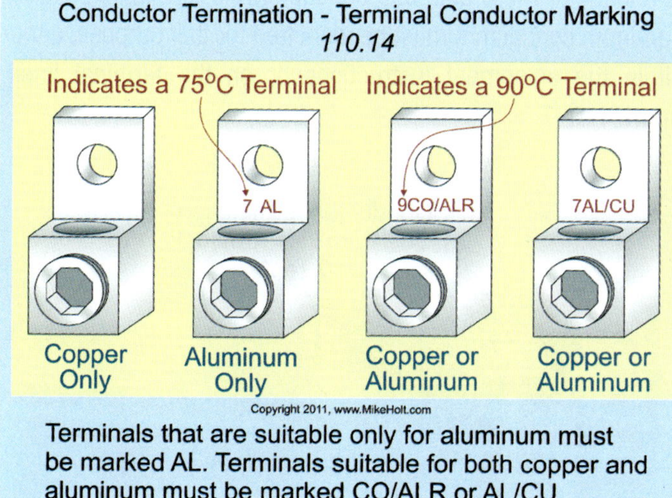

Figure 110–4

CAUTION: *When the insulation is stripped from an aluminum conductor and the conductor is exposed to air, an insulating film (aluminum oxide) immediately forms on the conductor. This film can create a poor connection and overheating at terminations. Unless the terminal or the device is manufactured with the right contacts designed to break through the film and ensure a good connection, overheating may occur. An oxide inhibiting paste can be applied to aluminum conductors at terminations to help improve the connection, but this isn't required.*

Connectors and terminals for conductors more finely stranded than Class B and Class C, as shown in Table 10 of Chapter 9, must be identified for the conductor class. **Figure 110–5**

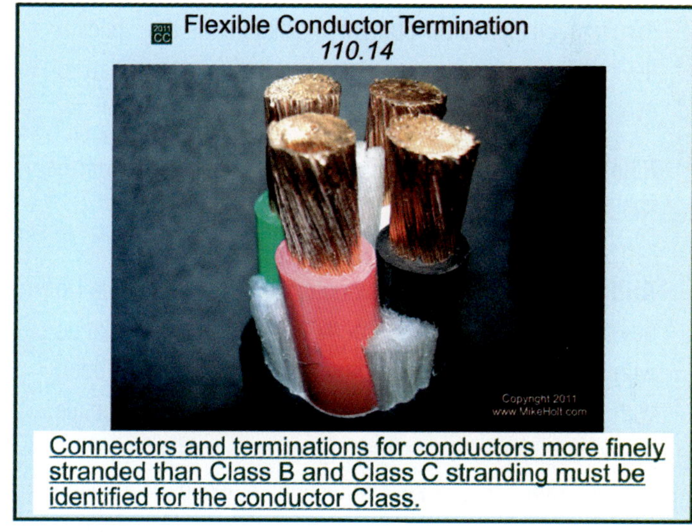

Figure 110–5

> **Author's Comment:** According to UL Standard 486 A-B, a terminal/lug/connector must be listed and marked for use with conductors stranded in other than Class B. With no marking or factory literature/instructions to the contrary, terminals may only be used with Class B stranded conductors.
>
> - Class B stranding (Standard) has 7 strands of wire per conductor in sizes 18-2 AWG, 19 strands in sizes 1-4/0 AWG, and 37 strands in sizes 250-500 kcmil.

- Class C stranding has 19 strands of wire per conductor in sizes 18-2 AWG, 37 strands in sizes 1-4/0 AWG, and 61 strands in sizes 250-500 kcmil.
- Class D stranding has 37 strands of wire per conductor in sizes 18-2 AWG, 61 strands in sizes 1-4/0 AWG, and 91 strands in sizes 250-500 kcmil.

Copper and Aluminum Mixed. Copper and aluminum conductors must not make contact with each other in a device unless the device is listed and identified for this purpose.

Author's Comment: Few terminations are listed for the mixing of aluminum and copper conductors, but if they are, that will be marked on the product package or terminal device. The reason copper and aluminum shouldn't be in contact with each other is because corrosion develops between the two different metals due to galvanic action, resulting in increased contact resistance at the splicing device. This increased resistance can cause the splice to overheat and cause a fire.

Note: Many terminations and equipment are marked with a tightening torque.

Author's Comment: Conductors must terminate in devices that have been properly tightened in accordance with the manufacturer's torque specifications included with equipment instructions. Failure to torque terminals can result in excessive heating of terminals or splicing devices due to a loose connection. A loose connection can also lead to arcing which increases the heating effect and also may lead to a short circuit or ground fault. Any of these can result in a fire or other failure, including an arc-flash event. In addition, this is a violation of 110.3(B), which requires all equipment to be installed in accordance with listing or labeling instructions. Figure 110–6

Author's Comment: Terminating conductors without a torque tool can result in an improper and unsafe installation. If a torque screwdriver isn't used, there's a good chance the conductors aren't properly terminated.

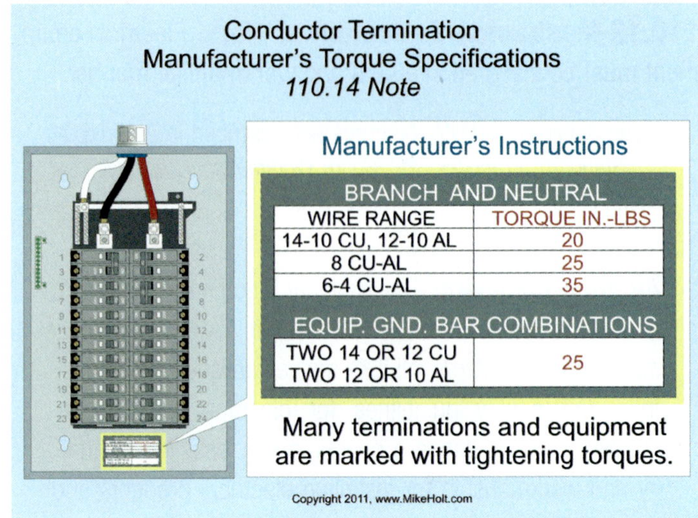

Figure 110–6

(A) Terminations. Conductor terminals must ensure a good connection without damaging the conductors and must be made by pressure connectors (including set screw type) or splices to flexible leads.

Author's Comment: See the definition of "Connector, Pressure" in Article 100.

Terminals for more than one conductor and terminals used for aluminum conductors must be identified for this purpose, either within the equipment instructions or on the terminal itself. Figure 110–7

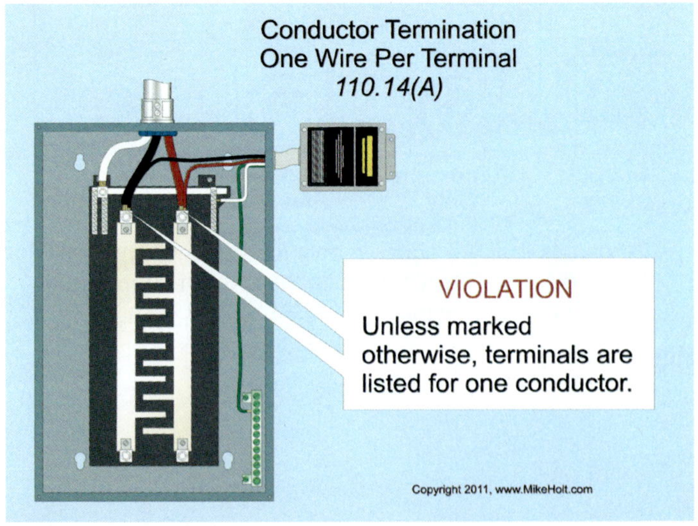

Figure 110–7

Author's Comments:

- Split-bolt connectors are commonly listed for only two conductors, although some are listed for three conductors. However, it's a common industry practice to terminate as many conductors as possible within a split-bolt connector, even though this violates the NEC. Figure 110–8
- Grounding and bonding terminals are also often listed for more than one conductor under the terminal.

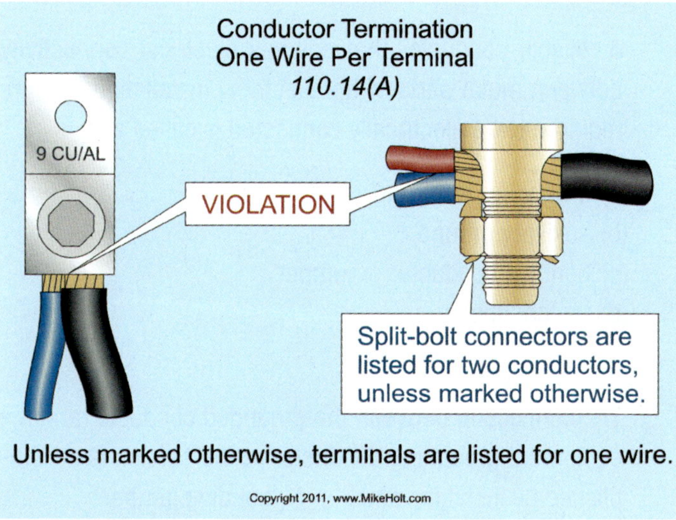

Figure 110–8

(B) Conductor Splices. Conductors must be spliced by a splicing device identified for the purpose or by exothermic welding.

Author's Comment: Conductors aren't required to be twisted together prior to the installation of a twist-on wire connector, unless specifically required in the installation instructions. Figure 110–9

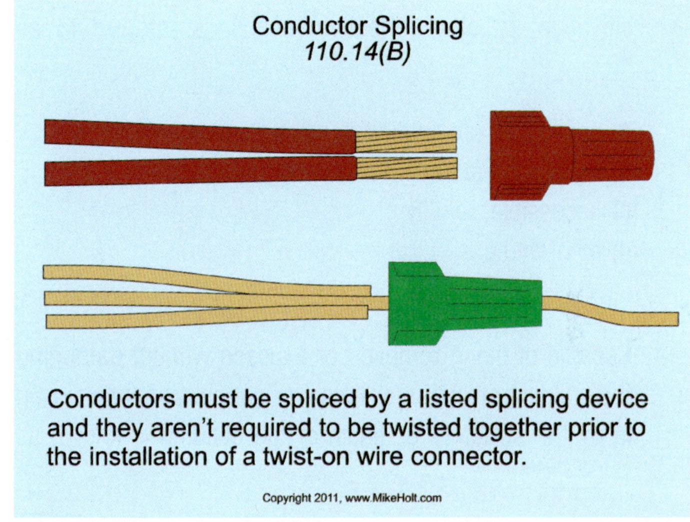

Figure 110–9

CHAPTER 1

Practice Questions

CHAPTER 1. GENERAL—PRACTICE QUESTIONS

Article 100. Definitions

1. Admitting close approach, not guarded by locked doors, elevation, or other effective means, is referred to as "______."

   (a) accessible (as applied to equipment)
   (b) accessible (as applied to wiring methods)
   (c) accessible, readily
   (d) all of these

2. Capable of being removed or exposed without damaging the building structure or finish, or not permanently closed in by the structure or finish of the building is known as "______."

   (a) accessible (as applied to equipment)
   (b) accessible (as applied to wiring methods)
   (c) accessible, readily
   (d) all of these

3. Acceptable to the authority having jurisdiction means ______.

   (a) identified
   (b) listed
   (c) approved
   (d) labeled

4. Where no statutory requirement exists, the authority having jurisdiction can be a property owner or his/her agent, such as an architect or engineer.

   (a) True
   (b) False

5. Bonded can be described as ______ to establish electrical continuity and conductivity.

   (a) isolated
   (b) guarded
   (c) connected
   (d) separated

6. A reliable conductor that ensures electrical conductivity between metal parts of the electrical installation that are required to be electrically connected is called a "______."

   (a) grounding electrode
   (b) auxiliary ground
   (c) bonding conductor or jumper
   (d) tap conductor

7. The connection between the grounded conductor and the equipment grounding conductor at the service is accomplished by installing a(n) ______ bonding jumper.

   (a) main
   (b) system
   (c) equipment
   (d) circuit

8. The connection between the grounded conductor and the supply-side bonding jumper or equipment grounding conductor, or both at a ______ is called a system bonding jumper.

   (a) service disconnect
   (b) separately derived system
   (c) motor control center
   (d) separate building or structure disconnect

9. The conductors between the final overcurrent device protecting the circuit and the outlet(s) are known as "______" conductors.

   (a) feeder
   (b) branch-circuit
   (c) home run
   (d) none of these

10. For a circuit to be considered a multiwire branch circuit, it shall have ______.

   (a) two or more ungrounded conductors with a voltage potential between them
   (b) a grounded conductor having equal voltage potential between it and each ungrounded conductor of the circuit
   (c) a grounded conductor connected to the neutral or grounded terminal of the system
   (d) all of these

11. The *NEC* defines a(n) "______" as a permanent structure having a roof and walls that stands alone or that is cut off from adjoining structures by fire walls or fire barriers, with all openings therein protected by approved fire doors and used to enclose an occupancy.

   (a) unit
   (b) apartment
   (c) building
   (d) utility

12. An enclosure for either surface mounting or flush mounting provided with a frame in which a door can be hung is called a(n) "______."

   (a) enclosure
   (b) outlet box
   (c) cutout box
   (d) cabinet

13. Communications equipment includes equipment used for the transmission of ______.

   (a) audio
   (b) video
   (c) data
   (d) any of these

14. A solderless pressure connector is a device that ______ between conductors or between conductors and a terminal by means of mechanical pressure.

   (a) provides access
   (b) protects the wiring
   (c) is never needed
   (d) establishes a connection

15. A(n) ______ is a device by which the conductors of a circuit can be disconnected from their source of supply.

   (a) feeder
   (b) enclosure
   (c) disconnecting means
   (d) conductor interrupter

16. A ______ is a single unit that provides independent living facilities for persons, including permanent provisions for living, sleeping, cooking, and sanitation.

   (a) one-family dwelling
   (b) two-family dwelling
   (c) dwelling unit
   (d) multifamily dwelling

17. Fixed, stationary, or portable self-contained, electrically illuminated equipment with words or symbols designed to convey information or attract attention describes ______.

   (a) electric signs
   (b) equipment
   (c) appliances
   (d) none of these

18. As used in the *NEC*, equipment includes ______.

(a) fittings
(b) appliances
(c) machinery
(d) all of these

19. When the term exposed, as it applies to live parts, is used in the *Code*, it refers to ______.

(a) being capable of being inadvertently touched or approached nearer than a safe distance by a person
(b) parts that are not suitably guarded, isolated, or insulated
(c) wiring on, or attached to, the surface or behind panels designed to allow access
(d) a and b

20. On or attached to the surface or behind access panels designed to allow access is known as "______."

(a) open
(b) uncovered
(c) exposed
(d) bare

21. The *NEC* defines a "______" as: all circuit conductors between the service equipment, the source of a separately derived system, or other power-supply source and the final branch-circuit overcurrent device.

(a) service
(b) feeder
(c) branch circuit
(d) all of these

22. An accessory, such as a locknut, intended to perform a mechanical function best describes ______.

(a) a part
(b) equipment
(c) a device
(d) a fitting

23. A(n) ______ is an unintentional, electrically conducting connection between an ungrounded conductor of an electrical circuit, and the normally non-current-carrying conductors, metallic enclosures, metallic raceways, metallic equipment, or earth.

(a) grounded conductor
(b) ground fault
(c) equipment ground
(d) bonding jumper

24. Connected to ground or to a conductive body that extends the ground connection is called "______."

(a) equipment grounding
(b) bonded
(c) grounded
(d) all of these

25. A circuit conductor that is intentionally grounded is called a(n) "______."

(a) grounding conductor
(b) unidentified conductor
(c) grounded conductor
(d) grounding electrode conductor

26. Connected to ground without the insertion of any resistor or impedance device is "______."

(a) grounded
(b) solidly grounded
(c) effectively grounded
(d) grounding conductor

27. A device intended for the protection of personnel that functions to de-energize a circuit or portion thereof within an established period of time when a current to ground exceeds the values established for a Class A device, is a(n) ______.

(a) dual-element fuse
(b) inverse time breaker
(c) ground-fault circuit interrupter
(d) safety switch

28. A Class A GFCI-protection device is designed to trip when the ground-fault current to ground is ______ or higher.

(a) 4 mA
(b) 5 mA
(c) 6 mA
(d) 7 mA

29. The installed conductive path that connects normally non-current-carrying metal parts of equipment together and to the system grounded conductor or to the grounding electrode conductor, or both, is known as a(n) "______."

(a) grounding electrode conductor
(b) grounding conductor
(c) equipment grounding conductor
(d) none of these

30. A conducting object through which a direct connection to the earth is established is a "______."

(a) bonding conductor
(b) grounding conductor
(c) grounding electrode
(d) grounded conductor

31. A conductor used to connect the system grounded conductor or equipment to a grounding electrode or to a point on the grounding electrode system is called the "______" conductor.

(a) main grounding
(b) common main
(c) equipment grounding
(d) grounding electrode

32. A handhole enclosure is an enclosure for use in underground systems, provided with an open or closed bottom, and sized to allow personnel to ______.

(a) enter and exit freely
(b) reach into but not enter
(c) have full working space
(d) examine it visually

33. Recognized as suitable for the specific purpose, function, use, environment, and application is the definition of "______."

(a) labeled
(b) identified (as applied to equipment)
(c) listed
(d) approved

34. A device that provides a means to connect bonding conductors for ______ systems to the building grounding electrode system is an intersystem bonding termination.

(a) limited-energy
(b) low-voltage
(c) communications
(d) power and lighting

35. Equipment or materials to which a symbol or other identifying mark of a product evaluation organization that is acceptable to the authority having jurisdiction has been attached is known as "_____."

(a) listed
(b) labeled
(c) approved
(d) identified

36. Equipment or materials included in a list published by a testing laboratory acceptable to the authority having jurisdiction are said to be _____.

(a) a book
(b) a digest
(c) a manifest
(d) listed

37. The term "Luminaire" includes an individual lampholder.

(a) True
(b) False

38. A neutral conductor is the conductor connected to the _____ of a system, which is intended to carry neutral current under normal conditions.

(a) grounding electrode
(b) neutral point
(c) intersystem bonding termination
(d) none of these

39. The common point on a wye-connection in a polyphase system describes a neutral point.

(a) True
(b) False

40. Outline lighting may include an arrangement of _____ to outline or call attention to the shape of a building.

(a) incandescent lamps
(b) electric-discharge lighting
(c) electrically powered light sources
(d) any of these

41. A panel, including buses and automatic overcurrent devices, designed to be placed in a cabinet or cutout box and accessible only from the front is known as a "_____."

(a) switchboard
(b) disconnect
(c) panelboard
(d) switch

42. Premises wiring includes _____ wiring from the service point or power source to the outlets.

(a) interior
(b) exterior
(c) underground
(d) all of these

43. NFPA 70E—*Standard for Electrical Safety in the Workplace,* provides information to help determine the electrical safety training requirements expected of a qualified person.

(a) True
(b) False

44. A raceway is an enclosure designed for the installation of wires, cables, or busbars.

(a) True
(b) False

45. A contact device installed at an outlet for the connection of an attachment plug is known as a(n) "______."

(a) attachment point
(b) tap
(c) receptacle
(d) wall plug

46. A single receptacle is a single contact device with no other contact device on the same ______.

(a) circuit
(b) yoke
(c) run
(d) equipment
(d) controller

47. A(n) "______" system is a premises wiring system whose power is derived from a source of electric energy other than a service and has no direct electrical connection to supply conductors originating in another system.

(a) separately derived
(b) classified
(c) direct
(d) emergency

48. The conductors and equipment from the electric utility that deliver electric energy to the wiring system of the premises is called a "______."

(a) branch circuit
(b) feeder
(c) service
(d) none of these

49. Service conductors originate at the service point and terminate at service disconnecting means.

(a) True
(b) False

50. The ______ is the necessary equipment, usually consisting of a circuit breaker(s) or switch(es) and fuse(s) and their accessories, connected to the load end of service conductors, and intended to constitute the main control and cutoff of the supply.

(a) service equipment
(b) service
(c) service disconnect
(d) service overcurrent device

51. The ______ is the point of connection between the facilities of the serving utility and the premises wiring.

(a) service entrance
(b) service point
(c) overcurrent protection
(d) beginning of the wiring system

52. The combination of all components and subsystems that convert solar energy into electrical energy is called a "______" system.

(a) solar
(b) solar voltaic
(c) separately derived source
(d) solar photovoltaic

53. Special permission is the written consent from the ______.

(a) testing laboratory
(b) manufacturer
(c) owner
(d) authority having jurisdiction

54. A structure is that which is built or constructed.

(a) True
(b) False

Article 110. Requirements for Electrical Installations

1. In judging equipment for approval, considerations such as the following shall be evaluated:

(a) Mechanical strength
(b) Wire-bending space
(c) Arcing effects
(d) all of these

2. Listed or labeled equipment shall be installed and used in accordance with any instructions included in the listing or labeling.

(a) True
(b) False

3. Conductors shall be ______ unless otherwise provided.

(a) bare
(b) stranded
(c) copper
(d) aluminum

4. Conductor sizes are expressed in American Wire Gage or ______.

(a) inches
(b) circular mils
(c) square inches
(d) cubic inches

5. Some cleaning and lubricating compounds can cause severe deterioration of many plastic materials used for insulating and structural applications in equipment.

(a) True
(b) False

6. The *NEC* requires that electrical work be ______.

(a) installed in a neat and workmanlike manner
(b) installed under the supervision of a licensed person
(c) completed before being inspected
(d) all of these

7. Accepted industry workmanship practices are described in ANSI/NECA 1-2006, *Standard Practices for Good Workmanship in Electrical Contracting*, and other ANSI-approved installation standards.

(a) True
(b) False

8. Internal parts of electrical equipment, including ______, shall not be damaged or contaminated by foreign materials such as paint, plaster, cleaners, abrasives, or corrosive residues.

(a) busbars
(b) wiring terminals
(c) insulators
(d) all of these

9. Connectors and terminals for conductors more finely stranded than Class B and Class C, as shown In Table 10 of Chapter 9, must be ______ for the specific conductor class or classes.

(a) listed
(b) approved
(c) identified
(d) all of these

10. Many terminations and equipment are marked with ______.

(a) an etching tool
(b) a removable label
(c) a tightening torque
(d) the manufacturer's initials

11. Connection of conductors to terminal parts shall ensure a thoroughly good connection without damaging the conductors and shall be made by means of ______.

    (a) solder lugs
    (b) pressure connectors
    (c) splices to flexible leads
    (d) any of these

12. Connection by means of wire-binding screws, studs, or nuts having upturned lugs or the equivalent shall be permitted for ______ or smaller conductors.

    (a) 12 AWG
    (b) 10 AWG
    (c) 8 AWG
    (d) 6 AWG

13. Soldered splices shall first be spliced or joined so as to be mechanically and electrically secure without solder and then be soldered.

    (a) True
    (b) False

Notes

CHAPTER

2 WIRING AND PROTECTION

INTRODUCTION TO CHAPTER 2—WIRING AND PROTECTION

Chapter 2 provides general rules for wiring and the protection of conductors. The rules in this chapter apply to all electrical installations covered by the *NEC*—except as modified in Chapters 5, 6, and 7 [90.3].

- **Article 250—Grounding and Bonding.** Article 250 covers the grounding requirements for providing a low-impedance path to the earth to reduce overvoltage from lightning, and the requirements for a low-impedance fault current path necessary to facilitate the operation of overcurrent devices in the event of a ground fault.

Notes

Grounding and Bonding

INTRODUCTION TO ARTICLE 250—GROUNDING AND BONDING

No other article can match Article 250 for misapplication, violation, and misinterpretation. Terminology used in this article has been a source for much confusion, but that has improved during the last few *NEC* revisions. It's very important to understand the difference between grounding and bonding in order to correctly apply the provisions of Article 250. Pay careful attention to the definitions that apply to grounding and bonding both here and in Article 100 as you begin the study of this important article. Article 250 covers the grounding requirements for providing a path to the earth to reduce overvoltage from lightning, and the bonding requirements for a low-impedance fault current path back to the source of the electrical supply to facilitate the operation of overcurrent devices in the event of a ground fault.

Over the past five Code cycles, this article was extensively revised to organize it better and make it easier to understand and implement. It's arranged in a logical manner, so it's a good idea to just read through Article 250 to get a big picture view—after you review the definitions. Next, study the article closely so you understand the details. The illustrations will help you understand the key points.

PART I. GENERAL

250.1 Scope. Article 250 contains the following grounding and bonding requirements:

(1) What systems and equipment are required to be grounded.

(3) Location of grounding connections.

(4) Types of electrodes and sizes of grounding and bonding conductors.

(5) Methods of grounding and bonding.

250.2 Definitions.

Bonding Jumper, Supply-Side. A conductor on the supply side or within a service or separately derived system to ensure the electrical conductivity between metal parts required to be electrically connected. **Figures 250–1 and 250–2**

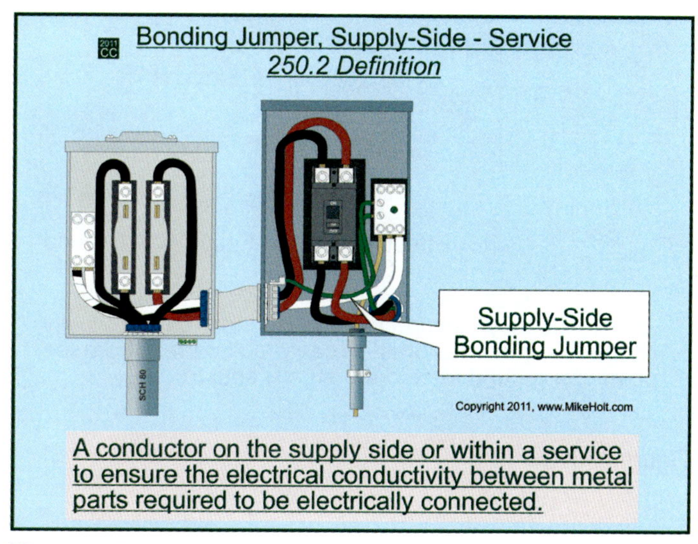

Figure 250–1

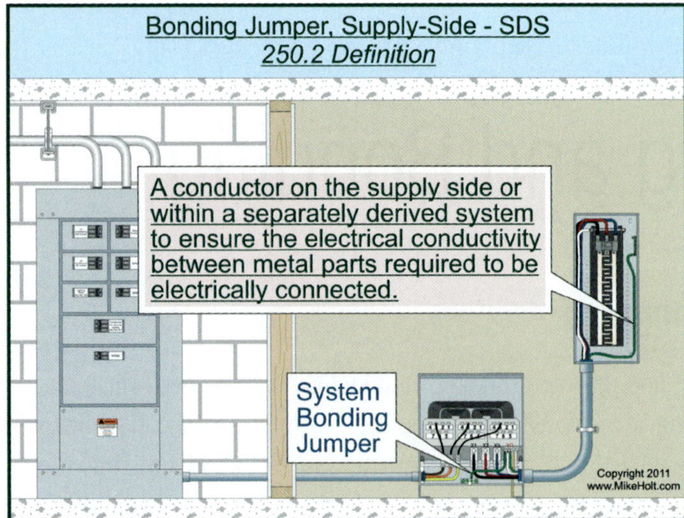

Figure 250–2

Effective Ground-Fault Current Path. An intentionally constructed low-impedance conductive path designed to carry fault current from the point of a ground fault on a wiring system to the electrical supply source. **Figure 250–3**

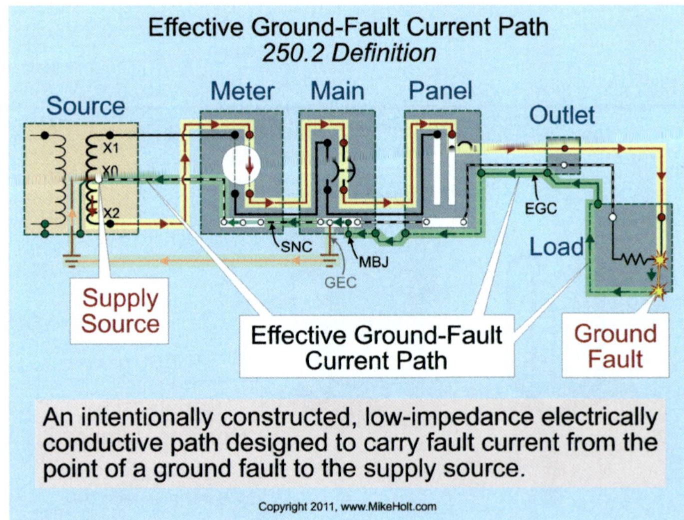

Figure 250–3

Author's Comment: In **Figure 250–3**, EGC represents the equipment grounding conductor [259.118], MBJ represents the main bonding jumper, SNC represents the service neutral conductor (grounded service conductor), GEC represents the grounding electrode conductor.

The current path shown between the supply source grounding electrode and the grounding electrode at the service main shows that some current will flow through the earth but the earth is not part of the effective ground-fault current path.

The effective ground-fault current path is intended to help remove dangerous voltage from a ground fault by opening the circuit overcurrent device. **Figure 250–4**

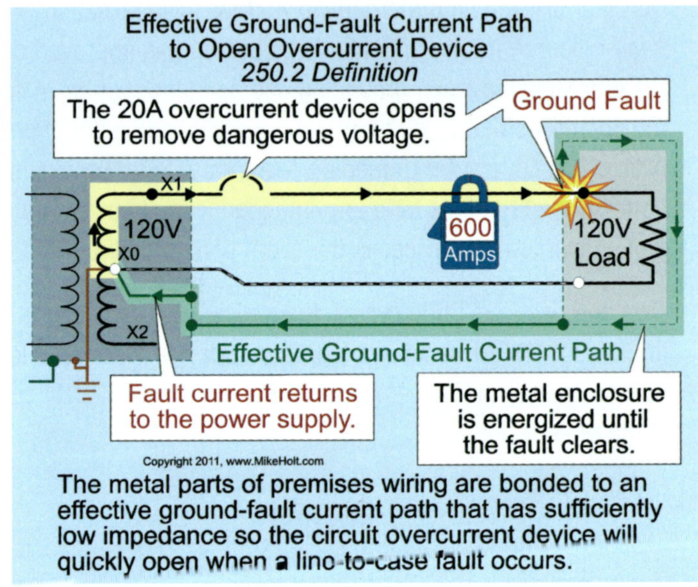

Figure 250–4

Ground-Fault Current Path. An electrically conductive path from a ground fault to the electrical supply source.

Note: The ground-fault current path could be metal raceways, cable sheaths, electrical equipment, or other electrically conductive materials, such as metallic water or gas piping, steel-framing members, metal ducting, reinforcing steel, or the shields of communications cables. **Figure 250–5**

Author's Comment: The difference between an "effective ground-fault current path" and a "ground-fault current path" is the effective ground-fault current path is "intentionally" constructed to provide a low-impedance fault current path to the electrical supply source for the purpose of clearing a ground fault. A ground-fault current path is all of the available conductive paths over which fault current flows on its return to the electrical supply source during a ground fault.

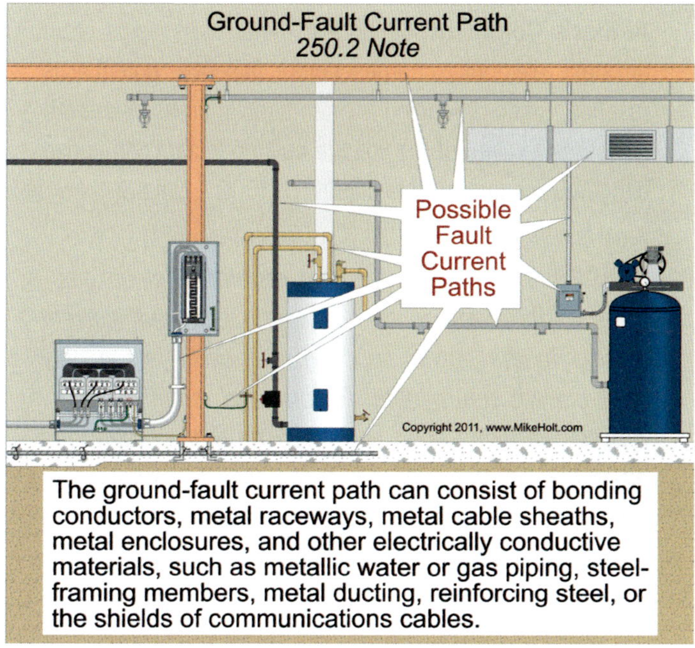

Figure 250–5

250.4 General Requirements for Grounding and Bonding.

(A) Solidly Grounded Systems.

(1) Electrical System Grounding. Electrical power systems, such as the secondary winding of a transformer are grounded (connected to the earth) to limit the voltage induced by lightning, line surges, or unintentional contact by higher-voltage lines. **Figure 250–6**

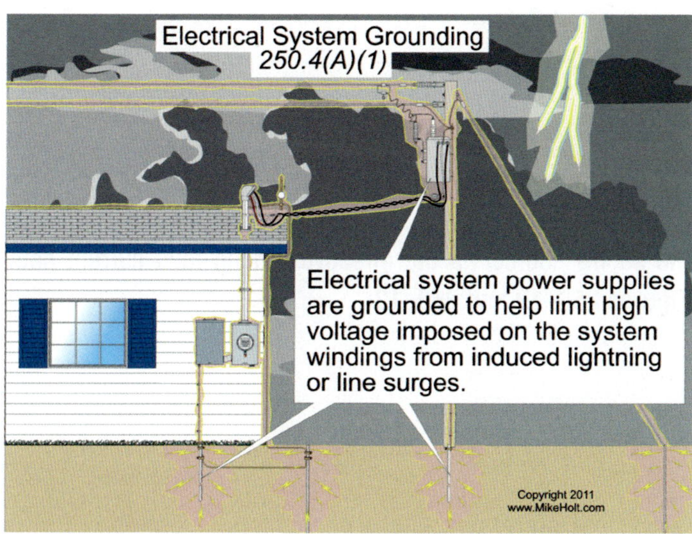

Figure 250–6

Author's Comment: System grounding helps reduce fires in buildings as well as voltage stress on electrical insulation, thereby ensuring longer insulation life for motors, transformers, and other system components. **Figure 250–7**

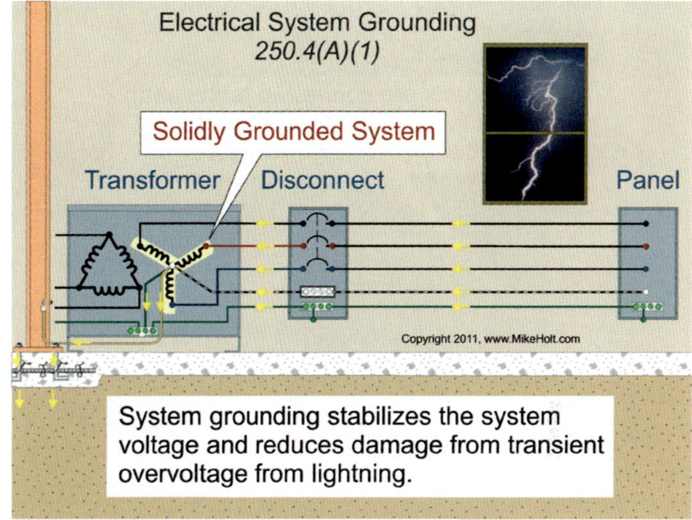

Figure 250–7

Note: An important consideration for limiting imposed voltage is to remember that grounding electrode conductors shouldn't be any longer than necessary and unnecessary bends and loops should be avoided. **Figure 250–8**

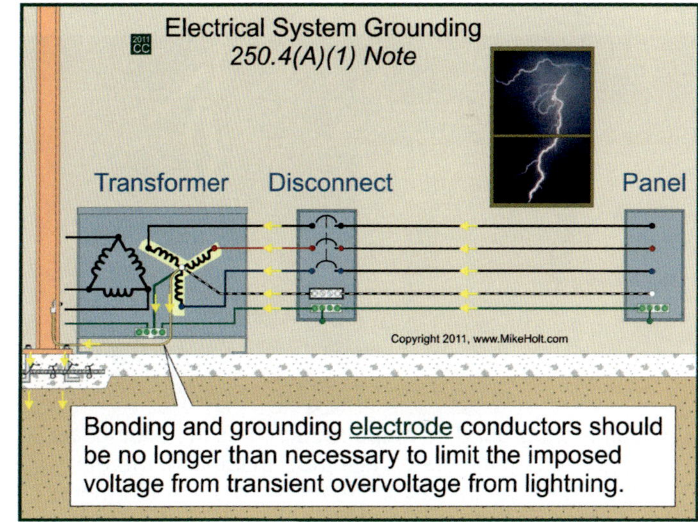

Figure 250–8

(2) Equipment Grounding. Metal parts of electrical equipment are grounded (connected to the earth) to reduce induced voltage on metal parts from exterior lightning so as to prevent fires from an arc within the building/structure. **Figure 250–9**

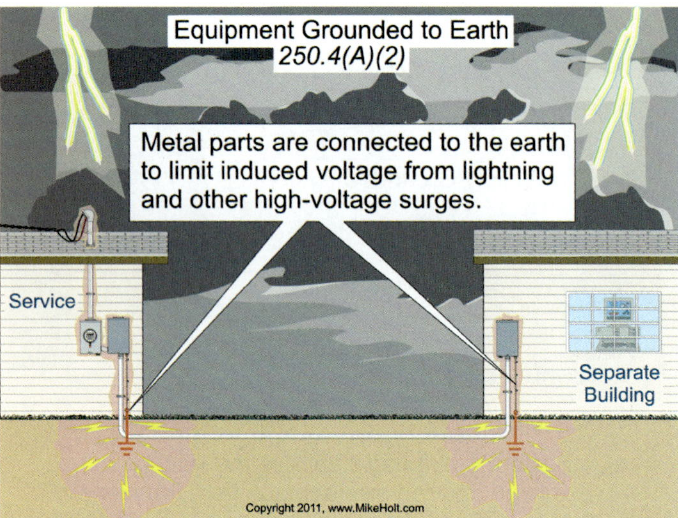

Figure 250–9

DANGER: *Failure to ground the metal parts can result in high voltage on metal parts from an indirect lightning strike to seek a path to the earth within the building—possibly resulting in a fire and/or electric shock.* **Figure 250–10**

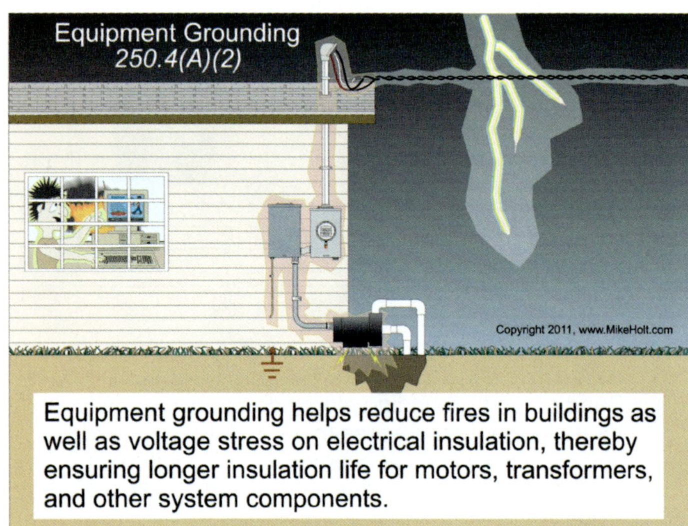

Figure 250–10

Author's Comment: Grounding metal parts helps drain off static electricity charges before flashover potential is reached. Static grounding is often used in areas where the discharge (arcing) of the voltage buildup (static) can cause dangerous or undesirable conditions [500.4 Note 3].

DANGER: *Because the contact resistance of an electrode to the earth is so high, very little fault current returns to the power supply if the earth is the only fault current return path. Result—the circuit overcurrent device won't open and clear the ground fault, and all metal parts associated with the electrical installation, metal piping, and structural building steel will become and remain energized.* **Figure 250–11**

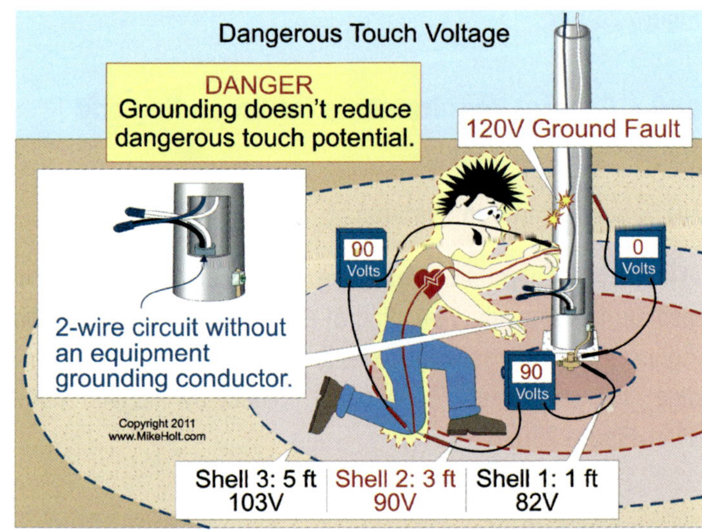

Figure 250–11

(3) Equipment Bonding. Metal parts of electrical raceways, cables, enclosures, and equipment must be connected to the supply source via the effective ground-fault current path. **Figures 250–12 and 250–13**

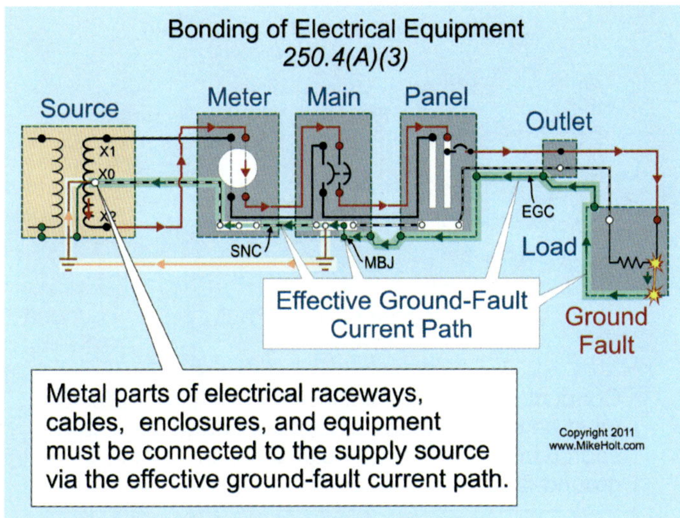

Figure 250–12

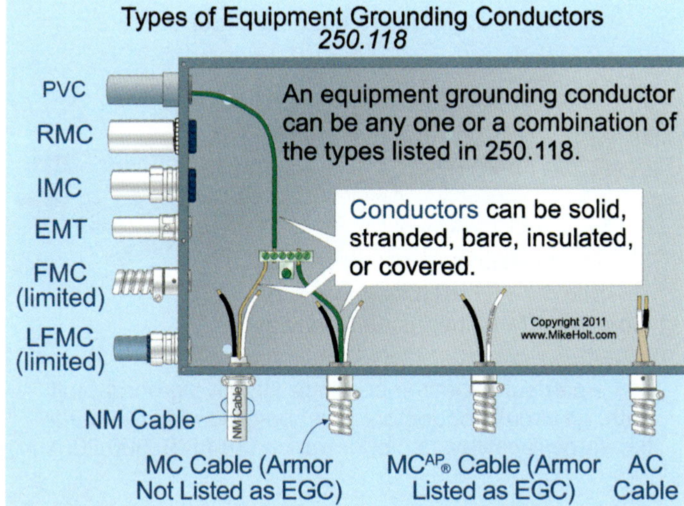

Figure 250–13

Author's Comments:

- To quickly remove dangerous touch voltage on metal parts from a ground fault, the fault current path must have sufficiently low impedance to the source so that fault current will quickly rise to a level that will open the branch-circuit overcurrent device. **Figure 250–14**

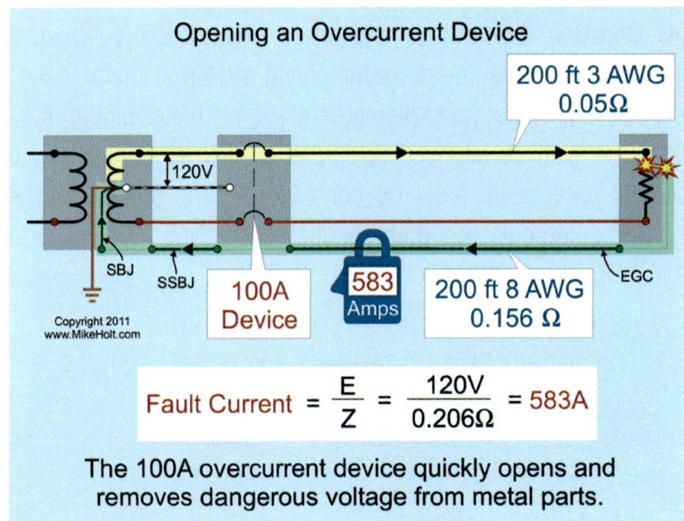

Figure 250–14

- The time it takes for an overcurrent device to open is inversely proportional to the magnitude of the fault current. This means the higher the ground-fault current value, the less time it will take for the overcurrent device to open and clear the fault. For example, a 20A circuit with an overload of 40A (two times the 20A rating) takes 25 to 150 seconds to open the overcurrent device. At 100A (five times the 20A rating) the 20A breaker trips in 5 to 20 seconds. **Figure 250–15**

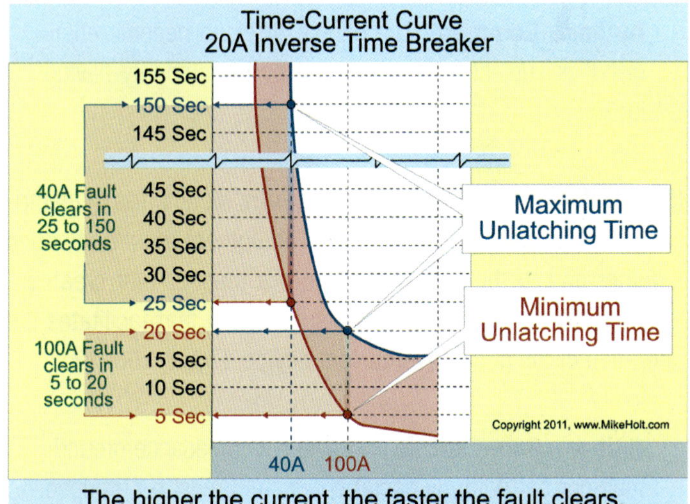

Figure 250–15

(4) Bonding Conductive Materials. Electrically conductive materials such as metal water piping systems, metal sprinkler piping, metal gas piping, and other metal-piping systems, as well as exposed structural steel members likely to become energized, must be connected to the supply source via an equipment grounding conductor of a type recognized in 250.118. **Figure 250–16**

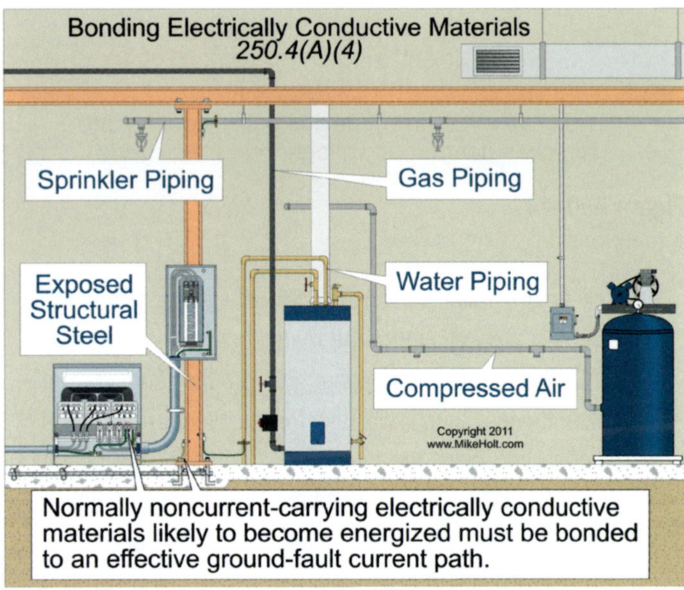

Figure 250–16

> **Author's Comment:** The phrase "likely to become energized" is subject to interpretation by the authority having jurisdiction.

(5) Effective Ground-Fault Current Path. Metal parts of electrical raceways, cables, enclosures, or equipment must be bonded together and to the supply system in a manner that creates a low-impedance path for ground-fault current that facilitates the operation of the circuit overcurrent device. **Figure 250–17**

> **Author's Comment:** To ensure a low-impedance ground-fault current path, all circuit conductors must be grouped together in the same raceway, cable, or trench [300.3(B), 300.5(I), and 300.20(A)]. **Figure 250–18**

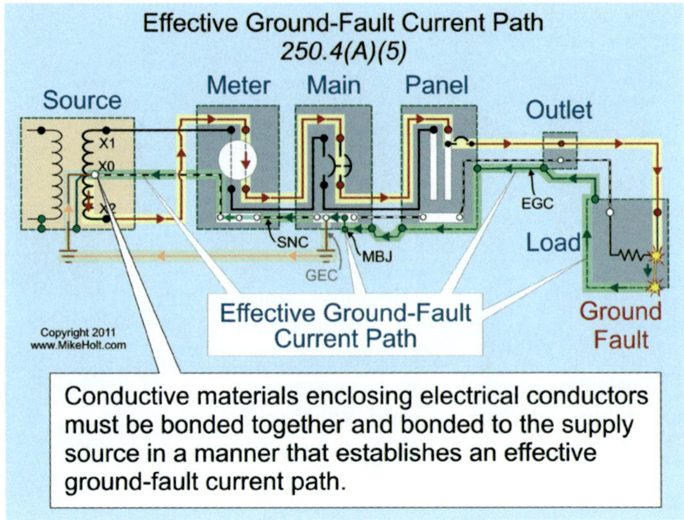

Figure 250–17

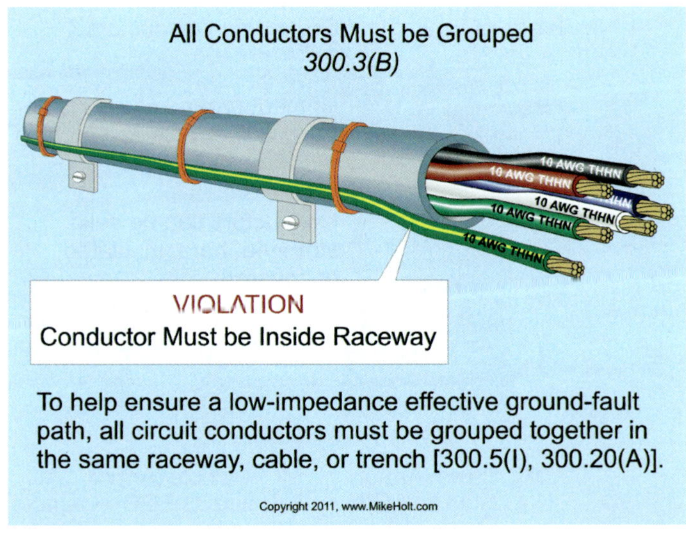

Figure 250–18

Because the earth isn't suitable to serve as the required effective ground-fault current path, an equipment grounding conductor is required to be installed with all circuits. **Figure 250–19**

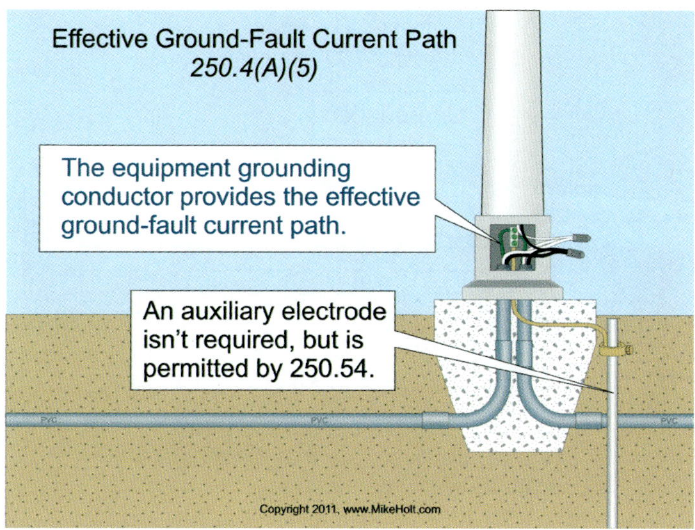

Figure 250–19

Question: *What's the maximum fault current that can flow through the earth to the power supply from a 120V ground fault to metal parts of a light pole that's grounded (connected to the earth) via a ground rod having a contact resistance to the earth of 25 ohms?* **Figure 250–20**

(a) 4.80A (b) 20A (c) 40A (d) 100A

Answer: *(a) 4.80A*

I = E/R

I = 120V/25 ohms

I = 4.80A

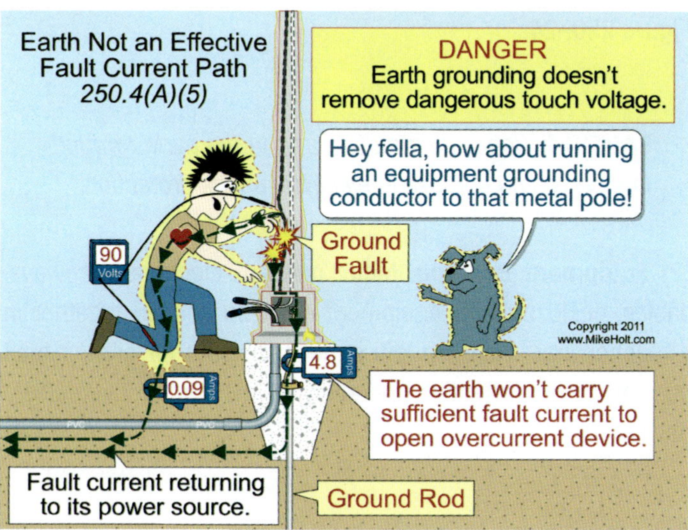

Figure 250–20

DANGER: *Because the contact resistance of an electrode to the earth is so high, very little fault current returns to the power supply if the earth is the only fault current return path. Result—the circuit overcurrent device won't open and all metal parts associated with the electrical installation, metal piping, and structural building steel will become and remain energized.* **Figure 250–21**

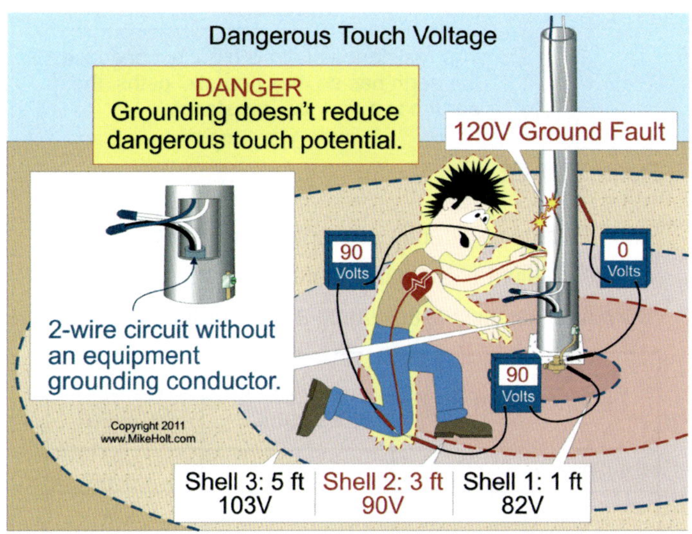

Figure 250–21

EARTH SHELLS

According to ANSI/IEEE 142, *Recommended Practice for Grounding of Industrial and Commercial Power Systems* (Green Book) [4.1.1], the resistance of the soil outward from a ground rod is equal to the sum of the series resistances of the earth shells. The shell nearest the rod has the highest resistance and each successive shell has progressively larger areas and progressively lower resistances. Don't be concerned if you don't understand this statement; just review the table below. **Figure 250–22**

Distance from Rod	Soil Contact Resistance
1 ft (Shell 1)	68% of total contact resistance
3 ft (Shells 1 and 2)	75% of total contact resistance
5 ft (Shells 1, 2, and 3)	86% of total contact resistance

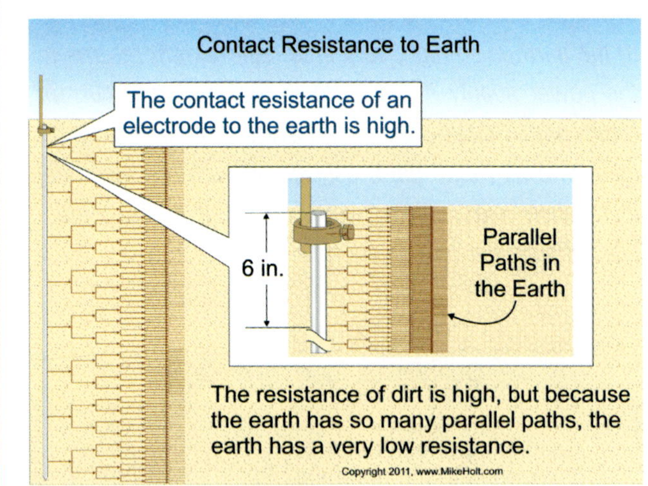

Figure 250–22

Since voltage is directly proportional to resistance, the voltage gradient of the earth around an energized ground rod will be as follows, assuming a 120V ground fault:

Distance from Rod	Soil Contact Resistance	Voltage Gradient
1 ft (Shell 1)	68%	82V
3 ft (Shells 1 and 2)	75%	90V
5 ft (Shells 1, 2, and 3)	86%	103V

(B) Ungrounded Systems.

Author's Comment: Ungrounded systems are those systems with no connection to the ground or to a conductive body that extends the ground connection [Article 100]. Figure 250–23

(1) Equipment Grounding. Metal parts of electrical equipment are grounded (connected to the earth) to reduce induced voltage on metal parts from exterior lightning so as to prevent fires from an arc within the building/structure. Figure 250–24

Author's Comment: Grounding metal parts helps drain off static electricity charges before an electric arc takes place (flashover potential). Static grounding is often used in areas where the discharge (arcing) of the voltage buildup (static) can cause dangerous or undesirable conditions [500.4 Note 3].

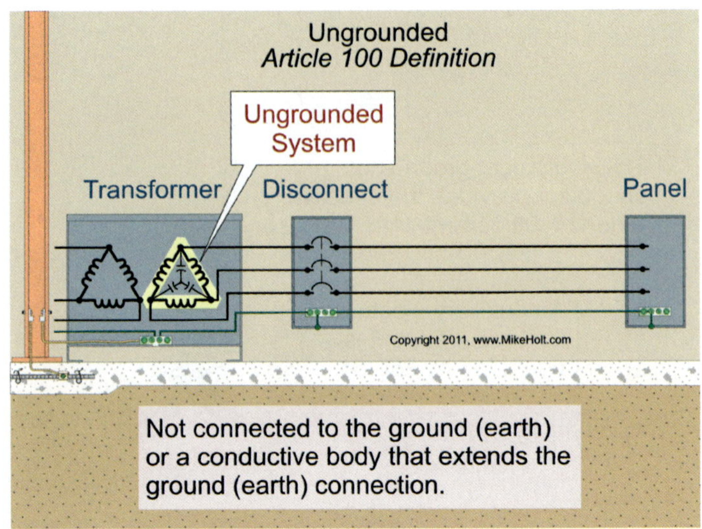

Figure 250–23

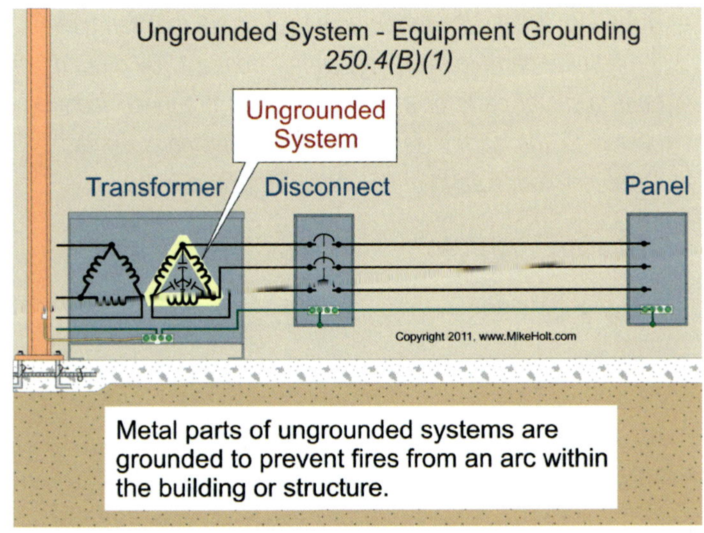

Figure 250–24

CAUTION: *Connecting metal parts to the earth (grounding) serves no purpose in electrical shock protection.*

(2) Equipment Bonding. Metal parts of electrical raceways, cables, enclosures, or equipment must be bonded together in a manner that creates a low-impedance path for ground-fault current to facilitate the operation of the circuit overcurrent device.

The fault current path must be capable of safely carrying the maximum ground-fault current likely to be imposed on it from any point on the wiring system where a ground fault may occur to the electrical supply source.

(3) Bonding Conductive Materials. Conductive materials such as metal water piping systems, metal sprinkler piping, metal gas piping, and other metal-piping systems, as well as exposed structural steel members likely to become energized must be bonded together in a manner that creates a low-impedance fault current path that's capable of carrying the maximum fault current likely to be imposed on it. Figure 250–25

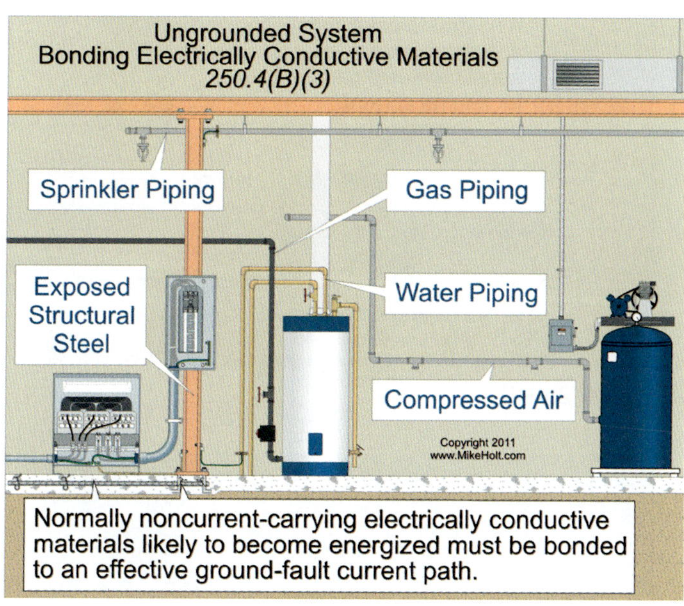

Figure 250–25

> **Author's Comment:** The phrase "likely to become energized" is subject to interpretation by the authority having jurisdiction.

(4) Fault Current Path. Electrical equipment, wiring, and other electrically conductive material likely to become energized must be installed in a manner that creates a low-impedance fault current path to facilitate the operation of overcurrent devices should a second ground fault from a different phase occur. Figure 250–26

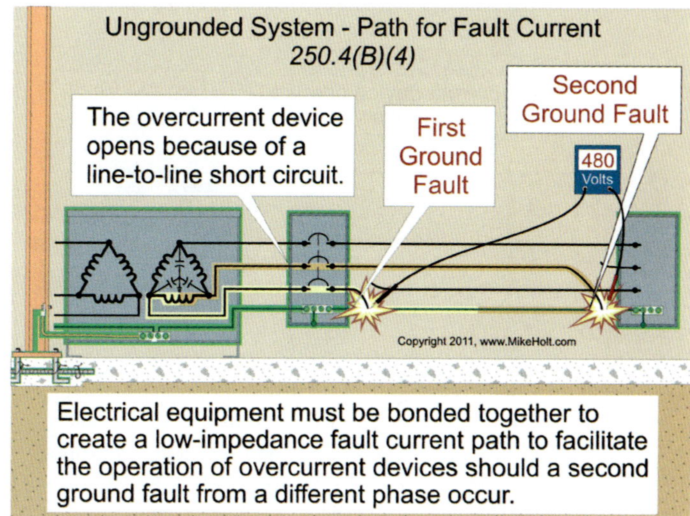

Figure 250–26

> **Author's Comment:** A single ground fault can't be cleared on an ungrounded system because there's no low-impedance fault current path to the power source. The first ground fault simply grounds the previously ungrounded system. However, a second ground fault on a different phase results in a line-to-line short circuit between the two ground faults. The conductive path, between the ground faults, provides the low-impedance fault current path necessary so the overcurrent device will open.

250.6 Objectionable Current.

(A) Preventing Objectionable Current. To prevent a fire, electric shock, or improper operation of circuit overcurrent devices or electronic equipment, electrical systems and equipment must be installed in a manner that prevents objectionable neutral current from flowing on metal parts.

(C) Temporary Currents Not Classified as Objectionable Currents. Temporary currents from abnormal conditions, such as ground faults, aren't to be classified as objectionable current. Figure 250–27

(D) Limitations to Permissible Alterations. Currents that introduce noise or data errors in electronic equipment are not considered objectionable currents for the purposes of this section. Circuits that supply electronic equipment must be connected to an equipment grounding conductor.

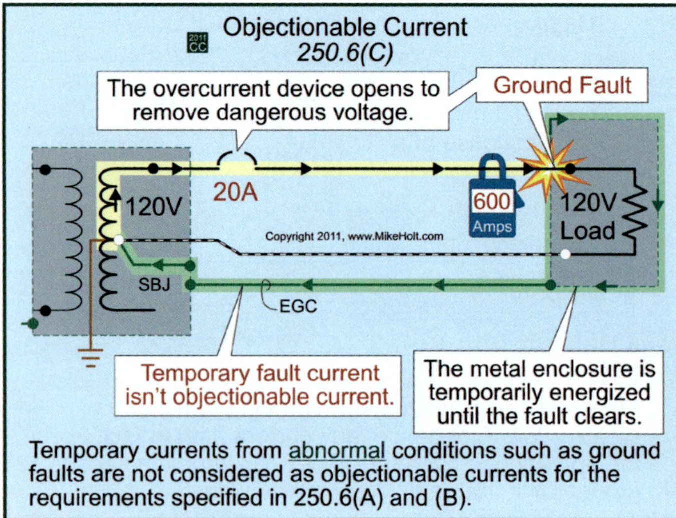

Figure 250–27

OBJECTIONABLE CURRENT

Objectionable neutral current occurs because of improper neutral-to-case connections or wiring errors that violate 250.142(B).

Improper Neutral-to-Case Connection [250.142]

Panelboards. Objectionable neutral current will flow when the neutral conductor is connected to the metal case of a panelboard that's not used as service equipment. **Figure 250–28**

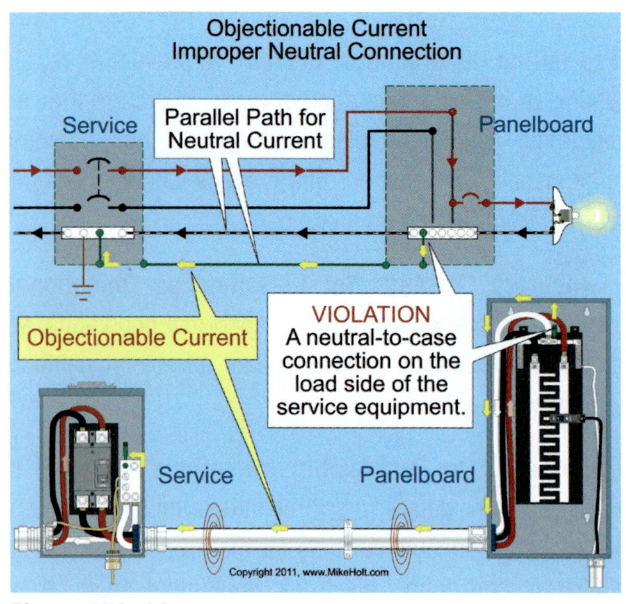

Figure 250–28

Separately Derived Systems. Objectionable neutral current will flow on conductive metal parts and conductors if the neutral conductor is connected to the circuit equipment grounding conductor on the load side of the system bonding jumper for a separately derived system. **Figures 250–29 and 250–30**

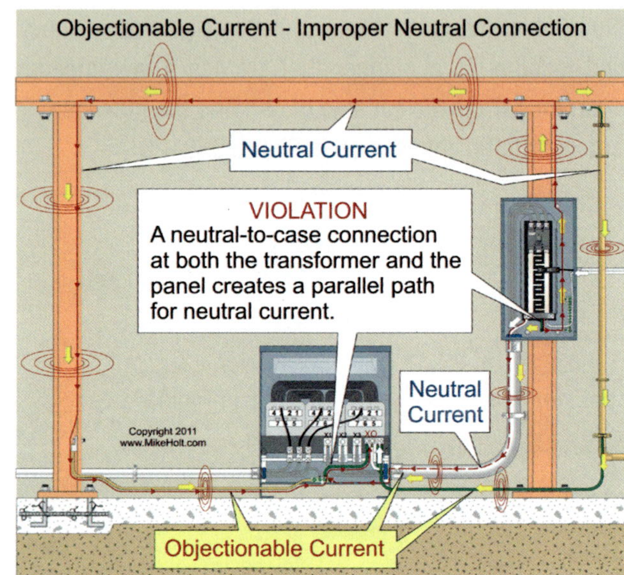

Figure 250–29

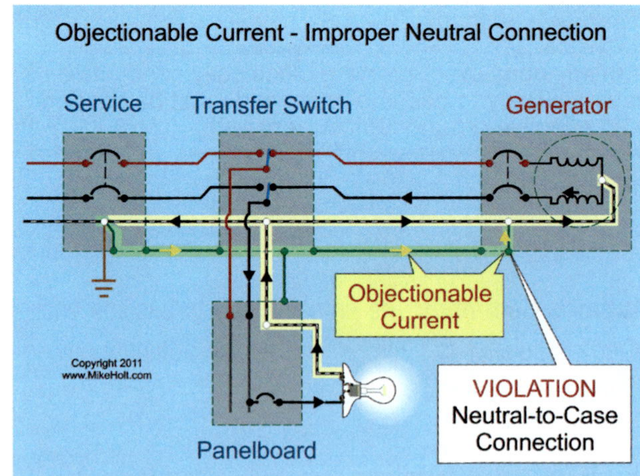

Figure 250-30

Disconnects. Objectionable neutral current will flow when the neutral conductor is connected to the metal case of a disconnecting means that's not part of the service equipment. **Figure 250–31**

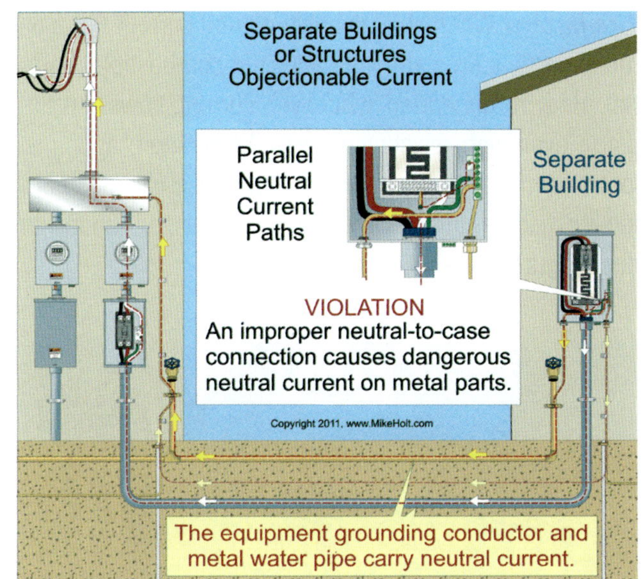

Figure 250–31

Wiring Errors. Objectionable neutral current will flow when the neutral conductor from one system is connected to a circuit of a different system. Figure 250–32

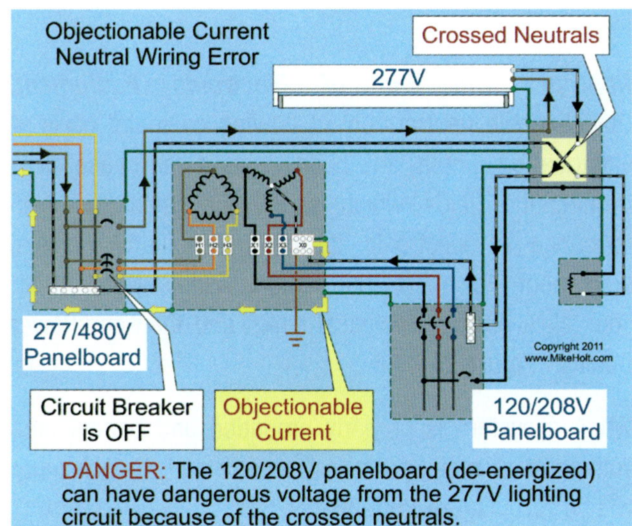

Figure 250–32

Objectionable neutral current will flow on metal parts when the circuit equipment grounding conductor is used as a neutral conductor such as where:

- A 230V time-clock motor is replaced with a 115V time-clock motor, and the circuit equipment grounding conductor is used for neutral return current.
- A 115V water filter is wired to a 240V well-pump motor circuit, and the circuit equipment grounding conductor is used for neutral return current. Figure 250–33

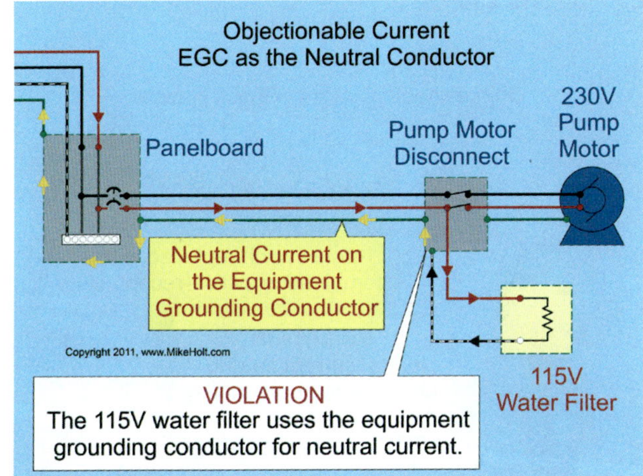

Figure 250–33

- The circuit equipment grounding conductor is used for neutral return current. Figure 250–34

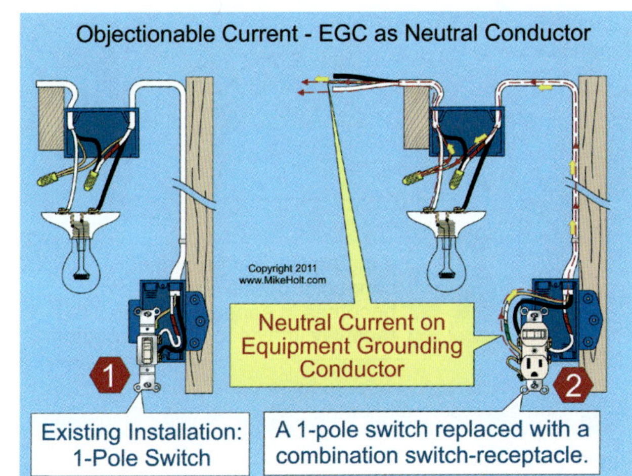

Figure 250–34

DANGERS OF OBJECTIONABLE CURRENT

Objectionable neutral current on metal parts can cause electric shock, fires, and improper operation of electronic equipment and overcurrent devices such as GFPs, GFCIs, and AFCIs.

Shock Hazard. When objectionable neutral current flows on metal parts, electric shock and even death can occur from the elevated voltage on those metal parts. **Figures 250–35 and 250–36**

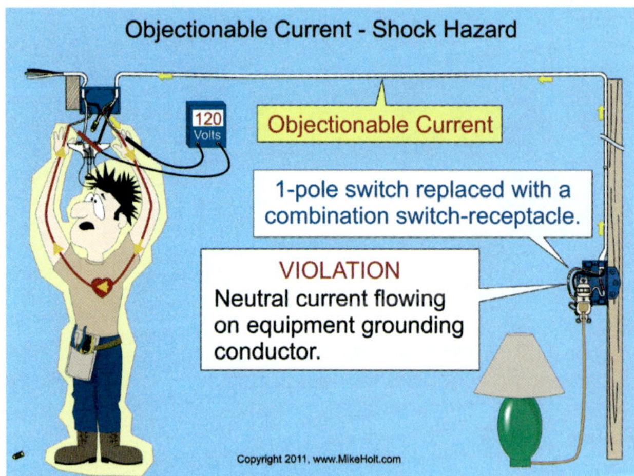

Figure 250–35

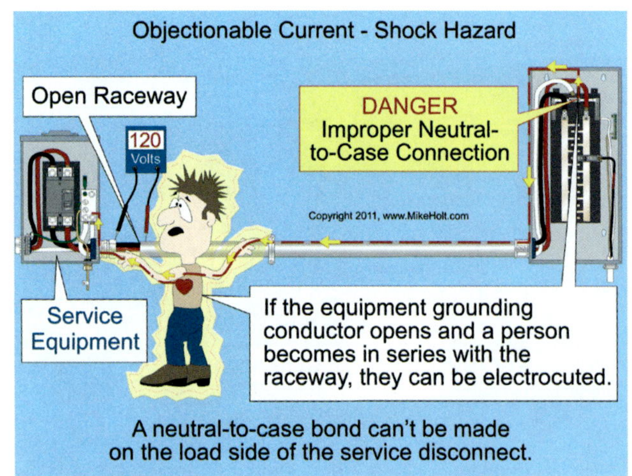

Figure 250–36

Fire Hazard. When objectionable neutral current flows on metal parts, a fire can ignite adjacent combustible material. Heat is generated whenever current flows, particularly over high-resistance parts. In addition, arcing at loose connections is especially dangerous in areas containing easily ignitible and explosive gases, vapors, or dust. **Figure 250–37**

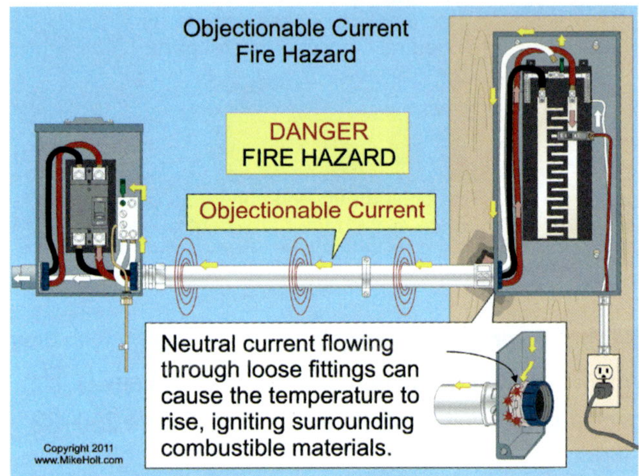

Figure 250–37

Improper Operation of Electronic Equipment. Objectionable neutral current flowing on metal parts of electrical equipment and building parts can cause electromagnetic fields which negatively affect the performance of electronic devices, particularly medical equipment. For more information, visit www.MikeHolt.com, click on the "Technical Link," and then on "Power Quality." **Figure 250–38**

When a system is properly grounded and bonded, the voltage of all metal parts to the earth and to each other will be zero. **Figure 250–39**

When objectionable neutral current travels on metal parts because of the improper bonding of the neutral to metal parts in violation of the *NEC*, a difference of potential will exist between all metal parts. This situation can cause some electronic equipment to operate improperly. **Figure 250–40**

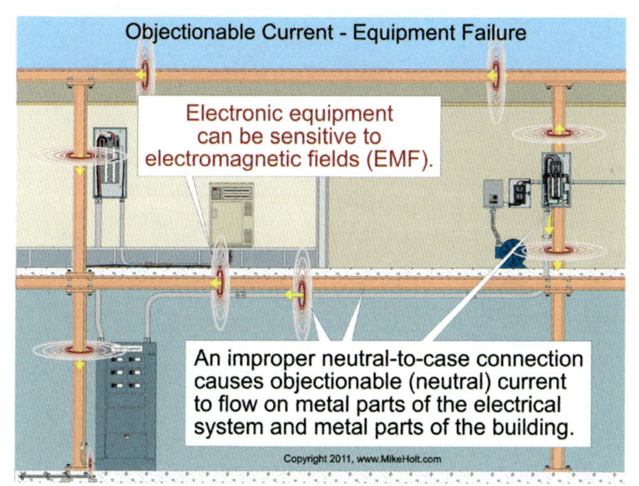

Figure 250–38

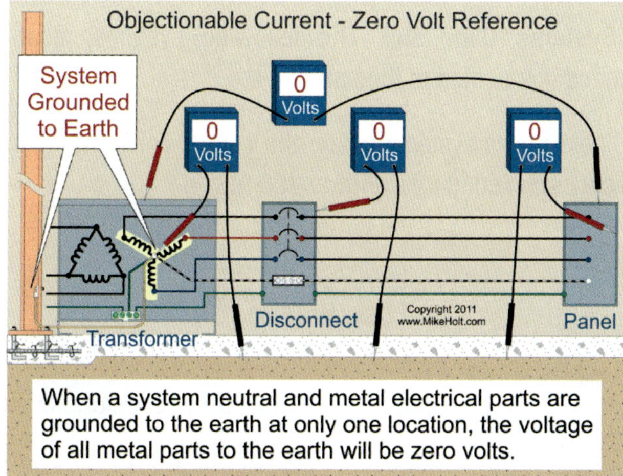

Figure 250–39

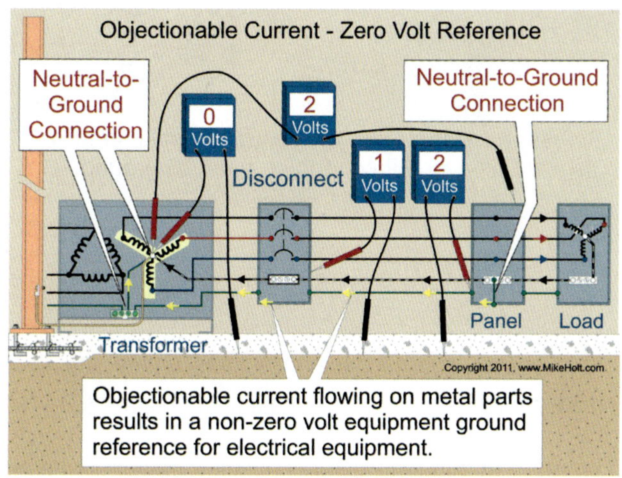

Figure 250–40

Operation of Overcurrent Devices. When objectionable neutral current travels on metal parts, tripping of electronic overcurrent devices equipped with ground-fault protection can occur because some neutral current flows on the circuit equipment grounding conductor instead of the neutral conductor.

250.8 Termination of Grounding and Bonding Conductors.

(A) Permitted Methods. Equipment grounding conductors, grounding electrode conductors, and bonding jumpers must terminate in one of the following methods:

(1) Listed pressure connectors

(2) Terminal bars

(3) Pressure connectors listed for direct burial or concrete encasement [250.70]

(4) Exothermic welding

(5) Machine screws that engage at least two threads or are secured with a nut, **Figure 250–41**

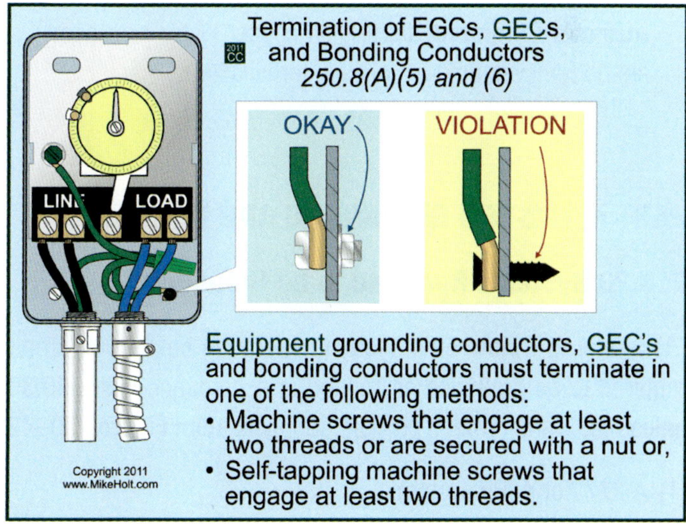

Figure 250–41

(6) Self-tapping machine screws that engage at least two threads

(7) Connections that are part of a listed assembly

(8) Other listed means

(B) Methods Not Permitted. Connection devices or fittings that depend solely on solder aren't allowed.

250.10 Protection of Fittings.

Grounding and bonding fittings must be protected from physical damage by:

(1) Locating the fittings so they aren't likely to be damaged.

(2) Enclosing the fittings in metal, wood, or an equivalent protective covering.

Author's Comment: Grounding and bonding fittings can be buried or encased in concrete if they're installed in accordance with 250.53(G), 250.68(A) Ex 1, and 250.70.

250.12 Clean Surfaces.

Nonconductive coatings, such as paint, must be removed to ensure good electrical continuity, or the termination fittings must be designed so as to make such removal unnecessary [250.53(A) and 250.96(A)].

Author's Comment: Tarnish on copper water pipe need not be removed before making a termination.

PART II. SYSTEM GROUNDING AND BONDING

250.20 Systems Required to be Grounded.

(A) Systems Below 50V. Systems operating below 50V aren't required to be grounded or bonded in accordance with 250.30 unless the transformer's primary supply is from: Figure 250–42

(1) A 277V or 480V system.

(2) An ungrounded system.

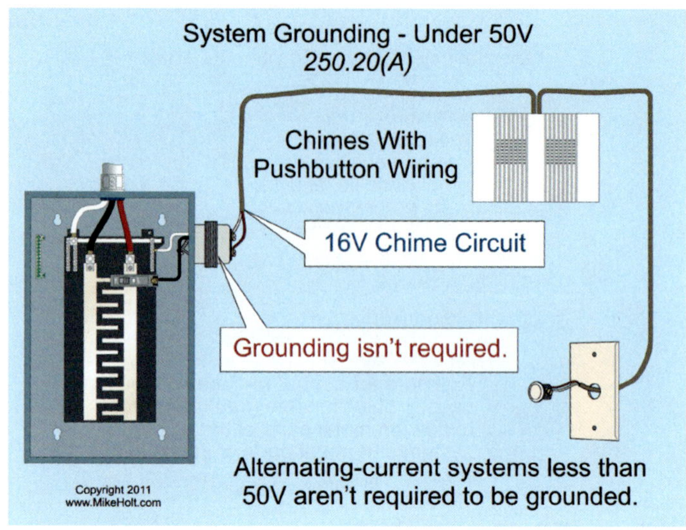

Figure 250–42

(B) Systems Over 50V. The following systems must be grounded (connected to the earth):

(1) Single-phase systems where the neutral conductor is used as a circuit conductor. Figure 250–43

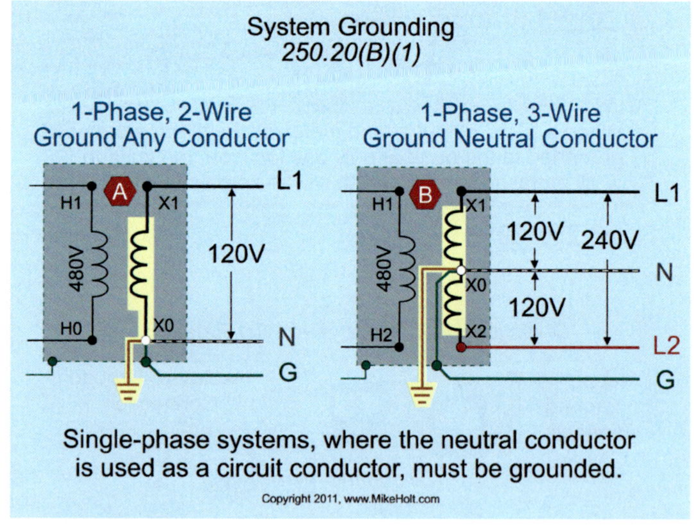

Figure 250–43

(2) Three-phase, wye-connected systems where the neutral conductor is used as a circuit conductor. Figure 250–44A

(3) Three-phase, high-leg delta-connected systems where the neutral conductor is used as a circuit conductor. Figure 250–44B

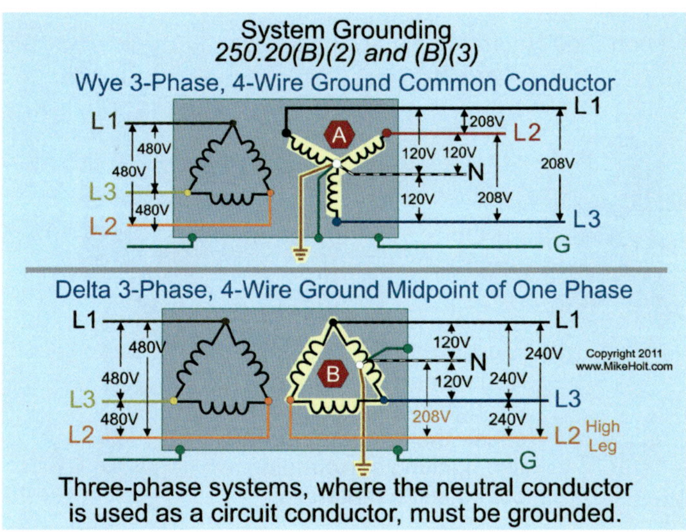

Figure 250–44

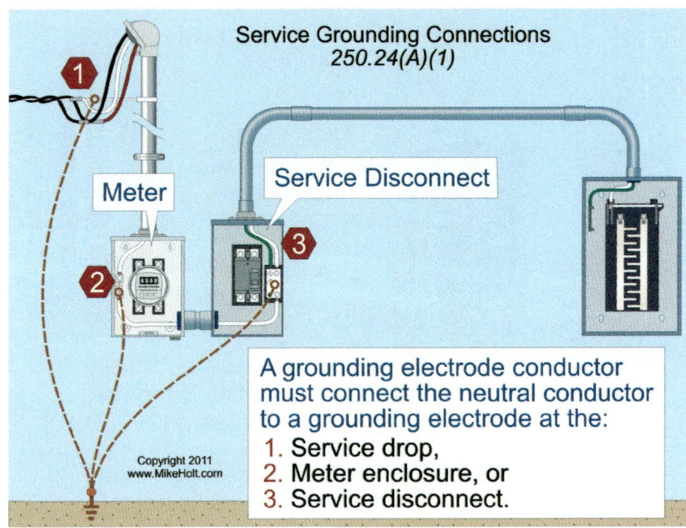

Figure 250–45

250.21 Ungrounded Systems—50V to Less Than 100V.

(B) Ground Detectors.

(1) Systems that aren't required to be grounded in accordance with 250.20(B) [250.21(A)(4)] must have ground detectors installed.

(2) The ground detection sensing equipment must be connected as close as practicable to where the system receives its supply.

(C) Marking. Ungrounded systems must be legibly marked "Ungrounded System" at the source or first disconnecting means of the system, with sufficient durability to withstand the environment involved.

250.24 Service Equipment—Grounding and Bonding.

(A) Grounded System. Service equipment supplied from a grounded system must have the neutral conductor terminate in accordance with (1) through (5).

(1) Grounding Location. A grounding electrode conductor must connect the service neutral conductor to the grounding electrode at any accessible location, from the load end of the service drop or service lateral, up to and including the service disconnecting means. Figure 250–45

> **Author's Comment:** Some inspectors require the service neutral conductor to be grounded (connected to the earth) from the meter socket enclosure, while other inspectors insist that the service neutral conductor be grounded (connected to the earth) only from the service disconnect.

(4) Grounding Termination. When the service neutral conductor is connected to the service disconnecting means [250.24(B)] by a wire or busbar [250.28], the grounding electrode conductor is permitted to terminate to either the neutral terminal or the equipment grounding terminal within the service disconnect.

(5) Neutral-to-Case Connection. A neutral-to-case connection isn't permitted on the load side of service equipment, except as permitted by 250.142(B). Figure 250–46

> **Author's Comment:** If a neutral-to-case connection is made on the load side of service equipment, dangerous objectionable neutral current will flow on conductive metal parts of electrical equipment [250.6(A)]. Objectionable neutral current on metal parts of electrical equipment can cause electric shock and even death from ventricular fibrillation, as well as a fire. Figures 250–47 and 250–48

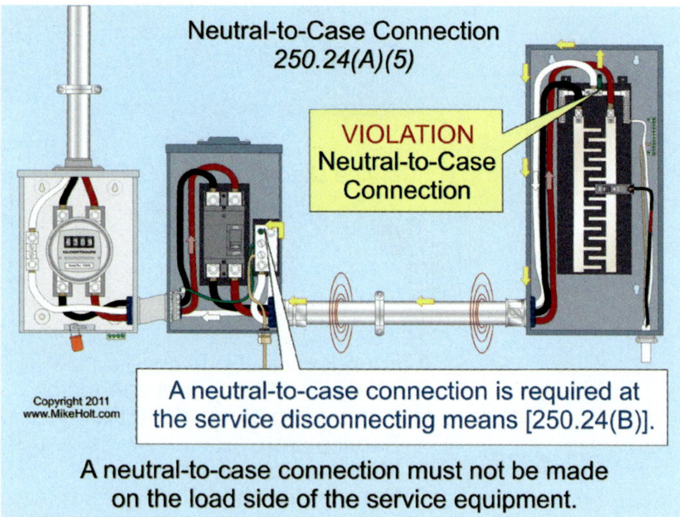

Figure 250–46

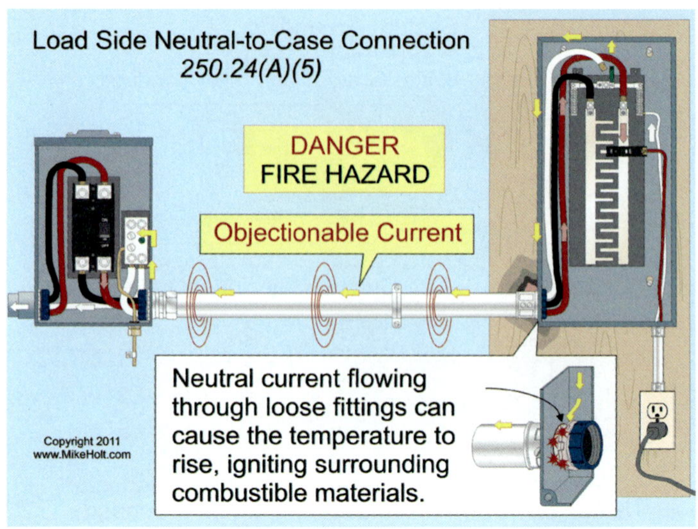

Figure 250–48

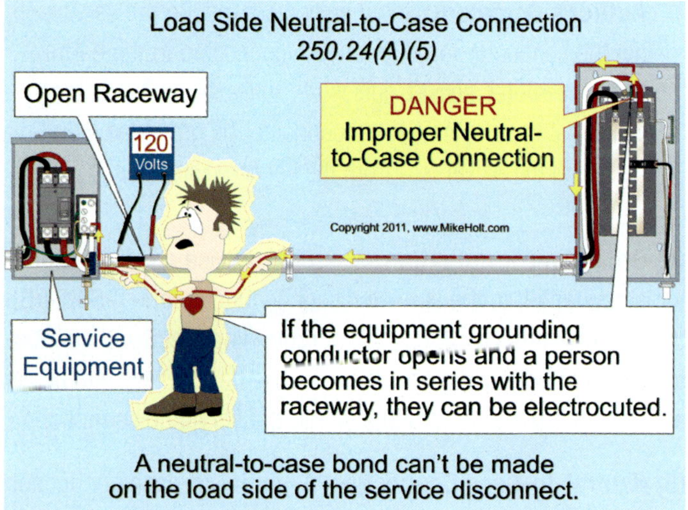

Figure 250–47

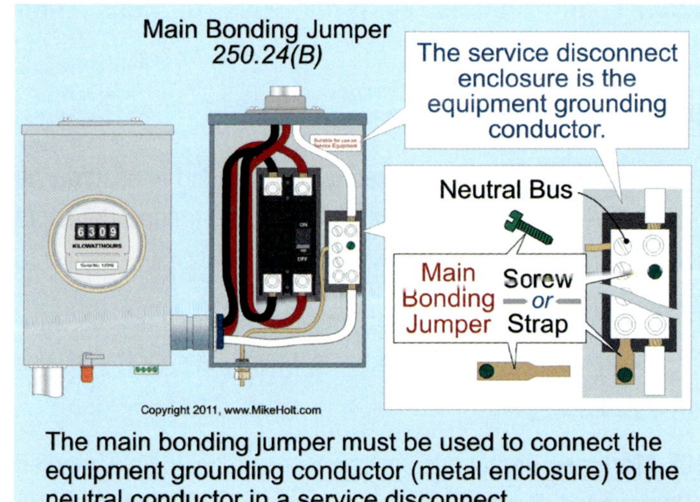

Figure 250–49

(B) Bonding. A main bonding jumper [250.28] must be installed for the purpose of connecting the neutral conductor to the metal parts of the service disconnecting means. **Figure 250–49**

(C) Grounded Conductor Brought to Service Equipment. A service neutral conductor from the electric utility must be routed with the ungrounded conductors and terminate to the service disconnecting means via a main bonding jumper [250.24(B)] that's installed between the service neutral conductor and the service disconnecting means enclosure [250.28]. **Figures 250–50 and 250–51**

Author's Comment: The service neutral conductor provides the effective ground-fault current path to the power supply to ensure that dangerous voltage from a ground fault will be quickly removed by opening the overcurrent device [250.4(A)(3) and 250.4(A)(5)]. **Figure 250–52**

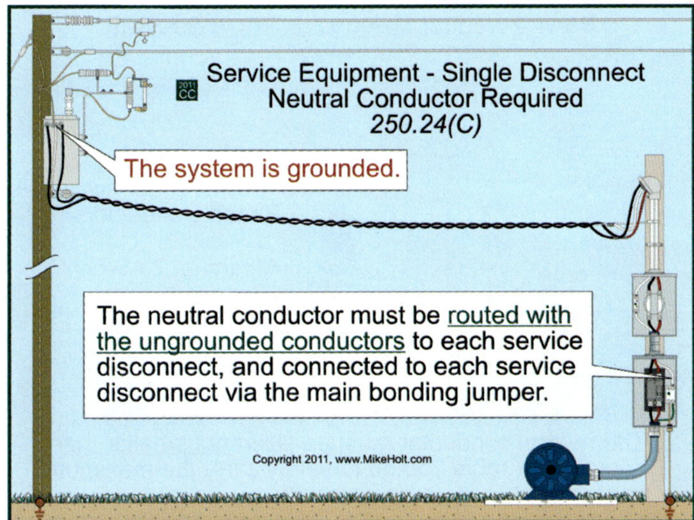

Figure 250–50

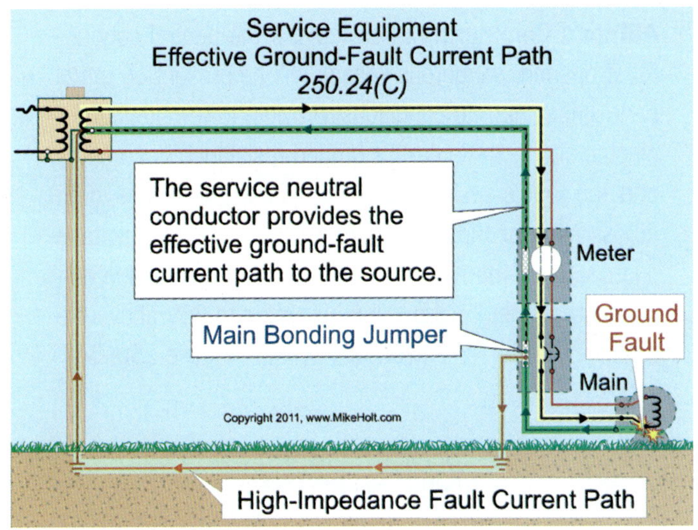

Figure 250–52

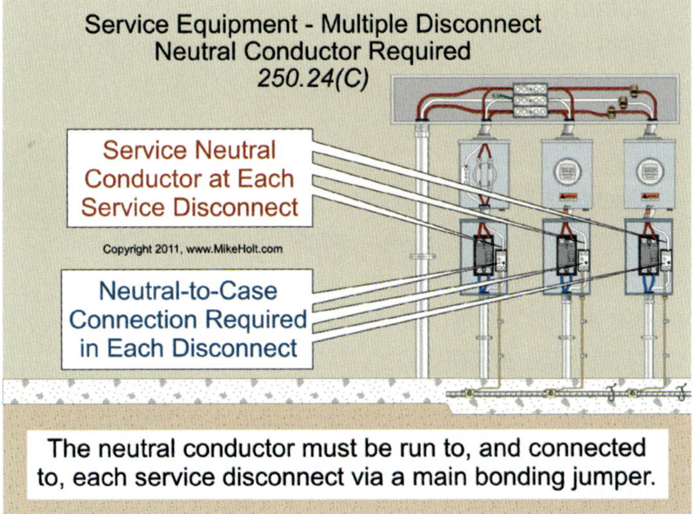

Figure 250–51

DANGER: *Dangerous voltage from a ground fault won't be removed from metal parts, metal piping, and structural steel if the service disconnecting means enclosure isn't connected to the service neutral conductor. This is because the contact resistance of a grounding electrode to the earth is so great that insufficient fault current returns to the power supply if the earth is the only fault current return path to open the circuit overcurrent device.* **Figure 250–53**

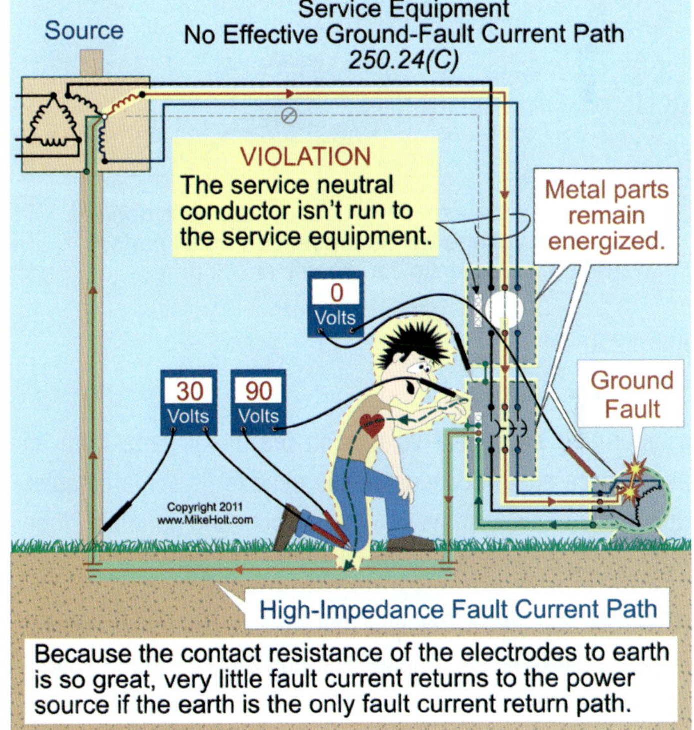

Figure 250–53

Author's Comment: For example, if the neutral conductor is opened, dangerous voltage will be present on metal parts under normal conditions, providing the potential for electric shock. If the earth's ground resistance is 25 ohms and the load's resistance is 25 ohms, the voltage drop across each of these resistors will be half of the voltage source. Since the neutral is connected to the service disconnect, all metal parts will be elevated to 60V above the earth's potential for a 120/240V system. **Figure 250–54**

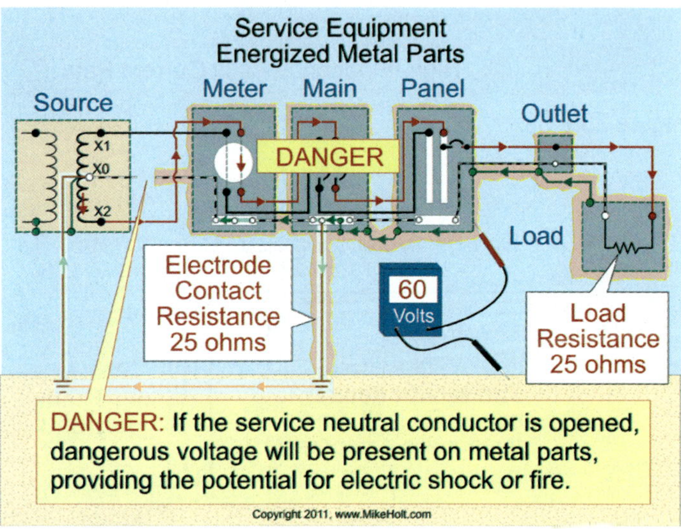

Figure 250–54

To determine the actual voltage on the metal parts from an open service neutral conductor, you need to do some complex math calculations. Visit www.MikeHolt.com and go to the "Free Stuff" link to download a spreadsheet for this purpose.

(1) Single Raceway. Because the service neutral conductor serves as the effective ground-fault current path to the source for ground faults, the neutral conductor must be sized so it can safely carry the maximum fault current likely to be imposed on it [110.10 and 250.4(A)(5)]. This is accomplished by sizing the neutral conductor not smaller than specified in Table 250.66, based on the cross-sectional area of the largest ungrounded service conductor. **Figure 250–55**

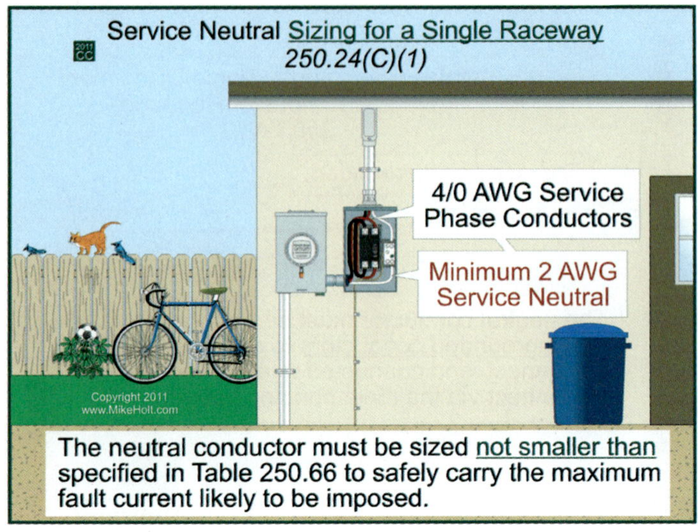

Figure 250–55

Author's Comment: In addition, the neutral conductors must have the capacity to carry the maximum unbalanced neutral current in accordance with 220.61.

Question: *What's the minimum size service neutral conductor required for a 240V, single-phase service installed in one raceway where the ungrounded service conductors are 500 kcmil and the maximum unbalanced load is 100A?* **Figure 250–56**

(a) 3 AWG (b) 2 AWG (c) 1 AWG (d) 1/0 AWG

Answer: *(d) 1/0 AWG [Table 250.66]*

The unbalanced load of 100A requires a 3 AWG service neutral conductor, which is rated 100A at 75°C in accordance with Table 310.15(B)(16) [220.61]. Table 250.66 requires a minimum of 1/0 AWG based on 500 kcmil ungrounded conductors.

(2) Parallel Conductors in Two or More Raceways. If service conductors are paralleled in two or more raceways, a neutral conductor must be installed in each of the parallel raceways. The size of the neutral conductor in each raceway must not be smaller than specified in Table 250.66, based on the cross-sectional area of the largest ungrounded service conductor in each raceway. In no case can the neutral conductor in each parallel set be sized smaller than 1/0 AWG [310.10(H)(1)].

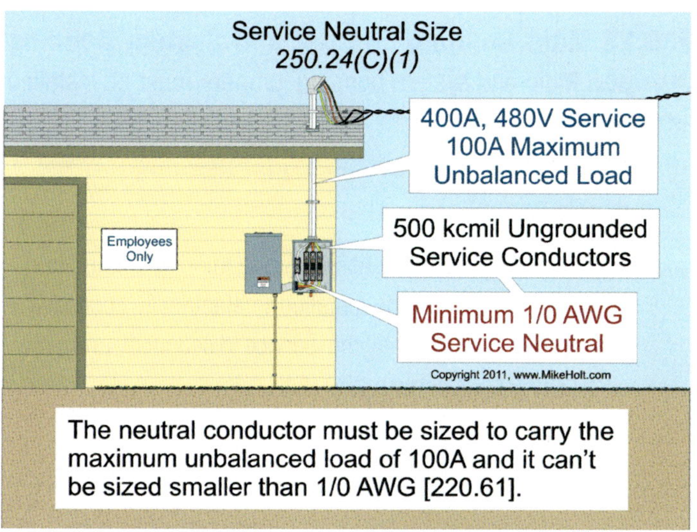

Figure 250–56

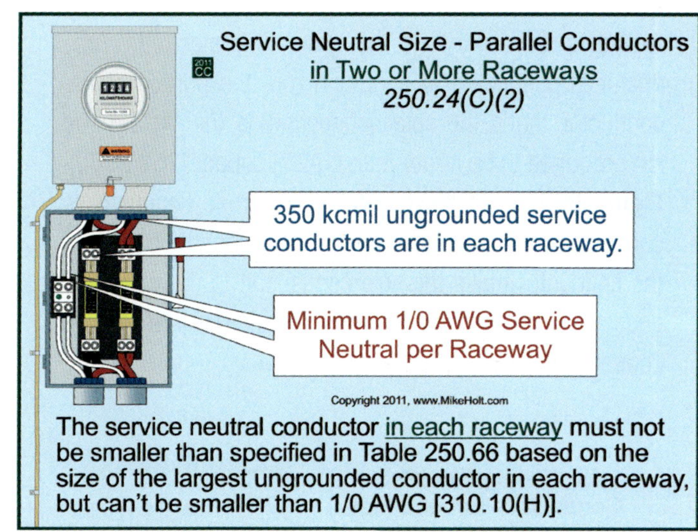

Figure 250–57

Author's Comment: In addition, the neutral conductors must have the capacity to carry the maximum unbalanced neutral current in accordance with 220.61.

Question: *What's the minimum size service neutral conductor required for a 250V, single-phase service installed in parallel in two raceways where the ungrounded service conductors in each of the raceways are 350 kcmil and the maximum unbalanced load is 100A?* **Figure 250–57**

(a) 3 AWG (b) 2 AWG (c) 1 AWG (d) 1/0 AWG

Answer: *(d) 1/0 AWG per raceway [Table 250.66 and 310.10(H)]*

The unbalanced load of 50A in each raceway requires an 8 AWG service neutral conductor, which is rated 50A at 75°C in accordance with Table 310.15(B)(16) [220.61]. Table 250.66 requires a minimum of 2 AWG, however, the smallest service neutral conductor permitted to be installed in parallel in each raceway must not be smaller than 1/0 AWG [310.10(H) and Table 310.15(B)(16)].

(D) Grounding Electrode Conductor. A grounding electrode conductor, sized in accordance with 250.66 based on the area of the ungrounded service conductor, must connect the metal parts of service equipment enclosures to a grounding electrode in accordance with Part III of Article 250.

Question: *What's the minimum size grounding electrode conductor for a 400A service where the ungrounded service conductors are sized at 500 kcmil?* **Figure 250–58**

(a) 3 AWG (b) 2 AWG (c) 1 AWG (d) 1/0 AWG

Answer: *(d) 1/0 AWG [Table 250.66]*

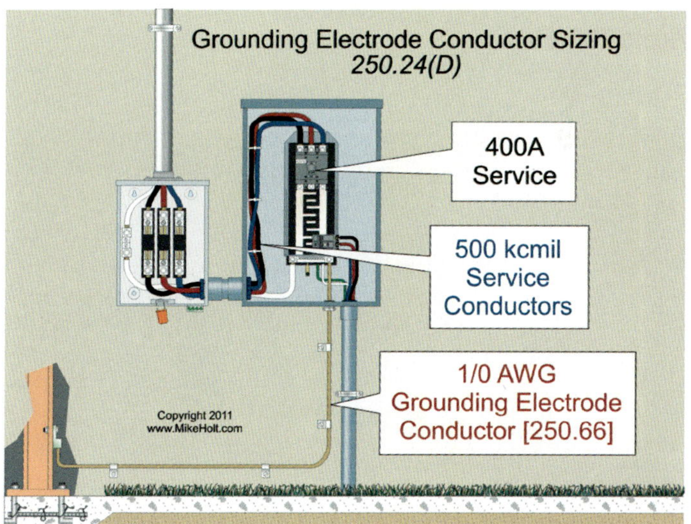

Figure 250–58

Author's Comment: If the grounding electrode conductor is connected to a ground rod, the portion of the conductor that's the sole connection to the ground rod isn't required to be larger than 6 AWG copper [250.66(A)], **Figure 250–59**. If the grounding electrode conductor is connected to a concrete-encased electrode, the portion of the conductor that's the sole connection to the concrete-encased electrode isn't required to be larger than 4 AWG copper [250.66(B)]. **Figure 250–60**

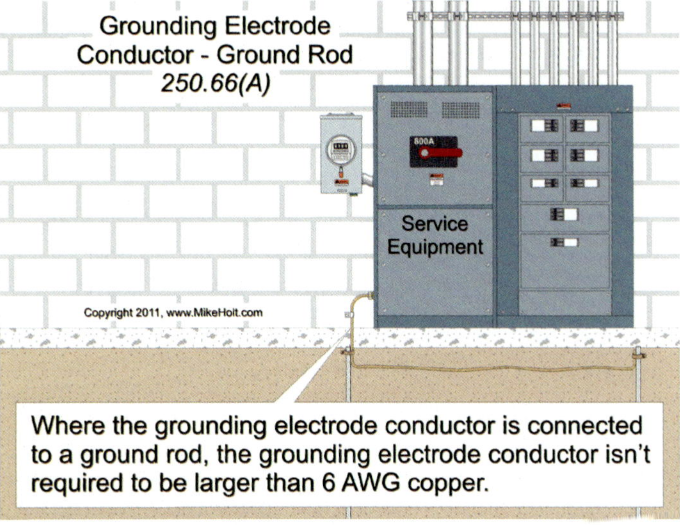

Figure 250–59

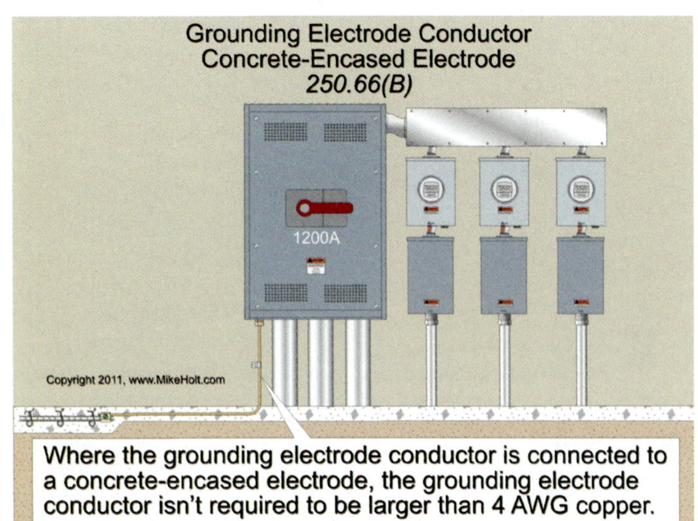

Figure 250–60

250.28 Main Bonding Jumper and System Bonding Jumper.

Main and system bonding jumpers must be installed as follows:

Author's Comments:

- Main Bonding Jumper. At service equipment, a main bonding jumper must be installed to electrically connect the neutral conductor to the service disconnect enclosure [250.24(B)]. **Figure 250–61**

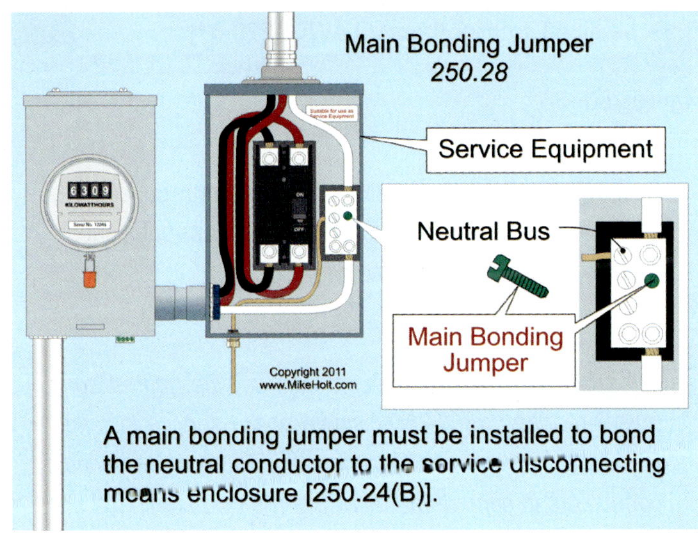

Figure 250–61

The main bonding jumper provides the low-impedance path necessary for fault current to travel back to the power supply to open the circuit overcurrent device to clear a ground fault [250.24(C)]. **Figure 250–62**

DANGER: *Metal parts of the electrical installation, as well as metal piping and structural steel, will become and remain energized with dangerous voltage from a ground fault if a main bonding jumper isn't installed at service equipment.* **Figure 250–63**

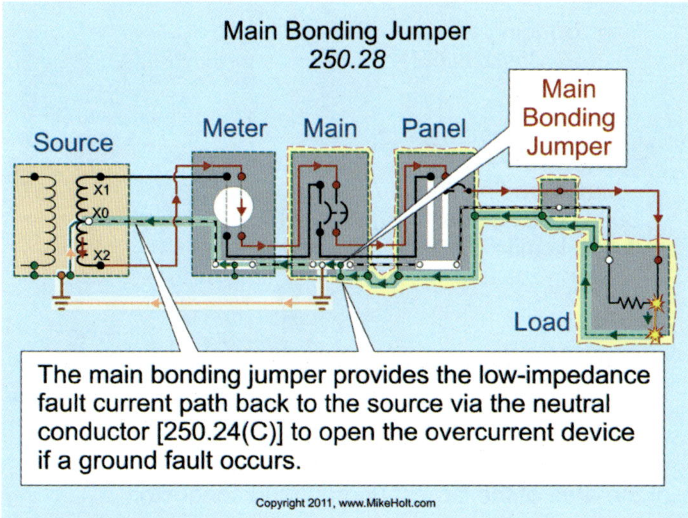

Figure 250–62

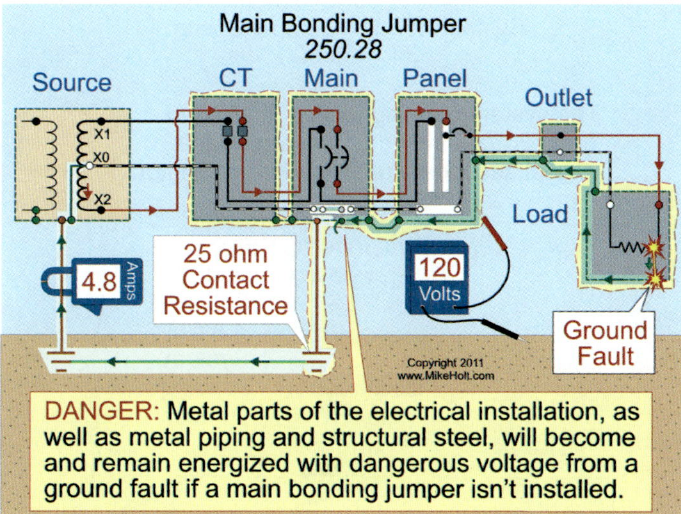

Figure 250–63

- System Bonding Jumper. A system bonding jumper must be installed between the neutral terminal of a separately derived system and the circuit equipment grounding conductor [Article 100 Bonding Jumper, System and 250.30(A)(1)]. **Figure 250–64**

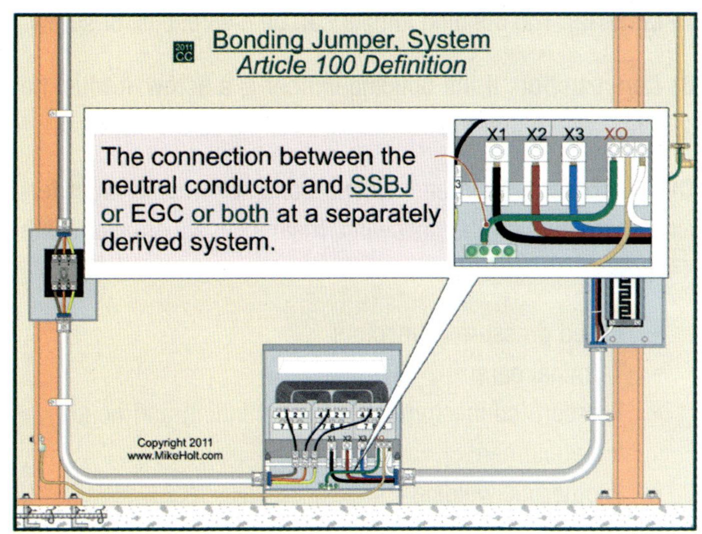

Figure 250–64

DANGER: *Metal parts of the electrical installation, as well as metal piping and structural steel, will become and remain energized with dangerous voltage from a ground fault if a system bonding jumper isn't installed at a separately derived system.* **Figure 250–65**

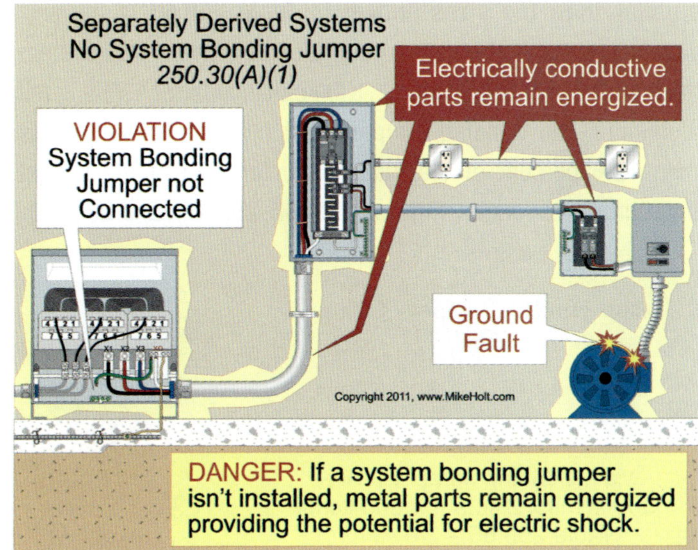

Figure 250–65

(A) Material. The bonding jumper can be a wire, bus, or screw.

(B) Construction. If the bonding jumper is a screw, it must be identified with a green finish visible with the screw installed.

(C) Attachment. Main and system bonding jumpers must terminate by one of the following means in accordance with 250.8(A):

- Listed pressure connectors
- Terminal bars
- Pressure connectors listed as grounding and bonding equipment
- Exothermic welding
- Machine screw-type fasteners that engage not less than two threads or are secured with a nut
- Thread-forming machine screws that engage not less than two threads in the enclosure
- Connections that are part of a listed assembly
- Other listed means

(D) Size.

(1) Main and system bonding jumpers must be sized not smaller than the sizes shown in Table 250.66. If the service or ungrounded conductors of a separately derived system have a total area larger than 1,100 kcmil copper or 1,750 kcmil aluminum, the bonding jumper must have an area not less than 12½ percent of the total conductor area of the largest ungrounded conductor. **Figures 250–66, 250–67, and 250–68**

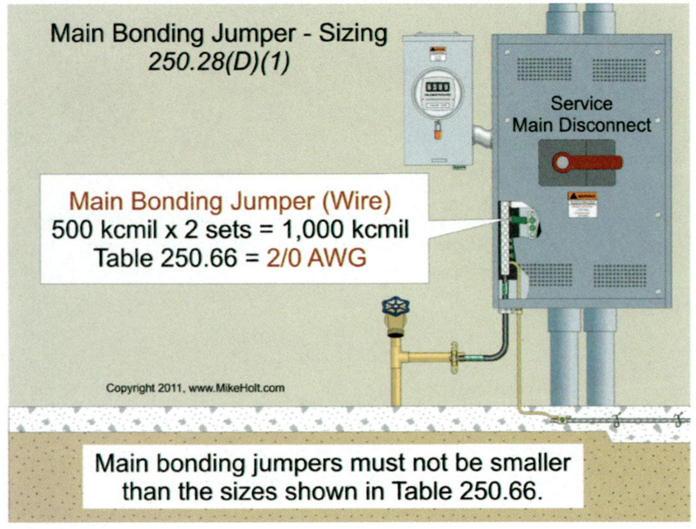

Figure 250–66

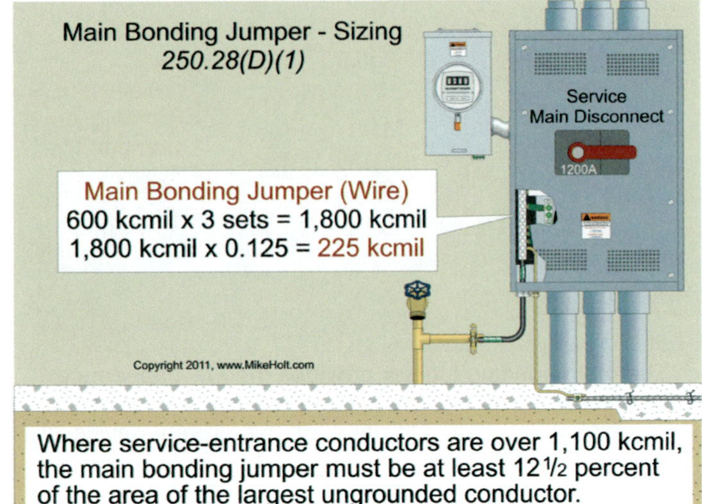

Figure 250–67

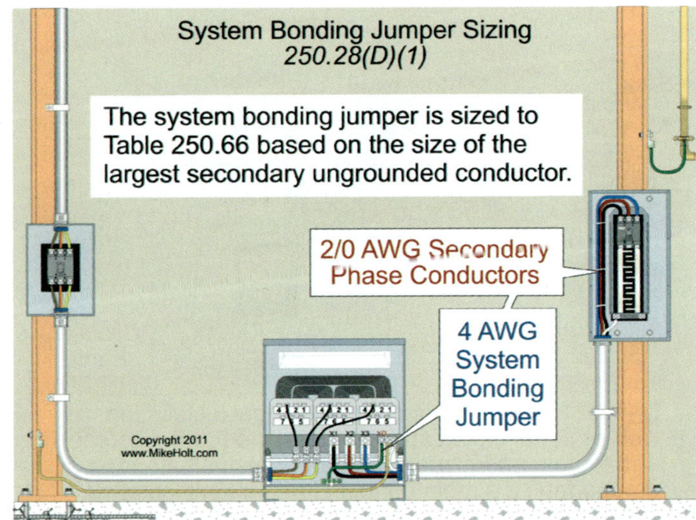

Figure 250–68

250.30 Separately Derived Systems—Grounding and Bonding.

<u>**Note 1:** An alternate alternating-current power source such as an on-site generator isn't a separately derived system if the neutral conductor is solidly interconnected to a service-supplied system neutral conductor. An example is a generator provided with a transfer switch that includes a neutral conductor that's not switched.</u> **Figure 250–69**

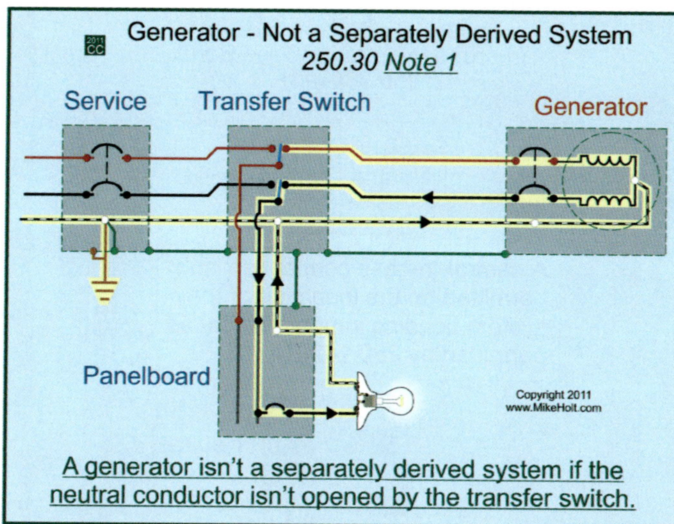

Figure 250–69

Author's Comments:

- According to Article 100, a separately derived system is a wiring system whose power is derived from a source where there's no direct electrical connection to the supply conductors of another system.
- Transformers are considered separately derived when the primary conductors have no direct electrical connection from circuit conductors of one system to circuit conductors of another system, other than connections through the earth, metal enclosures, metallic raceways, or equipment grounding conductors. **Figure 100-70**

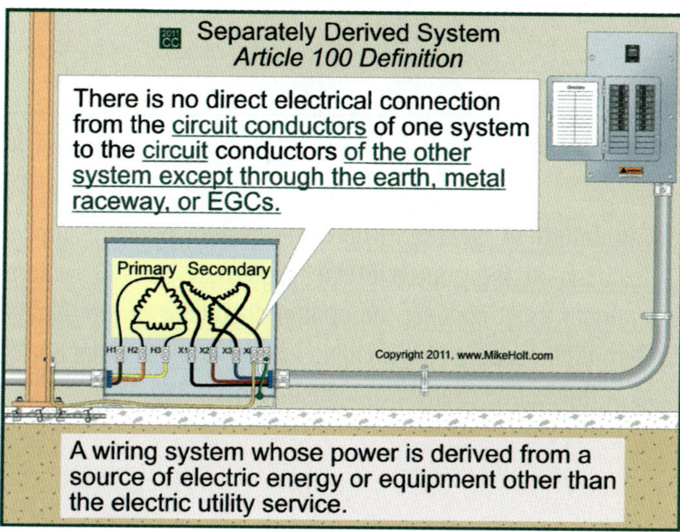

Figure 250–70

- A generator having transfer equipment that switches the neutral conductor, or one that has no neutral conductor at all, is a separately derived system and must be grounded and bonded in accordance with 250.30(A). **Figure 250–71**

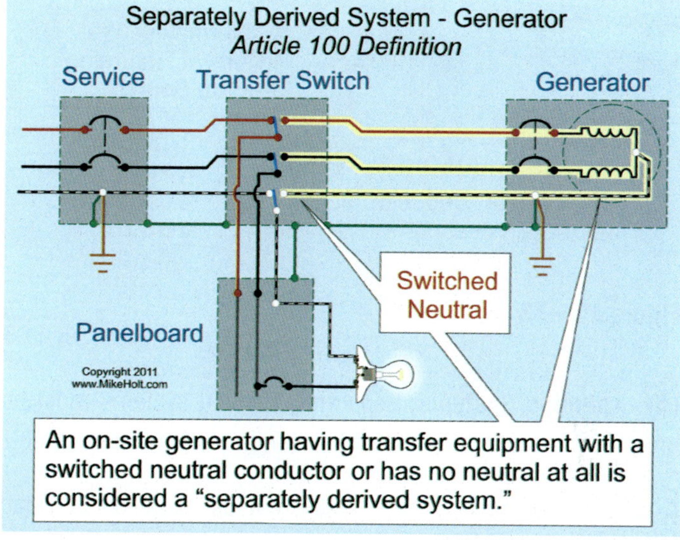

Figure 250–71

Note 2: For nonseparately derived systems, see 445.13 for the minimum size neutral conductors necessary to carry fault current. **Figures 250-72 and 250-73**

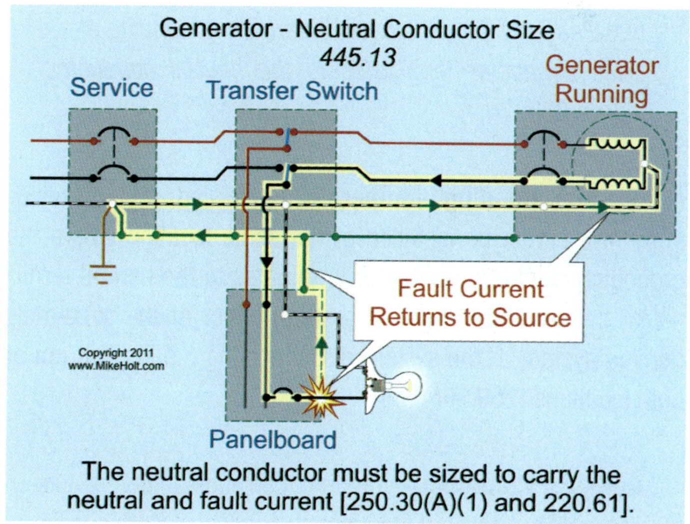

Figure 250–72

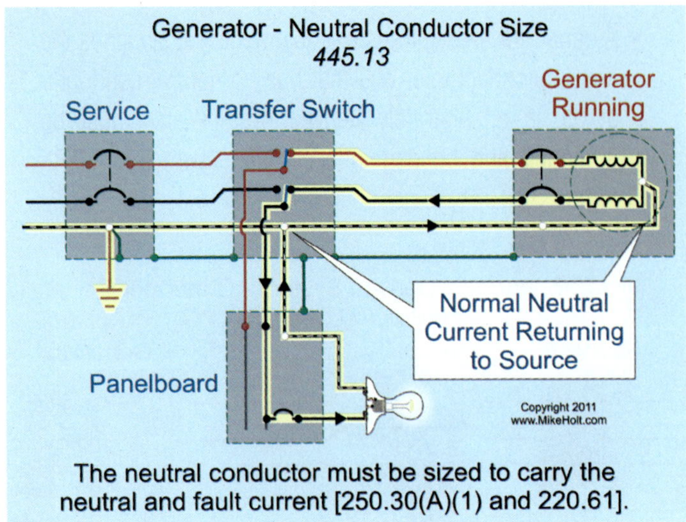

Figure 250–73

(A) Grounded Systems. Separately derived systems must be grounded and bonded in accordance with (A)(1) through (A)(8).

A neutral-to-case connection must not be made on the load side of the system bonding jumper, except as permitted by 250.142(B).

> **CAUTION:** *Dangerous objectionable neutral current will flow on conductive metal parts of electrical equipment as well as metal piping and structural steel, in violation of 250.6(A), if more than one system bonding jumper is installed, or if it's not located where the grounding electrode conductor terminates to the neutral conductor.* **Figure 250–74**

(1) System Bonding Jumper. An unspliced system bonding jumper must be installed at the same location where the grounding electrode conductor terminates to the neutral terminal of the separately derived system; either at the separately derived system or the system disconnecting means, but not at both locations [250.30(A)(5)].

> **Author's Comment:** A system bonding jumper is the connection between the neutral conductor and supply side bonding jumper or equipment grounding conductor or both at a separately derived system [Article 100]. **Figure 250-75**

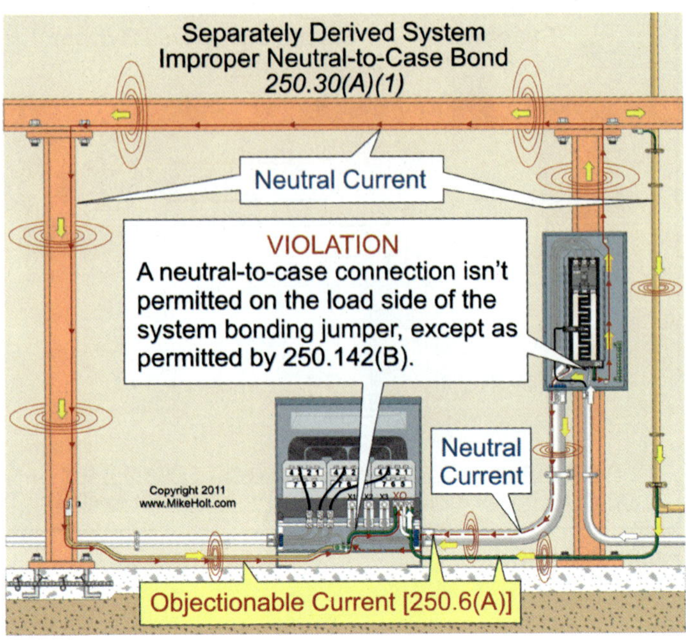

Figure 250–74

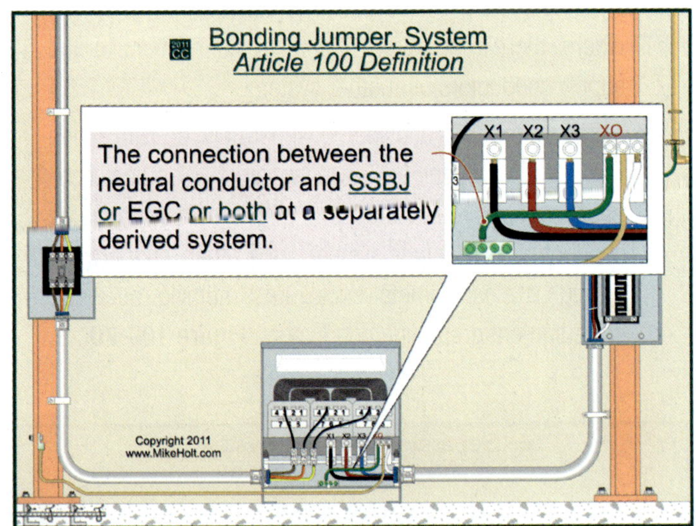

Figure 250–75

(a) Installed at Source. Where the system bonding jumper is installed at the source of the separately derived system, the jumper must connect the neutral conductor of the derived system to the supply-side bonding jumper and the metal enclosure of the source (transformer case). **Figure 250–76**

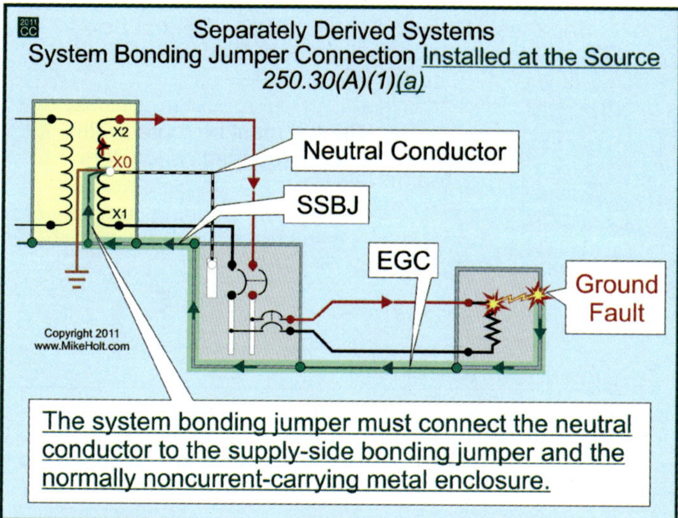

Figure 250–76

(b) Installed at First Disconnecting Means. Where the system bonding jumper is installed at the first disconnecting means of a separately derived system, the jumper must connect the neutral conductor of the derived system to the supply-side bonding jumper and the metal disconnecting means enclosure. **Figure 250–77**

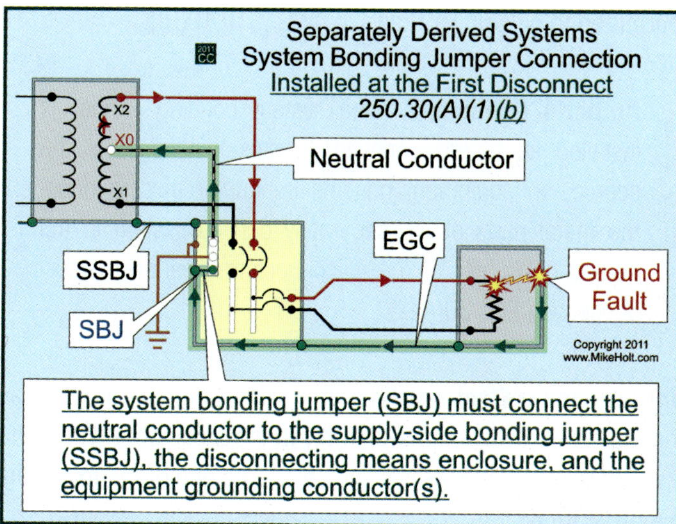

Figure 250–77

Author's Comment: A system bonding jumper is a conductor, screw, or strap that bonds the metal parts of a separately derived system to the system neutral point [Article 100 Bonding Jumper, System], and it's sized to Table 250.66 in accordance with 250.28(D).

DANGER: *During a ground fault, metal parts of electrical equipment, as well as metal piping and structural steel, will become and remain energized providing the potential for electric shock and fire if the system bonding jumper isn't installed.* **Figure 250–78**

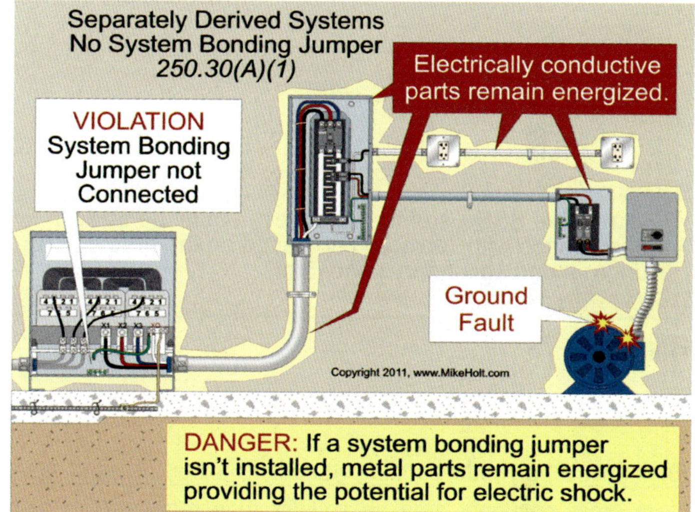

Figure 250–78

(2) Supply-Side Bonding Jumper. If the separately derived system and the first disconnecting means are located in separate enclosures, a supply-side bonding jumper must be run to the derived system disconnecting means. The supply-side bonding jumper can be a nonflexible metal raceway, a wire, or a bus.

(a) If the supply-side bonding jumper is of the wire type, it must be sized in accordance with Table 250.66, based on the area of the largest ungrounded derived system conductor in the raceway or cable.

Question: What size supply-side bonding jumper is required for flexible metal conduit containing 300 kcmil secondary conductors? **Figure 250–79**

(a) 3 AWG (b) 2 AWG (c) 1 AWG (d) 1/0 AWG

Answer: *(b) 2 AWG [Table 250.66]*

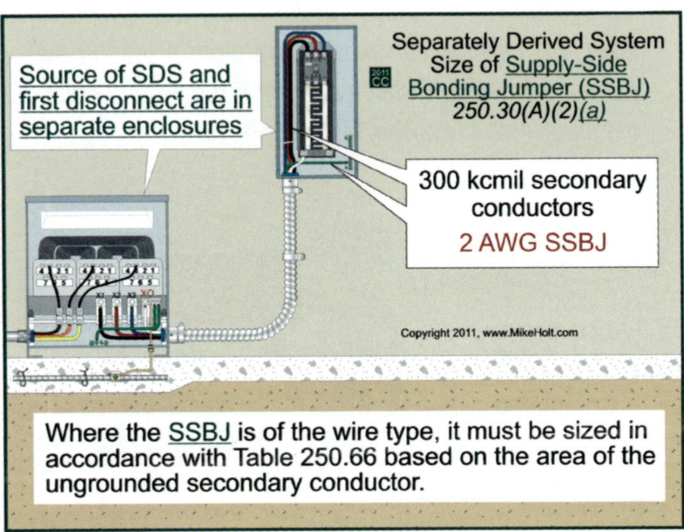

Figure 250–79

(b) If the supply-side bonding jumper is a bus, it must have a cross-sectional area no smaller than required by Table 250.66.

(3) System Neutral Conductor Size. If the system bonding jumper is installed at the disconnecting means instead of at the source, the following requirements apply:

(a) Sizing for Single Raceway. Because the neutral conductor of a derived system serves as the effective ground-fault current path for ground-fault current, it must be routed with the ungrounded conductors of the derived system and be sized not smaller than specified in Table 250.66, based on the area of the ungrounded conductor of the derived system. **Figure 250–80**

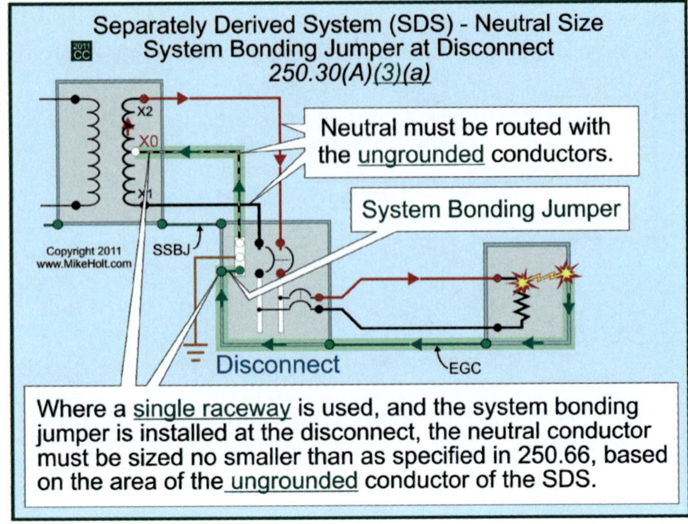

Figure 250–80

(b) Parallel Conductors in Two or More Raceways. If the conductors from the derived system are installed in parallel in two or more raceways, the neutral conductor of the derived system in each raceway or cable must be sized not smaller than specified in Table 250.66, based on the area of the largest ungrounded conductor of the derived system in the raceway or cable. In no case is the neutral conductor of the derived system permitted to be smaller than 1/0 AWG [310.10(H)].

Author's Comment: If the system bonding jumper is installed at the disconnecting means instead of at the source, an equipment bonding conductor must connect the metal parts of the separately derived system to the neutral conductor at the disconnecting means in accordance with 250.30(A)(2).

(4) Grounding Electrode. The grounding electrode must be as near as practicable, and preferably in the same area where the system bonding jumper is installed and be one of the following: **Figure 250–81**

(1) Metal water pipe electrode, within 5 ft of the entry to the building [250.52(A)(1)].

(2) Metal building frame electrode [250.52(A)(2)].

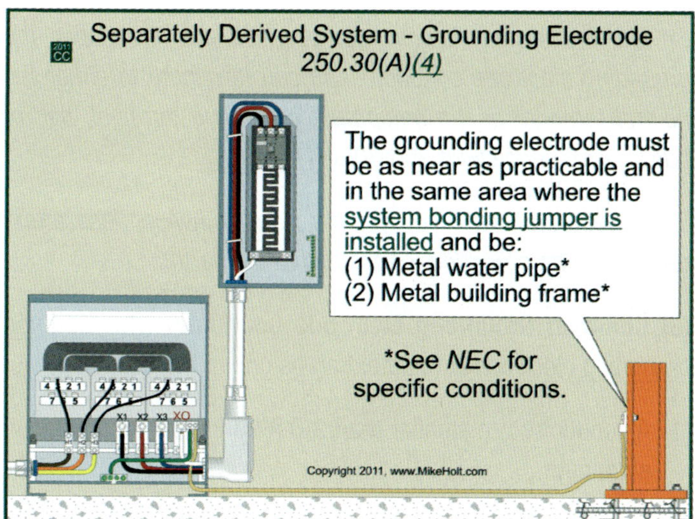

Figure 250–81

Ex 1: If the electrodes specified in 250.30(A)(4) aren't available, one of the following electrodes can be used:

- *A concrete-encased electrode encased by not less than 2 in. of concrete, located horizontally near the bottom or vertically, and within that portion of concrete foundation or footing that's in direct contact with the earth [250.52(A)(3)].*
- *A ground ring electrode encircling the building/structure, buried not less than 30 in. below grade, consisting of at least 20 ft of bare copper conductor not smaller than 2 AWG [250.52(A)(4) and 250.53(F)].*
- *A ground rod electrode having not less than 8 ft of contact with the soil meeting the requirements of 250.52(A)(5) and 250.53(G)].*
- *Other metal underground systems, piping systems, or underground tanks [250.52(A)(8)].*

Note 1: Interior metal water piping in the area served by separately derived systems must be bonded to the separately derived system in accordance with 250.104(D).

(5) Grounding Electrode Conductor, Single Separately Derived System. The grounding electrode conductor must be sized in accordance with 250.66, based on the area of the largest ungrounded conductor of the derived system. A grounding electrode conductor must connect the neutral terminal of a separately derived system to a grounding electrode of a type identified in 250.30(A)(4) at the same point on the separately derived system where the system bonding jumper is connected. Figure 250–82

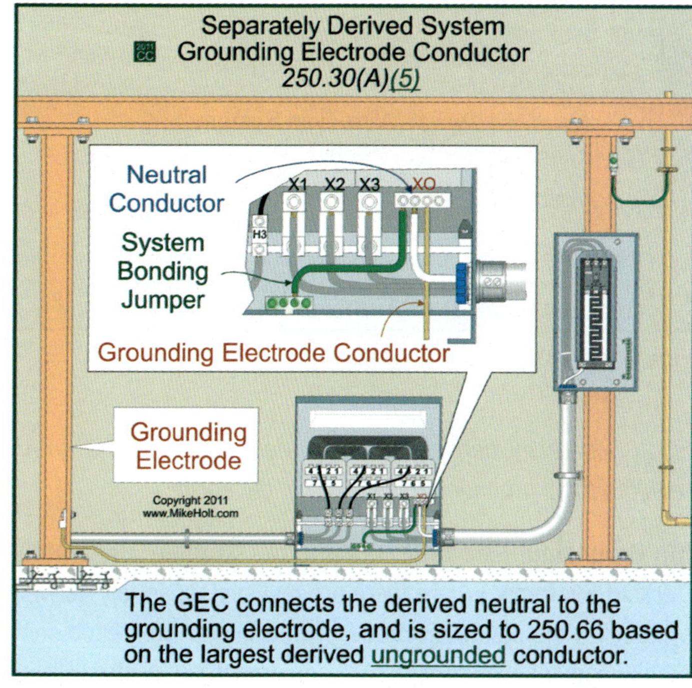

Figure 250–82

Author's Comments:

- System grounding also helps reduce fires in buildings as well as voltage stress on electrical insulation, thereby ensuring longer insulation life for motors, transformers, and other system components.
- To prevent objectionable neutral current from flowing [250.6] onto metal parts, the grounding electrode conductor must originate at the same point on the separately derived system where the system bonding jumper is connected [250.30(A)(1)].

Ex 1: If the system bonding jumper is a wire or busbar, the grounding electrode conductor is permitted to terminate to either the neutral terminal or the equipment grounding terminal, bar, or bus in accordance with 250.30(A)(1). Figure 250–83

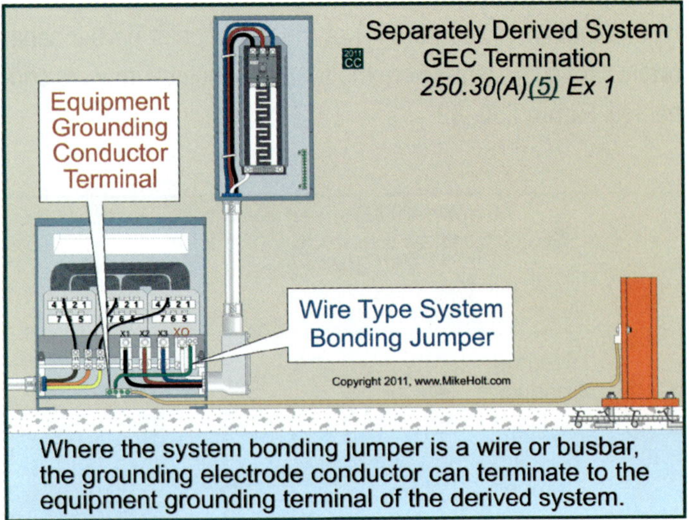

Figure 250–83

Ex 3: Separately derived systems rated 1 kVA or less aren't required to be grounded (connected to the earth).

(6) Grounding Electrode Conductor, Multiple Separately Derived Systems. Where there are multiple separately derived systems, a grounding electrode conductor tap from each separately derived system to a common grounding electrode conductor is permitted. This connection is to be made at the same point on the separately derived system where the system bonding jumper is connected [250.30(A)(1)]. **Figure 250–84**

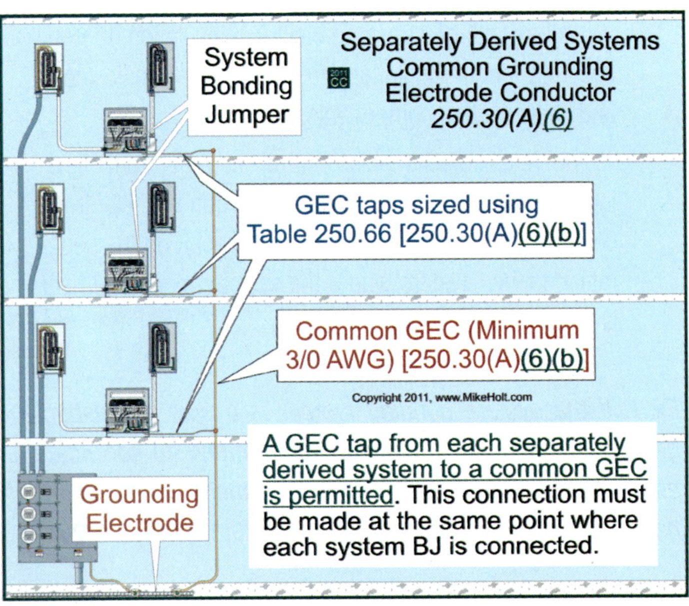

Figure 250–84

Ex 1: If the system bonding jumper is a wire or busbar, the grounding electrode conductor tap can terminate to either the neutral terminal or the equipment grounding terminal, bar, or bus in accordance with 250.30(A)(1).

Ex 2: Separately derived systems rated 1 kVA or less aren't required to be grounded (connected to the earth).

(a) Common Grounding Electrode Conductor. The common grounding electrode conductor can be one of the following:

(1) A conductor not smaller than 3/0 AWG copper or 250 kcmil aluminum.

(2) The metal frame of the building/structure that complies with 250.52(A)(2) or is connected to the grounding electrode system by a conductor not smaller than 3/0 AWG copper or 250 kcmil aluminum.

(b) Tap Conductor Size. Grounding electrode conductor taps must be sized in accordance with Table 250.66, based on the area of the largest ungrounded conductor of the given derived system.

(c) Connections. All tap connections to the common grounding electrode conductor must be made at an accessible location by one of the following methods:

(1) A connector listed as grounding and bonding equipment.

(2) Listed connections to aluminum or copper busbars not less than ¼ in. x 2 in.

(3) Exothermic welding.

Grounding electrode conductor taps must be connected to the common grounding electrode conductor so the common grounding electrode conductor isn't spliced.

(7) Installation. The grounding electrode conductor must comply with the following:

- Be of copper where within 18 in. of the earth [250.64(A)].
- Securely fastened to the surface on which it's carried [250.64(B)].

- Adequately protected if exposed to physical damage [250.64(B)].
- Metal enclosures enclosing a grounding electrode conductor must be made electrically continuous from the point of attachment to cabinets or equipment to the grounding electrode [250.64(E)].

(8) Structural Steel and Metal Piping. To ensure dangerous voltage from a ground fault is removed quickly, structural steel and metal piping in the area served by a separately derived system must be connected to the neutral conductor at the separately derived system in accordance with 250.104(D).

(C) Outdoor Source. If the separately derived system is located outside the building/structure, a connection to the grounding electrode must be made at the separately derived system location. Figure 250–85

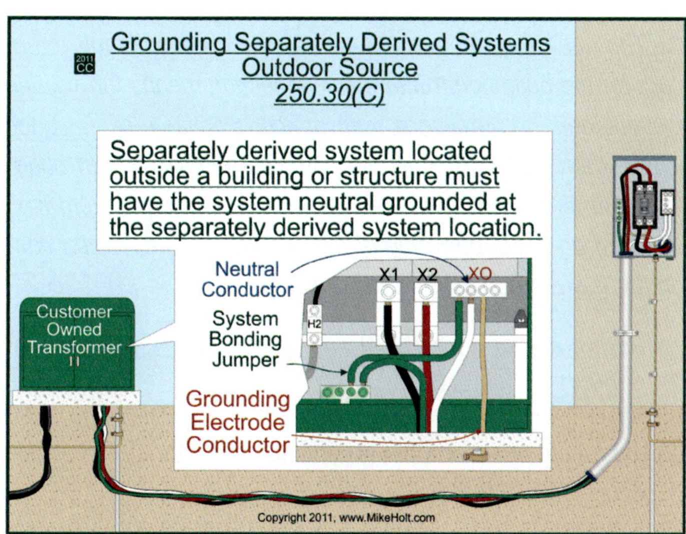

Figure 250–85

250.32 Buildings or Structures Supplied by a Feeder or Branch Circuit.

(A) Grounding Electrode. Each building/structure's disconnect must be connected to an electrode of a type identified in 250.52. Figure 250–86

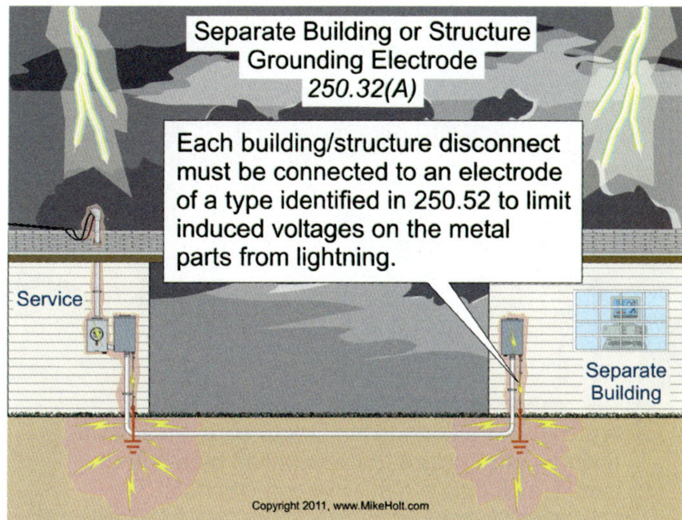

Figure 250–86

Author's Comments:

- The grounding of the building/structure disconnecting means to the earth is intended to help in limiting induced voltages on the metal parts from nearby lightning strikes [250.4(A)(1)].
- The *Code* prohibits the use of the earth to serve as an effective ground-fault current path [250.4(A)(5) and 250.4(B)(4)].

Ex: A grounding electrode isn't required where the building/structure is served with a 2-wire, 3-wire, or 4-wire multiwire branch circuit. Figure 250–87

(B) Equipment Grounding Conductor.

(1) Supplied by a Feeder or Branch Circuit. To quickly clear a ground fault and remove dangerous voltage from metal parts, the building/structure disconnecting means must be connected to the circuit equipment grounding conductor, which must be one of the types described in 250.118. If the supply circuit equipment grounding conductor is of the wire type, it must be sized in accordance with 250.122, based on the rating of the overcurrent device. Figure 250–88

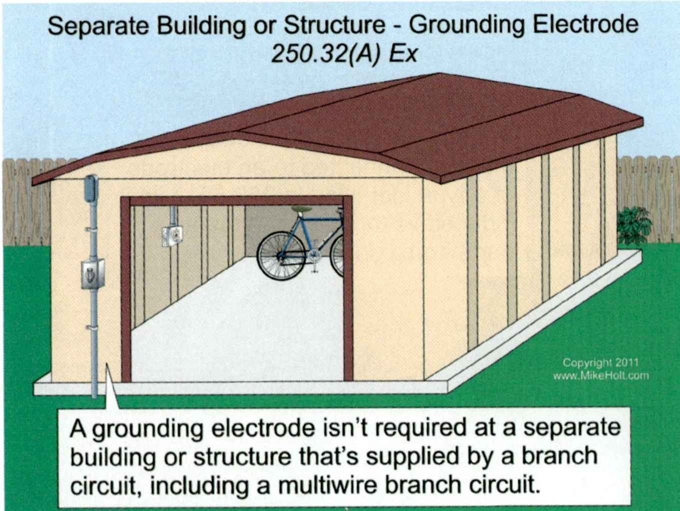

Figure 250–87

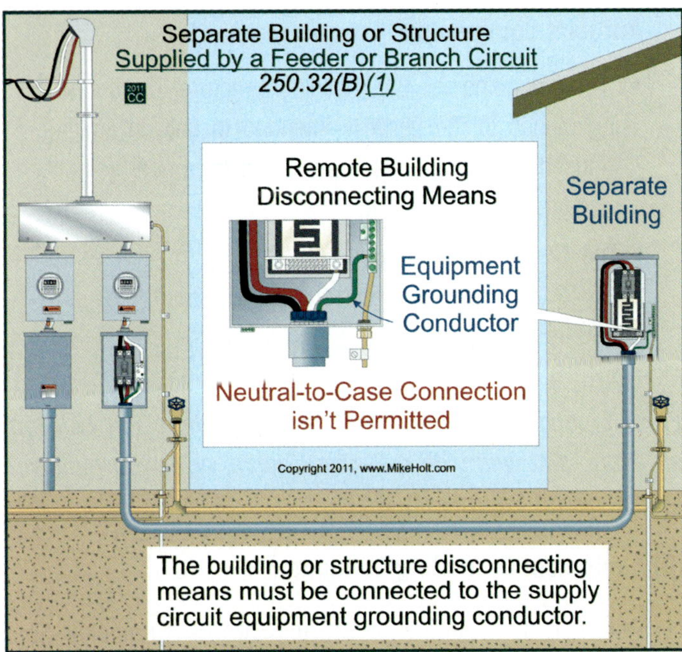

Figure 250–88

CAUTION: *To prevent dangerous objectionable neutral current from flowing onto metal parts [250.6(A)], the supply circuit neutral conductor isn't permitted to be connected to the remote building/structure disconnecting means [250.142(B)].* Figure 250–89

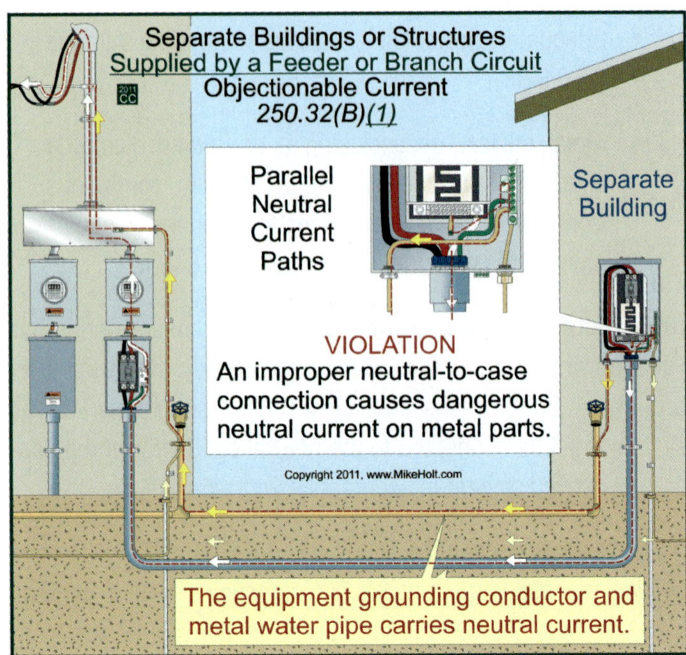

Figure 250–89

Ex: The neutral conductor can serve as the ground-fault return path for the building/structure disconnecting means for existing installations in compliance with previous editions of the Code where there are no continuous metallic paths between buildings and structures, ground-fault protection of equipment isn't installed on the supply side of the circuit, and the neutral conductor is sized no smaller than the larger of:

(1) The maximum unbalanced neutral load in accordance with 220.61.

(2) The minimum equipment grounding conductor size in accordance with 250.122.

(2) Supplied by Separately Derived System.

(a) With Overcurrent Protection. If overcurrent protection is provided where the conductors originate, the supply conductors must contain an equipment grounding conductor in accordance with 250.32(B)(1).

(b) Without Overcurrent Protection. If overcurrent protection isn't provided for the supply conductors to the building/structure as permitted by 240.21(C)(4), the installation must be grounded and bonded in accordance with 250.30(A).

(E) Grounding Electrode Conductor. The grounding electrode conductor must terminate to the grounding terminal of the disconnecting means, and it must be sized in accordance with 250.66, based on the conductor area of the ungrounded feeder conductor.

> ***Question:*** *What size grounding electrode conductor is required for a building disconnect supplied with a 3/0 AWG feeder?* **Figure 250–90**
>
> *(a) 4 AWG (b) 3 AWG (c) 2 AWG (d) 1 AWG*
>
> ***Answer:*** *(a) 4 AWG [Table 250.66]*

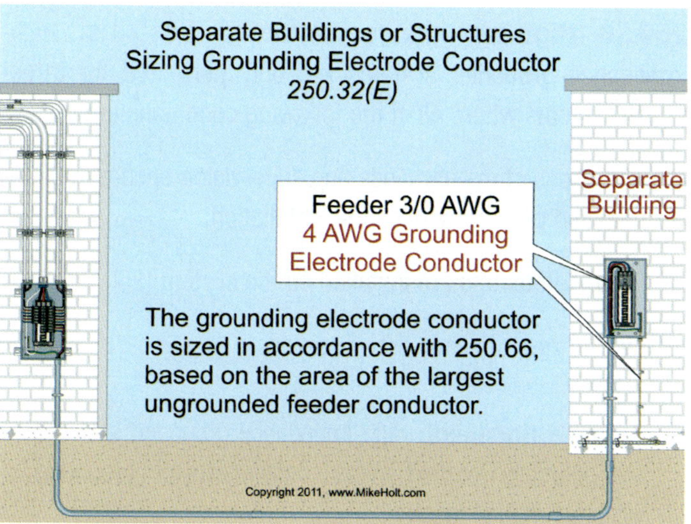

Figure 250–90

Author's Comment: If the grounding electrode conductor is connected to a ground rod, the portion of the conductor that's the sole connection to the ground rod isn't required to be larger than 6 AWG copper [250.66(A)]. If the grounding electrode conductor is connected to a concrete-encased electrode, the portion of the conductor that's the sole connection to the concrete-encased electrode isn't required to be larger than 4 AWG copper [250.66(B)].

250.34 Generators—Portable and Vehicle-Mounted.

(A) Portable Generators. The frame of a portable generator isn't required to be grounded (connected to the earth) if: **Figure 250–91**

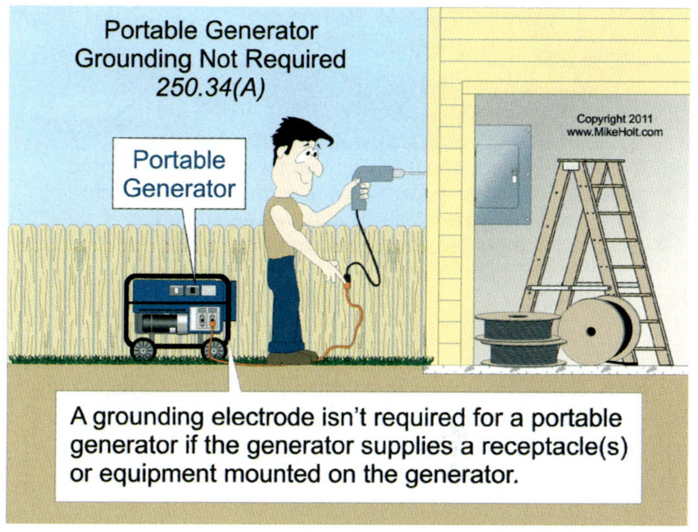

Figure 250–91

(1) The generator only supplies equipment or receptacles mounted on the generator, and

(2) The metal parts of the generator and the receptacle grounding terminal are connected to the generator frame.

(B) Vehicle-Mounted Generators. The frame of a vehicle-mounted generator isn't required to be grounded (connected to the earth) if: **Figure 250–92**

(1) The generator frame is bonded to the vehicle frame,

(2) The generator only supplies equipment or receptacles mounted on the vehicle or generator, and

(3) The metal parts of the generator and the receptacle grounding terminal are connected to the generator frame.

(C) Separately Derived Portable or Vehicle-Mounted Generator. A portable or vehicle-mounted generator used as a separately derived system to supply equipment or receptacles mounted on the vehicle or generator must have the neutral conductor connected to the generator frame.

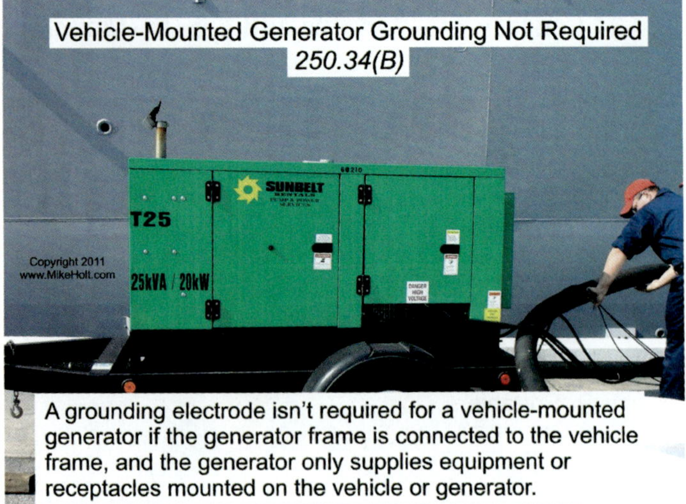

Figure 250–92

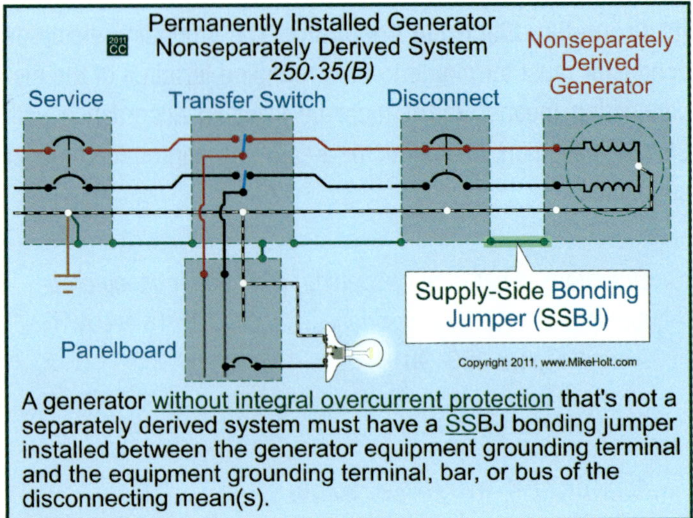

Figure 250–93

Note: A portable or vehicle-mounted generator supplying fixed wiring for a premises must be grounded (connected to the earth) and bonded in accordance with 250.30 for separately derived systems and 250.35 for nonseparately derived systems.

250.35 Permanently Installed Generators.

(A) Separately Derived System. If the generator is installed as a separately derived system, the system must be grounded (connected to the earth) and bonded in accordance with 250.30.

(B) Nonseparately Derived System. A generator without integral overcurrent protection that's not a separately derived system must have a supply-side bonding jumper installed between the generator equipment grounding terminal and the equipment grounding terminal, bar, or bus of the disconnecting mean(s). The supply-side bonding jumper is sized in accordance with 250.102(C), based on the size of the ungrounded circuit conductors of the generator. Figure 250–93

Author's Comment: The frame of a nonseparately derived system generator isn't required to be connected to a grounding electrode.

250.36 High-Impedance Grounded Systems.

High-impedance grounded systems are only permitted for three-phase systems where all of the following conditions are met:

(1) Conditions of maintenance and supervision ensure that only qualified persons service the installation.

(2) Ground detectors are installed on the system [250.21(B)].

(3) Line-to-neutral loads aren't served.

Author's Comment: High-impedance grounded systems are generally referred to as "high-resistance grounded systems" in the industry.

(A) Grounding Impedance Location. To limit fault current to a very low value, high-impedance grounded systems must have a resistor installed between the neutral point of the derived system and the grounding electrode conductor. Figure 250–94

Note: For more information on this topic see IEEE 142—*Recommended Practice for Grounding of Industrial and Commercial Power Systems* (Green Book).

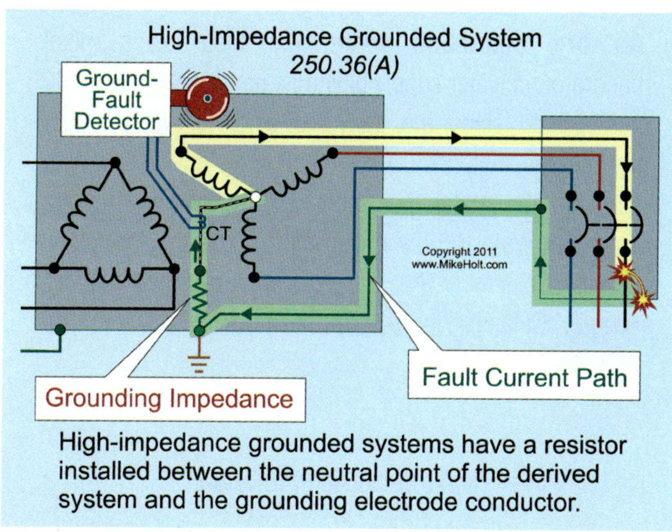

Figure 250–94

PART III. GROUNDING ELECTRODE SYSTEM AND GROUNDING ELECTRODE CONDUCTOR

250.50 Grounding Electrode System. Any grounding electrode described in 250.52(A)(1) through (A)(8) that's present at a building/structure must be bonded together to form the grounding electrode system. Figure 250–95

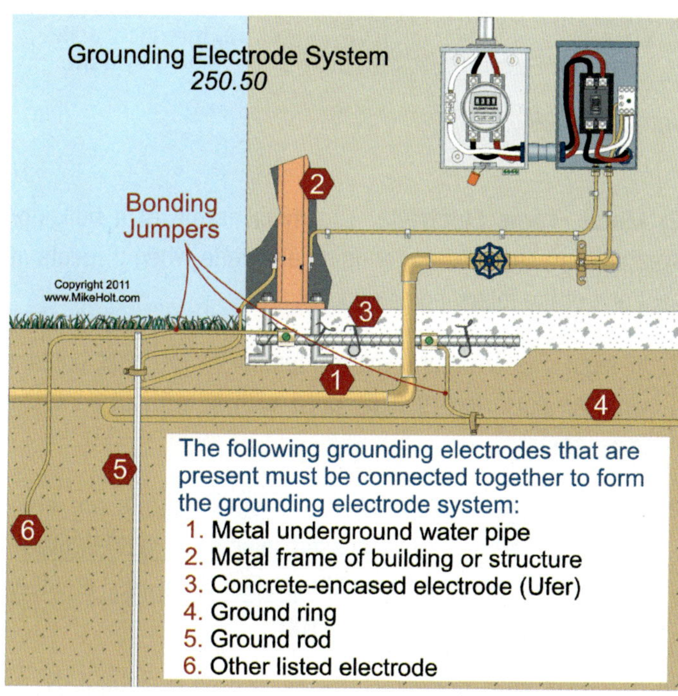

Figure 250–95

- Underground metal water pipe [250.52(A)(1)]
- Metal frame of the building/structure [250.52(A)(2)]
- Concrete-encased electrode [250.52(A)(3)]
- Ground ring [250.52(A)(4)]
- Ground rod [250.52(A)(5)]
- Other listed electrodes [250.52(A)(6)]
- Grounding plate [250.52(A)(7)]
- Metal underground systems, piping systems, or underground tanks [250.52(A)(8)].

Ex: Concrete-encased electrodes aren't required for existing buildings or structures where the conductive steel reinforcing bars aren't accessible without chipping up the concrete. Figure 250–96

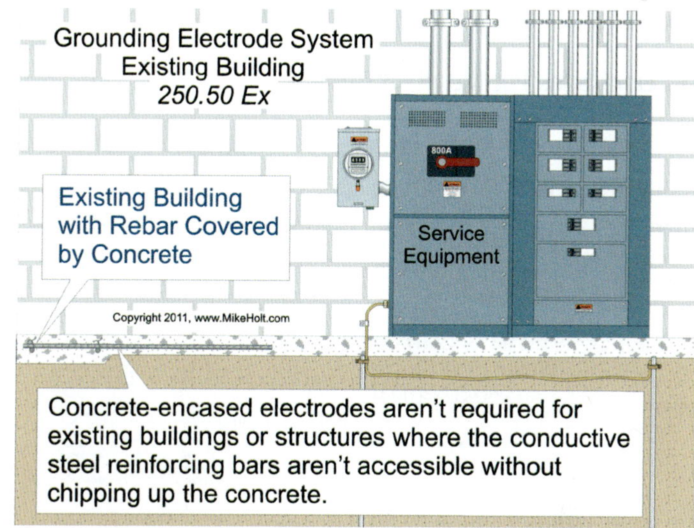

Figure 250–96

Author's Comment: When a concrete-encased electrode is used at a building/structure that doesn't have an underground metal water pipe electrode, no additional electrode is required. Figure 250–97

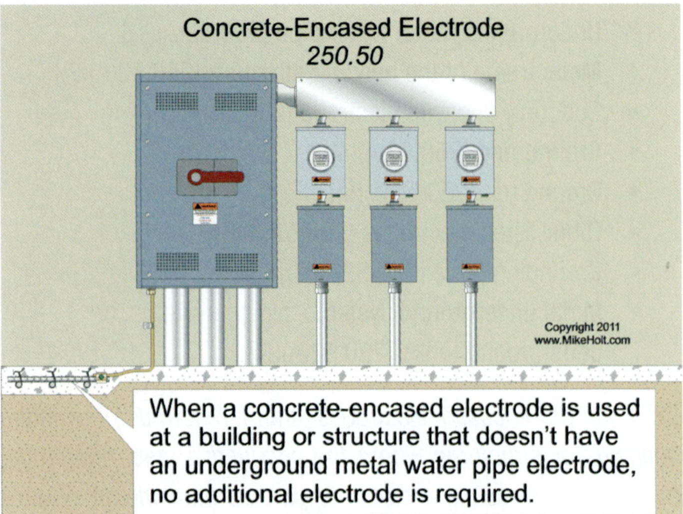

Figure 250–97

250.52 Grounding Electrode Types.

(A) Electrodes Permitted for Grounding.

(1) Underground Metal Water Pipe Electrode. Underground metal water pipe in direct contact with the earth for 10 ft or more can serve as a grounding electrode. Figure 250–98

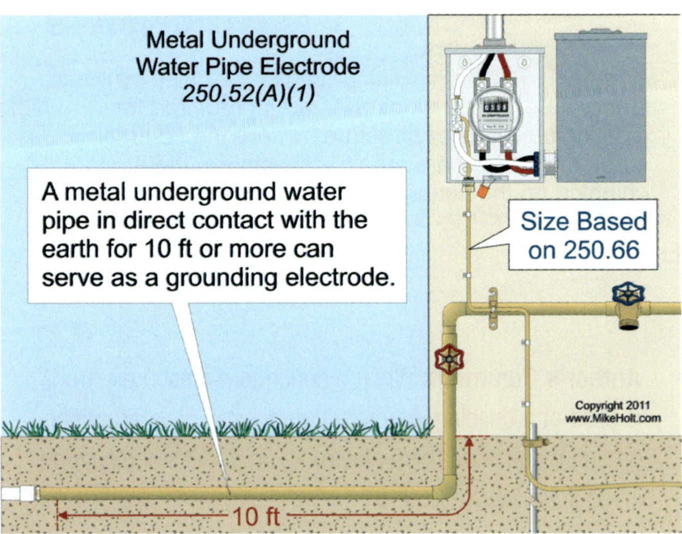

Figure 250–98

Author's Comment: Controversy about using metal underground water supply piping as a grounding electrode has existed since the early 1900s. The water industry believes that neutral current flowing on water piping corrodes the metal. For more information, contact the American Water Works Association about their report—*Effects of Electrical Grounding on Pipe Integrity and Shock Hazard*, Catalog No. 90702, 1.800.926.7337. Figure 250–99

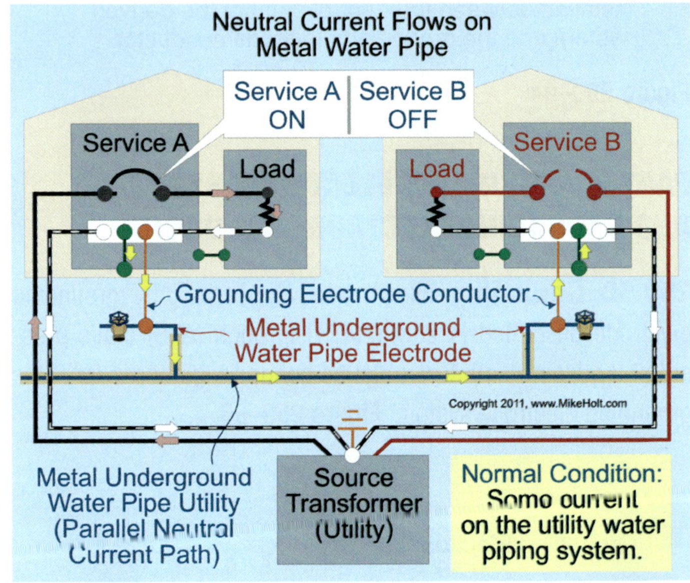

Figure 250–99

(2) Metal Frame Electrode. The metal frame of a building/structure can serve as a grounding electrode when it meets at least one of the following conditions:

(1) At least one structural metal member is in direct contact with the earth for 10 ft or more, with or without concrete encasement.

(2) The bolts securing the structural steel column are connected to a concrete-encased electrode [250.52(A)(3)] by welding, exothermic welding, steel tie wires, or other approved means. Figure 250–100

(3) Concrete-Encased Electrode. At least 20 ft of either (1) or (2): Figure 250–101

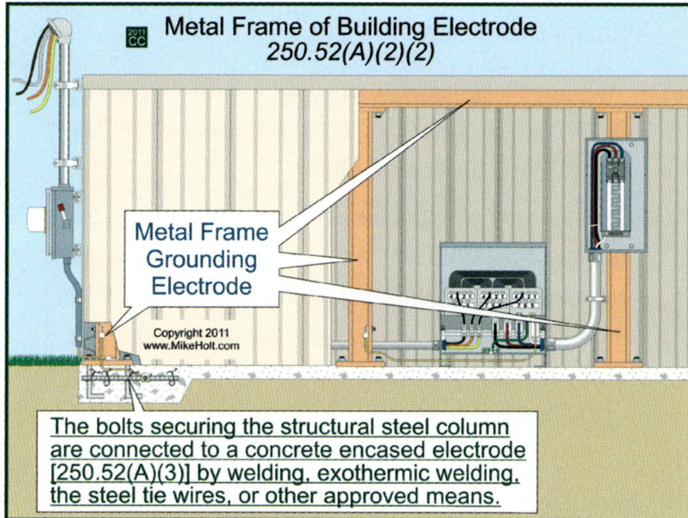

Figure 250–100

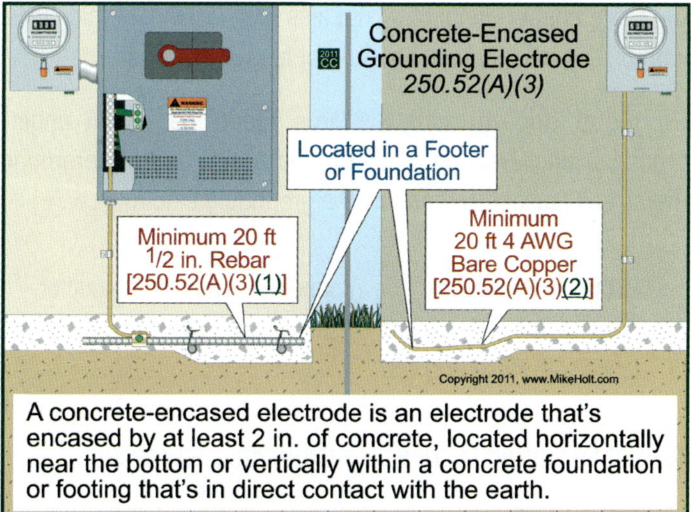

Figure 250–101

(1) One or more of bare, zinc-galvanized, or otherwise electrically conductive steel reinforcing bars of not less than ½ in. diameter, mechanically connected together by steel tie wires, welding, or other effective means, to create a 20 ft or greater length.

(2) Bare copper conductor not smaller than 4 AWG.

The reinforcing bars or bare copper conductor must be encased by at least 2 in. of concrete located horizontally near the bottom of a concrete footing or vertically within a concrete foundation that's in direct contact with the earth.

If multiple concrete-encased electrodes are present at a building/structure, only one is required to serve as a grounding electrode. Figure 250–102

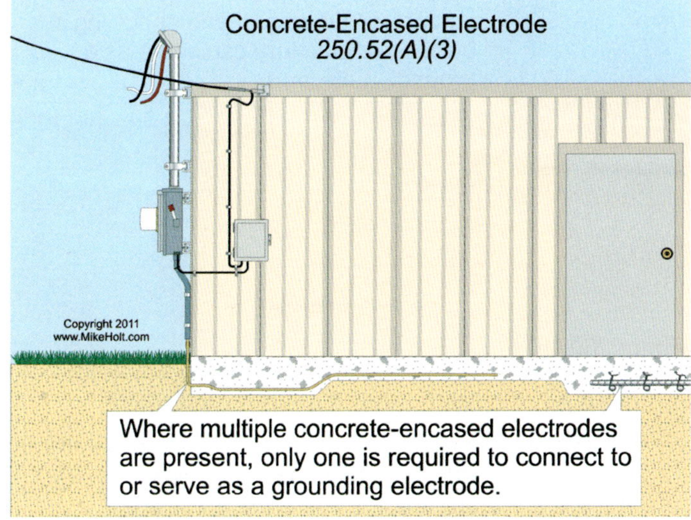

Figure 250–102

Note: Concrete containing insulation, vapor barriers, films or similar items separating it from the earth isn't considered to be in "direct contact" with the earth.

Author's Comments:

- The grounding electrode conductor to a concrete-encased grounding electrode isn't required to be larger than 4 AWG copper [250.66(B)].
- The concrete-encased grounding electrode is also called a "Ufer Ground," named after a consultant working for the U.S. Army during World War II. The technique Mr. Ufer came up with was necessary because the site needing grounding had no underground water table and little rainfall. The desert site was a series of bomb storage vaults in the area of Flagstaff, Arizona. This type of grounding electrode generally offers the lowest ground resistance for the cost.

(4) Ground Ring Electrode. A ground ring consisting of at least 20 ft of bare copper conductor not smaller than 2 AWG buried in the earth encircling a building/structure, can serve as a grounding electrode. Figure 250–103

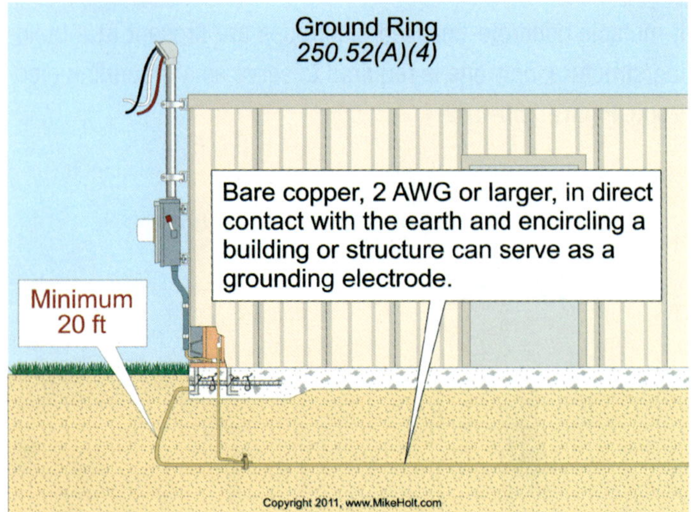

Figure 250–103

Author's Comment: The ground ring must be buried not less than 30 in. [250.53(F)], and the grounding electrode conductor to a ground ring isn't required to be larger than the ground ring conductor size [250.66(C)].

(5) Ground Rod and Pipe Electrode. Ground rod electrodes must not be less than 8 ft in length in contact with the earth [250.53(G)].

(b) Rod-type electrodes must have a diameter of at least ⅝ in., unless listed. Figure 250–104

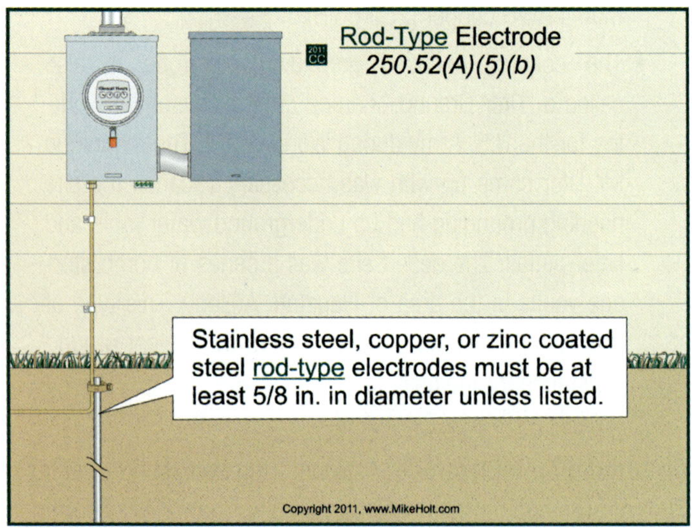

Figure 250–104

Author's Comments:

- The grounding electrode conductor, if it's the sole connection to the ground rod, isn't required to be larger than 6 AWG copper [250.66(A)].
- The diameter of a ground rod has an insignificant effect on the contact resistance of a ground rod to the earth. However, larger diameter ground rods (¾ in. and 1 in.) are sometimes installed where mechanical strength is desired, or to compensate for the loss of the electrode's metal due to corrosion.

(6) Listed Electrode. Other listed grounding electrodes.

(7) Ground Plate Electrode. A bare or conductively coated iron or steel plate with not less than ¼ in. of thickness, or a solid uncoated copper metal plate not less than 0.06 in. of thickness, with an exposed surface area of not less than 2 sq ft.

(8) Metal Underground Systems Electrode. Metal underground piping systems, underground tanks, and underground metal well casings can serve as a grounding electrode.

Author's Comment: The grounding electrode conductor to the metal underground system must be sized in accordance with Table 250.66.

(B) Not Permitted for Use as a Grounding Electrode.

(1) Underground metal gas-piping systems. Figure 250–105

(2) Aluminum

250.53 Grounding Electrode Installation Requirements.

(A) Rod, Pipe, or Plate Electrodes.

(1) Below Permanent Moisture Level. If practicable, rod, pipe, and plate electrodes must be embedded below the permanent moisture level and be free from nonconductive coatings such as paint or enamel.

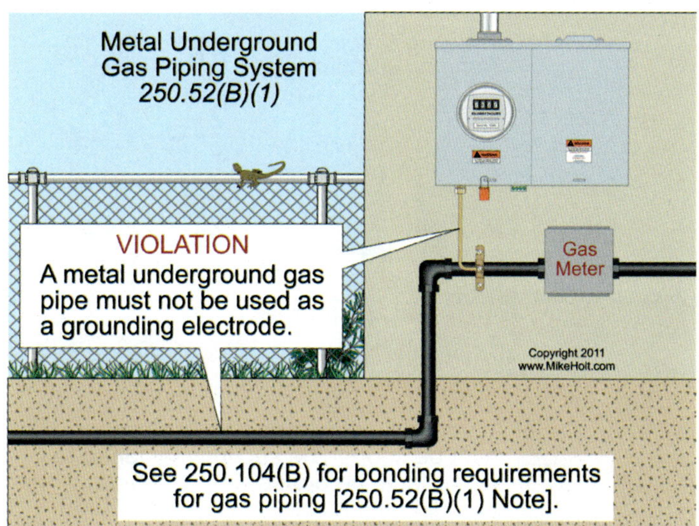

Figure 250–105

(2) Supplemental Electrode. A single rod, pipe or plate electrode must be supplemented by an additional electrode that's bonded to one of the following: **Figure 250–106**

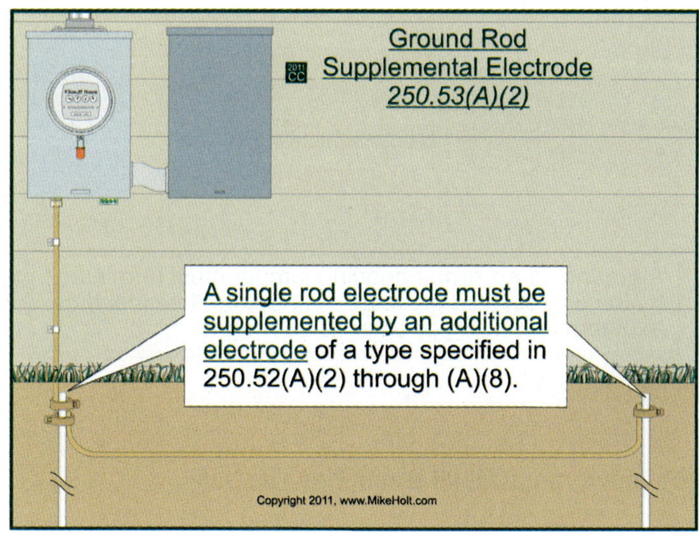

Figure 250–106

(1) The single rod, pipe, or plate electrode

(2) The grounding electrode conductor of the single electrode

(3) The neutral service-entrance conductor

(4) The nonflexible grounded service raceway

(5) The service enclosure

Ex: If a single rod, pipe, or plate grounding electrode has an earth contact resistance of 25 ohms or less, the supplemental electrode isn't required. **Figure 250–107**

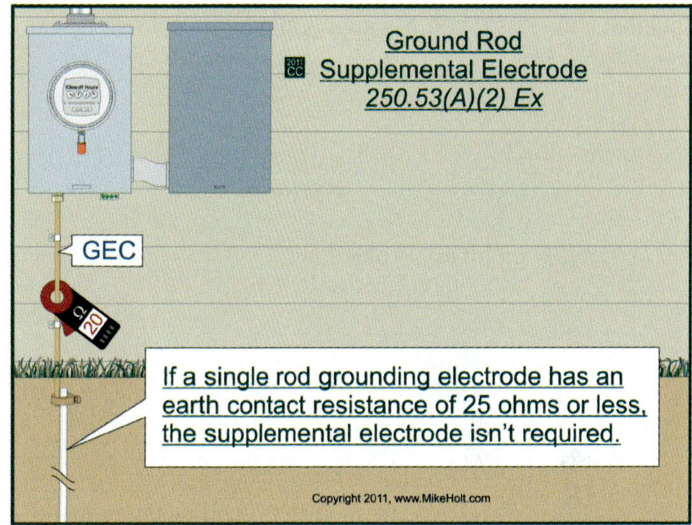

Figure 250–107

(3) Spacing. The supplemental electrode for a single rod, pipe, or plate electrode must be installed not less than 6 ft from the single electrode. **Figure 250–108**

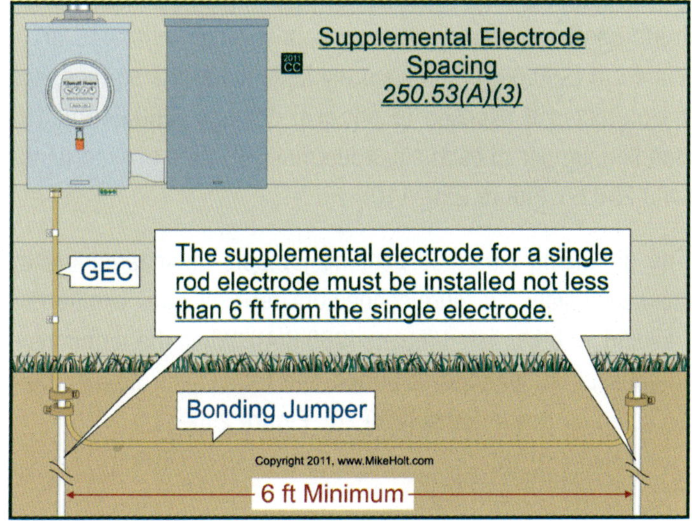

Figure 250–108

Note: The efficiency of paralleling electrodes is improved by spacing them at least twice the length of the longest rod.

(B) Electrode Spacing. Ground rods used as the required electrode for power systems must be located no closer than 6 ft from lighting protection or photovoltaic system grounding electrodes. Two or more grounding electrodes that are bonded together are considered a single grounding electrode system. Figure 250–109

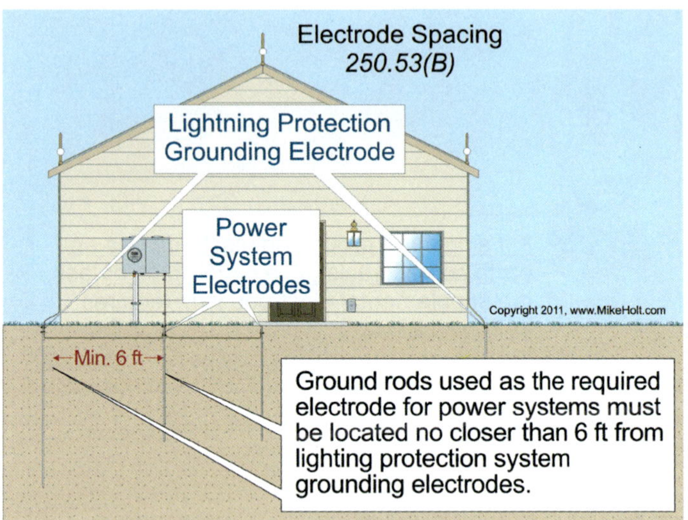

Figure 250–109

(C) Grounding Electrode Bonding Jumper. Grounding electrode bonding jumpers must be copper when within 18 in. of the earth [250.64(A)], be securely fastened to the surface, and be protected if exposed to physical damage [250.64(B)]. The bonding jumper to each electrode must be sized in accordance with 250.66. Figure 250–110

The grounding electrode bonding jumpers must terminate by the use of listed pressure connectors, terminal bars, exothermic welding, or other listed means [250.8(A)]. When the termination is encased in concrete or buried, the termination fittings must be listed for this purpose [250.70]. Figure 250–111

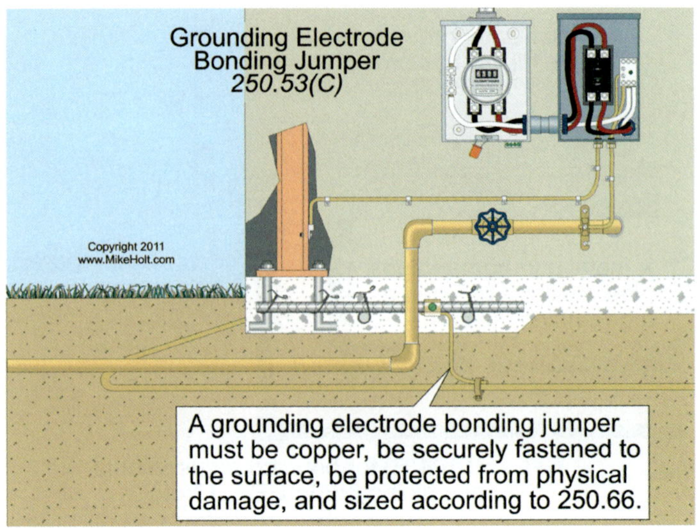

Figure 250–110

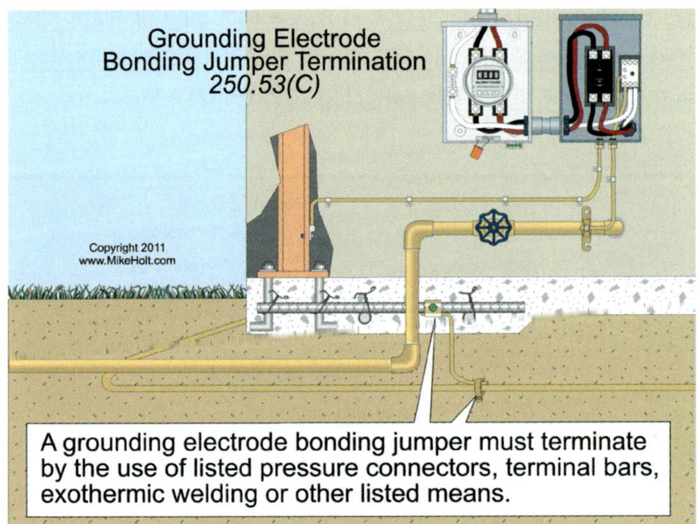

Figure 250–111

(D) Underground Metal Water Pipe Electrode.

(1) Continuity. The bonding connection to the interior metal water piping system, as required by 250.104(A), must not be dependent on water meters, filtering devices, or similar equipment likely to be disconnected for repairs or replacement. When necessary, a bonding jumper must be installed around insulated joints and equipment likely to be disconnected for repairs or replacement to assist in clearing and removing dangerous voltage on metal parts due to a ground fault [250.68(B)]. Figure 250–112

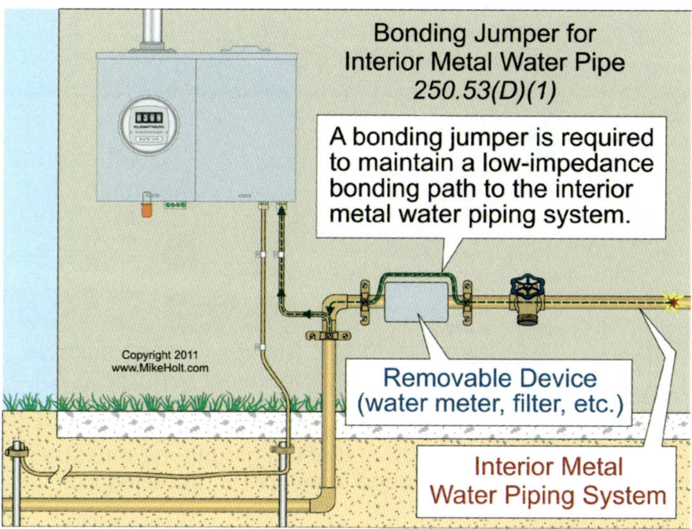

Figure 250–112

(2) Underground Metal Water Pipe Supplemental Electrode Required. When an underground metal water pipe grounding electrode is present [250.52(A)(1)], it must be supplemented by one of the following electrodes:

- Metal frame of the building/structure electrode [250.52(A)(2)]
- Concrete-encased electrode [250.52(A)(3)] Figure 250–113

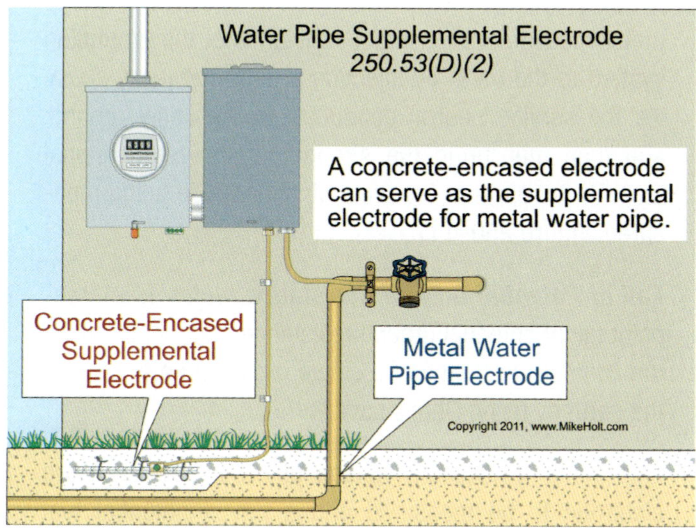

Figure 250–113

- Ground ring electrode [250.52(A)(4)]
- Ground rod electrode meeting the requirements of 250.52(A)(5)
- Other listed electrodes [250.52(A)(6)]
- Metal underground systems, piping systems, or underground tanks [250.52(A)(8)]

The termination of the supplemental grounding electrode conductor must be to one of the following locations: Figure 250–114

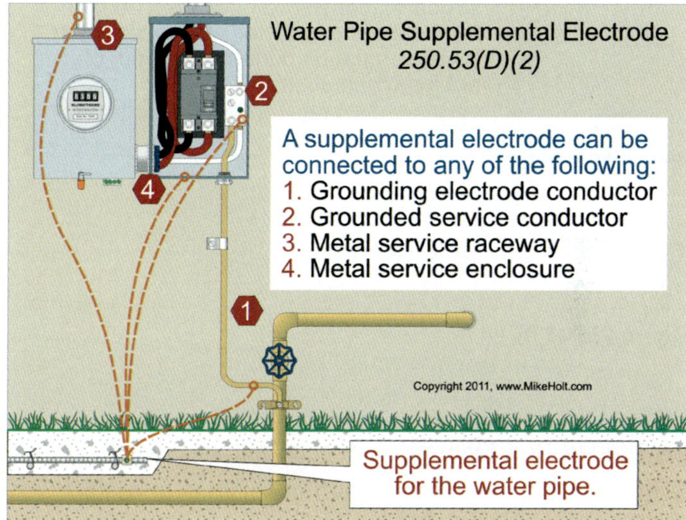

Figure 250–114

(1) Grounding electrode conductor

(2) Service neutral conductor

(3) Metal service raceway

(4) Service equipment enclosure

Ex: The supplemental electrode is permitted to be bonded to interior metal water piping located not more than 5 ft from the point of entrance to the building/structure [250.68(C)(1)].

(E) Supplemental Ground Rod Electrode. The grounding electrode conductor to a ground rod that serves as a supplemental electrode isn't required to be larger than 6 AWG copper.

(F) Ground Ring. A ground ring encircling the building/structure, consisting of at least 20 ft of bare copper conductor not smaller than 2 AWG, must be buried not less than 30 in. [250.52(A)(4)]. **Figure 250–115**

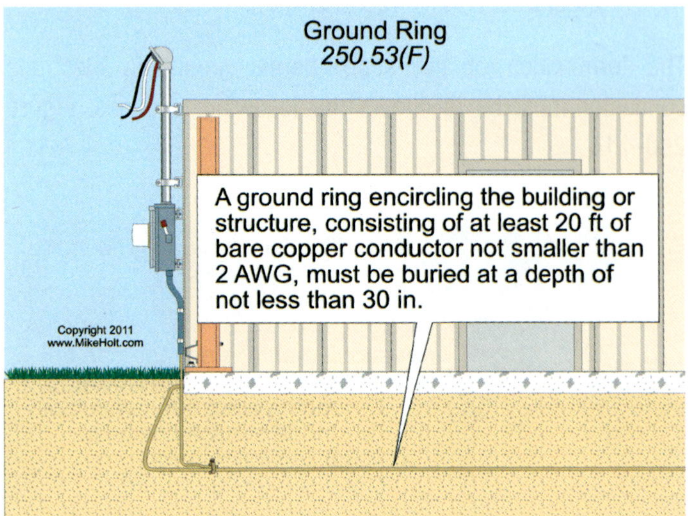

Figure 250–115

(G) Ground Rod Electrodes. Ground rod electrodes must be installed so that not less than 8 ft of length is in contact with the soil. If rock bottom is encountered, the ground rod must be driven at an angle not to exceed 45 degrees from vertical. If rock bottom is encountered at an angle up to 45 degrees from vertical, the ground rod can be buried in a minimum 30 in. deep trench. **Figure 250–116**

The upper end of the ground rod must be flush with or underground unless the grounding electrode conductor attachment is protected against physical damage as specified in 250.10.

> **Author's Comment:** When the grounding electrode attachment fitting is located underground, it must be listed for direct soil burial [250.68(A) Ex 1 and 250.70].

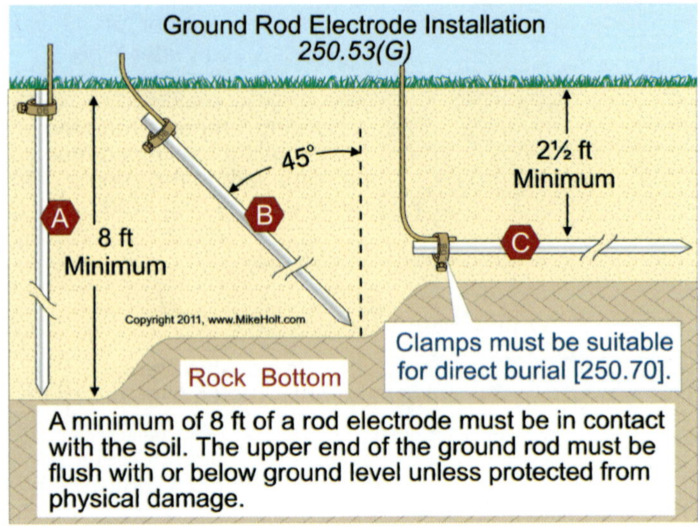

Figure 250–116

MEASURING THE GROUND RESISTANCE

Measuring the Ground Resistance

A ground resistance clamp meter, or a three-point fall of potential ground resistance meter, can be used to measure the contact resistance of a grounding electrode to the earth.

Ground Clamp Meter. The ground resistance clamp meter measures the contact resistance of the grounding system to the earth by injecting a high-frequency signal via the service neutral conductor to the utility ground, and then measuring the strength of the return signal through the earth to the grounding electrode being measured. **Figure 250–117**

Fall of Potential Ground Resistance Meter. The three-point fall of potential ground resistance meter determines the contact resistance of a single grounding electrode to the earth by using Ohm's Law: R=E/I.

This meter divides the voltage difference between the electrode to be measured and a driven potential test stake (P) by the current flowing between the electrode to be measured and a driven current test stake (C). The test stakes are typically made of ¼ in. diameter steel rods, 24 in. long, driven two-thirds of their length into the earth.

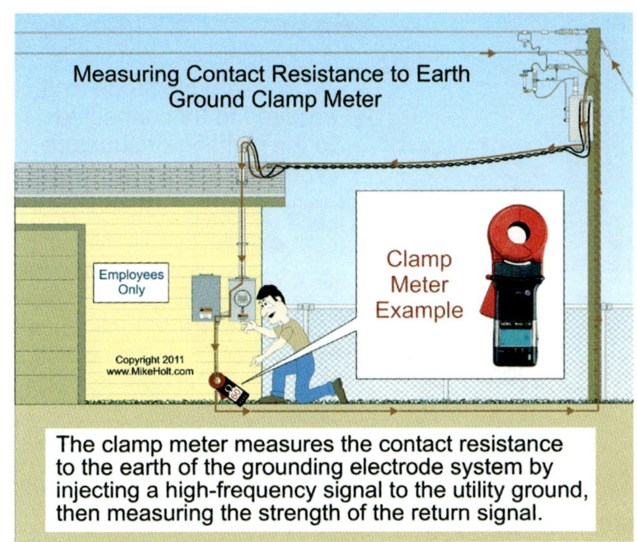

Figure 250–117

The distance and alignment between the potential and current test stakes, and the electrode, is extremely important to the validity of the earth contact resistance measurements. For an 8 ft ground rod, the accepted practice is to space the current test stake (C) 80 ft from the electrode to be measured.

The potential test stake (P) is positioned in a straight line between the electrode to be measured and the current test stake (C). The potential test stake should be located at approximately 62 percent of the distance the current test stake is located from the electrode. Since the current test stake (C) for an 8 ft ground rod is located 80 ft from the grounding electrode, the potential test stake (P) will be about 50 ft from the electrode to be measured.

Question: *If the voltage between the ground rod and the potential test stake (P) is 3V and the current between the ground rod and the current test stake (C) is 0.20A, then the earth contact resistance of the electrode to the earth will be ______.* **Figure 250–118**

(a) 5 ohms (b) 10 ohms (c) 15 ohms (d) 25 ohms

Answer: *(c) 15 ohms*

Resistance = Voltage/Current
E (Voltage) = 3V
I (Current) = 0.20A
R = E/I

Resistance = 3V/0.20A
Resistance = 15 ohms

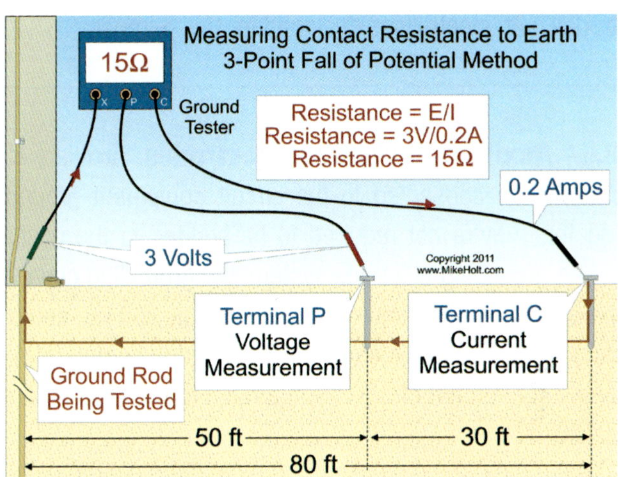

Figure 250–118

Author's Comment: The three-point fall of potential meter can only be used to measure the contact resistance of one electrode to the earth at a time, and this electrode must be independent and not connected to any part of the electrical system. The contact resistance of two electrodes bonded together must not be measured until they've been separated. The contact resistance of two separate electrodes to the earth is calculated as if they're two resistors connected in parallel.

Soil Resistivity

The earth's ground resistance is directly impacted by soil resistivity, which varies throughout the world. Soil resistivity is influenced by electrolytes, which consist of moisture, minerals, and dissolved salts. Because soil resistivity changes with moisture content, the resistance of any grounding system varies with the seasons of the year. Since moisture is stable at greater distances below the surface of the earth, grounding systems are generally more effective if the grounding electrode can reach the water table. In addition, placing the grounding electrode below the frost line helps to ensure less deviation in the system's contact resistance to the earth year round.

The contact resistance to the earth can be lowered by chemically treating the earth around the grounding electrodes with electrolytes designed for this purpose.

250.54 Auxiliary Grounding Electrodes. Auxiliary electrodes can be connected to the circuit equipment grounding conductor. They're not required to be bonded to the building/structure grounding electrode system, the grounding conductor to the electrode isn't required to be sized to 250.66, and their contact resistance to the earth isn't required to comply with the 25 ohm requirement of 250.53(A)(2) Ex. **Figures 250–119 and 250–120**

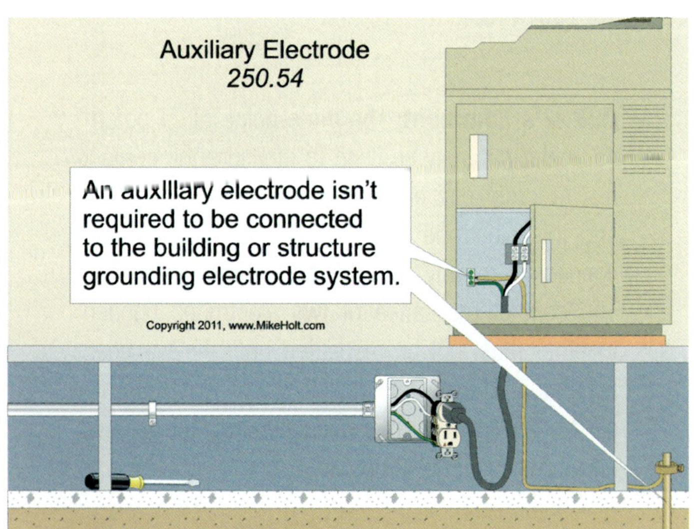

Figure 250–119

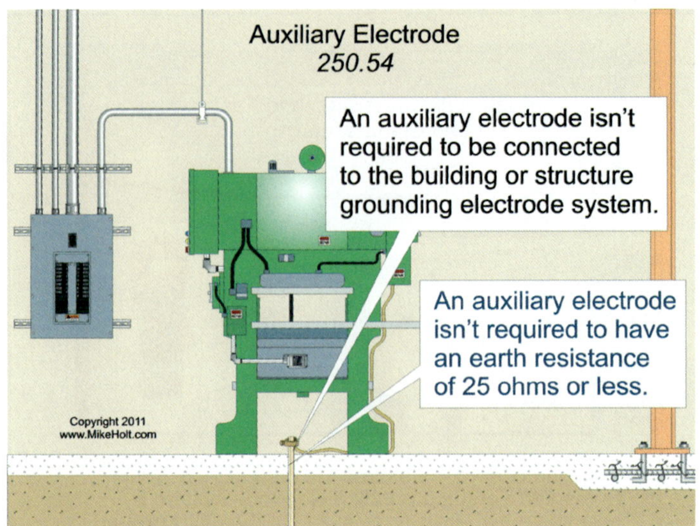

Figure 250–120

CAUTION: *An auxiliary electrode typically serves no useful purpose, and in some cases it may actually cause equipment failures by providing a path for lightning to travel through electronic equipment.* **Figure 250–121**

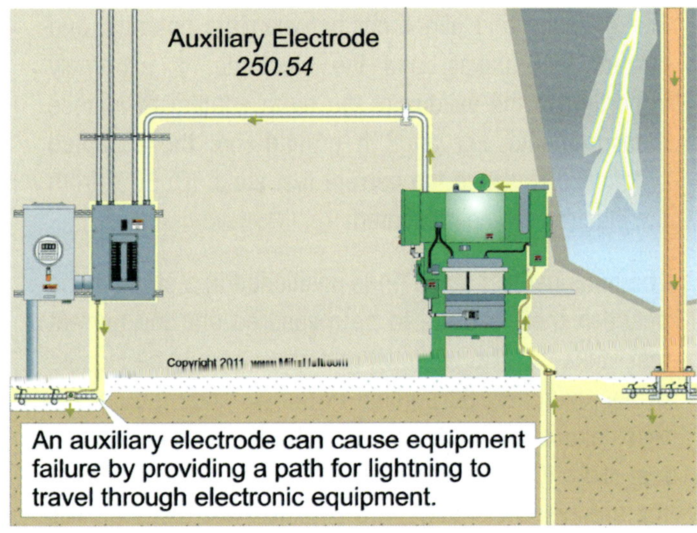

Figure 250–121

The earth must not be used as the effective ground-fault current path required by 250.4(A)(5). **Figure 250–122**

DANGER: *Because the contact resistance of an electrode to the earth is so great, very little fault current returns to the power supply if the earth is the only fault current return path. Result—the circuit overcurrent device won't open and clear the ground fault, and all metal parts associated with the electrical installation, metal piping, and structural building steel will become and remain energized.*

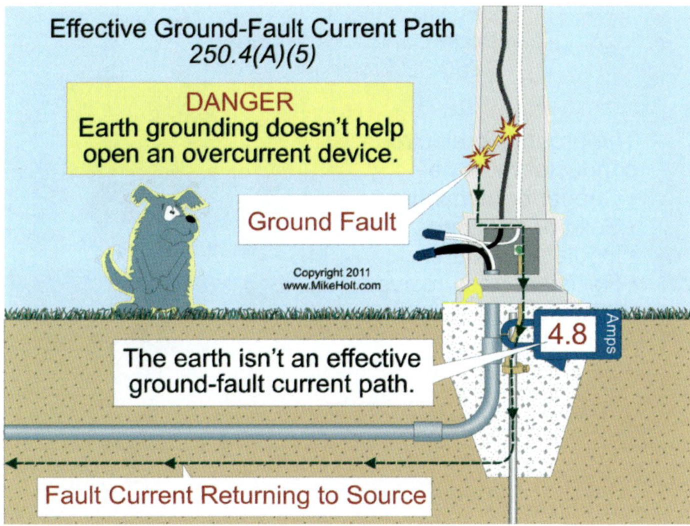

Figure 250–122

250.58 Common Grounding Electrode. Where an ac system is connected to a grounding electrode in or at a building or structure, the same grounding electrode must be used. If separate services, feeders, or branch circuits supply a building, the same grounding electrode must be used. Figure 250–123

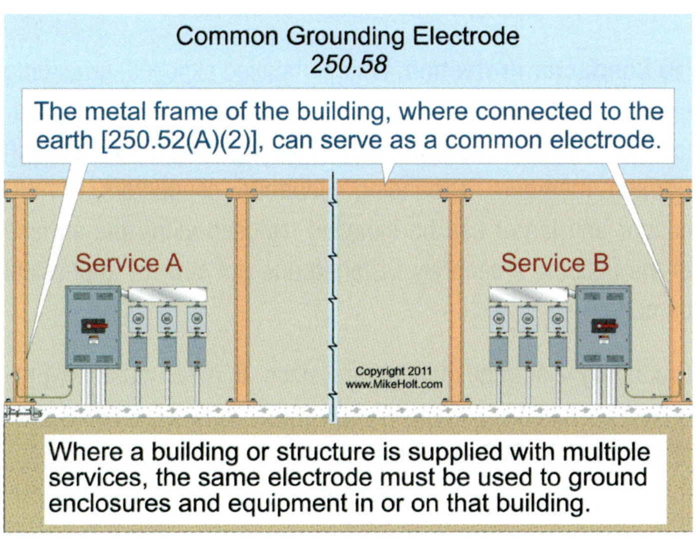

Figure 250–123

Two or more grounding electrodes that are bonded together will be considered as a single grounding electrode system in this sense.

Author's Comment: Metal parts of the electrical installation are grounded (connected to the earth) to reduce induced voltage on the metal parts from lightning so as to prevent fires from a surface arc within the building/structure. Grounding electrical equipment doesn't serve the purpose of providing a low-impedance fault current path to open the circuit overcurrent device in the event of a ground fault.

CAUTION: *Potentially dangerous objectionable neutral current flows on the metal parts when multiple service disconnecting means are connected to the same electrode. This is because neutral current from each service can return to the utility via the common grounding electrode and its conductors. This is especially a problem if a service neutral conductor is opened.* Figure 250–124

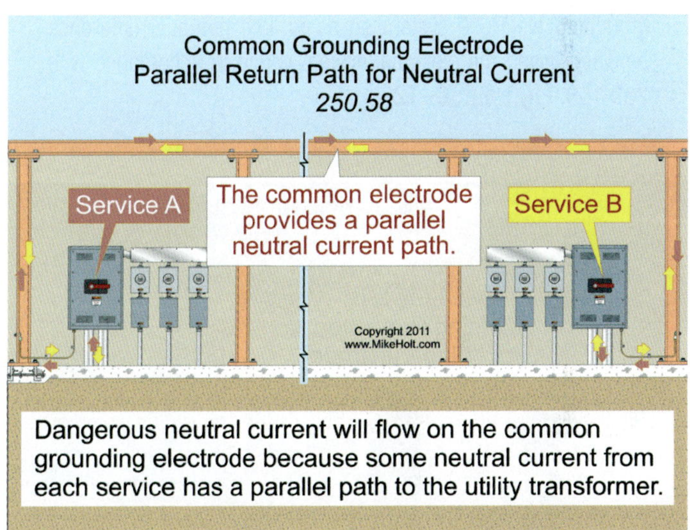

Figure 250–124

250.60 Lightning Protection Electrode. Conductors and electrodes used for strike termination devices of a lightning protection system aren't permitted to be used in lieu of the premises wiring grounding electrode system. Figure 250–125

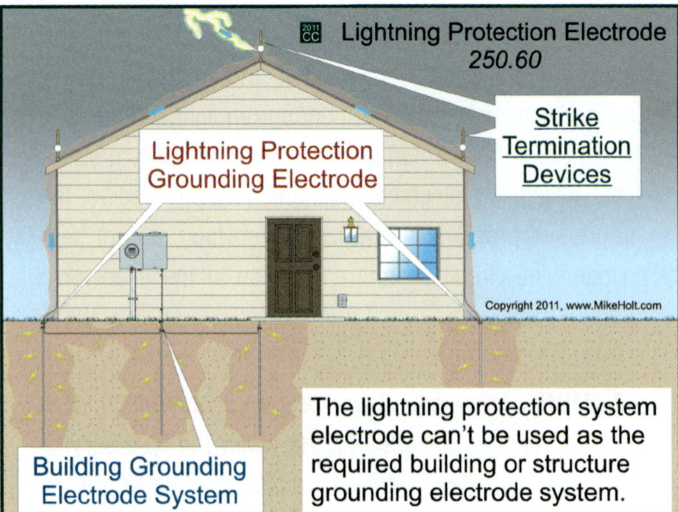

Figure 250–125

Note 2: If a lightning protection system is installed, the lightning protection system must be bonded to the building/structure grounding electrode system so as to limit potential difference between it and the electrical system wiring in accordance with 250.106. **Figure 250–126**

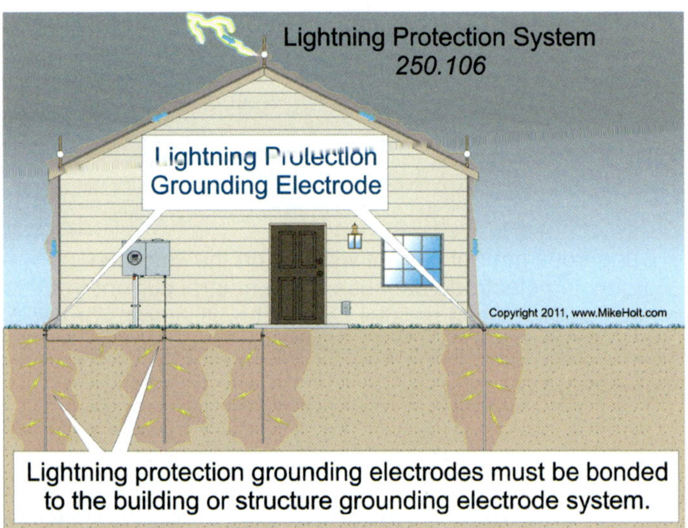

Figure 250–126

250.62 Grounding Electrode Conductor. The grounding electrode conductor must be solid or stranded, insulated or bare, and it must be copper if within 18 in. of the earth [250.64(A)]. **Figure 250–127**

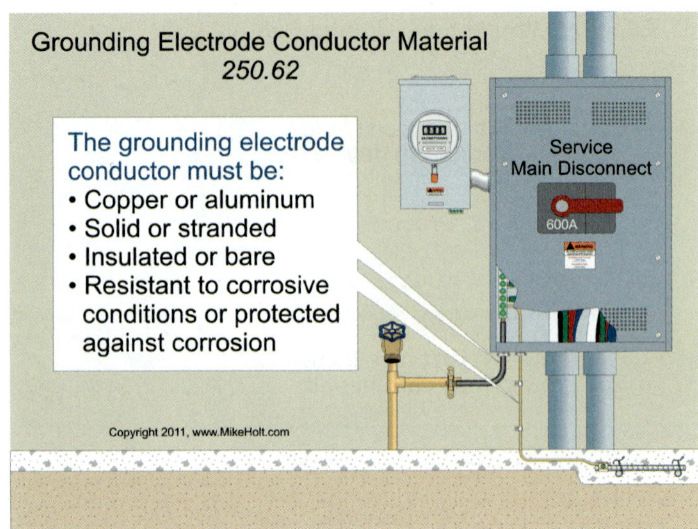

Figure 250–127

250.64 Grounding Electrode Conductor Installation. Grounding electrode conductors must be installed as specified in (A) through (F).

(A) Aluminum Conductors. Aluminum grounding electrode conductors must not be in contact with masonry, subject to corrosive conditions, or within 18 in. of the earth.

(B) Conductor Protection. Where installed exposed, grounding electrode conductors must be protected where subject to physical damage and are permitted to be installed on or through framing members. Grounding electrode conductors 6 AWG copper and larger can be installed exposed along the surface of the building if securely fastened and not subject to physical damage.

Grounding electrode conductors sized 8 AWG must be protected by installing them in rigid metal conduit, intermediate metal conduit, PVC conduit, electrical metallic tubing, or reinforced thermosetting resin conduit.

Author's Comment: A ferrous metal raceway containing a grounding electrode conductor must be made electrically continuous by bonding each end of that type of raceway to the grounding electrode conductor [250.64(E)], so it's best to use PVC conduit.

(C) Continuous. Grounding electrode conductor(s) must be installed without a splice or joint except: **Figures 250–128 and 250–129**

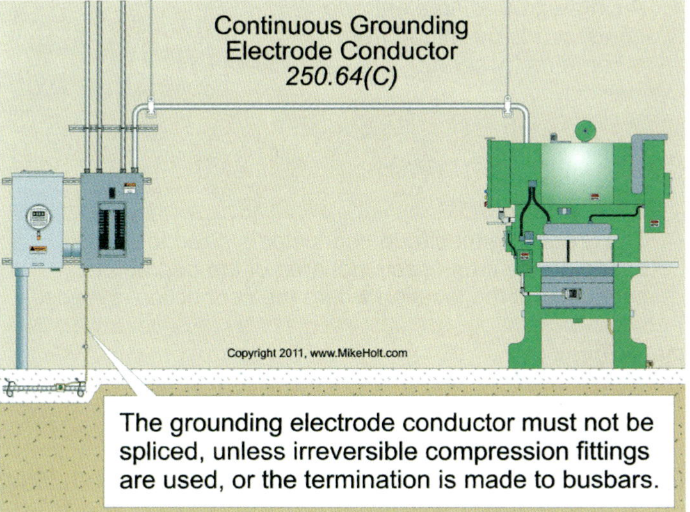

Figure 250–128

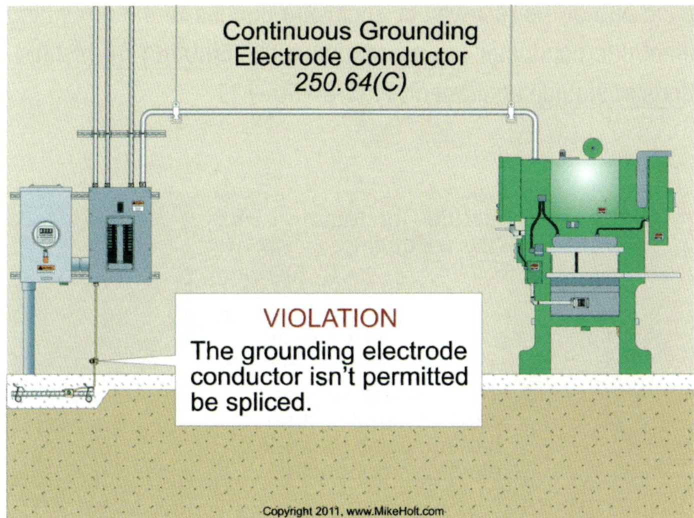

Figure 250–129

(1) By irreversible compression-type connectors or exothermic welding.

(2) Sections of busbars connected together to form a grounding electrode conductor.

(3) Bolted, riveted, or welded connections of structural metal frames of buildings or structures.

(4) Threaded, welded, brazed, soldered or bolted-flange connections of metal water piping.

(D) Grounding Electrode Conductor for Multiple Service Disconnects. If a service consists of more than a single enclosure, grounding electrode connections must be made in one of the following methods:

(1) Common Grounding Electrode Conductor and Taps. A grounding electrode conductor tap must extend to the inside of each service disconnecting means enclosure.

The common grounding electrode conductor must be sized in accordance with 250.66, based on the sum of the circular mil area of the largest ungrounded service-entrance conductors. **Figure 250–130**

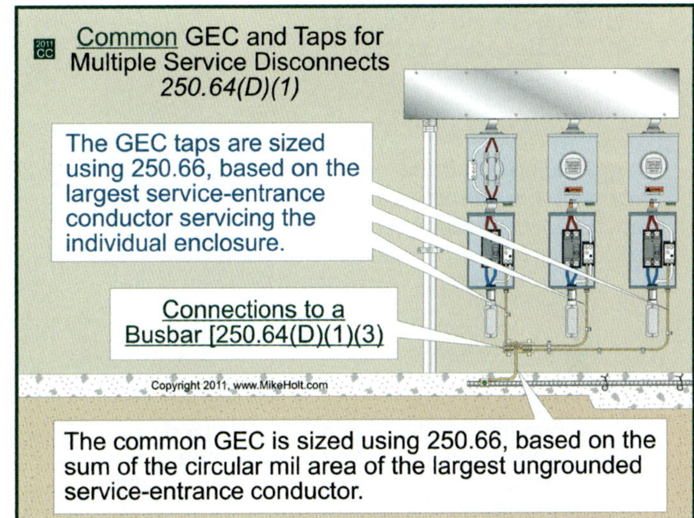

Figure 250–130

A grounding electrode conductor must extend from each service disconnecting means, sized not smaller than specified in Table 250.66, based on the area of the largest ungrounded conductor for each service disconnecting means.

The grounding electrode tap conductors must be connected to the common grounding electrode conductor, without splicing the common grounding electrode conductor, by one of the following methods:

(1) Exothermic welding.

(2) Connectors listed as grounding and bonding equipment.

(3) Connections to a busbar not less than ¼ in. × 2 in. that's securely fastened and installed in an accessible location.

(2) Individual Grounding Electrode Conductors. A grounding electrode conductor must be connected between the grounded conductor in each service equipment disconnecting means enclosure and the grounding electrode system, each sized in accordance with 250.66 based on the ungrounded service-entrance conductor(s) supplying the individual service disconnecting means. **Figure 250–131**

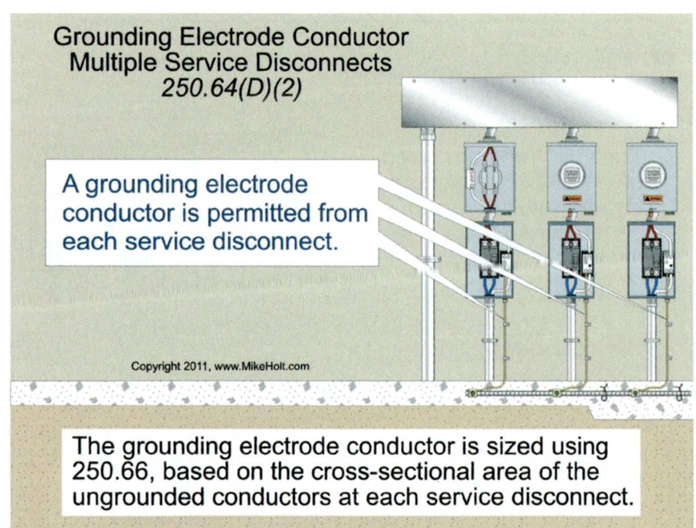

Figure 250–131

(3) Common Location. A single grounding electrode conductor is permitted from a common location, sized not smaller than specified in Table 250.66, based on the area of the ungrounded conductor at the location where the connection is made. **Figure 250–132**

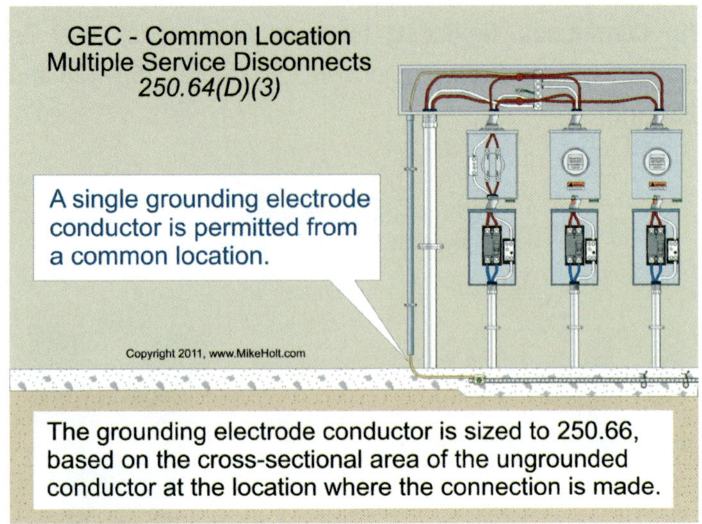

Figure 250–132

(E) Ferrous Metal Enclosures Containing Grounding Electrode Conductors. To prevent inductive choking of grounding electrode conductors, ferrous raceways and enclosures containing grounding electrode conductors must have each end of the raceway or enclosure bonded to the grounding electrode conductor in accordance with 250.92(B) for installations at service equipment. **Figure 250–133**

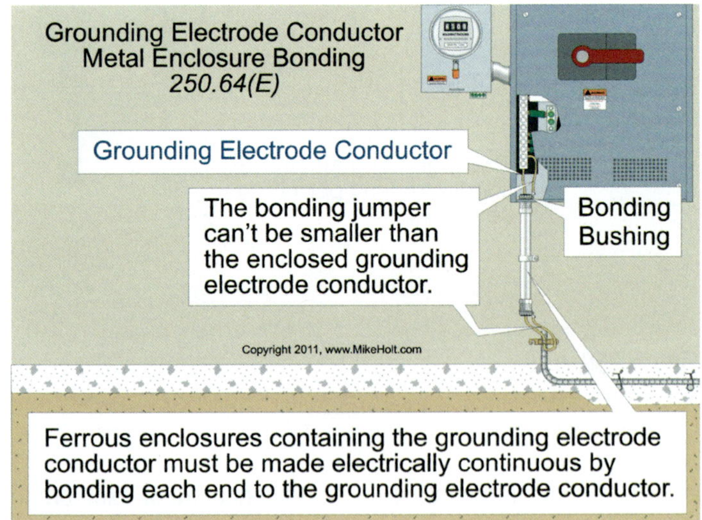

Figure 250–133

For other than service equipment locations, ferrous raceways and enclosures containing grounding electrode conductors must have each end of the raceway or enclosure bonded to the grounding electrode conductor in accordance with 250.92(B)(2) through (B)(4).

Author's Comment: Nonferrous metal raceways, such as aluminum rigid metal conduit, enclosing the grounding electrode conductor aren't required to meet the "bonding each end of the raceway to the grounding electrode conductor" provisions of this section.

CAUTION: *The effectiveness of a grounding electrode is significantly reduced if a ferrous metal raceway containing a grounding electrode conductor isn't bonded to the ferrous metal raceway at both ends. This is because a single conductor carrying high-frequency induced lightning current in a ferrous raceway causes the raceway to act as an inductor, which severely limits (chokes) the current flow through the grounding electrode conductor. ANSI/IEEE 142—Recommended Practice for Grounding of Industrial and Commercial Power Systems (Green Book) states: "An inductive choke can reduce the current flow by 97 percent."*

Author's Comment: To save a lot of time and effort, install the grounding electrode conductor exposed if it's not subject to physical damage [250.64(B)], or enclose it in PVC conduit suitable for the application [352.10(F)].

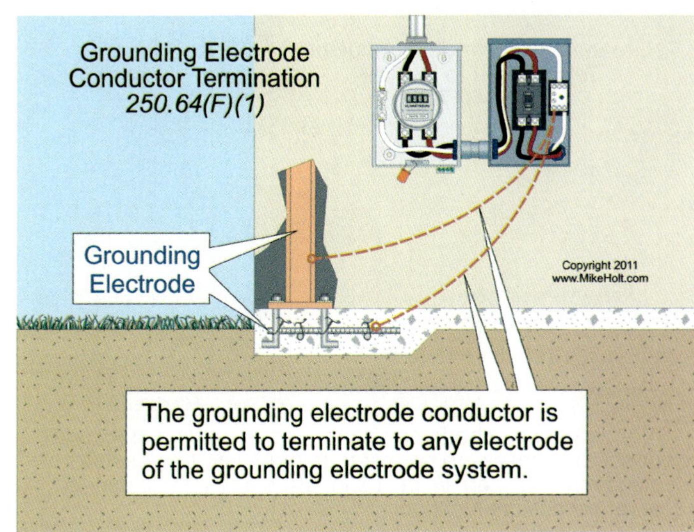

Figure 250–134

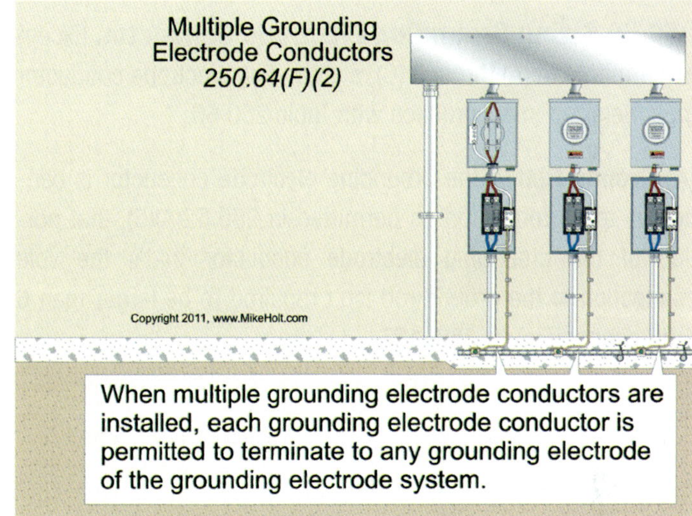

Figure 250–135

(F) Termination to Grounding Electrode.

(1) Single Grounding Electrode Conductor. A single grounding electrode conductor is permitted to terminate to any grounding electrode of the grounding electrode system. Figure 250–134

(2) Multiple Grounding Electrode Conductors. When multiple grounding electrode conductors are installed [250.64(D)(2)], each grounding electrode conductor is permitted to terminate to any grounding electrode of the grounding electrode system. Figure 250–135

(3) Termination to Busbar. A grounding electrode conductor and grounding electrode bonding jumpers are permitted to terminate to a busbar sized not less than ¼ in. × 2 in. that's securely fastened at an accessible location. The terminations to the busbar must be made by a listed connector or by exothermic welding. Figure 250–136

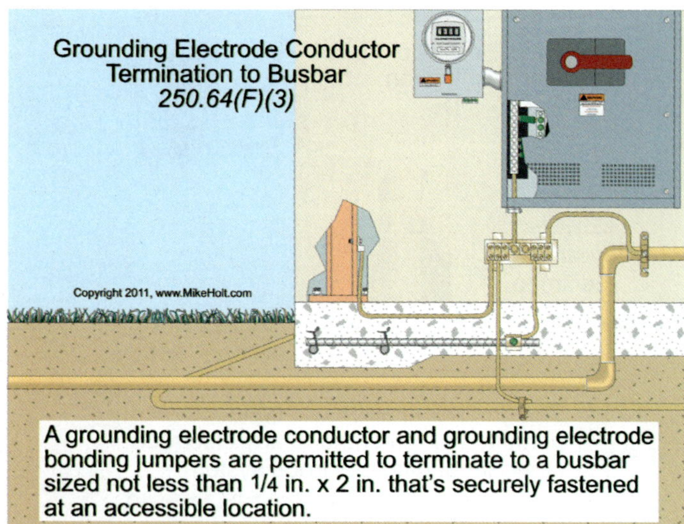

Figure 250–136

250.66 Sizing Grounding Electrode Conductor. Except as permitted in (A) through (C), a grounding electrode conductor must be sized in accordance with Table 250.66.

(A) Ground Rod. If the grounding electrode conductor is connected to a ground rod as permitted in 250.52(A)(5), that portion of the grounding electrode conductor that's the sole connection to the ground rod isn't required to be larger than 6 AWG copper. Figure 250–137

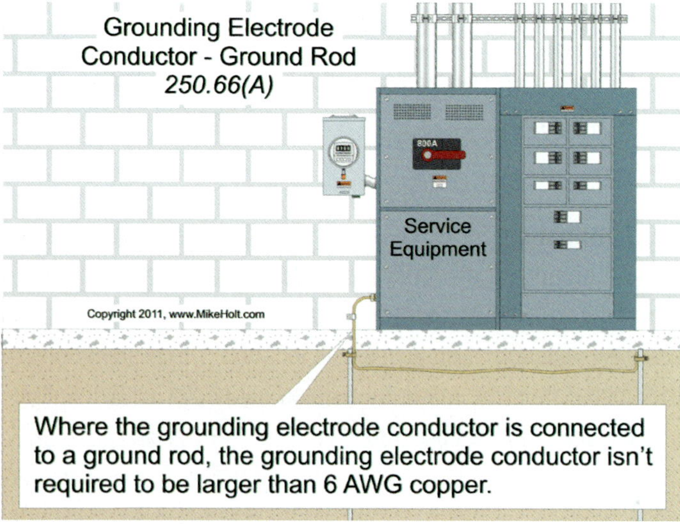

Figure 250–137

(B) Concrete-Encased Grounding Electrode. If the grounding electrode conductor is connected to a concrete-encased electrode, the portion of the grounding electrode conductor that's the sole connection to the concrete-encased electrode isn't required to be larger than 4 AWG copper. Figure 250–138

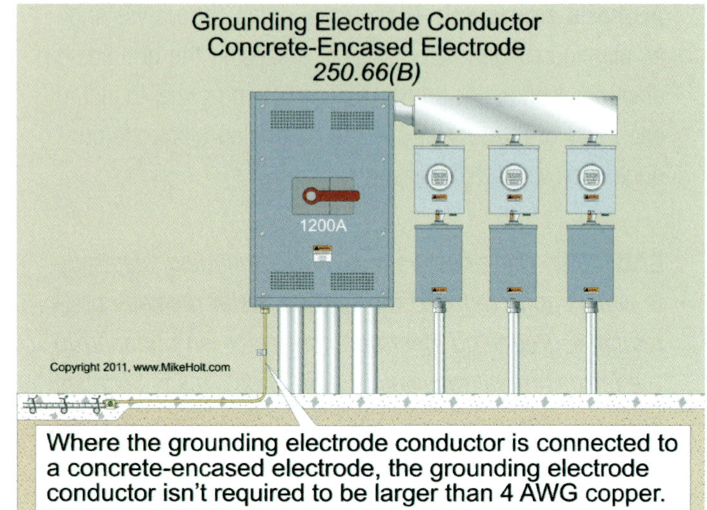

Figure 250–138

(C) Ground Ring. If the grounding electrode conductor is connected to a ground ring, the portion of the conductor that's the sole connection to the ground ring isn't required to be larger than the conductor used for the ground ring.

Author's Comments:

- A ground ring encircling the building/structure in direct contact with the earth must consist of at least 20 ft of bare copper conductor not smaller than 2 AWG [250.52(A)(4)]. See 250.53(F) for the installation requirements for a ground ring.
- Table 250.66 is used to size the grounding electrode conductor when the conditions of 250.66(A), (B), or (C) don't apply. Figure 250–139

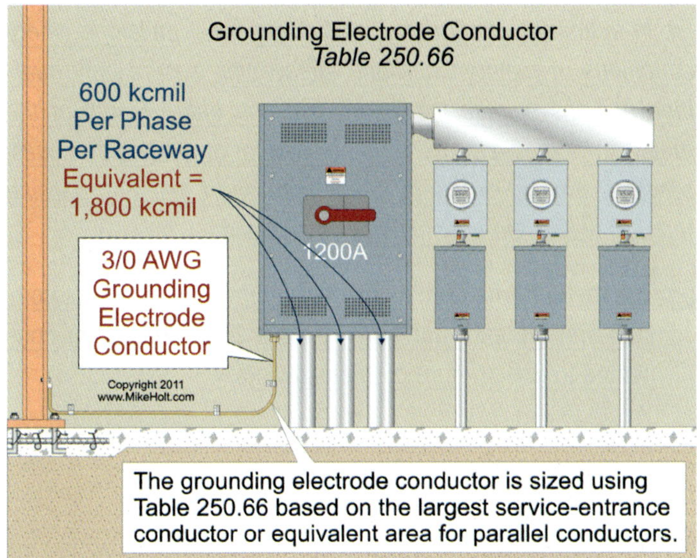

Figure 250–139

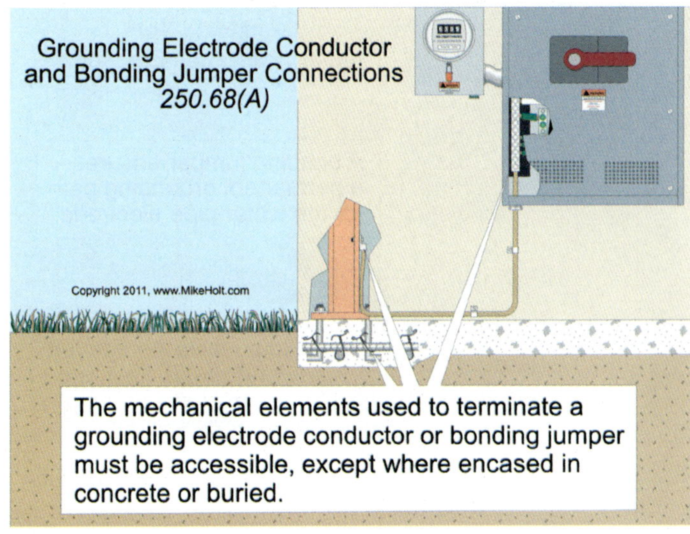

Figure 250–140

Table 250.66 Sizing Grounding Electrode Conductor	
Conductor or Area of Parallel Conductors	Copper Grounding Electrode Conductor
12 through 2 AWG	8 AWG
1 or 1/0 AWG	6 AWG
2/0 or 3/0 AWG	4 AWG
4/0 through 350 kcmil	2 AWG
400 through 600 kcmil	1/0 AWG
700 through 1,100 kcmil	2/0 AWG
1,200 kcmil and larger	3/0 AWG

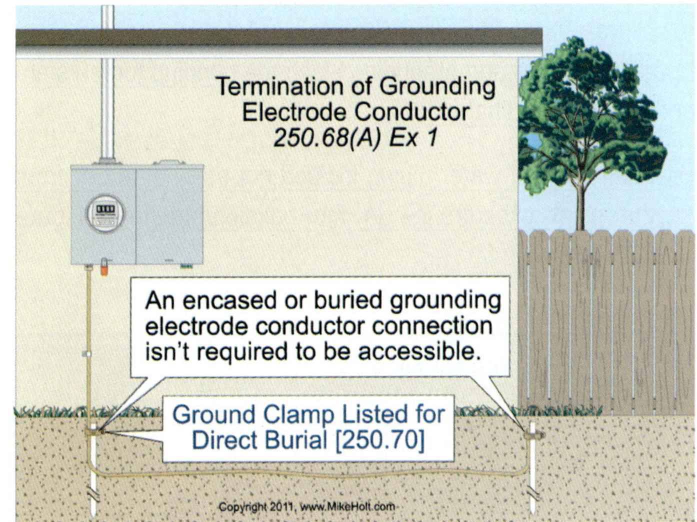

Figure 250–141

250.68 Termination to the Grounding Electrode.

(A) Accessibility. The mechanical elements used to terminate a grounding electrode conductor or bonding jumper to a grounding electrode must be accessible. Figure 250–140

Ex 1: The termination isn't required to be accessible if the termination to the electrode is encased in concrete or buried in the earth. Figure 250–141

> **Author's Comment:** If the grounding electrode attachment fitting is encased in concrete or buried in the earth, it must be listed for direct soil burial or concrete encasement [250.70].

Ex 2: Exothermic or irreversible compression connections, together with the mechanical means used to attach to fireproofed structural metal, aren't required to be accessible.

(B) Integrity of Underground Metal Water Pipe Electrode. A bonding jumper must be installed around insulated joints and equipment likely to be disconnected for repairs or replacement for an underground metal water piping system used as a grounding electrode. The bonding jumper must be of sufficient length to allow the removal of such equipment while retaining the integrity of the grounding path. Figure 250–142

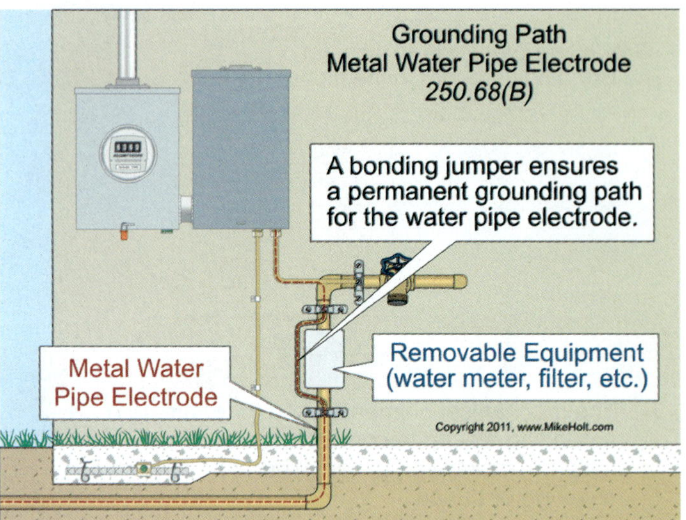

Figure 250–142

(C) Metal Water Pipe and Structural Metal. Grounding electrode conductors and grounding electrode bonding jumpers are permitted to terminate to:

(1) Interior metal water piping located not more than 5 ft from the point of entrance to the building/structure. Figure 250–143

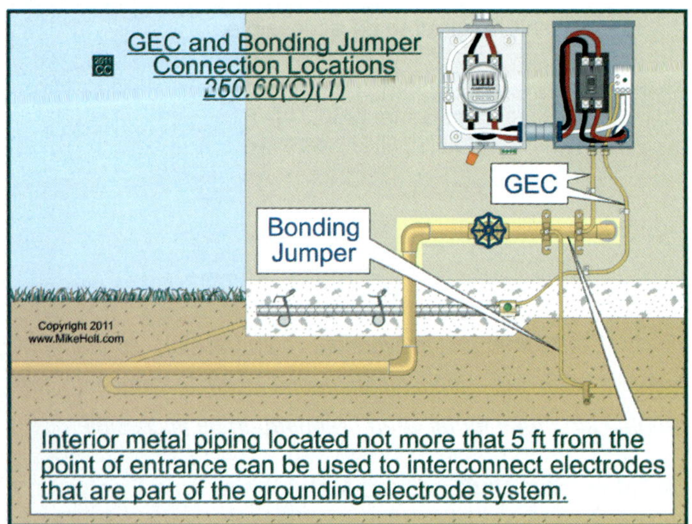

Figure 250–143

Ex: In industrial, institutional, and commercial buildings where conditions of maintenance and supervision ensure only qualified persons service the installation, the entire length of the metal water piping system can be used for grounding purposes, provided the entire length, other than short sections passing through walls, floors, or ceilings, is exposed.

(2) The metal frame of a building/structure that's in direct contact with the earth for 10 ft or more [250.52(A)(2)] or connected to one or more of the following:

(a) Concrete-encased electrode [250.52(A)(3)] or ground ring [250.52(A)(4)],

(b) Ground rod [250.52(A)(5)],

(c) Other approved earth connection.

250.70 Grounding Electrode Conductor Termination Fittings.

The grounding electrode conductor must terminate to the grounding electrode by exothermic welding, listed lugs, listed pressure connectors, listed clamps, or other listed means. In addition, fittings terminating to a grounding electrode must be listed for the materials of the grounding electrode.

When the termination to a grounding electrode is encased in concrete or buried in the earth, the termination fitting must be listed for direct soil burial or concrete encasement. No more than one conductor can terminate on a single clamp or fitting unless the clamp or fitting is listed for multiple connections. Figure 250–144

PART IV. GROUNDING ENCLOSURE, RACEWAY, AND SERVICE CABLE CONNECTIONS

250.80 Service Raceways and Enclosures. Metal enclosures and raceways containing service conductors must be connected to the neutral conductor at service equipment if the electrical system is grounded or to the grounding electrode conductor for electrical systems that aren't grounded.

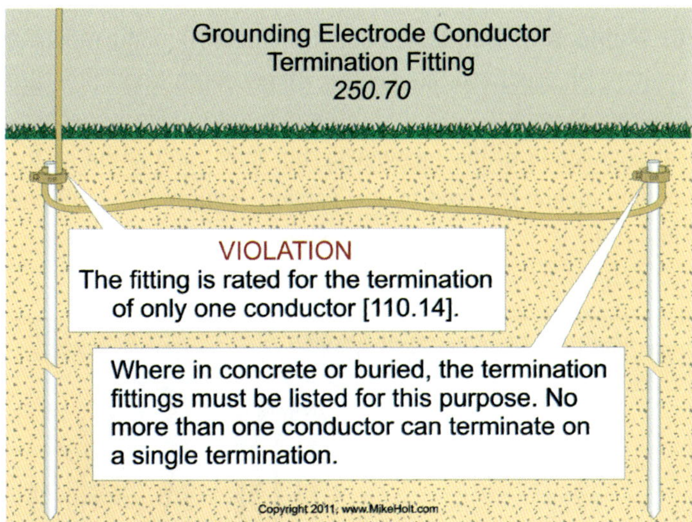

Figure 250–144

Ex: Metal elbows having a minimum of 18 in. of cover installed in an underground nonmetallic raceway system aren't required to be connected to the service neutral or grounding electrode conductor.

250.86 Other Enclosures. Metal raceways and enclosures containing electrical conductors operating at 50V or more [250.20(A)] must be connected to the circuit equipment grounding conductor. **Figure 250–145**

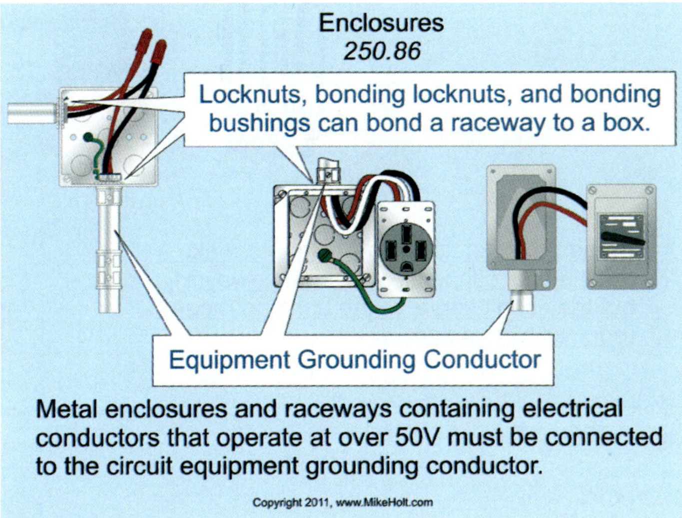

Figure 250–145

Ex 2: Short sections of metal raceways used for the support or physical protection of cables aren't required to be connected to the circuit equipment grounding conductor. **Figure 250–146**

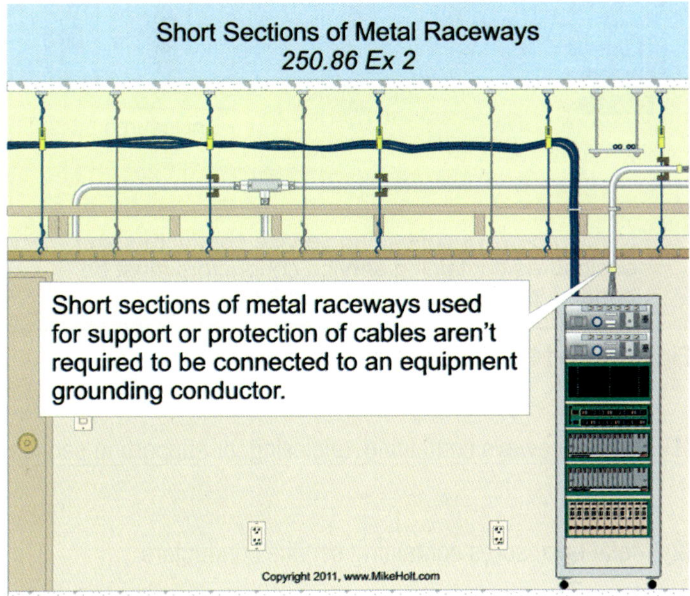

Figure 250–146

Ex 3: A metal elbow installed in a run of underground nonmetallic raceway having a minimum of 18 in. of cover or encased in not less than 2 in. of concrete.

PART V. BONDING

250.90 General. Bonding must be provided to ensure electrical continuity and the capacity to conduct safely any fault current likely to be imposed.

250.92 Bonding Equipment for Services.

(A) Bonding Requirements for Equipment for Services. The metal parts of equipment indicated below must be bonded together in accordance with 250.92(B). **Figure 250–147**

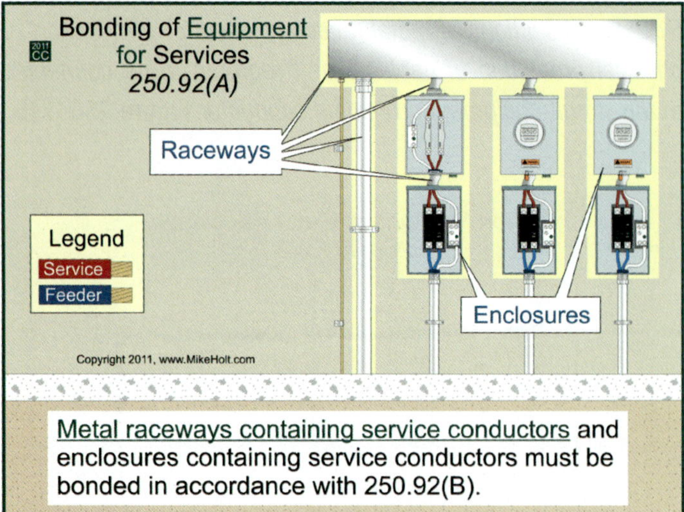

Figure 250–147

(1) Metal raceways containing, enclosing, or supporting service conductors.

(2) Metal enclosures containing service conductors.

Author's Comment: Metal raceways or metal enclosures containing feeder and branch-circuit conductors are required to be connected to the circuit equipment grounding conductor in accordance with 250.86. **Figure 250–148**

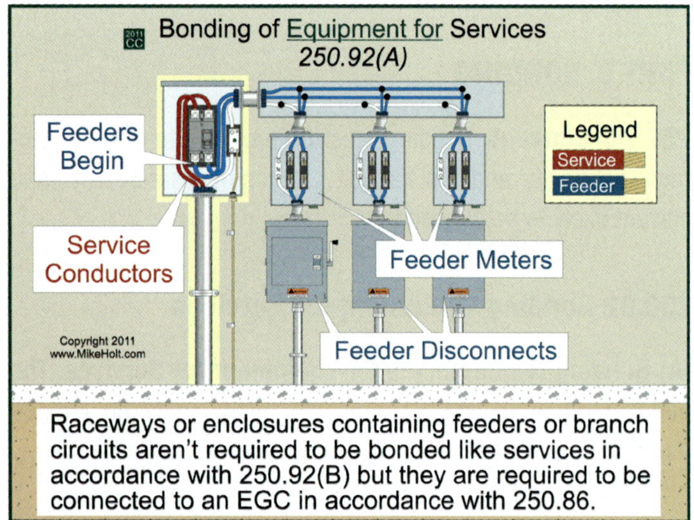

Figure 250–148

(B) Methods of Bonding. Bonding jumpers around reducing washers or oversized, concentric, or eccentric knockouts are required. Standard locknuts are permitted to make a mechanical connection of the raceway(s), but they can't serve as the bonding means required by this section. **Figures 250–149 and 250–150**

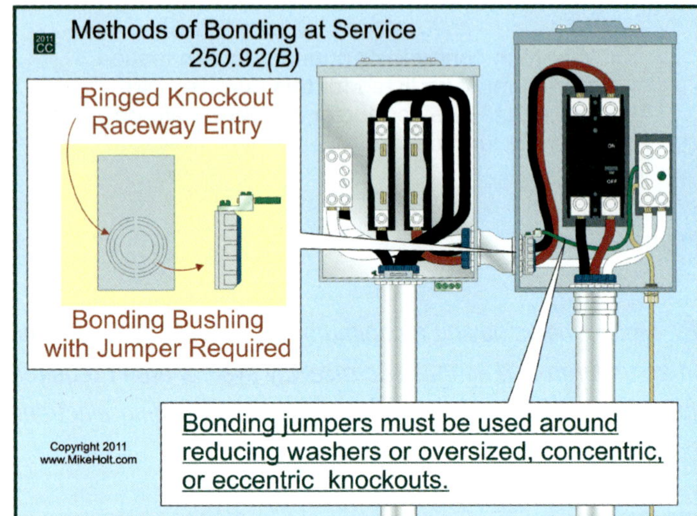

Figure 250–149

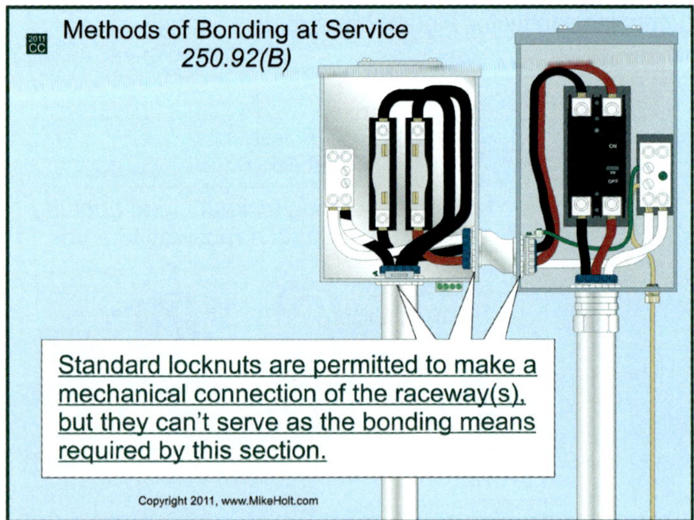

Figure 250–150

Electrical continuity at service equipment, service raceways, and service conductor enclosures must be ensured by one of the following methods:

(1) Neutral Conductor. By bonding the metal parts to the service neutral conductor. **Figure 250–151**

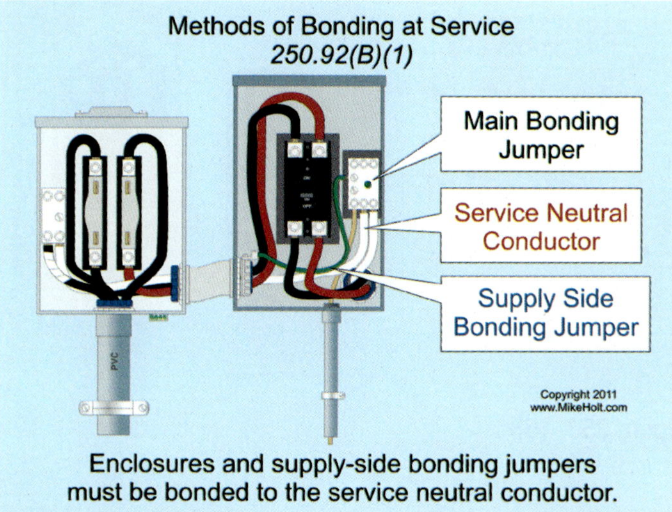

Figure 250–151

Author's Comments:

- A main bonding jumper is required to bond the service disconnect to the service neutral conductor [250.24(B) and 250.28].
- At service equipment, the service neutral conductor provides the effective ground-fault current path to the power supply [250.24(C)]; therefore, an equipment grounding conductor isn't required to be installed within PVC conduit containing service-entrance conductors [250.142(A)(1) and 352.60 Ex 2]. **Figure 250–152**

(2) Threaded Fittings. By terminating metal raceways to metal enclosures by threaded hubs on enclosures if made up wrenchtight. **Figure 250–153**

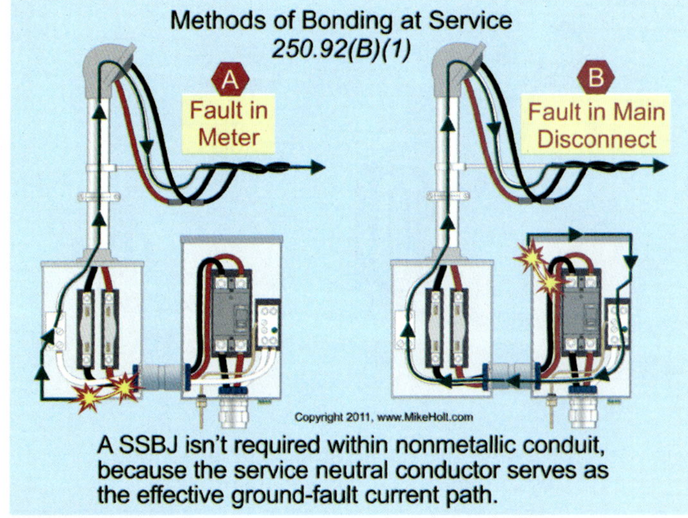

Figure 250–152

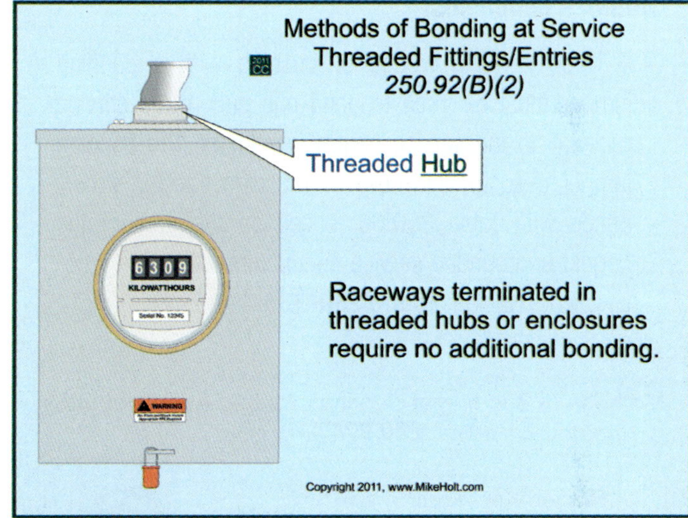

Figure 250–153

(3) Threadless Fittings. By terminating metal raceways to metal enclosures by threadless fittings if made up tight. **Figure 250–154**

(4) Other listed devices, such as bonding-type locknuts, bushings, wedges, or bushings with bonding jumpers.

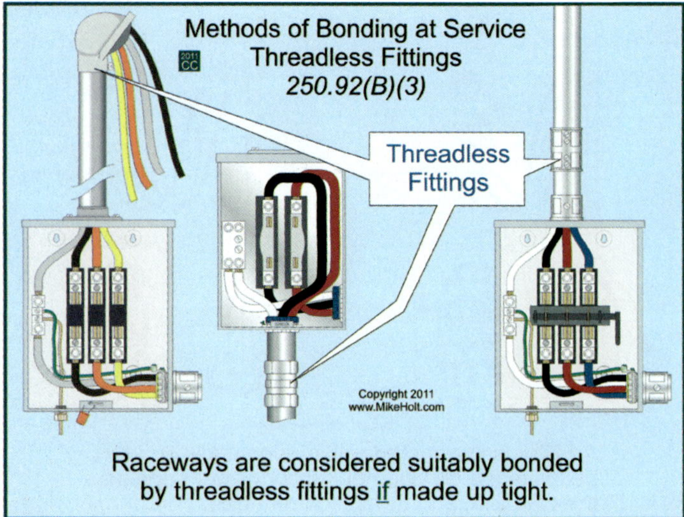

Figure 250–154

Author's Comments:

- A listed bonding wedge or bushing with a bonding jumper must be used to bond one end of the service raceway to the service neutral conductor. The bonding jumper used for this purpose must be sized in accordance with Table 250.66, based on the area of the largest ungrounded service conductors within the raceway [250.102(C)]. **Figure 250–155**

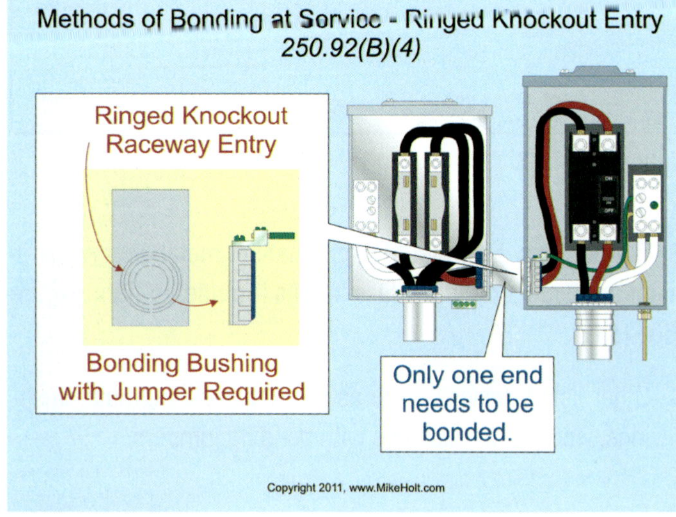

Figure 250–155

- When a metal raceway containing service conductors terminates to an enclosure without a ringed knockout, a bonding-type locknut can be used. **Figure 250–156**

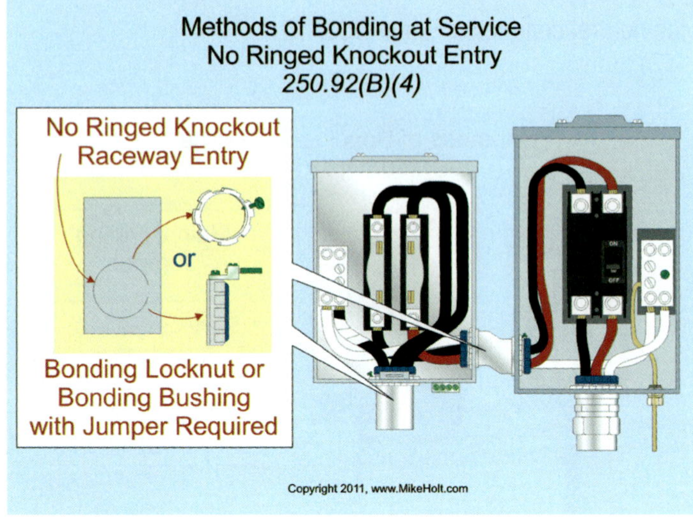

Figure 250–156

- A bonding locknut differs from a standard locknut in that it's a bonding screw with a sharp point that drives into the metal enclosure to ensure a solid connection.

- Bonding one end of a service raceway to the service neutral provides the low-impedance fault current path to the source. **Figure 250–157**

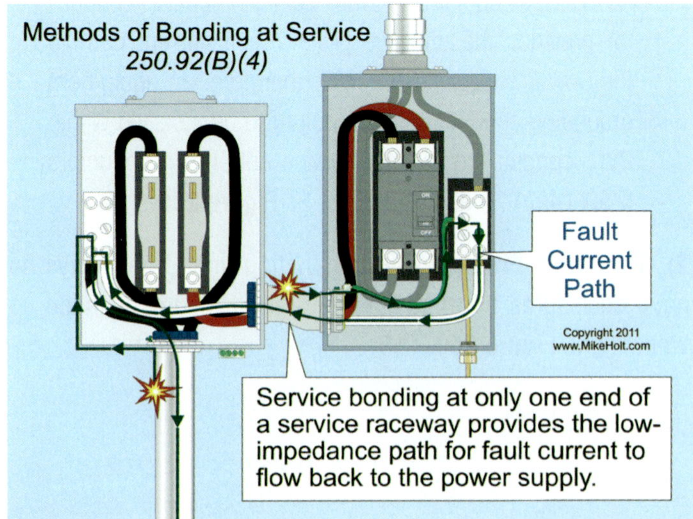

Figure 250–157

250.94 Intersystem Bonding Termination. An external accessible intersystem bonding termination for the connection of communications systems bonding conductors must be provided at service equipment or metering equipment enclosure and disconnecting means for buildings or structures supplied by a feeder, **Figure 250–158**. The intersystem bonding termination must:

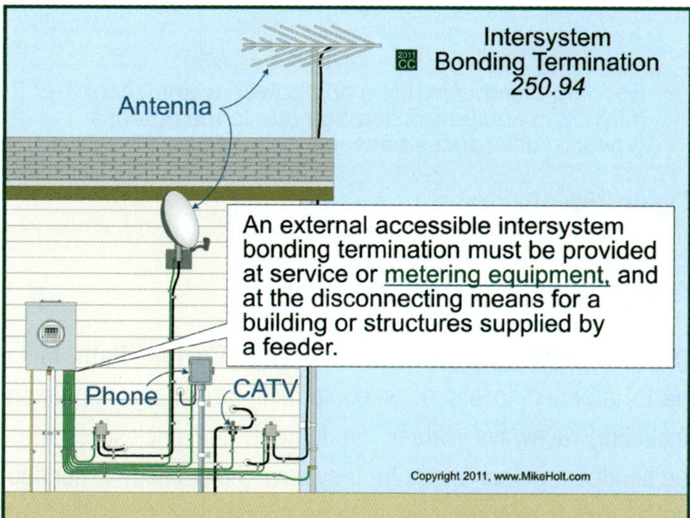

Figure 250–158

(1) Be accessible for connection and inspection. **Figure 250–159**

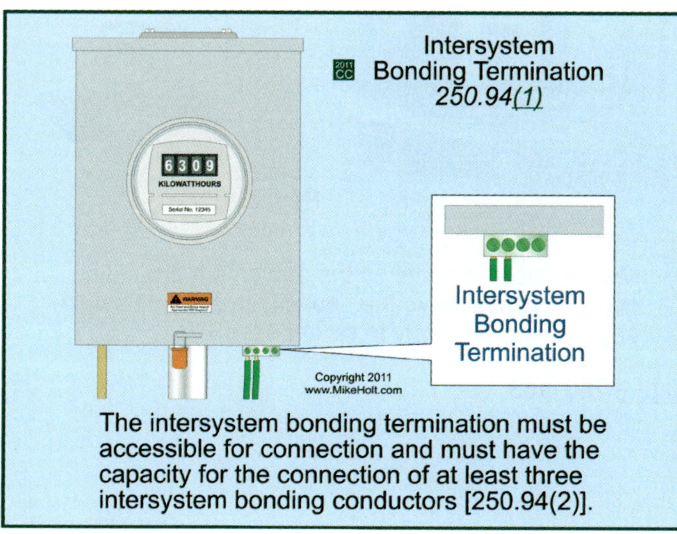

Figure 250–159

(2) Consist of a set of terminals with the capacity for connection of not less than three intersystem bonding conductors.

(3) Not interfere with opening the enclosure for a service, building/structure disconnecting means, or metering equipment.

(4) Be securely mounted and electrically connected to service equipment, the meter enclosure, or exposed nonflexible metallic service raceway, or be mounted at one of these enclosures and be connected to the enclosure or grounding electrode conductor with a minimum 6 AWG copper conductor.

(5) Be securely mounted to the building/structure disconnecting means, or be mounted at the disconnecting means and be connected to the metallic enclosure or grounding electrode conductor with a minimum 6 AWG copper conductor. **Figure 250–160**

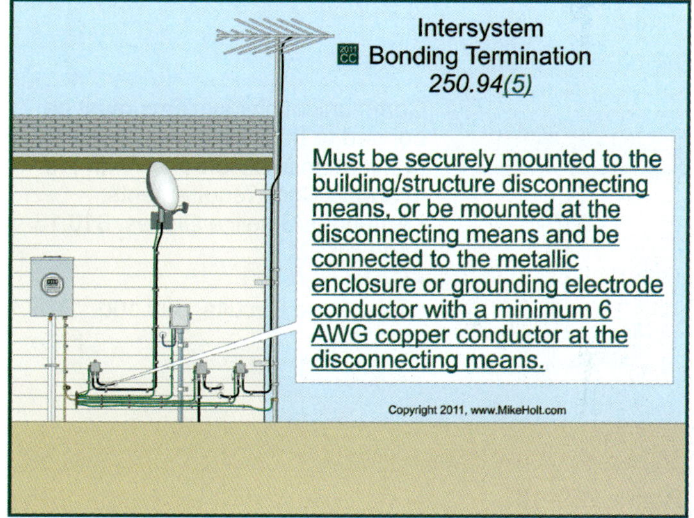

Figure 250–160

(6) The terminals must be listed as grounding and bonding equipment.

Author's Comment: According to Article 100, an intersystem bonding termination is a device that provides a means to connect communications systems grounding and bonding conductors to the building grounding electrode system.

Ex: At existing buildings or structures, an external accessible means for bonding communications systems together can be by the use of a:

(1) Nonflexible metallic raceway,

(2) Grounding electrode conductor, or

(3) Connection approved by the authority having jurisdiction.

Note 2: Communications systems must be bonded to the intersystem bonding termination in accordance with the following *Code* requirements: **Figure 250–161**

- Antennas/Satellite Dishes, 810.15 and 810.21
- CATV, 820.100
- Telephone Circuits, 800.100

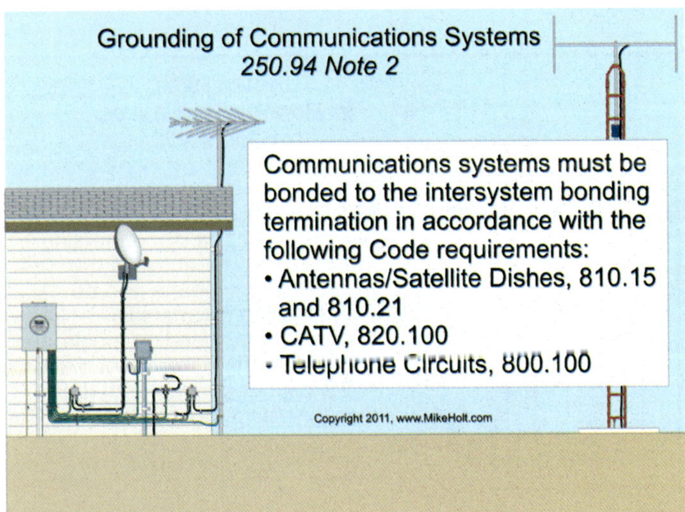

Figure 250–161

Author's Comment: All external communications systems must be connected to the intersystem bonding termination to minimize the damage to them from induced potential (voltage) differences between the systems from a lightning event. **Figure 250–162**

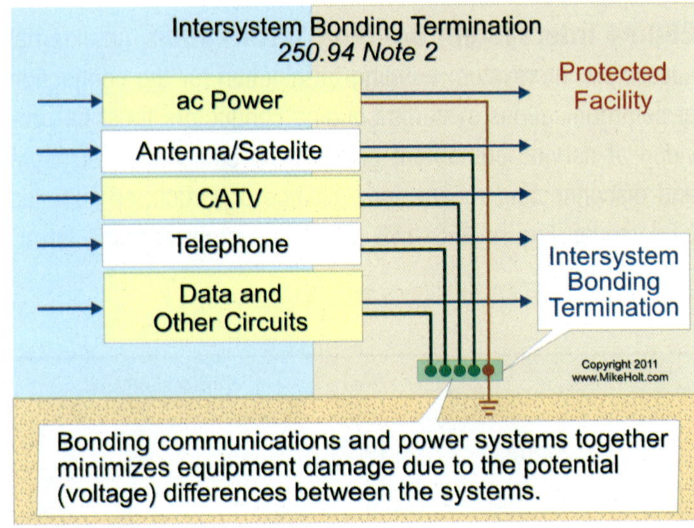

Figure 250–162

250.96 Bonding Other Enclosures.

(A) Maintaining Effective Ground-Fault Current Path. Metal parts intended to serve as equipment grounding conductors including raceways, cables, equipment, and enclosures must be bonded together to ensure they have the capacity to conduct safely any fault current likely to be imposed on them [110.10, 250.4(A)(5), and Note to Table 250.122]. **Figure 250–163**

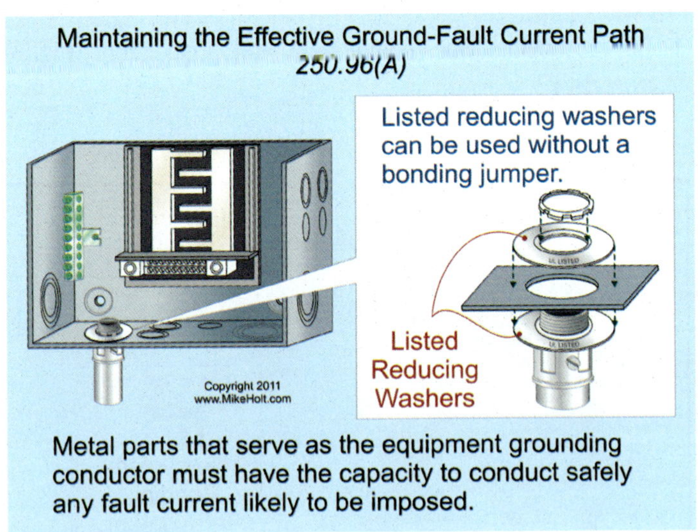

Figure 250–163

Nonconductive coatings such as paint, lacquer, and enamel on equipment must be removed to ensure an effective ground-fault current path, or the termination fittings must be designed so as to make such removal unnecessary [250.12].

Author's Comment: The practice of driving a locknut tight with a screwdriver and pliers is considered sufficient in removing paint and other nonconductive finishes to ensure an effective ground-fault current path.

(B) Isolated Grounding Circuits. An equipment enclosure can be isolated from a metal raceway by a nonmetallic raceway fitting located at the point of attachment of the raceway to the equipment enclosure. The metal raceway must contain an insulated equipment grounding conductor in accordance with 250.146(D). Figures 250–164 and 250–165

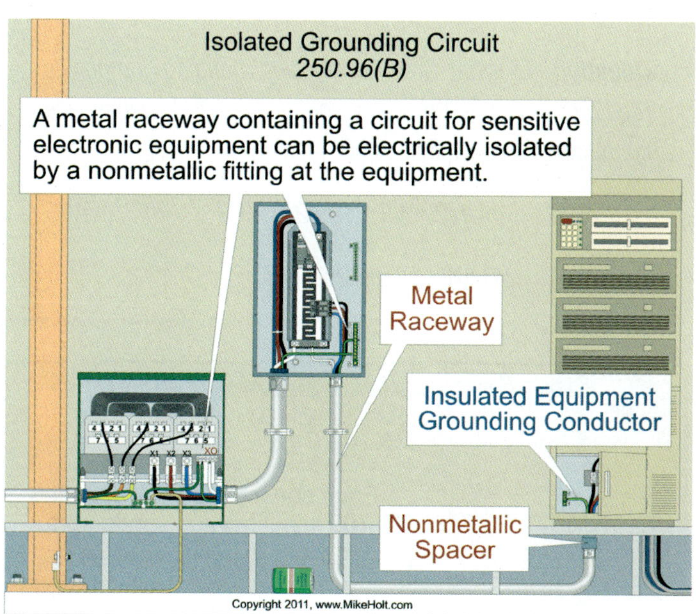

Figure 250–164

250.97 Bonding Metal Parts Containing 277V and 480V Circuits.

Metal raceways or cables containing 277V and/or 480V feeder or branch circuits terminating at ringed knockouts must be bonded to the metal enclosure with a bonding jumper sized in accordance with 250.122, based on the rating of the circuit overcurrent device [250.102(D)]. Figure 250–166

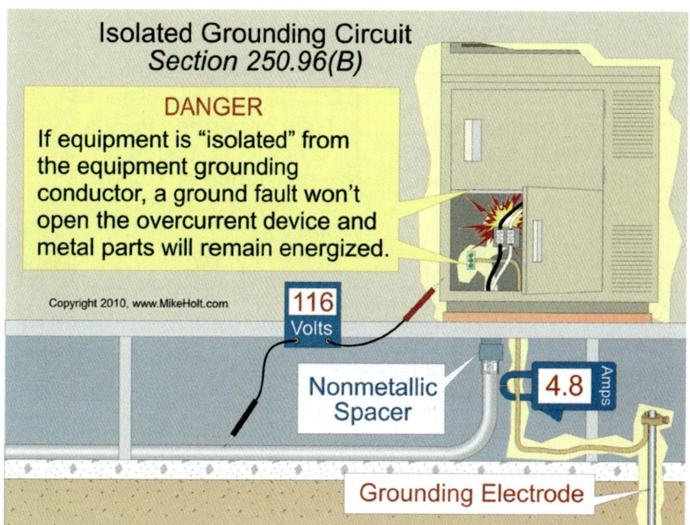

Figure 250–165

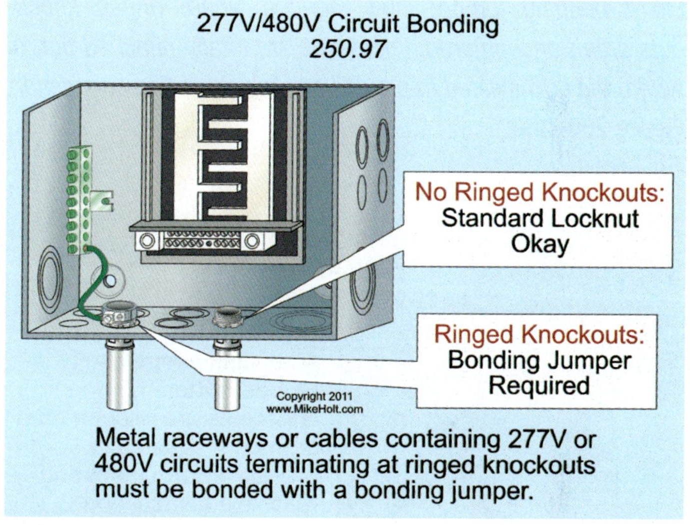

Figure 250–166

Author's Comments:

- Bonding jumpers for raceways and cables containing 277V or 480V circuits are required at ringed knockout terminations to ensure the ground-fault current path has the capacity to safely conduct the maximum ground-fault current likely to be imposed [110.10, 250.4(A)(5), and 250.96(A)].
- Ringed knockouts aren't listed to withstand the heat generated by a 277V ground fault, which generates five times as much heat as a 120V ground fault. Figure 250–167

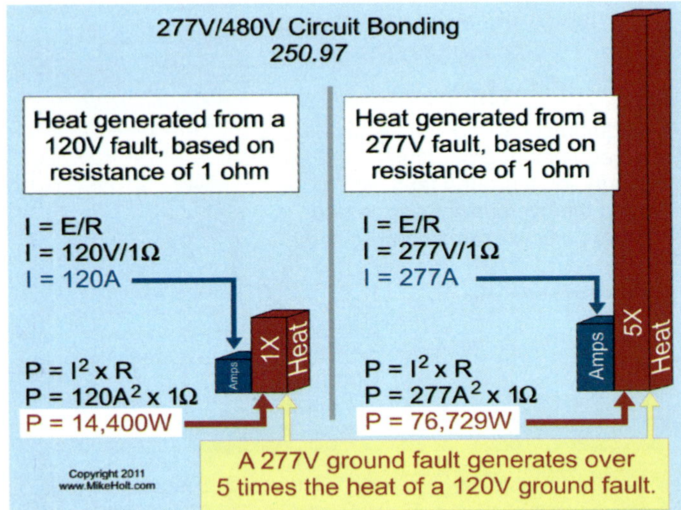

Figure 250–167

Ex: A bonding jumper isn't required where ringed knockouts aren't encountered, knockouts are totally punched out, or where the box is listed to provide a reliable bonding connection. **Figure 250–168**

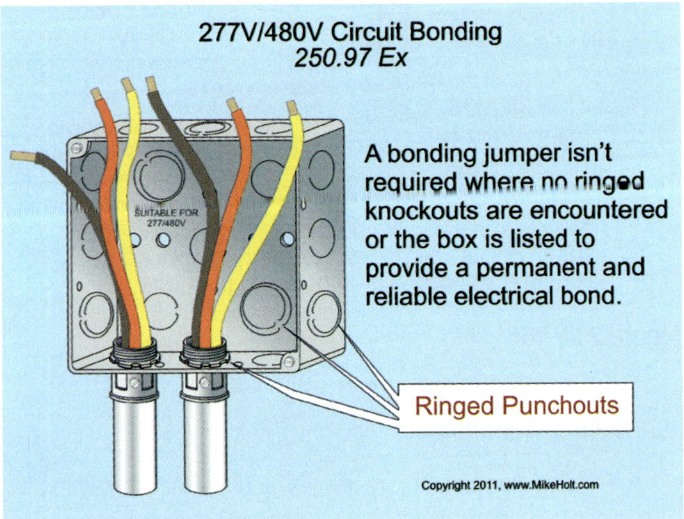

Figure 250–168

250.102 Bonding Conductors and Jumpers.

(A) Material. Equipment bonding jumpers must be copper.

(B) Termination. Equipment bonding jumpers must terminate by listed pressure connectors, terminal bars, exothermic welding, or other listed means [250.8(A)].

(C) Size for Supply-Side Bonding Jumper.

(1) Single Raceway Installations. The supply-side bonding jumper is sized to Table 250.66, based on the largest ungrounded conductor within the raceway. If the ungrounded supply conductors are larger than 1,100 kcmil copper or 1,750 kcmil aluminum, the supply-side bonding jumper must be sized not less than 12½ percent of the area of the largest set of ungrounded supply conductors.

(2) Parallel Conductor Installations. If the ungrounded supply conductors are paralleled in two or more raceways or cables, the size of the supply-side bonding jumper for each raceway or cable is sized in accordance with Table 250.66, based on the size of the largest ungrounded conductors in each raceway or cable. A single supply-side bonding jumper for bonding two or more raceways or cables must be sized in accordance with (C)(1).

Question 1: *What size supply-side bonding jumper is required for a metal raceway containing 700 kcmil service conductors?* **Figure 250–169**

(a) 1 AWG (b) 1/0 AWG (c) 2/0 AWG (d) 3/0 AWG

Answer: *(c) 2/0 AWG [Table 250.66]*

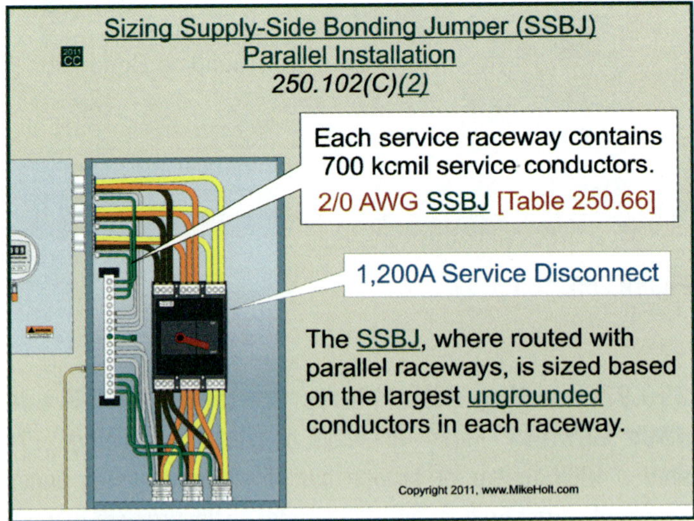

Figure 250–169

***Question 2:** What size single supply-side bonding jumper is required for three metal raceways containing 700 kcmil service conductors?* **Figure 250–170**

(a) 1 AWG (b) 1/0 AWG (c) 2/0 AWG (d) 300 AWG

***Answer:** (d) 300 kcmil [250.102(C)(1)]*

700 kcmil x 3 = 2,100 kcmil
2,100 kcmil x 0.125 = 263 kcmil
Chapter 9, Table 8, use 300 kcmil

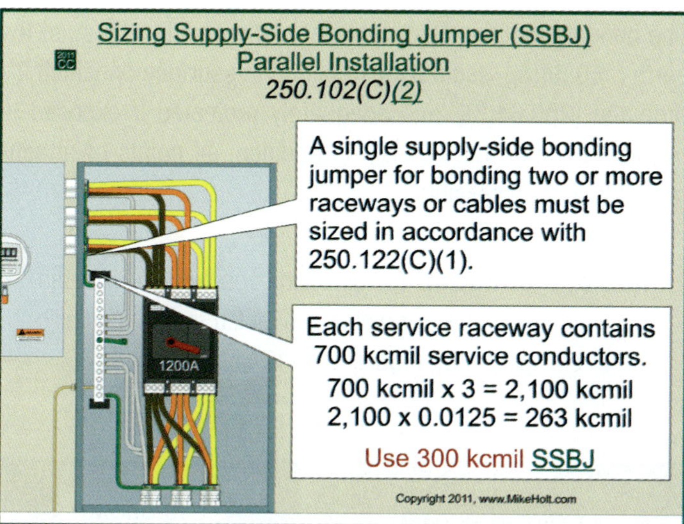

Figure 250–170

(3) Different Materials. If the ungrounded supply conductors and the supply-side bonding jumper are of different materials (copper or aluminum), the supply-side bonding jumper is sized on the assumed use of the same material.

(D) Load Side Equipment Bonding Jumper Sizing. Bonding jumpers on the load side of feeder and branch-circuit overcurrent devices are sized in accordance with 250.122, based on the rating of the circuit overcurrent device.

> **Author's Comment:** The equipment bonding jumper isn't required to be larger than the largest ungrounded circuit conductors [250.122(A)].

***Question:** What size equipment bonding jumper is required for a metal raceway where the circuit conductors are protected by a 1,200A overcurrent device?* **Figure 250–171**

(a) 1 AWG (b) 1/0 AWG (c) 2/0 AWG (d) 3/0 AWG

***Answer:** (d) 3/0 AWG [Table 250.122]*

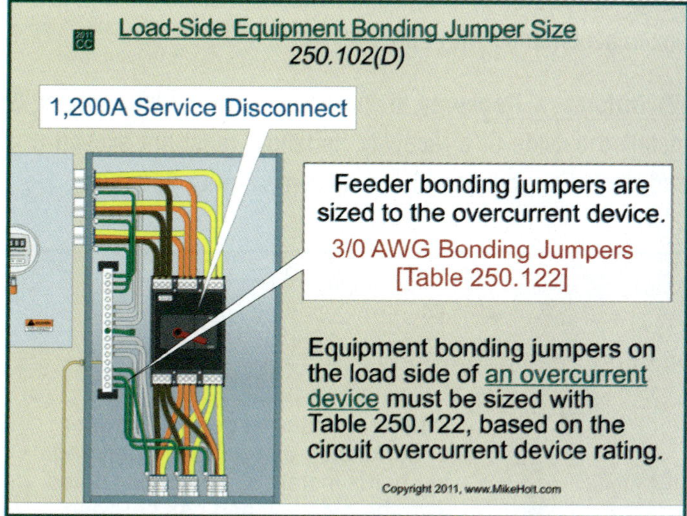

Figure 250–171

If a single equipment bonding jumper is used to bond two or more raceways, it must be sized in accordance with 250.122, based on the rating of the largest circuit overcurrent device. **Figure 250–172**

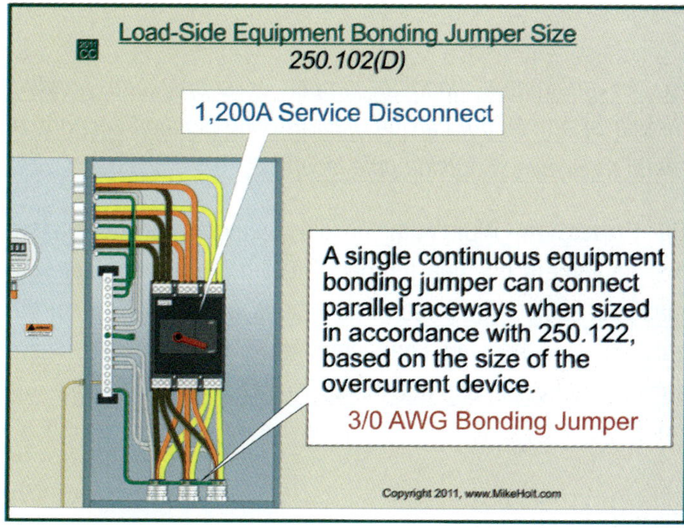

Figure 250–172

(E) Installation. Equipment bonding jumpers, as well as bonding jumpers or conductors can be installed inside or outside of a raceway.

(1) Inside a Raceway or Enclosure. If installed inside a raceway, the conductors must be identified in accordance with 250.119 and if circuit conductors are spliced or terminated on equipment within a metal box, the equipment grounding conductor associated with those circuits must be connected to the box in accordance with 250.148.

(2) Outside a Raceway. If the equipment bonding jumper is installed outside of a raceway, its length must not exceed 6 ft and it must be routed with the raceway. Figure 250–173

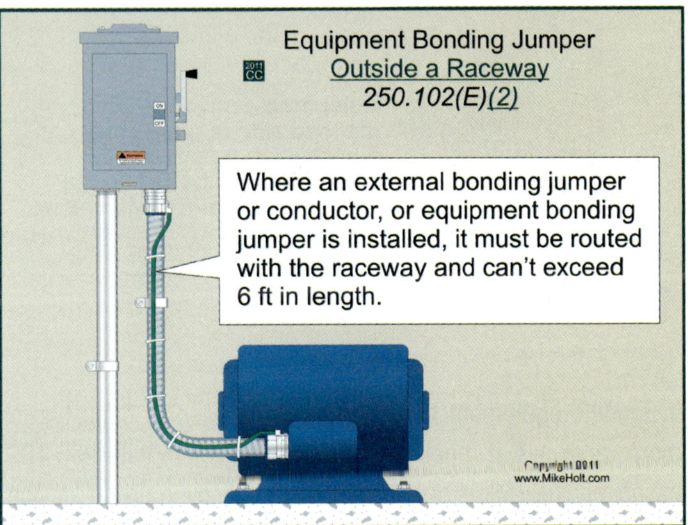

Figure 250–173

Ex: An equipment bonding jumper or supply-side bonding jumper of any length can be used to bond isolated sections of metal raceways at outside pole locations.

(3) Protection. Aluminum bonding jumpers or conductors and equipment bonding jumpers must not be in contact with masonry, subject to corrosive conditions, or within 18 in. of the earth [250.64(A)] and conductors must be protected where subject to physical damage in accordance with 250.64(B).

250.104 Bonding of Piping Systems and Exposed Structural Metal.

Author's Comment: To remove dangerous voltage on metal parts from a ground fault, electrically conductive metal water piping systems, metal sprinkler piping, metal gas piping, as well as exposed structural steel members likely to become energized, must be connected to an effective ground-fault current path [250.4(A)(4)].

(A) Metal Water Piping System. The metal water piping system must be bonded as required in (A)(1), (A)(2), or (A)(3). The bonding jumper must be copper where within 18 in. of the earth [250.64(A)], securely fastened to the surface on which it's mounted [250.64(B)], and adequately protected if exposed to physical damage [250.64(B)]. In addition, all points of attachment must be accessible.

Author's Comment: Bonding isn't required for isolated sections of metal water piping connected to a nonmetallic water piping system. Figure 250–174

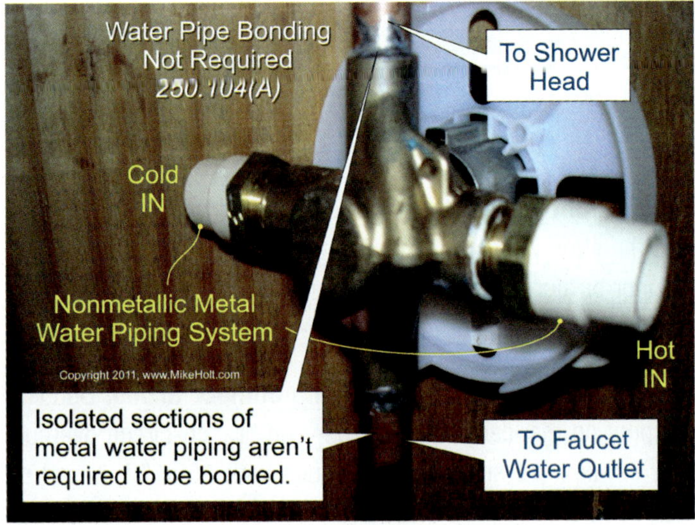

Figure 250–174

(1) Building/Structure Supplied by a Service. The metal water piping system, including the metal sprinkler water piping system of a building/structure supplied with service conductors must be bonded to the: **Figure 250–175**

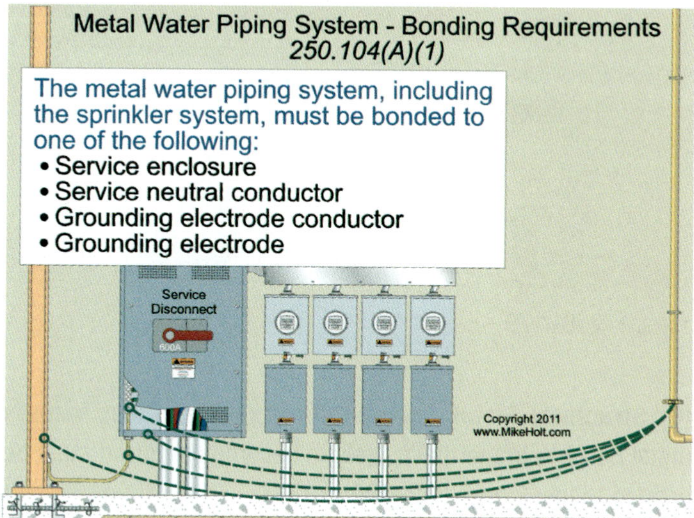

Figure 250–175

- Service equipment enclosure,
- Service neutral conductor,
- Grounding electrode conductor of sufficient size, or
- Grounding electrode system.

The metal water piping system bonding jumper must be sized in accordance with Table 250.66, based on the cross-sectional area of the ungrounded service conductors.

> ***Question:*** *What size bonding jumper is required for the metal water piping system if the 300 kcmil service conductors are paralleled in two raceways?* **Figure 250–176**
>
> *(a) 6 AWG (b) 4 AWG (c) 2 AWG (d) 1/0 AWG*
>
> ***Answer:*** *(d) 1/0 AWG, based on 600 kcmil conductors, in accordance with Table 250.66*

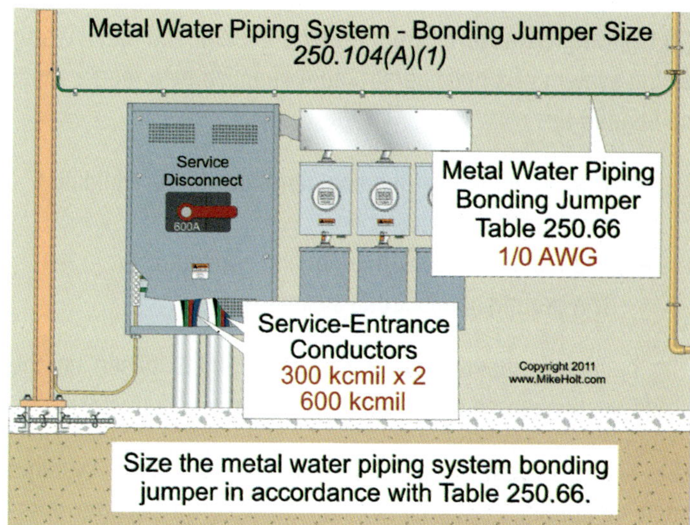

Figure 250–176

> **Author's Comment:** If hot and cold metal water pipes are electrically connected, only one bonding jumper is required, either to the cold or hot water pipe.

(2) Multiple Occupancy Building. When the metal water piping system in an individual occupancy is metallically isolated from other occupancies, the metal water piping system for that occupancy can be bonded to the equipment grounding terminal of the occupancy's panelboard. The bonding jumper must be sized in accordance with Table 250.122, based on the ampere rating of the occupancy's feeder overcurrent device. **Figure 250–177**

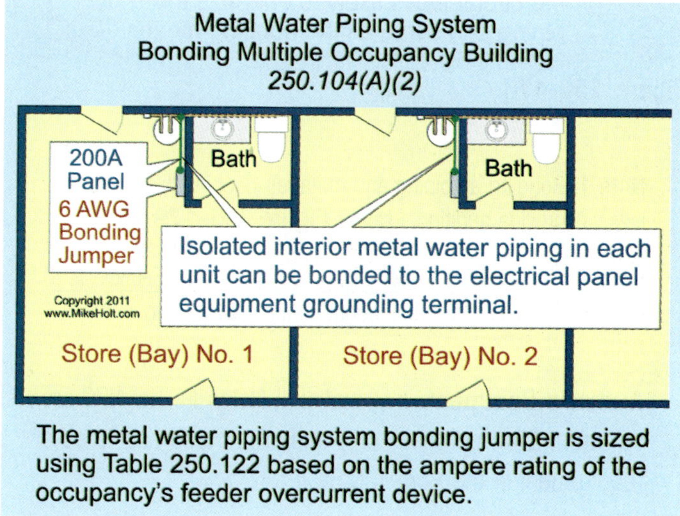

Figure 250–177

(3) Building/Structure Supplied by a Feeder. The metal water piping system of a building/structure supplied by a feeder must be bonded to:

- The equipment grounding terminal of the building disconnect enclosure,
- The feeder equipment grounding conductor, or
- The grounding electrode system.

The bonding jumper is sized to Table 250.66, based on the cross-sectional area of the ungrounded feeder conductor.

(B) Other Metal-Piping Systems. Metal-piping systems such as sprinkler, gas, or air that are likely to become energized must be bonded. The equipment grounding conductor for the circuit that's likely to energize the piping can serve as the bonding means. **Figure 250–178**

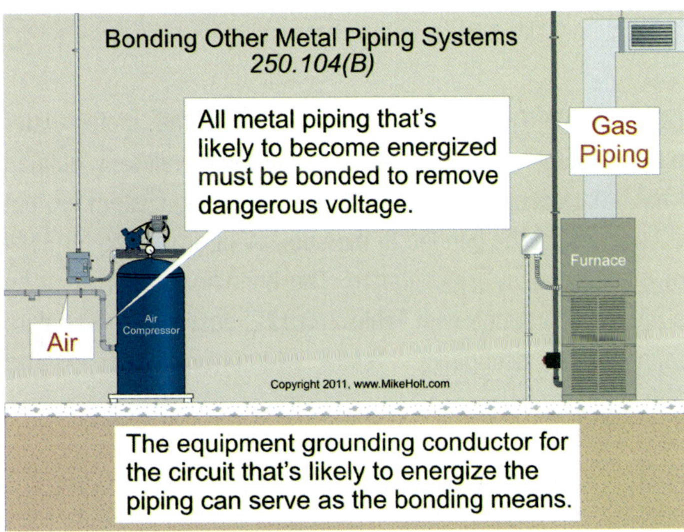

Figure 250–178

Note 1: Bonding all piping and metal air ducts within the premises will provide additional safety. **Figure 250–179**

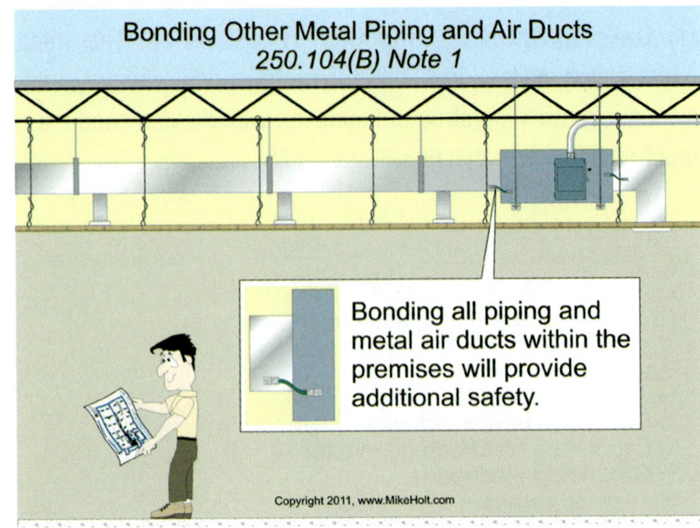

Figure 250–179

Note 2*: The National Fuel Gas Code, NFPA* 54, Section 7.13 contains further information about bonding gas piping.

Author's Comment: Informational Notes in the *NEC* are for information purposes only and aren't enforceable as a requirement of the *Code* [90.5(C)].

(C) Structural Metal. Exposed structural metal that forms a metal building frame that's likely to become energized must be bonded to the: **Figure 250–180**

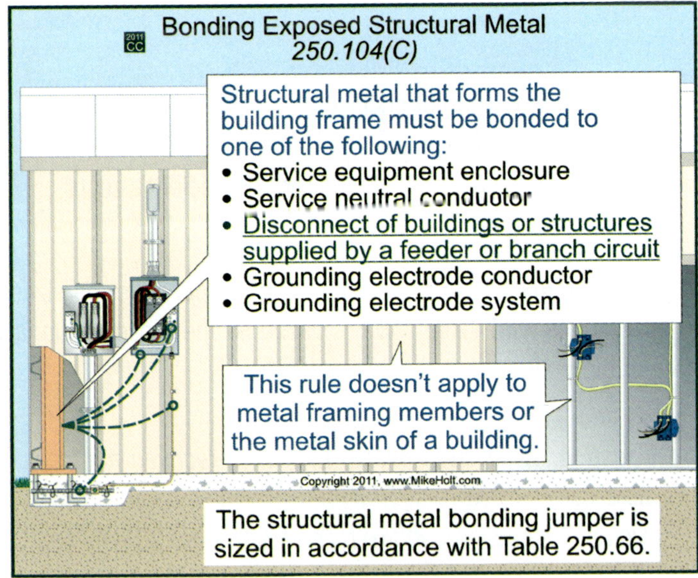

Figure 250–180

- Service equipment enclosure,
- Service neutral conductor,
- Building/structure disconnecting means for buildings or structures supplied by a feeder or branch circuit,

- Grounding electrode conductor if of sufficient size, or
- Grounding electrode system.

Author's Comment: This rule doesn't require the bonding of sheet metal framing members (studs) or the metal skin of a wood frame building.

The bonding jumper must be sized in accordance with Table 250.66, based on the area of the ungrounded supply conductors. The bonding jumper must be copper where within 18 in. of the earth [250.64(A)], securely fastened to the surface on which it's carried [250.64(B)], and adequately protected if exposed to physical damage [250.64(B)]. In addition, all points of attachment must be accessible, except as permitted in 250.68(A).

(D) Separately Derived Systems. Metal water piping systems and structural metal that forms a building frame must be bonded as required in (D)(1) through (D)(3).

(1) Metal Water Pipe. The nearest available point of the metal water piping system in the area served by a separately derived system must be bonded to the neutral point of the separately derived system where the grounding electrode conductor is connected. Figure 250–181

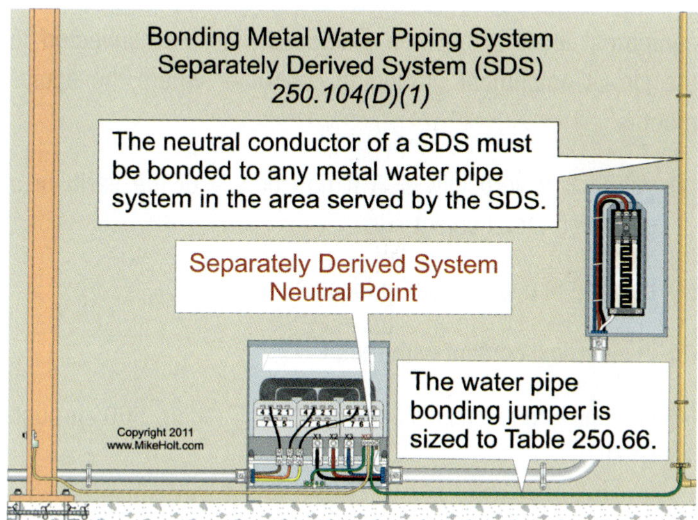

Figure 250–181

The bonding jumper must be sized in accordance with Table 250.66, based on the area of the ungrounded conductor of the derived system.

Ex 2: The metal water piping system is permitted to be bonded to the structural metal building frame if it serves as the grounding electrode [250.52(A)(1)] for the separately derived system. Figure 250–182

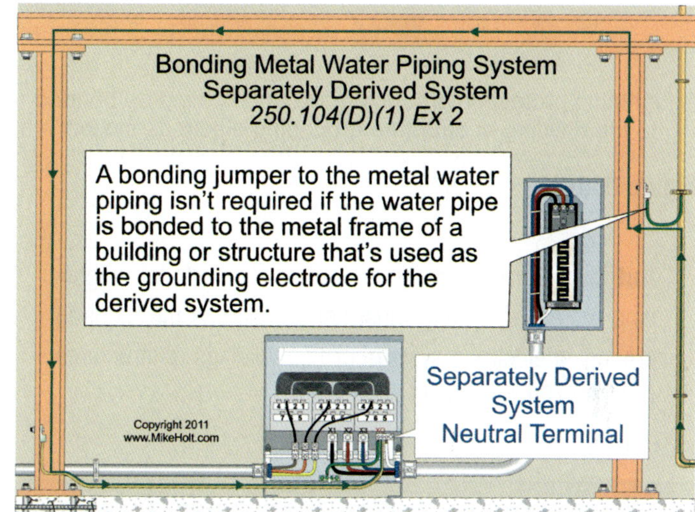

Figure 250–182

(2) Structural Metal. Exposed structural metal interconnected to form the building frame must be bonded to the neutral point of each separately derived system where the grounding electrode conductor is connected.

The bonding jumper must be sized in accordance with Table 250.66, based on the area of the ungrounded conductors of the derived system.

Ex 1: Bonding to the separately derived system isn't required if the metal structural frame serves as the grounding electrode [250.52(A)(2)] for the separately derived system.

250.106 Lightning Protection System. If a lightning protection system is installed on a building/structure, it must be bonded to the building/structure grounding electrode system. Figure 250–183

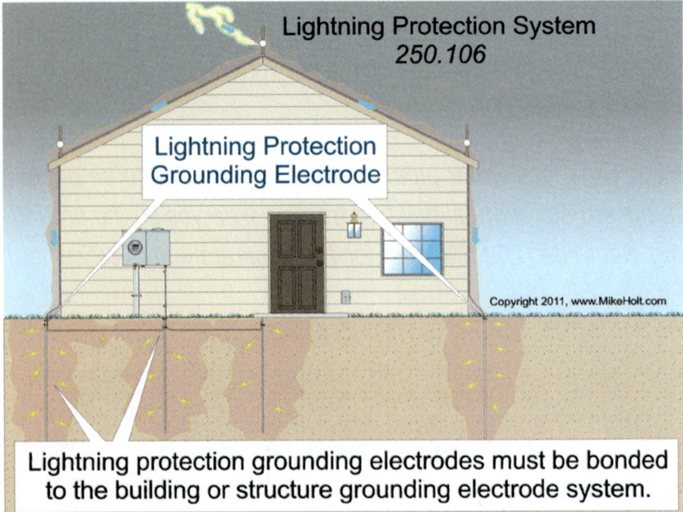

Figure 250–183

Author's Comment: The grounding electrode for a lightning protection system must not be used as the required grounding electrode system for the buildings or structures [250.60]. **Figure 250–184**

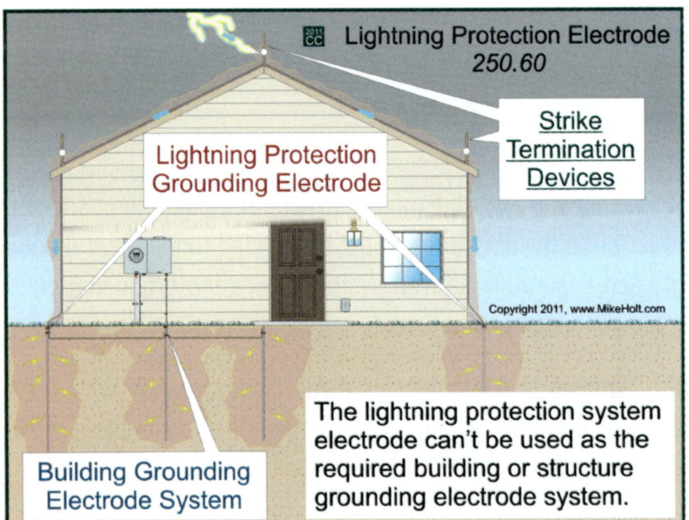

Figure 250–184

Note 1: See NFPA 780—*Standard for the Installation of Lightning Protection Systems,* which contains detailed information on grounding, bonding, and side-flash distance from lightning protection systems.

Note 2: To minimize the likelihood of arcing between metal parts because of induced voltage, metal raceways, enclosures, and other metal parts of electrical equipment may require bonding or spacing from the lightning protection conductors in accordance with NFPA 780—*Standard for the Installation of Lightning Protection Systems.* **Figure 250–185**

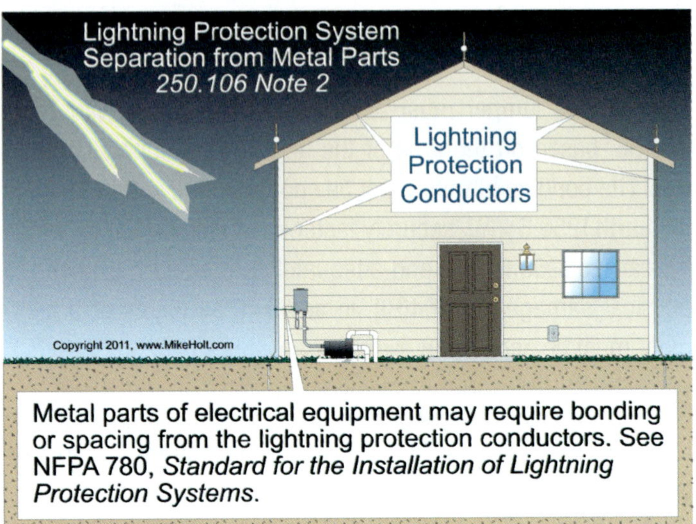

Figure 250–185

PART VI. EQUIPMENT GROUNDING AND EQUIPMENT GROUNDING CONDUCTORS

250.110 Fixed Equipment Connected by Permanent Wiring Methods—General. Exposed metal parts of fixed equipment likely to become energized must be connected to the circuit equipment grounding conductor where the equipment is:

(1) Within 8 ft vertically or 5 ft horizontally of the earth or a grounded metal object

(2) Located in a wet or damp location

(3) In electrical contact with metal

(4) In a hazardous (classified) location [Articles 500 through 517]

(5) Supplied by a wiring method that provides an equipment grounding conductor

(6) Supplied by a 277V or 480V circuit

Ex 3: Listed double-insulated equipment isn't required to be connected to the circuit equipment grounding conductor.

250.112 Specific Equipment Fastened in Place or Connected by Permanent Wiring Methods. Except as permitted in 250.112(I), exposed metal parts of equipment and enclosures must be connected to the circuit equipment grounding conductor. Figure 250–186

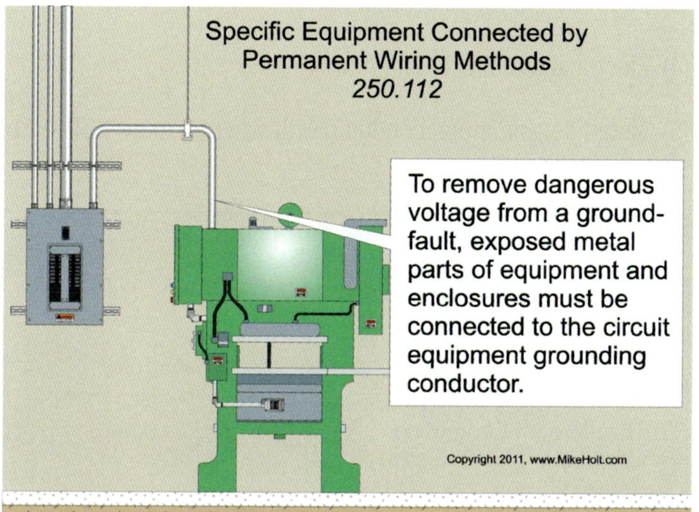

Figure 250–186

(I) Remote-Control, Signaling, and Fire Alarm Circuits. Equipment supplied by circuits operating at 50V or less isn't required to be connected to the circuit equipment grounding conductor. Figure 250–187

> **Author's Comment:** Class 1 power-limited circuits, Class 2, and Class 3 remote-control and signaling circuits, and fire alarm circuits operating at 50V or less don't need to have any metal parts connected to an equipment grounding conductor.

(K) Skid-Mounted Equipment. Electrical equipment permanently mounted on skids, and the skids themselves, must be connected to the equipment grounding conductor sized as required by 250.122.

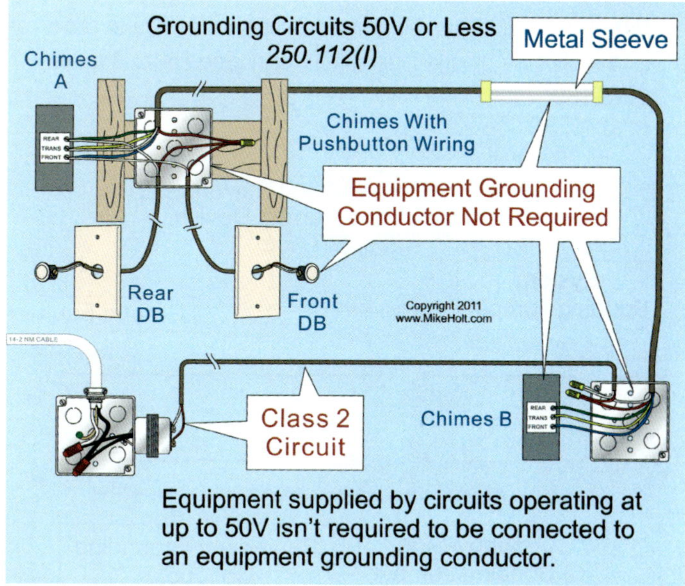

Figure 250–187

250.114 Cord-and-Plug-Connected Equipment. Metal parts of cord-and-plug-connected equipment must be connected to the circuit equipment grounding conductor.

Ex: Listed double-insulated equipment isn't required to be connected to the circuit equipment grounding conductor.

250.118 Types of Equipment Grounding Conductors. An equipment grounding conductor can be any one or a combination of the following: Figure 250–188

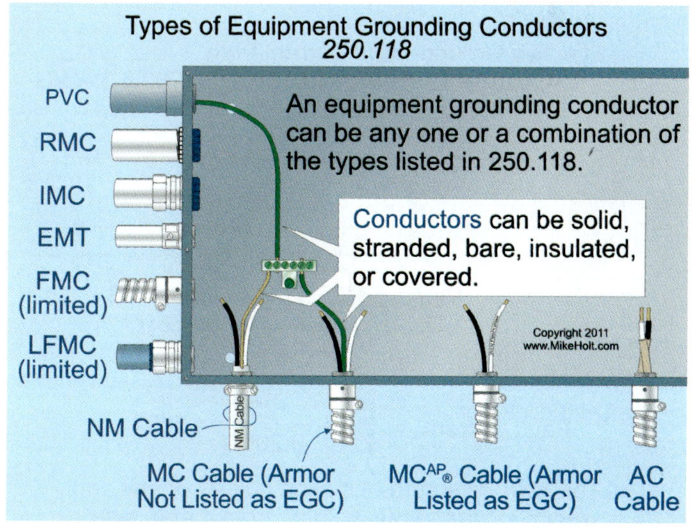

Figure 250–188

Note: The equipment grounding conductor is intended to serve as the effective ground-fault current path. See 250.2. **Figure 250–189**

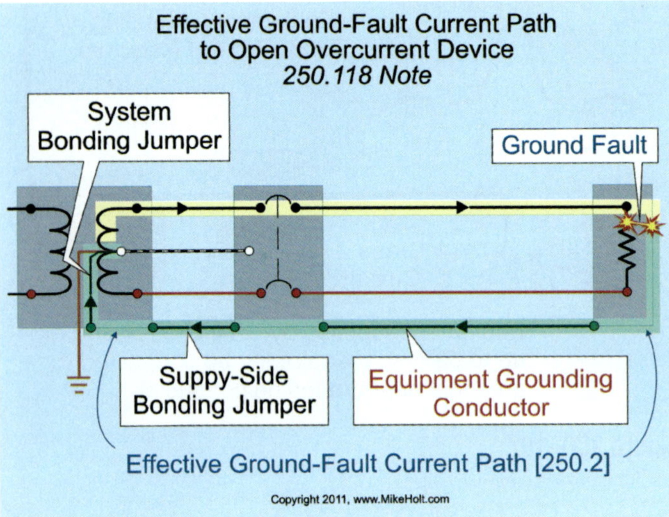

Figure 250–189

Author's Comment: The effective ground-fault path is an intentionally constructed low-impedance conductive path designed to carry fault current from the point of a ground fault on a wiring system to the electrical supply source. Its purpose is to quickly remove dangerous voltage from a ground fault by opening the circuit overcurrent device [250.2]. **Figure 250–190**

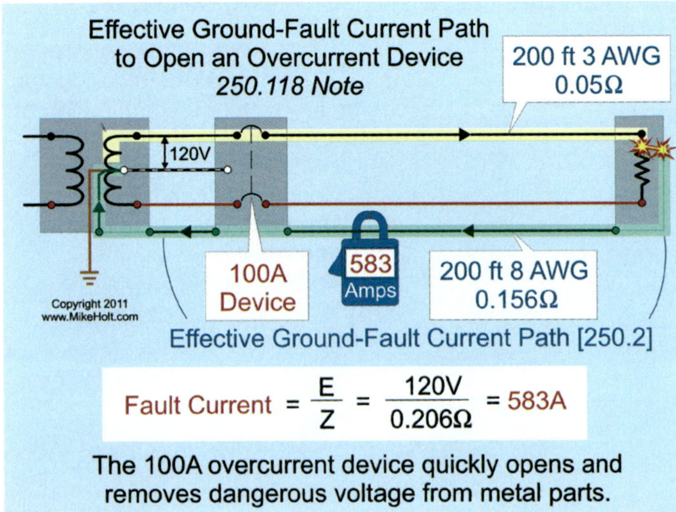

Figure 250–190

(1) A bare or insulated copper or aluminum conductor sized in accordance with 250.122.

Author's Comment: Examples include PVC conduit, Type NM cable, and Type MC cable with an equipment grounding conductor of the wire type.

(2) Rigid metal conduit (RMC).

(3) Intermediate metal conduit (IMC).

(4) Electrical metallic tubing (EMT).

(5) Listed flexible metal conduit (FMC) where: **Figure 250–191**

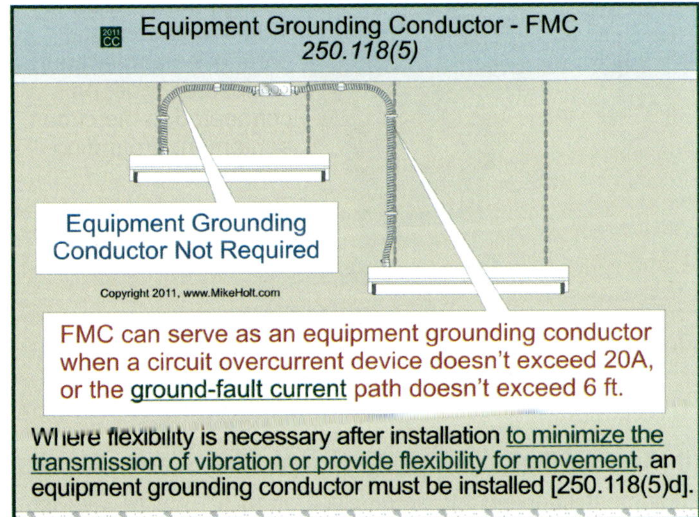

Figure 250–191

a. The raceway terminates in listed fittings.

b. The circuit conductors are protected by an overcurrent device rated 20A or less.

c. The combined length of the flexible conduit in the same ground-fault current path doesn't exceed 6 ft. **Figure 250–192**

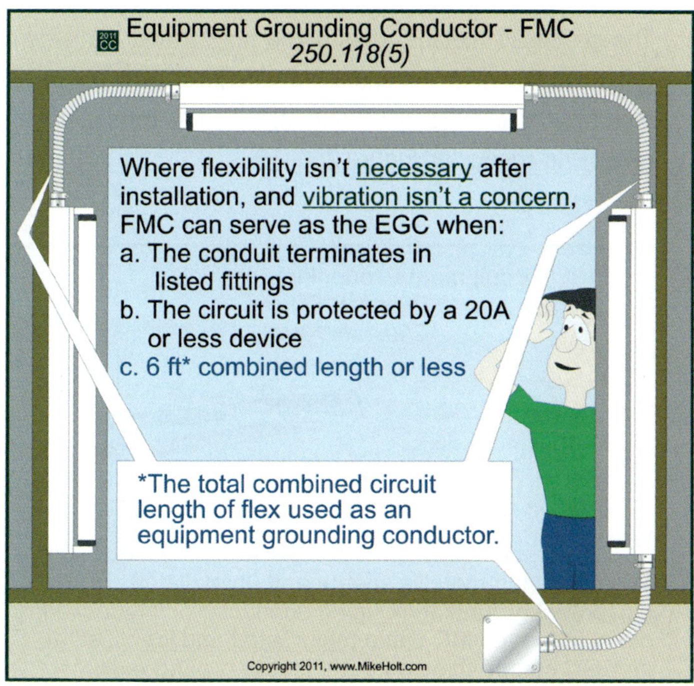

Figure 250–192

d. If flexibility is required to minimize the transmission of vibration from equipment or to provide flexibility for equipment that requires movement after installation, an equipment grounding conductor of the wire type must be installed with the circuit conductors in accordance with 250.102(E), and it must be sized in accordance with 250.122, based on the rating of the circuit overcurrent device.

(6) Listed liquidtight flexible metal conduit (LFMC) where: Figure 250–193

a. The raceway terminates in listed fittings.

b. For ⅜ in. through ½ in., the circuit conductors are protected by an overcurrent device rated 20A or less.

c. For ¾ in. through 1¼ in., the circuit conductors are protected by an overcurrent device rated 60A or less.

d. The combined length of the flexible conduit in the same ground-fault current path doesn't exceed 6 ft.

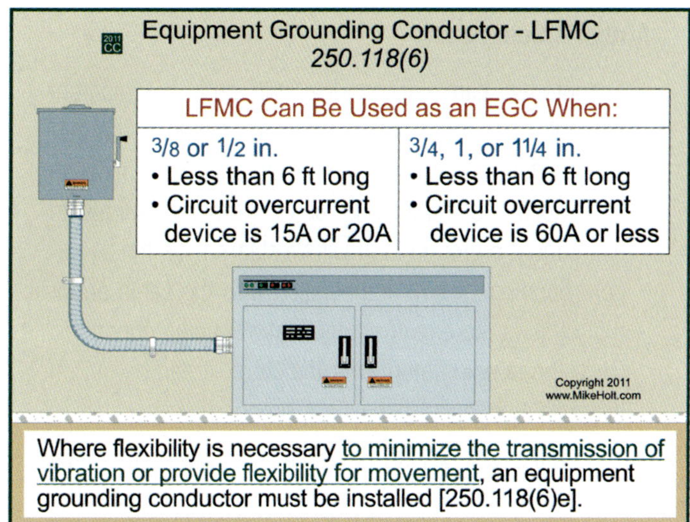

Figure 250–193

e. If flexibility is required to minimize the transmission of vibration from equipment or to provide flexibility for equipment that requires movement after installation, an equipment grounding conductor of the wire type must be installed with the circuit conductors in accordance with 250.102(E), and it must be sized in accordance with 250.122, based on the rating of the circuit overcurrent device.

(8) The sheath of Type AC cable containing an aluminum bonding strip. Figure 250–194

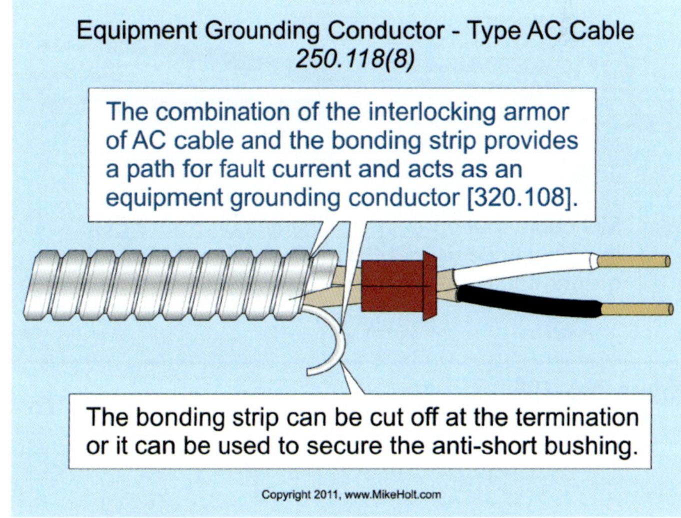

Figure 250–194

Author's Comments:

- The internal aluminum bonding strip isn't an equipment grounding conductor, but it allows the interlocked armor to serve as an equipment grounding conductor because it reduces the impedance of the armored spirals to ensure that a ground fault will be cleared. It's the aluminum bonding strip in combination with the cable armor that creates the circuit equipment grounding conductor. Once the bonding strip exits the cable, it can be cut off because it no longer serves any purpose.
- The effective ground-fault current path must be maintained by the use of fittings specifically listed for Type AC cable [320.40]. See 300.12, 300.15, and 320.100.

(9) The copper sheath of Type MI cable.

(10) Type MC cable that provides an effective ground-fault current path in accordance with one or more of the following:

(a) It contains an insulated or uninsulated equipment grounding conductor in compliance with 250.118(1). **Figure 250–195**

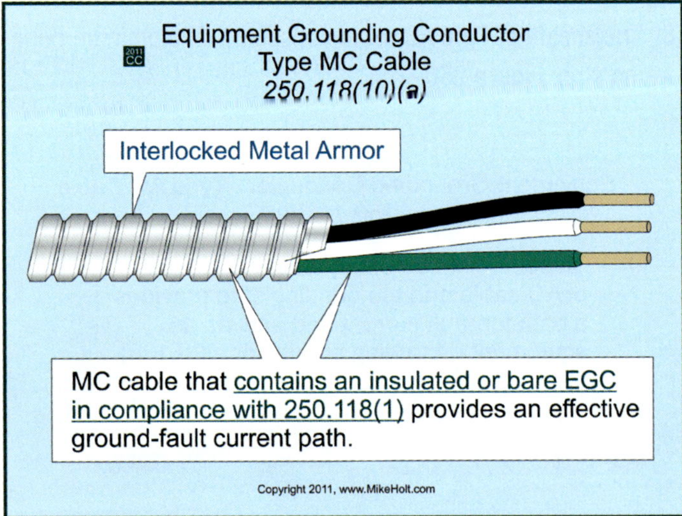

Figure 250–195

(b) The combined metallic sheath and uninsulated equipment grounding/bonding conductor of interlocked metal tape-type MC cable that's listed and identified as an equipment grounding conductor. **Figure 250–196**

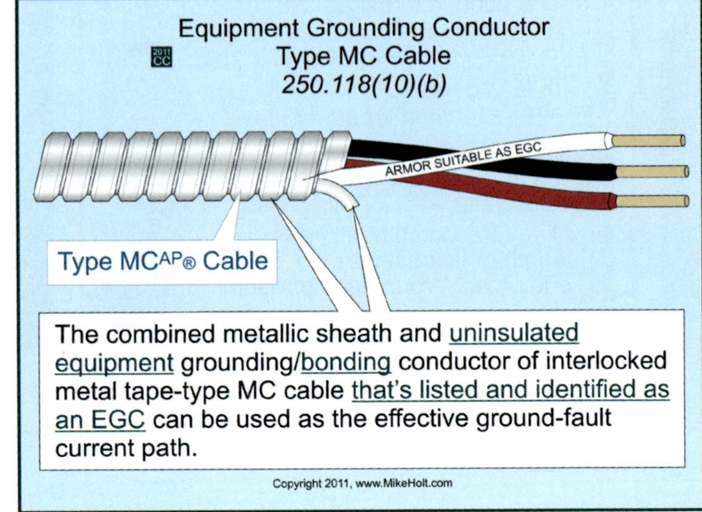

Figure 250–196

Author's Comment: Once the bare aluminum grounding/bonding conductor exits the cable, it can be cut off because it no longer serves any purpose. The effective ground-fault current path must be maintained by the use of fittings specifically listed for Type MCAP® cable [330.40]. See 300.12, 300.15, and 330.100. **Figure 250–197**

(c) The metallic sheath or the combined metallic sheath and equipment grounding conductors of the smooth or corrugated tube-type MC cable that's listed and identified as an equipment grounding conductor.

(11) Metallic cable trays where continuous maintenance and supervision ensure only qualified persons will service the cable tray, with cable tray and fittings identified for grounding and the cable tray, fittings [392.10], and raceways are bonded using bolted mechanical connectors or bonding jumpers sized and installed in accordance with 250.102 [392.60]. **Figure 250–198**

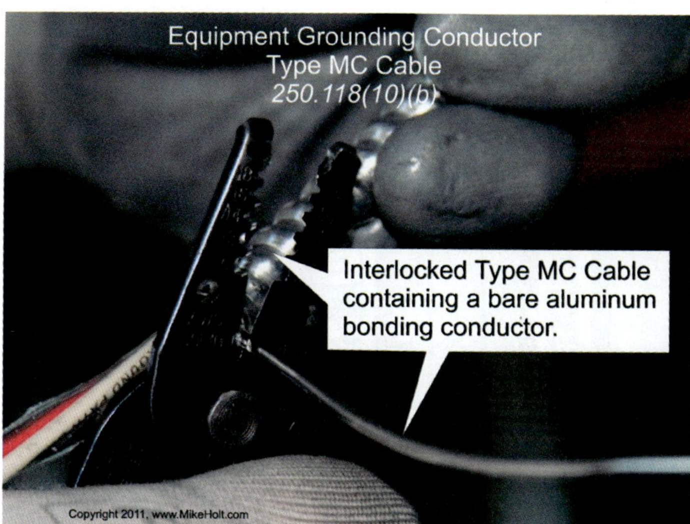

Figure 250–197

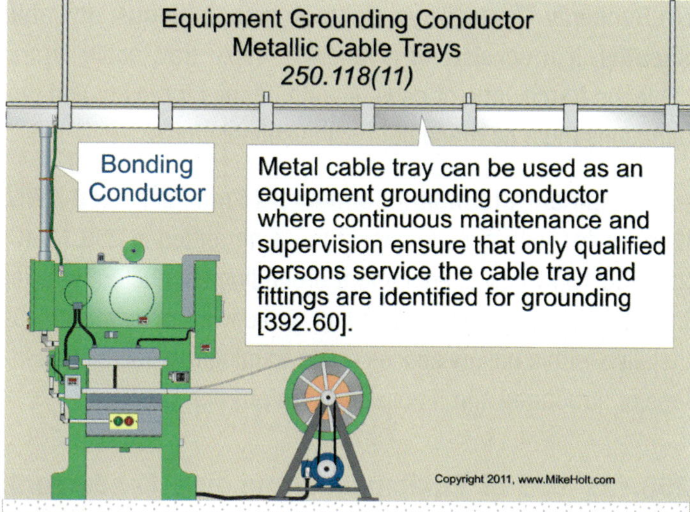

Figure 250–198

(13) Listed electrically continuous metal raceways, such as metal wireways [Article 376] or strut-type channel raceways [384.60].

(14) Surface metal raceways listed for grounding [Article 386].

250.119 Identification of Equipment Grounding Conductors.

Unless required to be insulated, equipment grounding conductors can be bare, covered, or insulated. Insulated equipment grounding conductors must have a continuous outer finish that's either green or green with one or more yellow stripes.

Conductors with insulation that's green, or green with one or more yellow stripes must not be used for an ungrounded or neutral conductor. **Figure 250–199**

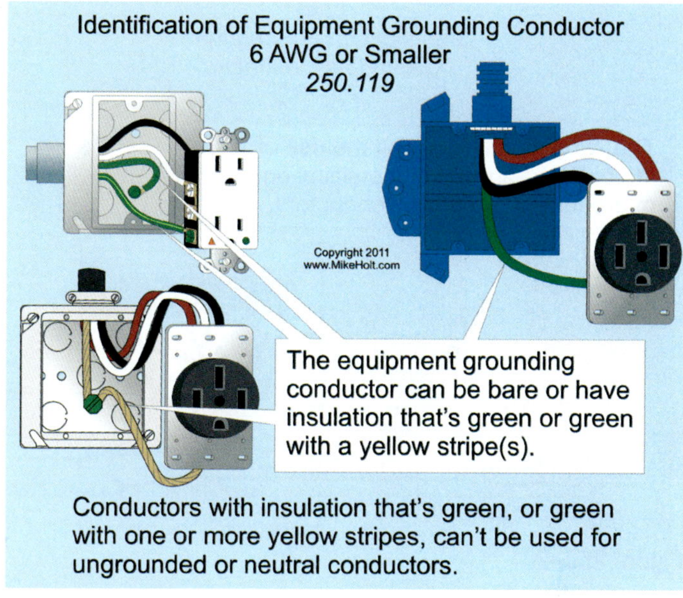

Figure 250–199

Ex: Power-limited, Class 2 or Class 3 cables, power-limited fire alarm cables, or communications cables containing circuits operating at less than 50 volts can use conductors with insulated green or green with one or more yellow stripes for other than equipment grounding conductors [250.20(A) and 250.112(I)]. **Figure 250–200**

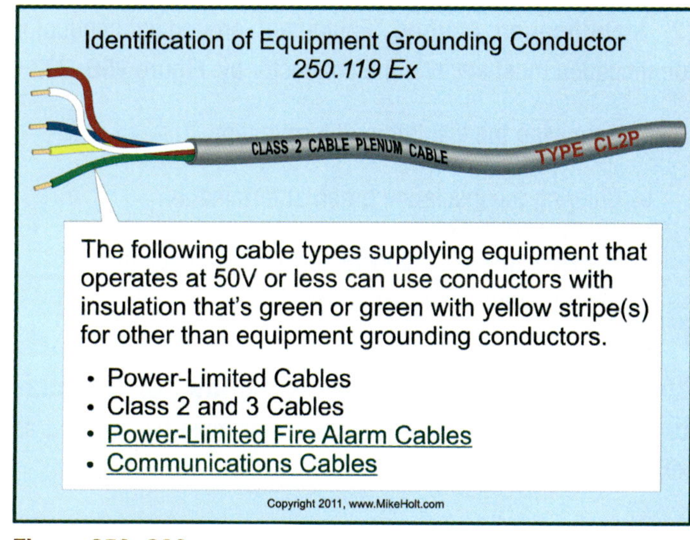

Figure 250–200

Author's Comment: The *NEC* neither requires nor prohibits the use of the color green for the identification of grounding electrode conductors. **Figure 250–201**

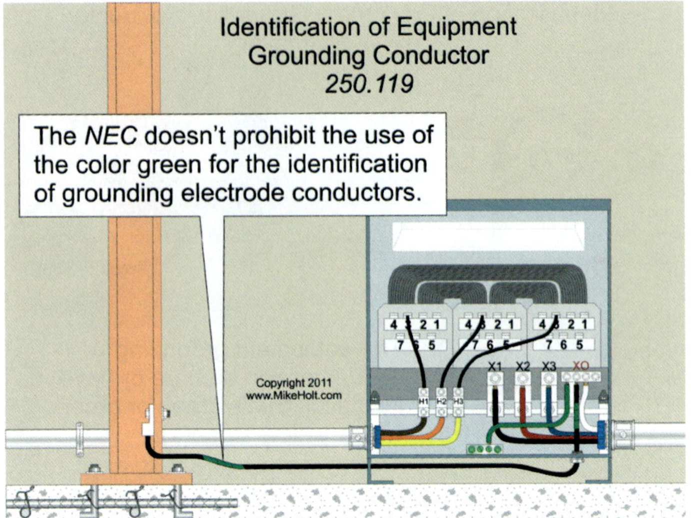

Figure 250–201

(A) Conductors Larger Than 6 AWG.

(1) Identified if Accessible. Insulated equipment grounding conductors larger than 6 AWG can be permanently reidentified at the time of installation at every point where the conductor is accessible.

Ex: Identification of equipment grounding conductors larger than 6 AWG in conduit bodies isn't required.

(2) Identification Method. Equipment grounding conductor identification must encircle the conductor by: **Figure 250–202**

a. Removing the insulation at termination

b. Coloring the insulation green at termination

c. Marking the insulation at termination with green tape or green adhesive labels

250.120 Equipment Grounding Conductor Installation. An equipment grounding conductor must be installed as follows:

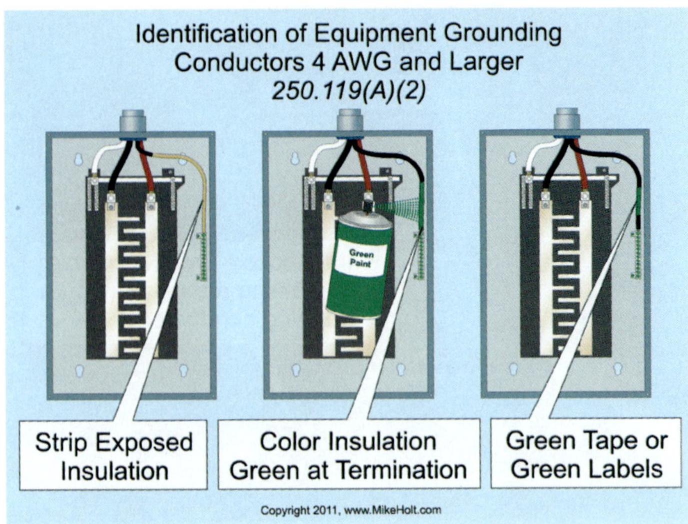

Figure 250–202

(A) Raceway, Cable Trays, Cable Armor, Cablebus, or Cable Sheaths. If it consists of a raceway, cable tray, cable armor, cablebus framework, or cable sheath, fittings for joints and terminations must be made tight using suitable tools.

(C) Equipment Grounding Conductors Smaller Than 6 AWG. If not routed with circuit conductors as permitted in 250.130(C) and 250.134(B) Ex 2, equipment grounding conductors smaller than 6 AWG must be installed in a raceway or cable unless installed within hollow spaces of the framing members of buildings or structures and if not subject to physical damage.

250.121 Use of Equipment Grounding Conductors. An equipment grounding conductor isn't permitted to be used as a grounding electrode conductor.

Author's Comment: For photovoltaic systems, 690.47(C) permits a combined equipment grounding/grounding electrode conductor if sized to the larger of 250.122 or 250.166 and installed in accordance with 250.64(E). **Figure 250–203**

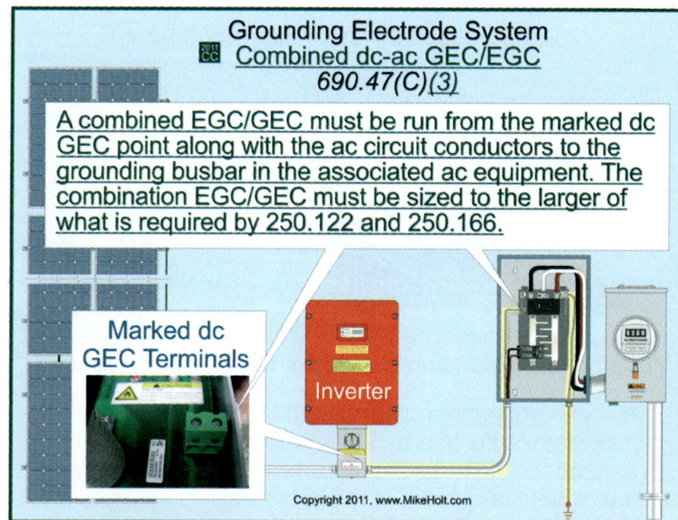

Figure 690-203

250.122 Sizing Equipment Grounding Conductor.

(A) General. Equipment grounding conductors of the wire type must be sized not smaller than shown in Table 250.122, based on the rating of the circuit overcurrent device; however, the circuit equipment grounding conductor isn't required to be larger than the circuit conductors. **Figure 250–204**

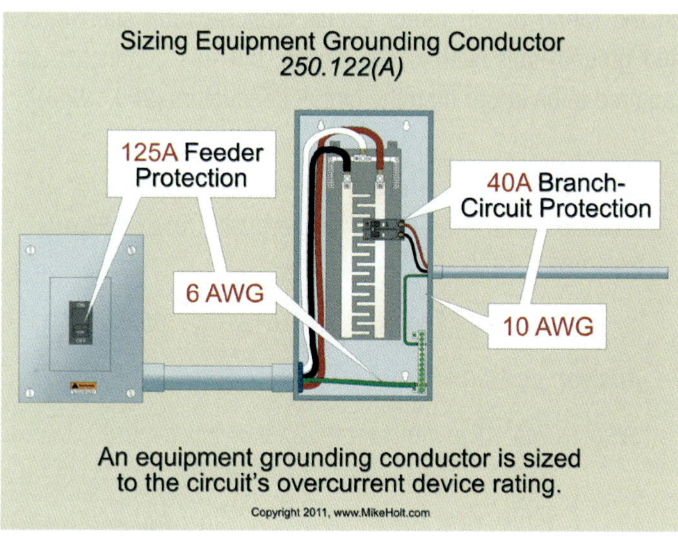

Figure 250–204

Equipment grounding conductors can be sectioned within a multiconductor cable, provided the combined circular mil area complies with Table 250.122.

Table 250.122 Sizing Equipment Grounding Conductor

Overcurrent Device Rating	Copper Conductor
15A	14 AWG
20A	12 AWG
30A—60A	10 AWG
70A—100A	8 AWG
110A—200A	6 AWG
225A—300A	4 AWG
350A—400A	3 AWG
450A—500A	2 AWG
600A	1 AWG
700A—800A	1/0 AWG
1,000A	2/0 AWG
1,200A	3/0 AWG

(B) Increased in Size. If ungrounded conductors are increased in size from the minimum size, equipment grounding conductors must be proportionately increased in size according to the circular mil area of the ungrounded conductors.

> **Author's Comment:** Ungrounded conductors are sometimes increased in size to accommodate conductor voltage drop, harmonic current heating, short-circuit rating, or simply for future capacity.

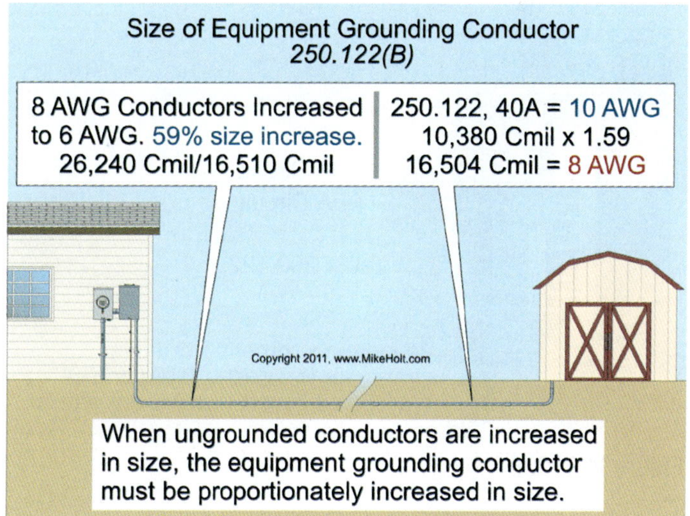

Figure 250–205

Question: *If the ungrounded conductors for a 40A circuit are increased in size from 8 AWG to 6 AWG, the circuit equipment grounding conductor must be increased in size from 10 AWG to ______.* **Figure 250–205** (previous page)

(a) 10 AWG (b) 8 AWG (c) 6 AWG (d) 4 AWG

Answer: *(b) 8 AWG*

The circular mil area of 6 AWG is 59 percent more than 8 AWG (26,240 Cmil/16,510 Cmil) [Chapter 9, Table 8].

According to Table 250.122, the circuit equipment grounding conductor for a 40A overcurrent device will be 10 AWG (10,380 Cmil), but the circuit equipment grounding conductor for this circuit must be increased in size by a multiplier of 1.59.

Conductor Size = 10,380 Cmil x 1.59
Conductor Size = 16,504 Cmil
Conductor Size = 8 AWG, Chapter 9, Table 8

(C) Multiple Circuits. When multiple circuits are installed in the same raceway, cable, or cable tray, only one equipment grounding conductor is required for the multiple circuits, sized in accordance with 250.122, based on the rating of the largest circuit overcurrent device. **Figures 250–206 and 250–207**

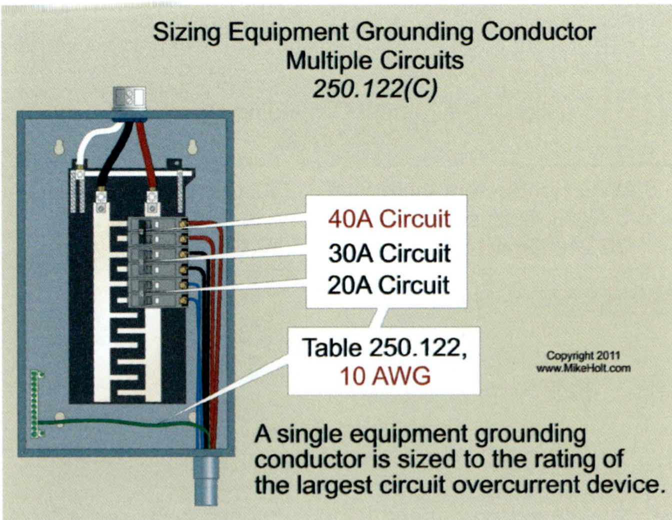

Figure 250–206

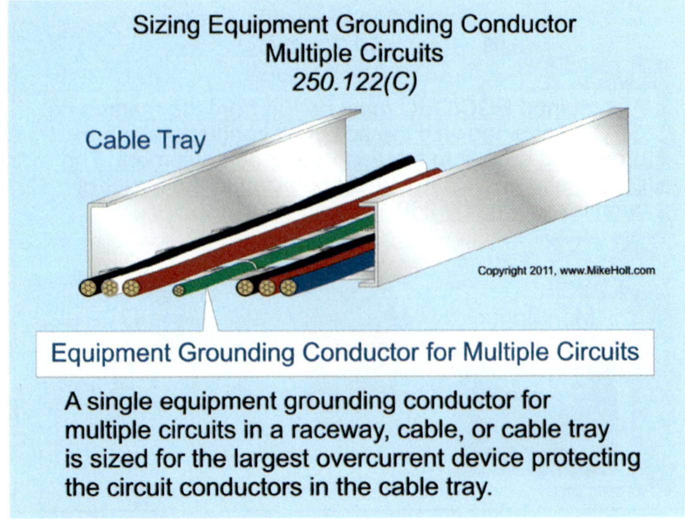

Figure 250–207

Author's Comment: Single conductors used as equipment grounding conductors in cable trays must be sized 4 AWG and larger [392.10(B)(1)(c)].

(D) Motor Branch Circuits.

(1) General. The equipment grounding conductor of the wire type must be sized in accordance with Table 250.122, based on the rating of the motor circuit branch-circuit short-circuit and ground-fault overcurrent device, but this conductor isn't required to be larger than the circuit conductors [250.122(A)].

Question: *What size equipment grounding conductor is required for a 2 hp, 230V, single-phase motor?* **Figure 250–208**

(a) 14 AWG (b) 12 AWG (c) 10 AWG (d) 8 AWG

Answer: *(a) 14 AWG*

Step 1: *Determine the branch-circuit conductor size [430.22(A) and Table 310.15(B)(16)]*

2 hp, 230V Motor FLC = 12A [Table 430.248]

12A x 1.25 = 15A, 14 AWG, rated 20A at 75°C [Table 310.15(B)(16)]

Step 2: *Determine the branch-circuit protection [240.6(A), 430.52(C)(1), and Table 430.248]*

12A x 2.50 = 30A

Step 3: The circuit equipment grounding conductor must be sized to the 30A overcurrent device—10 AWG [Table 250.122], but it's not required to be sized larger than the circuit conductors—14 AWG.

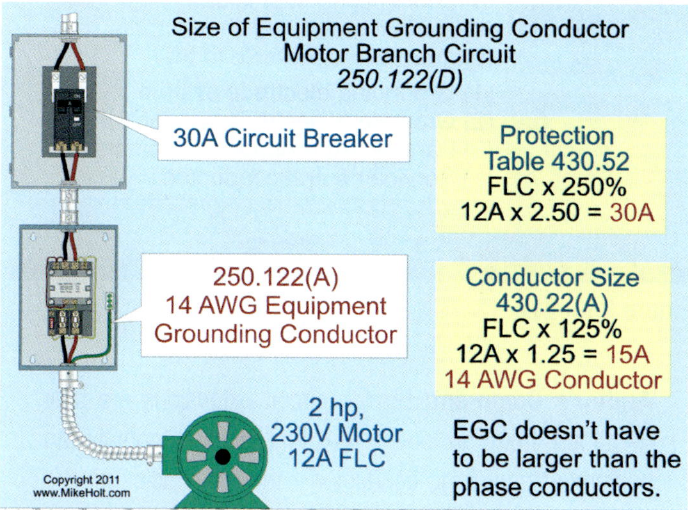

Figure 250–208

(F) Parallel Runs. If circuit conductors are installed in parallel in separate raceways as permitted by 310.10(H), an equipment grounding conductor must be installed for each parallel conductor set, Figure 250–209. Where conductors are installed in parallel in the same raceway or cable tray, a single equipment grounding conductor is permitted. Figure 250–210

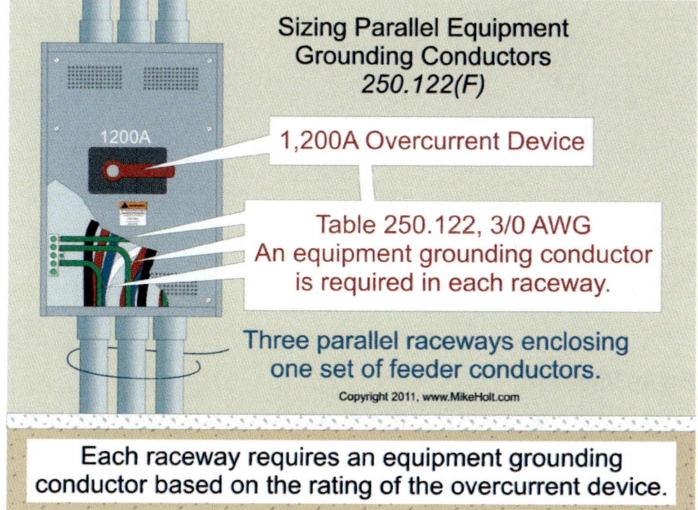

Figure 250–209

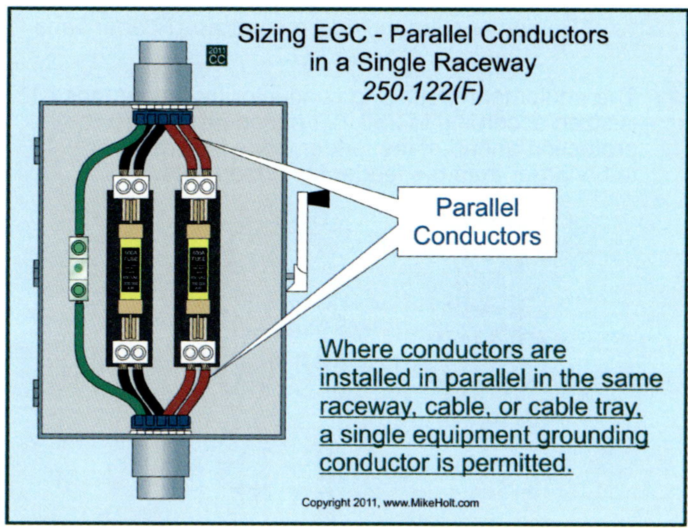

Figure 250–210

Each equipment grounding conductor must be sized in accordance with Table 250.122, based on the rating of the circuit overcurrent device, but it's not required to be larger than the circuit conductors [250.122(A)].

> **Author's Comment:** In cable trays, single-conductor equipment grounding conductors can be insulated, covered, or bare, but must be sized 4 AWG and larger [392.10(B)(1)(c)].

(G) Feeder Tap Conductors. Equipment grounding conductors for feeder taps must be sized in accordance with Table 250.122, based on the ampere rating of the overcurrent device ahead of the feeder, but in no case is it required to be larger than the feeder tap conductors. Figure 250–211

250.126 Identification of Wiring Device Terminals.

The terminal of a wiring device for the connection of the equipment grounding conductor must be identified by a green:

(1) Not readily removable terminal screw with a hexagonal head.

(2) Hexagonal, not readily removable terminal nut.

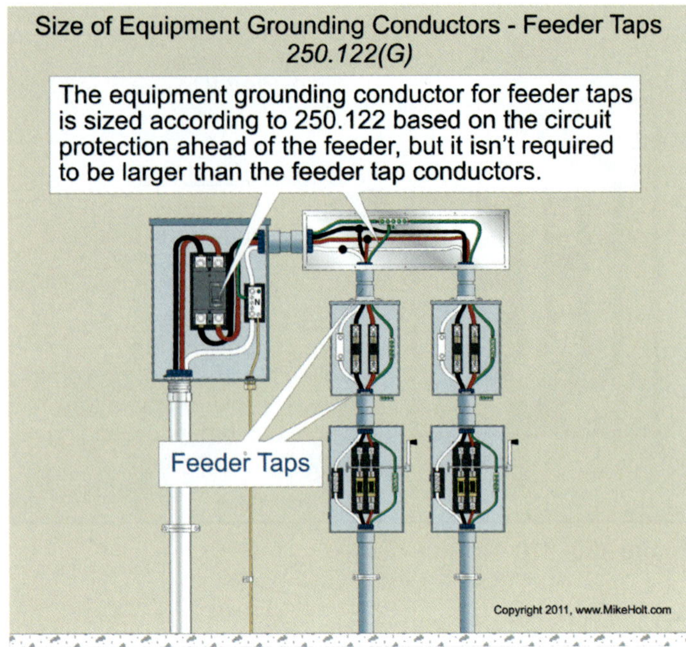

Figure 250–211

(3) Pressure wire connector. If the terminal for the grounding conductor isn't visible, the conductor entrance hole must be marked with the word "green" or "ground," the letters "G" or "GR," a grounding symbol, or otherwise identified by a distinctive green color.

PART VII. METHODS OF EQUIPMENT GROUNDING

250.130 Replacing Nongrounding Receptacles.

(C) Nongrounding Receptacle Replacement. If a nongrounding receptacle is replaced with a grounding-type receptacle from an outlet box that doesn't contain an equipment grounding conductor, the grounding contacts of the receptacle must be connected to one of the following: Figure 250–212

(1) Grounding electrode system [250.50]

(2) Grounding electrode conductor

(3) Panelboard equipment grounding terminal

(4) Service neutral conductor

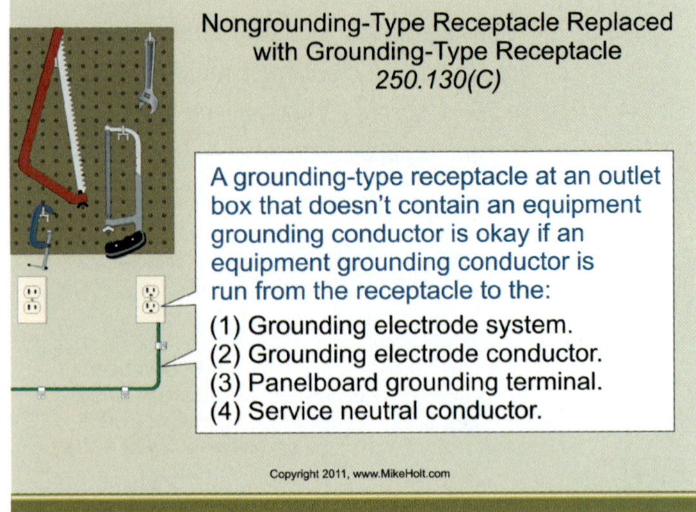

Figure 250–212

Author's Comment: Branch circuit extensions are only permitted from an outlet box that doesn't contain an equipment grounding conductor if the receptacles on the extension have the grounding contacts connected to the grounding electrode system, grounding electrode conductor, panelboard equipment grounding terminal, or service neutral conductor in accordance with 250.130(C). Figure 250–213

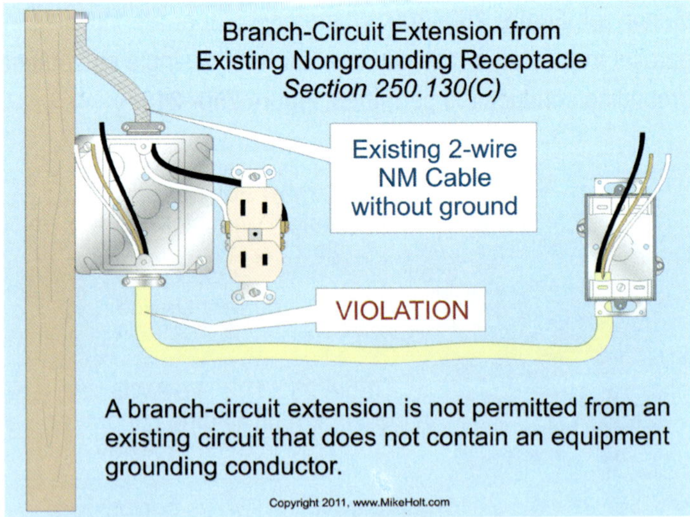

Figure 250–213

Note: A grounding-type receptacle can replace a nongrounding type receptacle, without having the grounding terminal connected to an equipment grounding conductor, if the receptacle is GFCI protected and marked in accordance with 406.4(D)(2). Figure 250–214

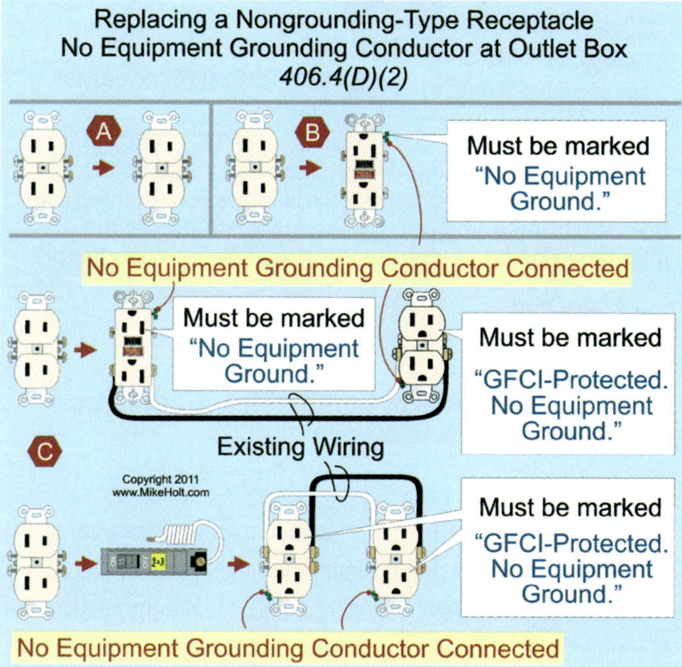

Figure 250–214

250.134 Equipment Fastened in Place or Connected by Wiring Methods.

Unless connected to the neutral conductor at services or separately derived systems as permitted or required by 250.142, metal parts of equipment, raceways, and enclosures must be connected to an equipment grounding conductor by one of the following methods:

(A) Equipment Grounding Conductor Types. By connecting to equipment grounding conductors identified in 250.118.

(B) With Circuit Conductors. If an equipment grounding conductor of the wire type is installed, it must be installed in the same raceway, cable tray, trench, cable, or cord with the circuit conductors in accordance with 300.3(B), except as permitted by 250.102(E). Figures 250–215 and 250–216

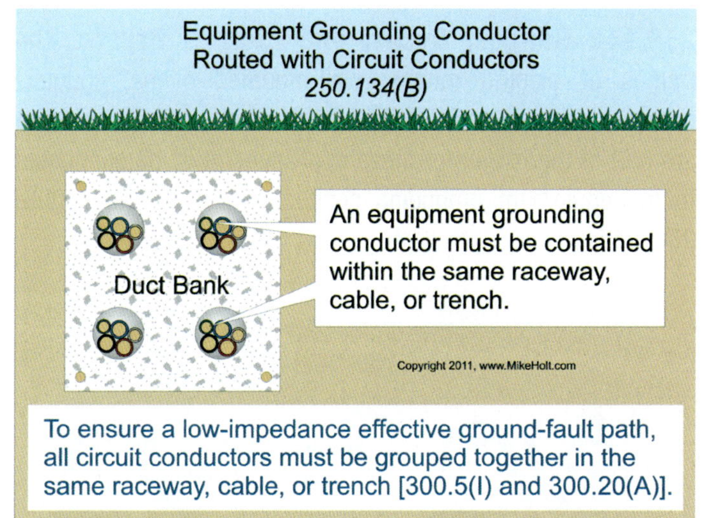

Figure 250–215

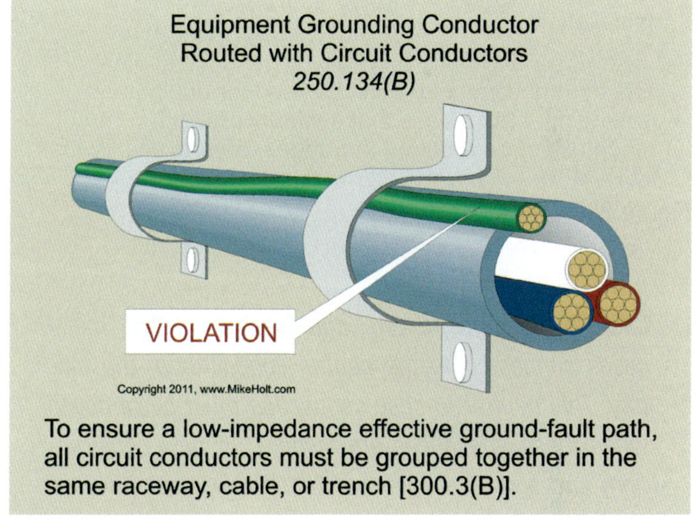

Figure 250–216

250.136 Equipment Considered Grounded.

(A) Equipment Secured to Grounded Metal Supports. The structural metal frame of a building must not be used as the required equipment grounding conductor.

250.138 Cord-and-Plug-Connected Equipment.

(A) Equipment Grounding Conductor. Metal parts of cord-and-plug-connected equipment must be connected to an equipment grounding conductor that terminates to a grounding-type attachment plug.

250.140 Ranges, Ovens, and Clothes Dryers. The frames of electric ranges, wall-mounted ovens, counter-mounted cooking units, clothes dryers, and outlet boxes that are part of the circuit for these appliances must be connected to the equipment grounding conductor [250.134(A)]. Figure 250–217

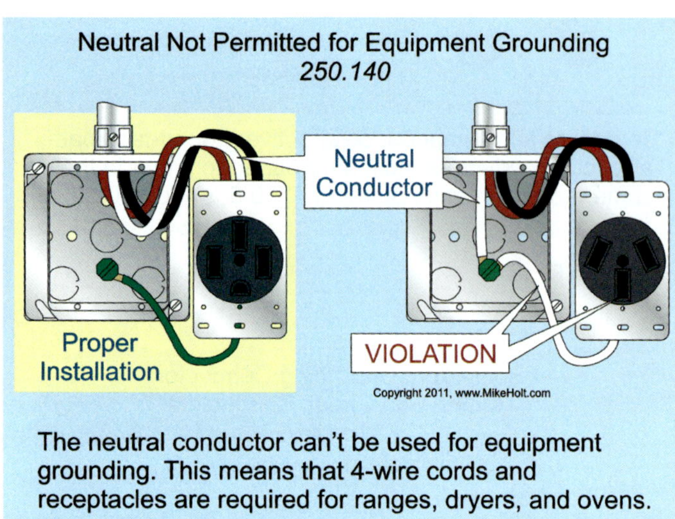

Figure 250–217

CAUTION: *Ranges, dryers, and ovens have their metal cases connected to the neutral conductor at the factory. This neutral-to-case connection must be removed when these appliances are installed in new construction, and a 4-wire cord and receptacle must be used [250.142(B)].*

Ex: For existing installations if an equipment grounding conductor isn't present in the outlet box, the frames of electric ranges, wall-mounted ovens, counter-mounted cooking units, clothes dryers, and outlet boxes that are part of the circuit for these appliances may be connected to the neutral conductor. Figure 250–218

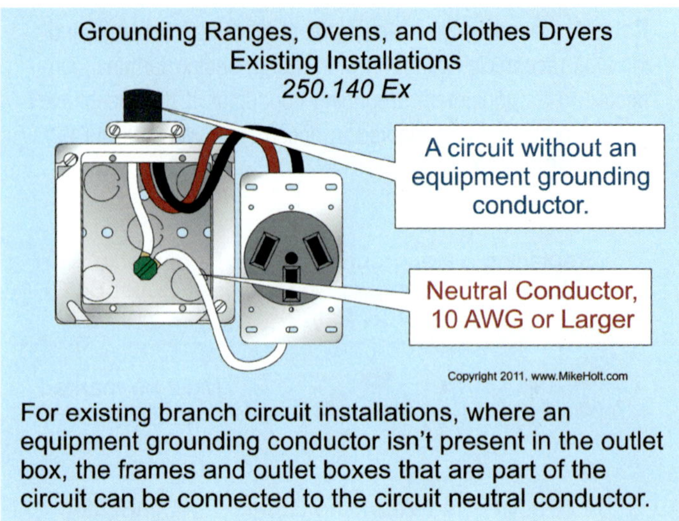

Figure 250–218

250.142 Use of Neutral Conductor for Equipment Grounding.

Author's Comment: To remove dangerous voltage on metal parts from a ground fault, the metal parts of electrical raceways, cables, enclosures, and equipment must be connected to an equipment grounding conductor of a type recognized in 250.118 in accordance with 250.4(A)(3).

(A) Supply-Side Equipment. The neutral conductor can be used as the circuit equipment grounding conductor for metal parts of equipment, raceways, and enclosures at the following locations:

(1) Service Equipment. On the supply side or within the enclosure of the service disconnect in accordance with 250.24(B). Figure 250–219

(3) Separately Derived Systems. At the source of a separately derived system or within the enclosure of the system disconnecting means in accordance with 250.30(A)(1).

DANGER: *Failure to install the system bonding jumper as required by 250.30(A)(1) creates a condition where dangerous touch voltage from a ground fault won't be removed.*

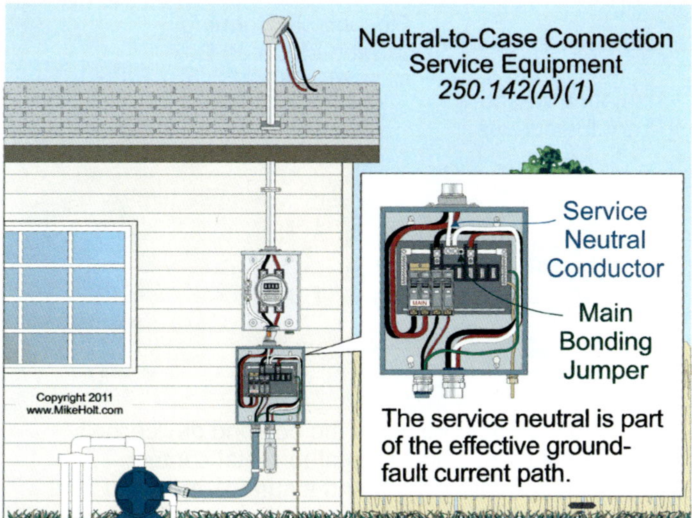

Figure 250–219

(B) Load-Side Equipment. Except as permitted in 250.30(A)(1) for separately derived systems and 250.32(B) Ex, for separate buildings/structures, the neutral conductor isn't permitted to serve as an equipment grounding conductor on the load side of service equipment.

Ex 1: In existing installations, the frames of ranges, wall-mounted ovens, counter-mounted cooking units, and clothes dryers can be connected to the neutral conductor in accordance with 250.140 Ex.

Ex 2: The neutral conductor can be connected to meter socket enclosures on the load side of the service disconnecting means if: Figure 250–220

(1) Ground-fault protection isn't provided on service equipment,

(2) Meter socket enclosures are immediately adjacent to the service disconnecting means, and

(3) The neutral conductor is sized in accordance with 250.122, based on the ampere rating of the occupancy's feeder overcurrent device.

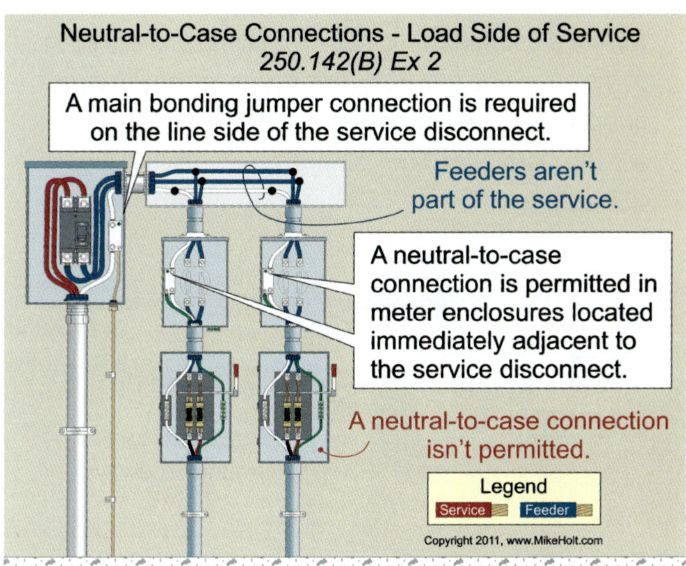

Figure 250–220

250.146 Connecting Receptacle Grounding Terminal to Metal Enclosure.

An equipment bonding jumper sized in accordance with 250.122, based on the rating of the circuit overcurrent device, must connect the grounding terminal of a receptacle to a metal box, except as permitted for (A) through (D). Figure 250–221

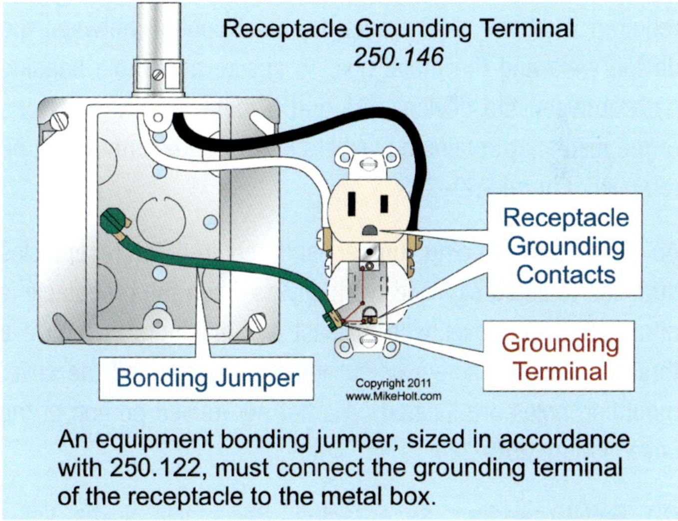

Figure 250–221

Author's Comment: The *NEC* doesn't restrict the position of the receptacle grounding terminal; it can be up, down, or sideways. *Code* proposals to specify the mounting position of receptacles have always been rejected. **Figure 250–222**

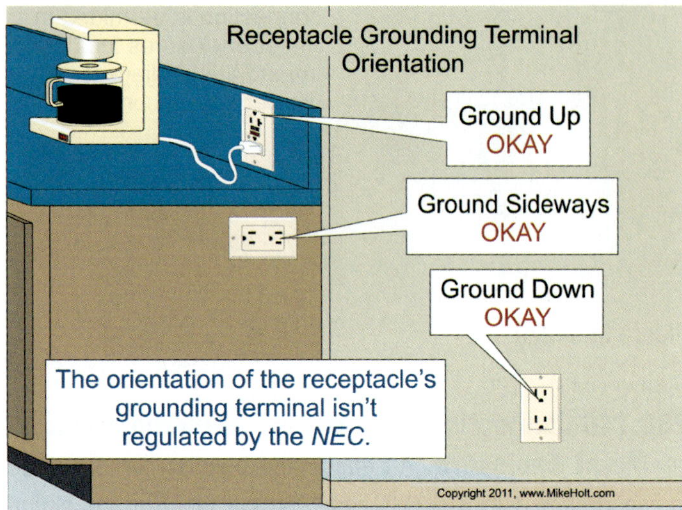

Figure 250–222

(A) Surface-Mounted Box. An equipment bonding jumper from a receptacle to a metal box that's surface mounted isn't required if there's direct metal-to-metal contact between the device yoke and the metal box. To ensure a suitable bonding path between the device yoke and a metal box, at least one of the insulating retaining washers on the yoke screw must be removed. **Figure 250–223**

An equipment bonding jumper isn't required for receptacles attached to listed exposed work covers when the receptacle is attached to the cover with at least two fasteners that have a thread locking or screw or nut locking means, and the cover mounting holes are located on a flat non-raised portion of the cover. **Figure 250–224**

(B) Self-Grounding Receptacles. Receptacle yokes listed as self-grounding are designed to establish the bonding path between the device yoke and a metal box via the two metal mounting screws. **Figure 250–225**

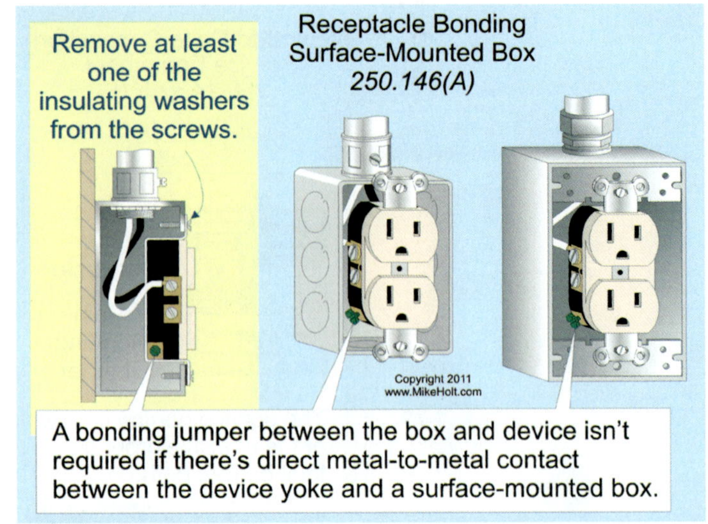

Figure 250–223

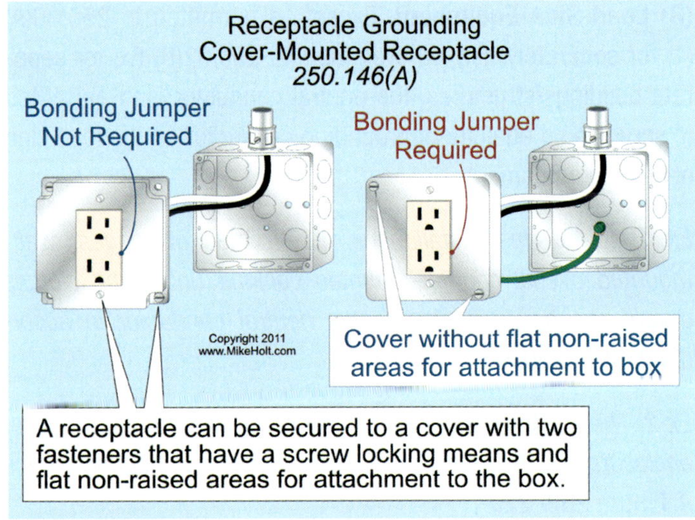

Figure 250–224

(C) Floor Boxes. Listed floor boxes are designed to establish the bonding path between the device yoke and a metal box.

(D) Isolated Ground Receptacles. If installed for the reduction of electrical noise, the grounding terminal of an isolated ground receptacle must be connected to an insulated equipment grounding conductor run with the circuit conductors. **Figure 250–226**

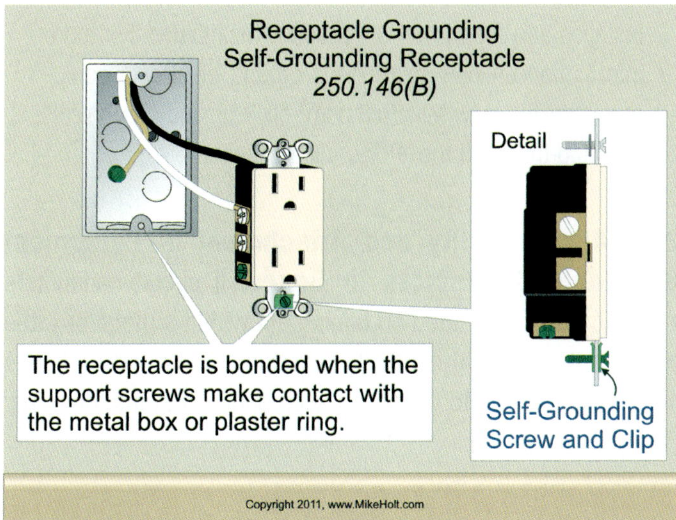

Figure 250–225

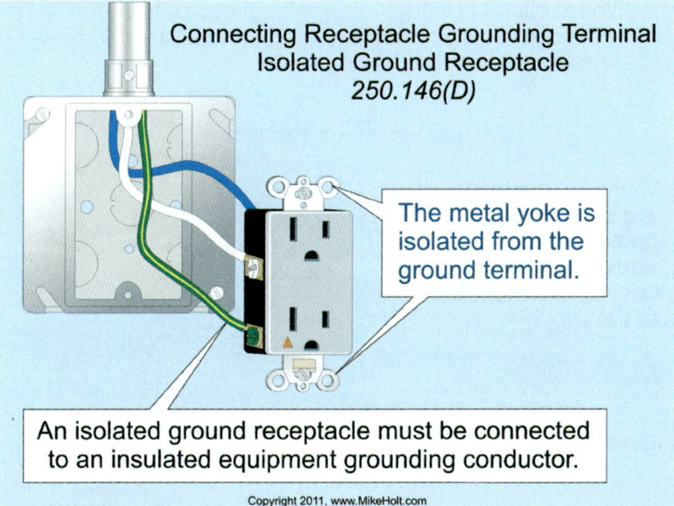

Figure 250–226

The circuit equipment grounding conductor is permitted to pass through panelboards [408.40 Ex], boxes, wireways, or other enclosures [250.148 Ex] without a connection to the enclosure as long as it terminates at an equipment grounding conductor terminal of the derived system or service.

CAUTION:

Type AC Cable—Type AC cable containing an insulated equipment grounding conductor of the wire type can be used to supply receptacles having insulated grounding terminals because the metal armor of the cable is listed as an equipment grounding conductor [250.118(8)]. **Figure 250–227**

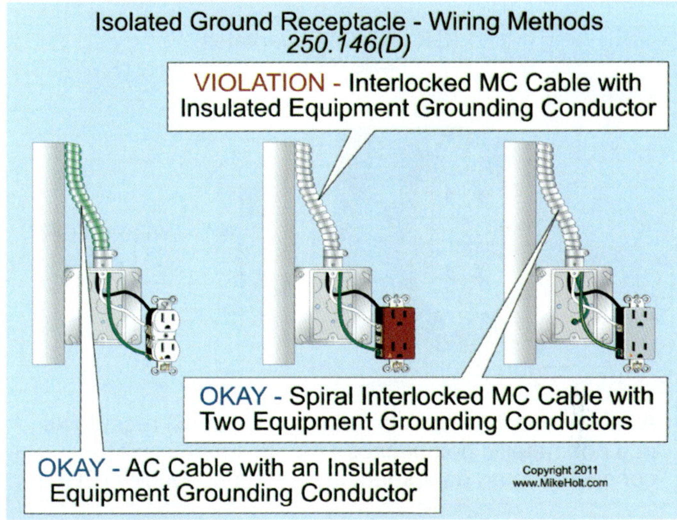

Figure 250–227

Type MC Cable—The metal armor sheath of interlocked Type MC cable containing an insulated equipment grounding conductor isn't listed as an equipment grounding conductor. Therefore, this wiring method with a single equipment grounding conductor can't supply an isolated ground receptacle installed in a metal box (because the box isn't connected to an equipment grounding conductor). However, Type MC cable with two insulated equipment grounding conductors is acceptable, since one equipment grounding conductor connects to the metal box and the other to the isolated ground receptacle. See **Figure 250–227**

The armor assembly of interlocked Type MCAP® cable with a 10 AWG bare aluminum grounding/bonding conductor running just below the metal armor is listed to serve as an equipment grounding conductor in accordance with 250.118(10)(b).

Nonmetallic Boxes—Because the grounding terminal of an isolated ground receptacle is insulated from the metal mounting yoke, a metal faceplate must not be used when an isolated ground receptacle is installed in a nonmetallic box. The reason is that the metal faceplate isn't connected to an equipment grounding conductor [406.3(D)(2)]. **Figure 250–228**

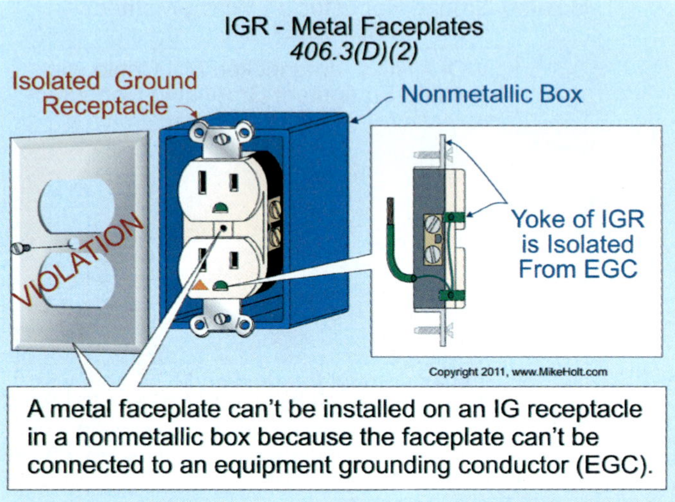

Figure 250–228

Author's Comment: When should an isolated ground receptacle be installed and how should the isolated ground system be designed? These questions are design issues and must not be answered based on the *NEC* alone [90.1(C)]. In most cases, using isolated ground receptacles is a waste of money. For example, IEEE 1100—*Powering and Grounding Electronic Equipment* (Emerald Book) states: "The results from the use of the isolated ground method range from no observable effects, the desired effects, or worse noise conditions than when standard equipment bonding configurations are used to serve electronic load equipment [8.5.3.2]."

In reality, few electrical installations truly require an isolated ground system. For those systems that can benefit from an isolated ground system, engineering opinions differ as to what's a proper design. Making matters worse—of those properly designed, few are correctly installed and even fewer are properly maintained. For more information on how to properly ground electronic equipment, go to: www.MikeHolt.com, click on the "Technical" link, and then visit the "Power Quality" page.

250.148 Continuity and Attachment of Equipment Grounding Conductors in Boxes. If circuit conductors are spliced or terminated on equipment within a metal box, the equipment grounding conductor associated with those circuits must be connected to the box in accordance with the following: **Figure 250–229**

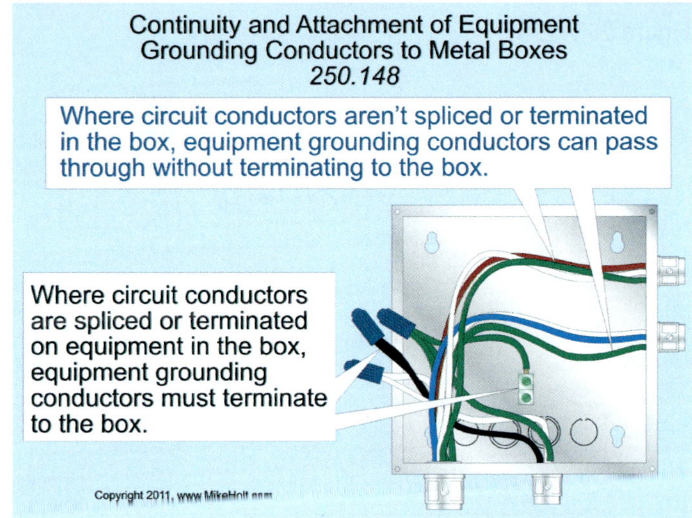

Figure 250–229

Ex: The circuit equipment grounding conductor for an isolated ground receptacle installed in accordance with 250.146(D) isn't required to terminate to a metal box. **Figure 250–230**

(A) Splicing. Equipment grounding conductors must be spliced together with a device listed for the purpose [110.14(B)]. **Figure 250–231**

Author's Comment: Wire connectors of any color can be used with equipment grounding conductor splices, but green wire connectors can only be used with equipment grounding conductors.

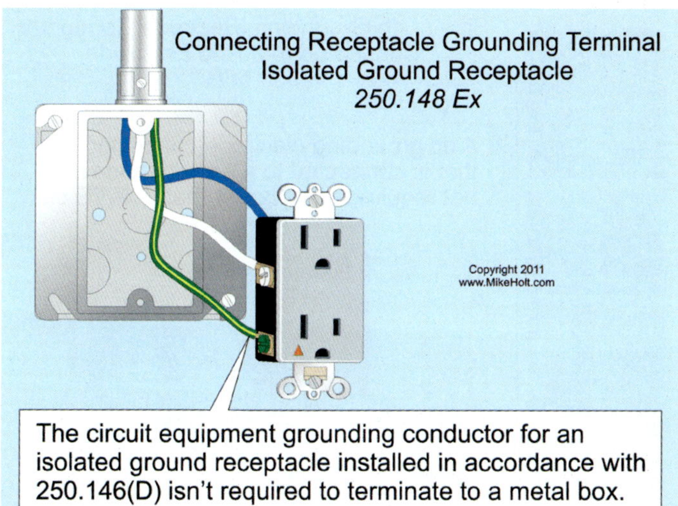

Figure 250–230

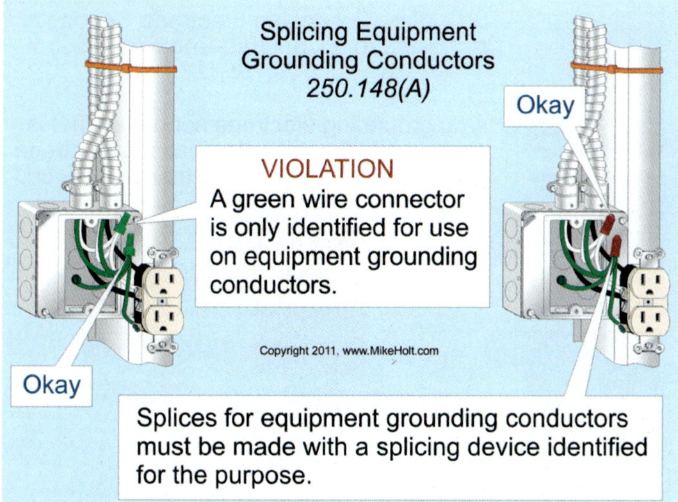

Figure 250–231

(B) Equipment Grounding Continuity. Equipment grounding conductors must terminate in a manner such that the disconnection or the removal of a receptacle, luminaire, or other device won't interrupt the grounding continuity. Figure 250–232

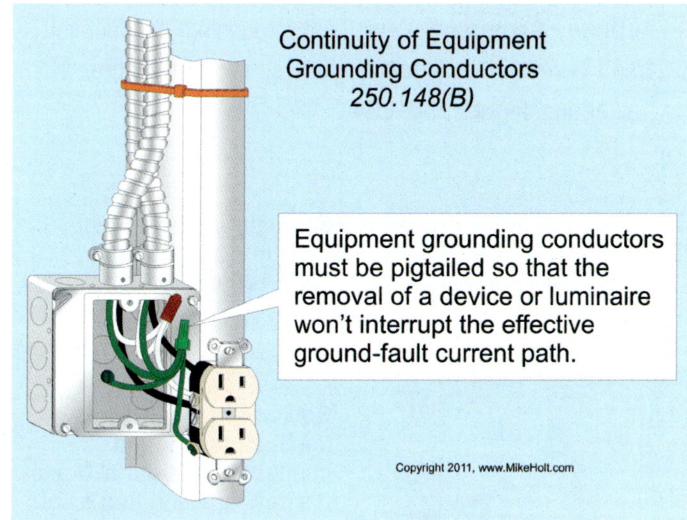

Figure 250–232

(C) Metal Boxes. Equipment grounding conductors within metal boxes must be connected to the metal box with a grounding screw that's not used for any other purpose, an equipment fitting listed for grounding, or a listed grounding device such as a ground clip. Figure 250–233

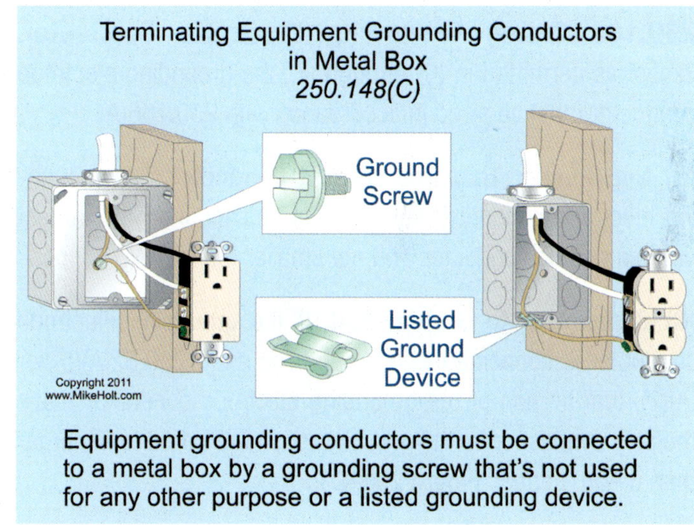

Figure 250–233

Author's Comment: Equipment grounding conductors aren't permitted to terminate to a screw that secures a plaster ring. Figure 250–234

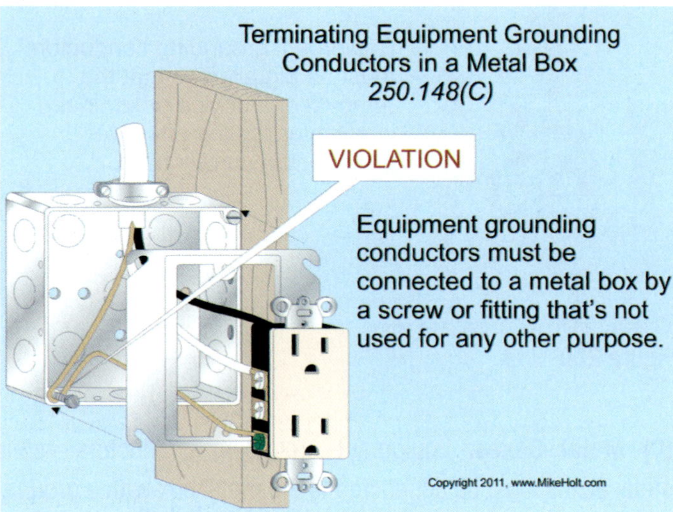

Figure 250–234

PART VIII. DIRECT-CURRENT SYSTEMS

250.166 Sizing Grounding Electrode Conductor.

Except as permitted in (C) through (E), the grounding electrode conductor must be sized in accordance with 250.166(A).

(B) Not Smaller Than the Largest Conductor. The grounding electrode conductor must not be smaller than the largest ungrounded dc conductor, and not smaller than 8 AWG copper.

(C) Connection to Ground Rod. If the grounding electrode conductor is connected to a ground rod as in 250.52(A)(5), or (A)(7), that portion of the grounding electrode conductor that's the sole connection to the ground rod isn't required to be larger than 6 AWG copper. Figure 250–235

(D) Connection to Concrete-Encased Grounding Electrode. If the grounding electrode conductor is connected to a concrete-encased electrode as in 250.52(A)(3), the portion of the grounding electrode conductor that's the sole connection to the concrete-encased electrode isn't required to be larger than 4 AWG copper. Figure 250–236

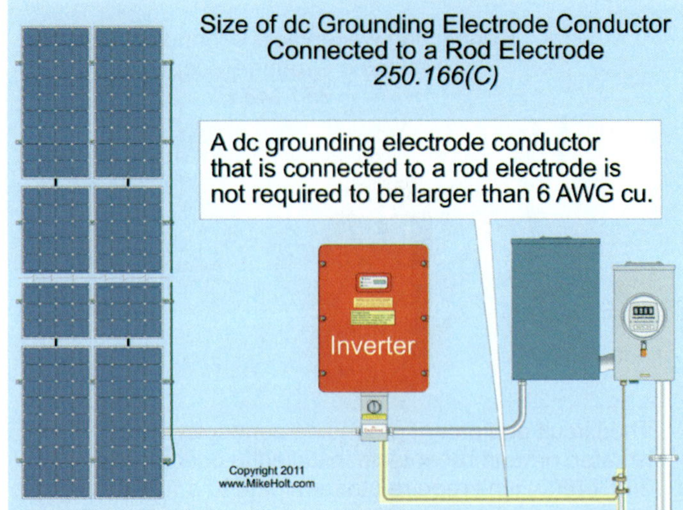

Figure 250–235

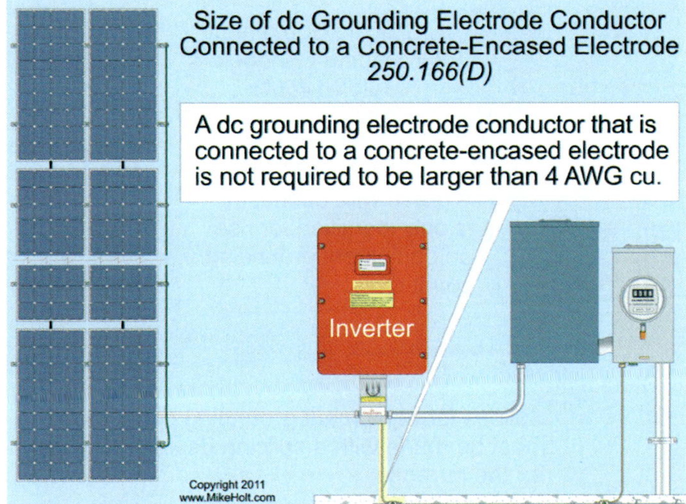

Figure 250–236

CHAPTER 2

Practice Questions

CHAPTER 2. WIRING AND PROTECTION—PRACTICE QUESTIONS

Article 250. Grounding and Bonding

Part I. General

1. A conductor on the supply side of a service or within a service equipment enclosure or separately derived system to ensure the electrical conductivity between metal parts required to be electrically connected is known as the "______."

(a) supply-side bonding jumper
(b) ungrounded conductor
(c) the electrical supply source
(d) grounding electrode conductor

2. An effective ground-fault current path is an intentionally constructed, permanent, low-impedance path designed and intended to carry fault current from the point of a ground fault on a wiring system to the ______.

(a) ground
(b) earth
(c) electrical supply source
(d) none of these

3. A ground-fault current path is an electrically conductive path from the point of a ground fault through normally non-current-carrying conductors, equipment, or the earth to the ______.

(a) ground
(b) earth
(c) electrical supply source
(d) none of these

4. Examples of ground-fault current paths include any combination of conductive materials including ______.

(a) equipment grounding conductors
(b) metallic raceways
(c) metal water and gas piping
(d) all of these

5. Grounded electrical systems shall be connected to earth in a manner that will ______.

(a) limit voltages due to lightning, line surges, or unintentional contact with higher-voltage lines
(b) stabilize the voltage-to-ground during normal operation
(c) facilitate overcurrent device operation in case of ground faults
(d) a and b

6. An important consideration for limiting imposed voltage on electrical systems is to remember that bonding and grounding electrode conductors shouldn't be any longer than necessary and unnecessary bends and loops should be avoided.

(a) True
(b) False

7. For grounded systems, normally non-current-carrying conductive materials enclosing electrical conductors or equipment shall be connected to earth so as to limit the voltage-to-ground on these materials.

(a) True
(b) False

8. For grounded systems, non-current-carrying conductive materials enclosing electrical conductors or equipment, or forming part of such equipment, shall be connected together and to the ______ to establish an effective ground-fault current path.

   (a) ground
   (b) earth
   (c) electrical supply source
   (d) none of these

9. In grounded systems, normally non-current-carrying electrically conductive materials that are likely to become energized shall be ______ in a manner that establishes an effective ground-fault current path.

   (a) connected together
   (b) connected to the electrical supply source
   (c) connected to the closest grounded conductor
   (d) a and b

10. For grounded systems, electrical equipment and conductive material likely to become energized, shall be installed in a manner that creates a ______ from any point on the wiring system where a ground fault may occur to the electrical supply source.

   (a) circuit facilitating the operation of the overcurrent device
   (b) low-impedance path
   (c) path capable of safely carrying the ground-fault current likely to be imposed on it
   (d) all of these

11. For grounded systems, electrical equipment and electrically conductive material likely to become energized, shall be installed in a manner that creates a low-impedance circuit capable of safely carrying the maximum ground-fault current likely to be imposed on it from where a ground fault may occur to the ______.

   (a) ground
   (b) earth
   (c) electrical supply source
   (d) none of these

12. For grounded systems, the earth is considered an effective ground-fault current path.

   (a) True
   (b) False

13. For ungrounded systems, non-current-carrying conductive materials enclosing electrical conductors or equipment shall be connected to the ______ in a manner that will limit the voltage imposed by lightning or unintentional contact with higher-voltage lines.

   (a) ground
   (b) earth
   (c) electrical supply source
   (d) none of these

14. For ungrounded systems, non-current-carrying conductive materials enclosing electrical conductors or equipment, or forming part of such equipment, shall be connected together and to the supply system equipment in a manner that creates a low-impedance path for ground-fault current that is capable of carrying ______.

   (a) the maximum branch-circuit current
   (b) at least twice the maximum ground-fault current
   (c) the maximum fault current likely to be imposed on it
   (d) the equivalent to the main service rating

15. Electrically conductive materials that are likely to ______ in ungrounded systems shall be connected together and to the supply system grounded equipment in a manner that creates a low-impedance path for ground-fault current that is capable of carrying the maximum fault current likely to be imposed on it.

(a) become energized
(b) require service
(c) be removed
(d) be coated with paint or nonconductive materials

16. In ungrounded systems, electrical equipment, wiring, and other electrically conductive material likely to become energized shall be installed in a manner that creates a low-impedance circuit from any point on the wiring system to the electrical supply source to facilitate the operation of overcurrent devices should a(n) ______ fault from a different phase occur on the wiring system.

(a) isolated ground
(b) second ground
(c) arc
(d) high impedance

17. The grounding of electrical systems, circuit conductors, surge arresters, surge protective devices, and conductive normally non-current-carrying metal parts of equipment shall be installed and arranged in a manner that will prevent objectionable current.

(a) True
(b) False

18. Temporary currents resulting from abnormal conditions, such as ground faults, are not considered to be objectionable currents.

(a) True
(b) False

19. Currents that introduce noise or data errors in electronic equipment are considered objectionable currents.

(a) True
(b) False

20. Equipment grounding conductors, grounding electrode conductors, and bonding jumpers shall be connected by ______.

(a) listed pressure connectors
(b) terminal bars
(c) exothermic welding
(d) any of these

21. Grounding and bonding connection devices shall not depend solely on ______.

(a) pressure connections
(b) solder
(c) lugs
(d) approved clamps

22. Ground clamps and fittings shall be protected from physical damage by being enclosed in ______ where there may be a possibility of physical damage.

(a) metal
(b) wood
(c) the equivalent of a or b
(d) none of these

23. ______ on equipment to be grounded shall be removed from contact surfaces to ensure good electrical continuity.

(a) Paint
(b) Lacquer
(c) Enamel
(d) any of these

Part II. System Grounding

1. Alternating-current circuits of less than 50V shall be grounded if supplied by a transformer whose supply system exceeds 150 volts-to-ground.

   (a) True
   (b) False

2. Alternating-current systems of 50V to 1,000V that supply premises wiring systems shall be grounded where the system is three-phase, 4-wire, wye connected with the neutral conductor used as a circuit conductor.

   (a) True
   (b) False

3. Alternating-current systems of 50V to 1,000V that supply premises wiring systems shall be grounded where supplied by a three-phase, 4-wire, delta-connected system in which the midpoint of one phase winding is used as a circuit conductor.

   (a) True
   (b) False

4. ______ alternating-current systems operating at 480V shall have ground detectors installed on the system.

   (a) Grounded
   (b) Solidly grounded
   (c) Effectively grounded
   (d) Ungrounded

5. Alternating-current systems from 50V to less than 1,000V that aren't required to be grounded in accordance with 250.20(b) must have ______.

   (a) ground detectors installed
   (b) the ground detection sensing equipment connected as close as practicable to where the system receives its supply
   (c) a and b
   (d) ground-fault protection for equipment

6. Alternating-current systems from 50V to less than 1,000V that are ungrounded systems must be legibly marked "Ungrounded System" at ______ of the system, with sufficient durability to withstand the environment involved.

   (a) the source
   (b) the first disconnecting means
   (c) every junction box
   (d) a or b

7. The grounding electrode conductor shall be connected to the grounded service conductor at the ______.

   (a) load end of the service drop or service lateral
   (b) load end of the service lateral
   (c) service disconnecting means
   (d) any of these

8. Where the main bonding jumper is installed from the grounded conductor terminal bar to the equipment grounding terminal bar in service equipment, the ______ conductor is permitted to be connected to the equipment grounding terminal bar.

   (a) grounding
   (b) grounded
   (c) grounding electrode
   (d) none of these

9. For a grounded system, an unspliced ______ shall be used to connect the equipment grounding conductor(s) and the service disconnecting means to the grounded conductor of the system within the enclosure for each service disconnect.

   (a) grounding electrode
   (b) main bonding jumper
   (c) busbar
   (d) insulated copper conductor

10. Where an alternating-current system operating at less than 1,000V is grounded at any point, the ______ conductor(s) shall be routed with the ungrounded conductors to each service disconnecting means and shall be connected to each disconnecting means grounded conductor(s) terminal or bus.

    (a) ungrounded
    (b) grounded
    (c) grounding
    (d) none of these

11. The grounded conductor of an alternating-current system operating at less than 1,000V shall be routed with the ungrounded conductors and connected to each disconnecting means grounded conductor terminal or bus, which is then connected to the service disconnecting means enclosure via a(n) ______ that's installed between the service neutral conductor and the service disconnecting means enclosure.

    (a) equipment bonding conductor
    (b) main bonding jumper
    (c) grounding electrode
    (d) intersystem bonding terminal

12. The grounded conductor brought to service equipment shall be routed with the phase conductors and shall not be smaller than specified in Table ______ when the service-entrance conductors are 1,100 kcmil copper and smaller.

    (a) 250.66
    (b) 250.122
    (c) 310.16
    (d) 430.52

13. When service-entrance conductors exceed 1,100 kcmil for copper, the required grounded conductor for the service shall be sized not less than ______ percent of the circular mil area of the largest set of ungrounded service-entrance conductor(s).

    (a) 9
    (b) 11
    (c) 12½
    (d) 15

14. Where service-entrance phase conductors are installed in parallel in two or more raceways, the size of the grounded conductor in each raceway shall be based on the total circular mil area of the parallel ungrounded service-entrance conductor in the raceway, sized in accordance with 250.24(C)(1), but not smaller than ______.

    (a) 1/0 AWG
    (b) 2/0 AWG
    (c) 3/0 AWG
    (d) 4/0 AWG

15. A grounding electrode conductor, sized in accordance with 250.66, shall be used to connect the equipment grounding conductors, the service equipment enclosures, and, where the system is grounded, the grounded service conductor to the grounding electrode(s).

    (a) True
    (b) False

16. A main bonding jumper shall be a ______ or similar suitable conductor.

(a) wire
(b) bus
(c) screw
(d) any of these

17. Where a main bonding jumper is a screw only, the screw shall be identified by a(n) ______ that shall be visible with the screw installed.

(a) silver or white finish
(b) etched ground symbol
(c) hexagonal head
(d) green finish

18. Main bonding jumpers and system bonding jumpers shall not be smaller than the sizes shown in ______.

(a) Table 250.66
(b) Table 250.122
(c) Table 310.15(B)(16)
(d) Chapter 9, Table 8

19. Where the supply conductors are larger than 1,100 kcmil copper or 1,750 kcmil aluminum, the main bonding jumper shall have an area that is ______ the area of the largest phase conductor when of the same material.

(a) at least equal to
(b) at least 50 percent of
(c) not less than 12½ percent of
(d) not more than 12½ percent of

20. A grounded conductor shall not be connected to normally non-current-carrying metal parts of equipment on the ______ side of the system bonding jumper of a separately derived system, except as otherwise permitted in Article 250.

(a) supply
(b) grounded
(c) high-voltage
(d) load

21. An unspliced ______ that is sized based on the derived phase conductors shall be used to connect the grounded conductor and the supply-side bonding jumper, or the equipment grounding conductor, or both, at a separately derived system.

(a) system bonding jumper
(b) equipment grounding conductor
(c) grounded conductor
(d) grounding electrode conductor

22. The connection of the system bonding jumper for a separately derived system shall be made ______ on the separately derived system from the source to the first system disconnecting means or overcurrent device.

(a) in at least two locations
(b) in every location that the grounded conductor is present
(c) at any single point
(d) none of these

23. Where a supply-side bonding jumper of the wire type is run with the derived phase conductors from the source of a separately derived system to the first disconnecting means, it shall be sized in accordance with 250.102(C), based on ______.

(a) the size of the primary conductors
(b) the size of the secondary overcurrent protection
(c) the size of the derived phase conductors
(d) one third the size of the primary grounded conductor

24. The grounding electrode for a separately derived system shall be as near as practicable to, and preferably in the same area as, the grounding electrode conductor connection to the system.

(a) True
(b) False

25. For a single separately derived system, the grounding electrode conductor connects the grounded conductor of the derived system to the grounding electrode at the same point on the separately derived system where the ______ is connected.

(a) metering equipment
(b) transfer switch
(c) system bonding jumper
(d) largest circuit breaker

26. The grounding electrode conductor for a single separately derived system is used to connect the grounded conductor of the derived system to the grounding electrode.

(a) True
(b) False

27. Grounding electrode conductor taps from a separately derived system to a common grounding electrode conductor are permitted when a building or structure has multiple separately derived systems, provided that the taps terminate at the same point as the system bonding jumper.

(a) True
(b) False

28. The common grounding electrode conductor installed for multiple separately derived systems shall not be smaller than ______ copper when using a wire-type conductor.

(a) 1/0 AWG
(b) 2/0 AWG
(c) 3/0 AWG
(d) 4/0 AWG

29. Each tap conductor to a common grounding electrode conductor for multiple separately derived systems shall be sized in accordance with ______, based on the derived phase conductors of the separately derived system it serves.

(a) 250.66
(b) 250.118
(c) 250.122
(d) 310.15

30. Tap connections to a common grounding electrode conductor for multiple separately derived systems shall be made at an accessible location by ______.

(a) a connector listed as grounding and bonding equipment
(b) listed connections to aluminum or copper busbars
(c) the exothermic welding process
(d) any of these

31. Tap connections to a common grounding electrode conductor for multiple separately derived systems may be made to a copper or aluminum busbar that is ______.

(a) not over ½ in. x 4 in.
(b) not over ¼ in. x 2 in.
(c) at least ¼ in. x 2 in.
(d) a and c

32. In an area served by a separately derived system, the ______ shall be connected to the grounded conductor of the separately derived system.

(a) structural steel
(b) metal piping
(c) metal building skin
(d) a and b

33. A grounding electrode shall be required if a building or structure is supplied by a feeder.

(a) True
(b) False

34. A grounding electrode at a separate building or structure shall be required where one multiwire branch circuit serves the building or structure.

(a) True
(b) False

35. When supplying a grounded system at a separate building or structure, an equipment grounding conductor shall be run with the supply conductors and connected to the building or structure disconnecting means.

(a) True
(b) False

36. For a separate building or structure supplied by a feeder or branch circuit, the neutral conductor can serve as the ground-fault return path for the building/structure disconnecting means for existing installations made in compliance with previous editions of the *Code* where the conditions continue to be met and ______.

(a) there are no continuous metallic paths between buildings and structures
(b) ground-fault protection of equipment isn't installed on the supply side of the circuit
(c) the neutral conductor is sized no smaller than the larger required by 220.61 or 250.122
(d) all of these

37. For a separate building or structure supplied by a separately derived system when overcurrent protection is provided where the conductors originate, the supply conductors must contain ______.

(a) an equipment grounding conductor
(b) a copper conductors only
(c) GFI protection for the feeder
(d) all of these

38. For a separate building or structure supplied by a separately derived system when overcurrent protection isn't provided for the supply conductors to the building/structure as permitted by 240.21(C)(4), the installation must be ______ in accordance with 250.30(A).

(a) AFCI protected
(b) grounded and bonded
(c) isolated
(d) all of these

39. The size of the grounding electrode conductor for a building or structure supplied by a feeder shall not be smaller than that identified in ______, based on the largest ungrounded supply conductor.

(a) Table 250.66
(b) Table 250.122
(c) Table 310.15(B)(16)
(d) none of these

40. The frame of a portable generator shall not be required to be connected to a(n) ______ if the generator only supplies equipment mounted on the generator or cord-and-plug-connected equipment using receptacles mounted on the generator.

(a) grounding electrode
(b) grounded conductor
(c) ungrounded conductor
(d) equipment grounding conductor

41. The frame of a vehicle-mounted generator shall not be required to be connected to a(n) ______ if the generator only supplies equipment mounted on the vehicle or cord-and-plug-connected equipment, using receptacles mounted on the vehicle.

(a) grounding electrode
(b) grounded conductor
(c) ungrounded conductor
(d) equipment grounding conductor

42. When a permanently installed generator ______, the requirements of 250.30 apply.

(a) is a separately derived system
(b) is not a separately derived system
(c) supplies only cord-and-plug-connected loads
(d) none of these

43. High-impedance grounded neutral systems shall be permitted for three-phase ac systems of 480 volts to 1,000 volts where ______.

(a) the conditions of maintenance ensure that only qualified persons service the installation
(b) ground detectors are installed on the system
(c) line-to-neutral loads are not served
(d) all of these

Part III. Grounding Electrode System and Grounding Electrode Conductor

1. Concrete-encased electrodes of ______ shall not be required to be part of the grounding electrode system where the steel reinforcing bars or rods aren't accessible for use without disturbing the concrete.

(a) hazardous (classified) locations
(b) health care facilities
(c) existing buildings or structures
(d) agricultural buildings with equipotential planes

2. In order for a metal underground water pipe to be used as a grounding electrode, it shall be in direct contact with the earth for ______.

(a) 5 ft
(b) 10 ft or more
(c) less than 10 ft
(d) 20 ft or more

3. The metal frame of a building shall be considered a grounding electrode where one of the *NEC*-prescribed methods for connection of the metal frame to earth has been met.

(a) True
(b) False

4. A bare 4 AWG copper conductor installed horizontally near the bottom or vertically, and within that portion of a concrete foundation or footing that is in direct contact with the earth, can be used as a grounding electrode when the conductor is at least ______ in length.

(a) 10 ft
(b) 15 ft
(c) 20 ft
(d) 25 ft

5. An electrode encased by at least 2 in. of concrete, located horizontally near the bottom or vertically and within that portion of a concrete foundation or footing that is in direct contact with the earth, shall be permitted as a grounding electrode when it consists of ______.

(a) at least 20 ft of ½ in. or larger steel reinforcing bars or rods
(b) at least 20 ft of bare copper conductor of 4 AWG or larger
(c) a or b
(d) none of these

6. Reinforcing bars for use as a concrete-encased electrode can be bonded together by the usual steel tie wires or other effective means.

(a) True
(b) False

7. Where more than one concrete-encased electrode is present at a building or structure, it shall be permitted to connect to only one of them.

(a) True
(b) False

8. A ground ring encircling the building or structure can be used as a grounding electrode when the ______.

(a) ring is in direct contact with the earth
(b) ring consists of at least 20 ft of bare conductor
(c) bare copper conductor is not smaller than 2 AWG
(d) all of these

9. Grounding electrodes that are driven rods require a minimum of ______ in contact with the soil.

(a) 6 ft
(b) 8 ft
(c) 10 ft
(d) 12 ft

10. Grounding electrodes of the rod type less than ______ in. in diameter shall be listed.

(a) ½ in.
(b) ⅝ in.
(c) ¾ in.
(d) none of these

11. A buried iron or steel plate used as a grounding electrode shall expose not less than ______ of surface area to exterior soil.

(a) 2 sq ft
(b) 4 sq ft
(c) 9 sq ft
(d) 10 sq ft

12. Local metal underground systems or structures such as ______ are permitted to serve as grounding electrodes.

(a) piping systems
(b) underground tanks
(c) underground metal well casings
(d) any of these

13. _____ shall not be used as grounding electrodes.

(a) Underground gas piping systems
(b) Aluminum
(c) Metal well casings
(d) a and b

14. Where practicable, rod, pipe, and plate electrodes shall be installed _____.

(a) directly below the electrical meter
(b) on the north side of the building
(c) below the permanent moisture level
(d) all of these

15. Where the resistance-to-ground of 25 ohms or less is not achieved for a single rod electrode, _____.

(a) other means besides electrodes shall be used in order to provide grounding
(b) the single rod electrode shall be supplemented by one additional electrode
(c) no additional electrodes are required
(d) none of these

16. Two or more grounding electrodes bonded together are considered a single grounding electrode system.

(a) True
(b) False

17. Where a metal underground water pipe is used as a grounding electrode, the continuity of the grounding path or the bonding connection to interior piping shall not rely on _____ and similar equipment.

(a) bonding jumpers
(b) water meters or filtering devices
(c) grounding clamps
(d) any of these

18. Where the supplemental electrode is a rod, that portion of the bonding jumper that is the sole connection to the supplemental grounding electrode shall not be required to be larger than _____ AWG.

(a) 8
(b) 6
(c) 4
(d) 1

19. When a ground ring is used as a grounding electrode, it shall be buried at a depth below the earth's surface of not less than _____.

(a) 18 in.
(b) 24 in.
(c) 30 in.
(d) 8 ft

20. Ground rod electrodes shall be installed so that at least _____ of the length is in contact with the soil.

(a) 5 ft
(b) 8 ft
(c) one-half
(d) 80 percent

21. The upper end of a ground rod electrode shall be _____ ground level unless the aboveground end and the grounding electrode conductor attachment are protected against physical damage.

(a) above
(b) flush with
(c) below
(d) b or c

22. Where rock bottom is encountered when driving a ground rod at an angle up to 45 degrees, the electrode can be buried in a trench that is at least ______ deep.

(a) 18 in.
(b) 30 in.
(c) 4 ft
(d) 8 ft

23. Auxiliary grounding electrodes can be connected to the ______.

(a) equipment grounding conductor
(b) grounded conductor
(c) a and b
(d) none of these

24. When installing auxiliary electrodes, the earth shall not be used as an effective ground-fault current path.

(a) True
(b) False

25. Buildings or structures supplied by multiple services or feeders must use the same ______ to ground enclosures and equipment in or on that building.

(a) service
(b) disconnect
(c) grounding electrode system
(d) any of these

26. The grounding electrode used for grounding strike termination devices of a lightning protection system can be used as a grounding electrode system for the buildings or structures.

(a) True
(b) False

27. Grounding electrode conductors shall be made of ______ wire.

(a) solid
(b) stranded
(c) insulated or bare
(d) any of these

28. Where used outside, aluminum or copper-clad aluminum grounding electrode conductors shall not be terminated within ______ of the earth.

(a) 6 in.
(b) 12 in.
(c) 15 in.
(d) 18 in.

29. Bare aluminum or copper-clad aluminum grounding electrode conductors shall not be used where in direct contact with ______ or where subject to corrosive conditions.

(a) masonry or the earth
(b) bare copper conductors
(c) wooden framing members
(d) all of these

30. Grounding electrode conductors ______ and larger that are not subject to physical damage can be run exposed along the surface of the building construction.

(a) 10 AWG
(b) 8 AWG
(c) 6 AWG
(d) 4 AWG

31. Grounding electrode conductors smaller than ______ shall be in rigid metal conduit, IMC, PVC conduit, electrical metallic tubing, or cable armor.

(a) 10 AWG
(b) 8 AWG
(c) 6 AWG
(d) 4 AWG

32. Grounding electrode conductors shall be installed in one continuous length without a splice or joint, unless spliced by ______.

(a) connecting together sections of a busbar
(b) irreversible compression-type connectors listed as grounding and bonding equipment
(c) the exothermic welding process
(d) any of these

33. Where service equipment consists of more than one enclosure, grounding electrode connections shall be permitted to be ______.

(a) multiple individual grounding electrode conductors
(b) one grounding electrode conductor at a common location
(c) a common grounding electrode conductor and taps
(d) any of these

34. Ferrous metal enclosures for grounding electrode conductors shall be electrically continuous, from the point of attachment to cabinets or equipment, to the grounding electrode.

(a) True
(b) False

35. A grounding electrode conductor shall be permitted to be run to any convenient grounding electrode available in the grounding electrode system where the other electrodes, if any, are connected by bonding jumpers in accordance with 250.53(C).

(a) True
(b) False

36. A service consisting of 12 AWG service-entrance conductors requires a grounding electrode conductor sized no less than ______.

(a) 10 AWG
(b) 8 AWG
(c) 6 AWG
(d) 4 AWG

37. The largest size grounding electrode conductor required is ______ copper.

(a) 6 AWG
(b) 1/0 AWG
(c) 3/0 AWG
(d) 250 kcmil

38. What size copper grounding electrode conductor is required for a service that has three sets of 600 kcmil copper conductors per phase?

(a) 1 AWG
(b) 1/0 AWG
(c) 2/0 AWG
(d) 3/0 AWG

39. In an ac system, the size of the grounding electrode conductor to a concrete-encased electrode shall not be required to be larger than a(n) ______ copper conductor.

(a) 10 AWG
(b) 8 AWG
(c) 6 AWG
(d) 4 AWG

40. Mechanical elements used to terminate a grounding electrode conductor to a grounding electrode shall be accessible.

(a) True
(b) False

41. Grounding electrode conductor connections to a concrete-encased or buried grounding electrode shall be accessible.

(a) True
(b) False

42. The connection of the grounding electrode conductor to a buried grounding electrode (driven ground rod) shall be made with a listed terminal device that is accessible.

(a) True
(b) False

43. Exothermic or irreversible compression connections, together with the mechanical means used to attach to fireproofed structural metal shall not be required to be accessible.

(a) True
(b) False

44. When an underground metal water piping system is used as a grounding electrode, bonding shall be provided around insulated joints and around any equipment that is likely to be disconnected for repairs or replacement.

(a) True
(b) False

45. Interior metal water piping located more than ______ from the point of entrance to the building shall be permitted to be used as a conductor to interconnect electrodes that are part of the grounding electrode system.

(a) 2 ft
(b) 4 ft
(c) 5 ft
(d) 6 ft

46. Where conditions of maintenance and supervision ensure only qualified persons service the installation in ______ buildings, the entire length of the metal water piping system can be used for grounding purposes, provided the entire length, other than short sections passing through walls, floors, or ceilings, is exposed.

(a) industrial
(b) institutional
(c) commercial
(d) any of these

47. Grounding electrode conductors and grounding electrode bonding jumpers are permitted to terminate to the metal frame of a building/structure that's in direct contact with the earth for 10 ft or more [250.52(A)(2)] or connected to ______.

(a) a concrete-encased electrode or ground ring
(b) a ground rod
(c) another approved earth connection
(d) any of these

48. The grounding conductor connection to the grounding electrode shall be made by ______.

(a) listed lugs
(b) exothermic welding
(c) listed pressure connectors
(d) any of these

Part IV. Grounding Enclosure, Raceway, and Service Cable Connections

1. Metal enclosures and raceways containing service conductors shall be connected to the grounded system conductor if the electrical system is grounded.

   (a) True
   (b) False

2. Metal enclosures and raceways for other than service conductors shall be connected to the neutral conductor.

   (a) True
   (b) False

3. Short sections of metal enclosures or raceways used to provide support or protection of ______ from physical damage shall not be required to be connected to the equipment grounding conductor.

   (a) conduit
   (b) feeders under 600V
   (c) cable assemblies
   (d) none of these

Part V. Bonding

1. Bonding shall be provided where necessary to ensure ______ and the capacity to conduct safely any fault current likely to be imposed.

   (a) electrical continuity
   (b) fiduciary responsibility
   (c) listing requirements
   (d) electrical demand

2. The non-current-carrying metal parts of service equipment, such as ______, shall be bonded together.

   (a) service raceways or service cable armor
   (b) service equipment enclosures containing service conductors, including meter fittings, boxes, or the like, interposed in the service raceway or armor
   (c) service cable trays
   (d) all of these

3. Bonding jumpers for service raceways shall be used around impaired connections such as ______.

   (a) concentric knockouts
   (b) eccentric knockouts
   (c) reducing washers
   (d) any of these

4. Electrical continuity at service equipment, service raceways, and service conductor enclosures shall be ensured by ______.

   (a) bonding equipment to the grounded service conductor
   (b) connections utilizing threaded couplings on enclosures, if made up wrenchtight
   (c) listed bonding devices with bonding jumpers
   (d) any of these

5. Service raceways threaded into metal service equipment such as bosses (hubs) are considered to be effectively ______ to the service metal enclosure.

   (a) attached
   (b) bonded
   (c) grounded
   (d) none of these

6. Service metal raceways and metal-clad cables are considered effectively bonded when using threadless couplings and connectors that are ______.

 (a) nonmetallic
 (b) made up tight
 (c) sealed
 (d) classified

7. A means external to enclosures for connecting intersystem ______ conductors shall be provided at the service equipment or metering equipment enclosure and disconnecting means of buildings or structures supplied by a feeder.

 (a) bonding
 (b) ungrounded
 (c) secondary
 (d) a and b

8. The intersystem bonding termination shall ______.

 (a) be accessible for connection and inspection
 (b) consist of a set of terminals with the capacity for connection of not less than three intersystem bonding conductors
 (c) not interfere with opening the enclosure for a service, building/structure disconnecting means, or metering equipment
 (d) all of these

9. The intersystem bonding termination shall ______.

 (a) be securely mounted and electrically connected to service equipment, the meter enclosure or exposed nonflexible metallic service raceway, or be mounted at one of these enclosures and be connected to the enclosure or grounding electrode conductor with a minimum 6 AWG copper conductor
 (b) be securely mounted to the building/structure disconnecting means, or be mounted at the disconnecting means and be connected to the metallic enclosure or grounding electrode conductor with a minimum 6 AWG copper conductor
 (c) use terminals that are listed as grounding and bonding equipment
 (d) all of these

10. At existing buildings or structures, an intersystem bonding termination is not required if other acceptable means of bonding exist. An external accessible means for bonding communications systems together can be by the use of a ______.

 (a) nonflexible metallic raceway
 (b) grounding electrode conductor
 (c) connection approved by the authority having jurisdiction
 (d) any of these

11. When bonding enclosures, metal raceways, frames, and fittings; any nonconductive paint, enamel, or similar coating shall be removed at ______.

 (a) contact surfaces
 (b) threads
 (c) contact points
 (d) all of these

12. Where installed to reduce electrical noise for electronic equipment, the metal raceway can terminate to a(n) ______ nonmetallic fitting(s) or spacer on the electronic equipment. The metal raceway shall be supplemented by an internal insulated equipment grounding conductor.

    (a) listed
    (b) labeled
    (c) identified
    (d) marked

13. For circuits over 250 volts-to-ground, electrical continuity can be maintained between a box or enclosure where no oversized concentric or eccentric knockouts are encountered, and a metal conduit by ______.

    (a) threadless fittings for cables with metal sheath
    (b) double locknuts on threaded conduit (one inside and one outside the box or enclosure)
    (c) fittings that have shoulders that seat firmly against the box with a locknut on the inside or listed fittings
    (d) any of these

14. Equipment bonding jumpers shall be of copper or other corrosion-resistant material.

    (a) True
    (b) False

15. Equipment bonding jumpers on the supply side of the service shall be no smaller than the sizes shown in ______.

    (a) Table 250.66
    (b) Table 250.122
    (c) Table 310.15(B)(16)
    (d) Table 310.15(B)(6)

16. The supply-side bonding jumper on the supply side of services shall be sized according to the ______.

    (a) overcurrent device rating
    (b) ungrounded supply conductor size
    (c) service-drop size
    (d) load to be served

17. Where ungrounded supply conductors are paralleled in two or more raceways or cables, the bonding jumper for each raceway or cable shall be based on the size of the ______ in each raceway or cable.

    (a) overcurrent protection for conductors
    (b) grounded conductors
    (c) ungrounded supply conductors
    (d) sum of all conductors

18. What is the minimum size copper supply-side bonding jumper for a service raceway containing 4/0 THHN aluminum conductors?

    (a) 6 AWG aluminum
    (b) 4 AWG aluminum
    (c) 4 AWG copper
    (d) 3 AWG copper

19. A service is supplied by three metal raceways, each containing 600 kcmil ungrounded conductors. Determine the copper supply-side bonding jumper size for each service raceway.

    (a) 1/0 AWG
    (b) 3/0 AWG
    (c) 250 kcmil
    (d) 500 kcmil

20. What is the minimum size copper equipment bonding jumper for a circuit rated 40A?

(a) 14 AWG
(b) 12 AWG
(c) 10 AWG
(d) 8 AWG

21. An equipment bonding jumper can be installed on the outside of a raceway, providing the length of the equipment bonding jumper is not more than _____ and the equipment bonding jumper is routed with the raceway.

(a) 12 in.
(b) 24 in.
(c) 36 in.
(d) 72 in.

22. Metal water piping system(s) shall be bonded to the _____.

(a) grounded conductor at the service
(b) service equipment enclosure
(c) equipment grounding bar or bus at any panelboard within a single occupancy building
(d) a or b

23. The bonding jumper used to bond the metal water piping system shall be sized in accordance with _____.

(a) Table 250.66
(b) Table 250.122
(c) Table 310.15(B)(16)
(d) Table 310.15(B)(6)

24. Where isolated metal water piping systems are installed in a multiple-occupancy building, the water pipes can be bonded with bonding jumpers sized in accordance with Table 250.122, based on the size of the _____.

(a) service-entrance conductors
(b) feeder conductors
(c) rating of the service equipment overcurrent device
(d) rating of the overcurrent device supplying the occupancy

25. A building or structure that is supplied by a feeder shall have the interior metal water piping system bonded with a conductor sized in accordance with _____.

(a) Table 250.66
(b) Table 250.122
(c) Table 310.15(B)(16)
(d) none of these

26. Metal gas piping shall be considered bonded by the equipment grounding conductor of the circuit that is likely to energize the piping.

(a) True
(b) False

27. Exposed structural metal interconnected to form a metal building frame that is not intentionally grounded and is likely to become energized, shall be bonded to the _____.

(a) service equipment enclosure or building disconnecting means
(b) grounded conductor at the service
(c) grounding electrode conductor where of sufficient size
(d) any of these

28. Lightning protection system ground terminals ______ be bonded to the building grounding electrode system.

    (a) shall
    (b) shall not
    (c) shall be permitted to
    (d) none of these

Part VI. Equipment Grounding and Equipment Grounding Conductors

1. Exposed non-current-carrying metal parts of fixed equipment likely to become energized shall be connected to the equipment conductor where located ______.

    (a) within 8 ft vertically or 5 ft horizontally of ground or grounded metal objects and subject to contact by persons
    (b) in wet or damp locations and not isolated
    (c) in electrical contact with metal
    (d) any of these

2. Electrical equipment permanently mounted on skids, and the skids themselves, shall be connected to the equipment grounding conductor sized as required by ______.

    (a) 250.50
    (b) 250.66
    (c) 250.122
    (d) 310.15

3. Which of the following appliances installed in residential occupancies need not be connected to an equipment grounding conductor?

    (a) A toaster.
    (b) An aquarium.
    (c) A dishwasher.
    (d) A refrigerator.

4. Listed FMC can be used as the equipment grounding conductor if the length in any ground return path does not exceed 6 ft and the circuit conductors contained in the conduit are protected by overcurrent devices rated at ______ or less.

    (a) 15A
    (b) 20A
    (c) 30A
    (d) 60A

5. Listed FMC and LFMC shall contain an equipment grounding conductor if the raceway is installed for the reason of ______.

    (a) physical protection
    (b) flexibility after installation
    (c) minimizing transmission of vibration from equipment
    (d) b or c

6. The *Code* requires the installation of an equipment grounding conductor of the wire type in ______.

    (a) rigid metal conduit (RMC)
    (b) intermediate metal conduit (IMC)
    (c) electrical metallic tubing (EMT)
    (d) listed flexible metal conduit (FMC) over 6 ft in length

7. Listed liquidtight flexible metal conduit (LFMC) is acceptable as an equipment grounding conductor when it terminates in listed fittings and is protected by an overcurrent device rated 60A or less for trade sizes ⅜ through ½.

    (a) True
    (b) False

8. The armor of Type AC cable containing an aluminum bonding strip is recognized by the *NEC* as an equipment grounding conductor.

    (a) True
    (b) False

9. Type MC cable provides an effective ground-fault current path and is recognized by the *Code* as an equipment grounding conductor when ______.

(a) it contains an insulated or uninsulated equipment grounding conductor in compliance with 250.118(1)
(b) the combined metallic sheath and uninsulated equipment grounding/bonding conductor of interlocked metal tape-type MC cable is listed and identified as an equipment grounding conductor
(c) a or b
(d) it is hospital grade Type MC cable only

10. An equipment grounding conductor shall be identified by ______.

(a) a continuous outer finish that is green
(b) being bare
(c) a continuous outer finish that is green with one or more yellow stripes
(d) any of these

11. Conductors with the color ______ insulation shall not be used for ungrounded or grounded conductors.

(a) green
(b) green with one or more yellow stripes
(c) a or b
(d) white

12. An equipment grounding conductor is permitted to be used as a grounding electrode conductor.

(a) True
(b) False

13. The equipment grounding conductor shall not be required to be larger than the circuit conductors.

(a) True
(b) False

14. When ungrounded circuit conductors are increased in size, the equipment grounding conductor must be proportionately increased in size according to the ______ of the ungrounded conductors.

(a) ampacity
(b) circular mil area
(c) diameter
(d) none of these

15. When a single equipment grounding conductor is used for multiple circuits in the same raceway, cable or cable tray, the single equipment grounding conductor shall be sized according to the ______.

(a) combined rating of all the overcurrent devices
(b) largest overcurrent device of the multiple circuits
(c) combined rating of all the loads
(d) any of these

16. Equipment grounding conductors for motor branch circuits shall be sized in accordance with Table 250.122, based on the rating of the ______ device.

(a) motor overload
(b) motor over-temperature
(c) motor short-circuit and ground-fault protective
(d) feeder overcurrent protection

17. Where conductors are run in parallel in multiple raceways or cables and include an EGC of the wire type, the equipment grounding conductor must be installed with each parallel conductor, sized in accordance with 250.122.

(a) True
(b) False

18. Equipment grounding conductors for feeder taps are not required to be larger than the tap conductors.

(a) True
(b) False

19. The terminal of a wiring device for the connection of the equipment grounding conductor shall be identified by a green-colored, ______.

    (a) not readily removable terminal screw with a hexagonal head
    (b) hexagonal, not readily removable terminal nut
    (c) pressure wire connector
    (d) any of these

Part VII. Methods of Equipment Grounding

1. The structural metal frame of a building can be used as the required circuit equipment grounding conductor.

    (a) True
    (b) False

2. Metal parts of cord-and-plug-connected equipment shall be connected to an equipment grounding conductor that terminates to a grounding-type attachment plug.

    (a) True
    (b) False

3. A grounded circuit conductor is permitted to ground non-current-carrying metal parts of equipment, raceways, and other enclosures on the supply side or within the enclosure of the ac service disconnecting means.

    (a) True
    (b) False

4. It shall be permissible to ground meter enclosures located near the service disconnecting means to the ______ circuit conductor on the load side of the service disconnect, if service ground-fault protection is not provided.

    (a) grounding
    (b) bonding
    (c) grounded
    (d) phase

5. A(n) ______ shall be used to connect the grounding terminal of a grounding-type receptacle to a grounded box.

    (a) equipment bonding jumper
    (b) grounded conductor jumper
    (c) a or b
    (d) a and b

6. Where the box is mounted on the surface, direct metal-to-metal contact between the device yoke and the box shall be permitted to ground the receptacle to the box if at least ______ of the insulating washers of the receptacle is(are) removed.

    (a) one
    (b) two
    (c) three
    (d) four

7. A listed exposed work cover can be the grounding and bonding means when the device is attached to the cover with at least ______ fastener(s) and the cover-mounting holes are located on a non-raised portion of the cover.

    (a) one
    (b) two
    (c) three
    (d) four

8. Receptacle yokes designed and ______ as self-grounding can establish the grounding circuit between the device yoke and a grounded outlet box.

    (a) approved
    (b) advertised
    (c) listed
    (d) installed

9. The receptacle grounding terminal of an isolated ground receptacle shall be connected to a(n) _____ equipment grounding conductor run with the circuit conductors.

   (a) insulated
   (b) covered
   (c) bare
   (d) solid

10. Where circuit conductors are spliced or terminated on equipment within a box, any equipment grounding conductors associated with those circuit conductors shall be connected to the box with devices suitable for the use.

   (a) True
   (b) False

11. The arrangement of grounding connections shall be such that the disconnection or the removal of a receptacle, luminaire, or other device does not interrupt the grounding continuity.

   (a) True
   (b) False

12. A connection between equipment grounding conductors and a metal box shall be by _____.

   (a) a grounding screw used for no other purpose
   (b) equipment listed for grounding
   (c) a listed grounding device
   (d) any of these

CHAPTER

3

WIRING METHODS AND MATERIALS

INTRODUCTION TO CHAPTER 3—WIRING METHODS AND MATERIALS

Chapter 3 covers wiring methods and materials, and provides some very specific installation requirements for conductors, cables, boxes, raceways, and fittings. This chapter includes detailed information about the installation and restrictions involved with wiring methods.

Wiring Method Articles

- **Article 300—Wiring Methods.** Article 300 contains the general requirements for all wiring methods included in the *NEC*, except for signaling and communications systems, which are covered in Chapters 7 and 8.
- **Article 314—Outlet, Device, Pull and Junction Boxes; Conduit Bodies; Fittings; and Handhole Enclosures.** Installation requirements for outlet boxes, pull and junction boxes, as well as conduit bodies, and handhole enclosures are contained in this article.

Cable Tray

- **Article 392—Cable Trays.** A cable tray system is a unit or assembly of units or sections with associated fittings that form a structural system used to securely fasten or support cables and raceways. A cable tray isn't a raceway; it's a support system for raceways, cables, and enclosures.

Notes

Wiring Methods

INTRODUCTION TO ARTICLE 300—WIRING METHODS

Article 300 contains the general requirements for all wiring methods included in the *NEC.* However, it doesn't apply to communications systems, which are covered in Chapter 8, except when Article 300 is specifically referenced in Chapter 8.

This article is primarily concerned with how to install, route, splice, protect, and secure conductors and raceways. How well you conform to the requirements of Article 300 will generally be evident in the finished work, because many of the requirements tend to determine the appearance of the installation. Because of this, it's often easy to spot Article 300 problems if you're looking for *Code* violations. For example, you can easily see when someone runs an equipment grounding conductor outside a raceway instead of grouping all conductors of a circuit together, as required by 300.3(B).

A good understanding of Article 300 will start you on the path to correctly installing the wiring methods included in Chapter 3. Be sure to carefully consider the accompanying illustrations, and refer to the definitions in Article 100 as needed.

300.3 Conductors.

(B) Circuit Conductors Grouped Together. All conductors of a circuit must be installed in the same raceway, cable, trench, cord, or cable tray. **Figure 300–1**

Circuit Conductors Grouped Together
300.3(B)
VIOLATION
Copyright 2011, www.MikeHolt.com
All conductors of a circuit must be installed in the same raceway, cable, trench, cord, or cable tray to minimize induction heating of metallic raceways and enclosures, and to maintain a low-impedance ground-fault current path.

Figure 300–1

Author's Comment: All conductors of a circuit must be installed in the same raceway, cable, trench, cord, or cable tray to minimize the induction heating of ferrous metal raceways and enclosures, and to maintain a low-impedance ground-fault current path [250.4(A)(3)].

300.10 Electrical Continuity. Metal raceways, cables, boxes, fittings, cabinets, and enclosures for conductors must be metallically joined together to form a continuous, low-impedance fault current path capable of carrying any fault current likely to be imposed on it [110.10, 250.4(A)(3), and 250.122]. **Figure 300–2**

Metal raceways and cable assemblies must be mechanically secured to boxes, fittings, cabinets, and other enclosures.

Ex 1: Short lengths of metal raceways used for the support or protection of cables aren't required to be electrically continuous, nor are they required to be connected to an equipment grounding conductor of a type recognized in 250.118 [250.86 Ex 2 and 300.12 Ex]. **Figure 300–3**

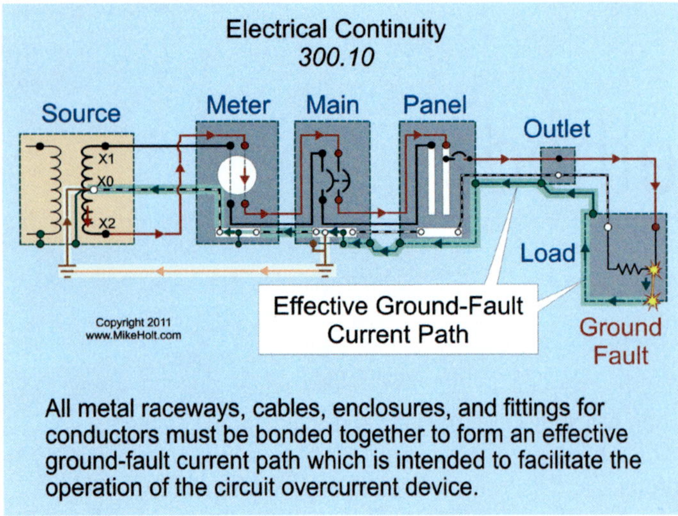

Figure 300–2

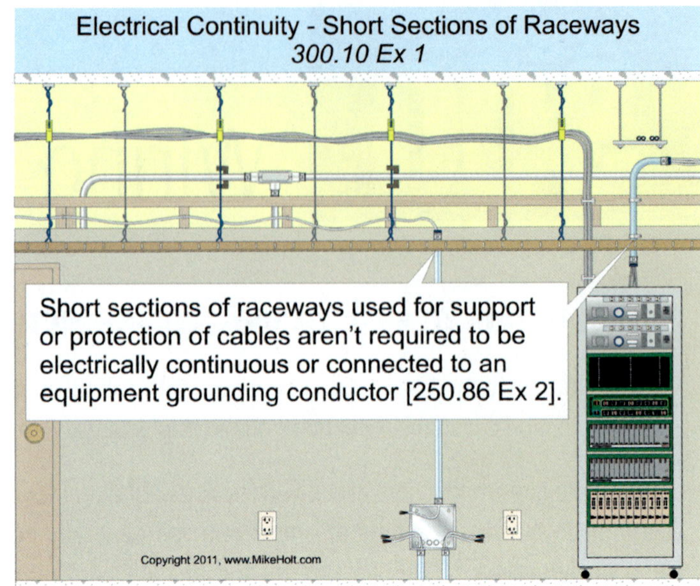

Figure 300–3

Outlet, Device, Pull and Junction Boxes; Conduit Bodies; and Handhole Enclosures

INTRODUCTION TO ARTICLE 314—OUTLET, DEVICE, PULL AND JUNCTION BOXES; CONDUIT BODIES; AND HANDHOLE ENCLOSURES

Article 314 contains installation requirements for outlet boxes, pull and junction boxes, conduit bodies, and handhole enclosures.

This article provides guidance for selecting and installing outlet, and device boxes, pull and junction boxes, conduit bodies, and handhole enclosures. Information in Article 314 will help you size an outlet box using the proper cubic-inch capacity as well as calculating the minimum dimensions for larger pull boxes. There are limits on the amount of weight that can be supported by an outlet box and rules on how to support a device or outlet box to various surfaces. This article will help you understand these types of rules so that your installation will be compliant with the *NEC.* As always, the clear illustrations in this unit will help you visualize the finished installation.

PART I. SCOPE AND GENERAL

314.1 Scope. Article 314 contains the installation requirements for outlet boxes, conduit bodies, pull and junction boxes, and handhole enclosures. Figure 314–1

Outlet Boxes, Conduit Bodies, Pull/Junction Boxes, and Handhole Enclosures
314.1

Outlet Boxes
Junction Box
Conduit Body
Handhole Enclosure
Copyright 2011
www.MikeHolt.com

Article 314 contains the installation requirements for outlet boxes, conduit bodies, pull and junction boxes, and handhole enclosures.

Figure 314–1

314.3 Nonmetallic Boxes. Nonmetallic boxes can only be used with nonmetallic cables and raceways because there's no way to maintain the electrical continuity of the effective ground-fault current path [250.2 and 250.4(A)(3)].

Ex 1: Metal raceways and metal cables can be used with nonmetallic boxes, but only if an internal bonding means is provided in the box between all metal entries.

314.4 Metal Boxes. Metal boxes containing circuits that operate at 50V or more must be connected to an equipment grounding conductor of a type listed in 250.118 [250.112(I)]. Figure 314–2

PART II. INSTALLATION

314.25 Covers and Canopies. When the installation is complete, each outlet box must be provided with a cover or faceplate, unless covered by a fixture canopy, lampholder, or similar device. Figure 314–3

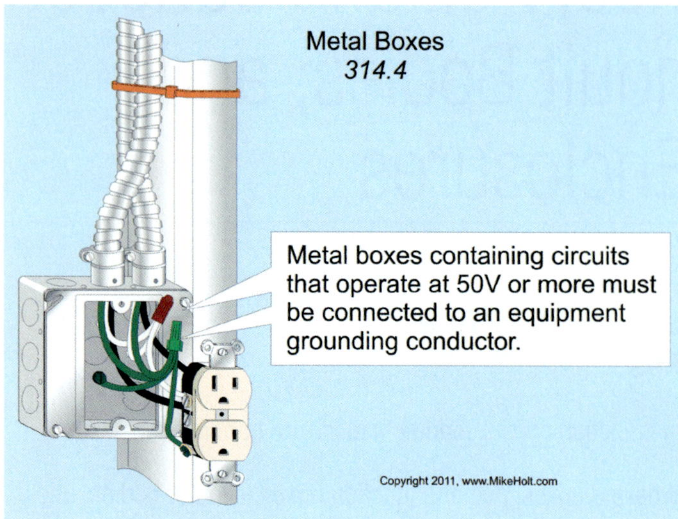

Figure 314–2

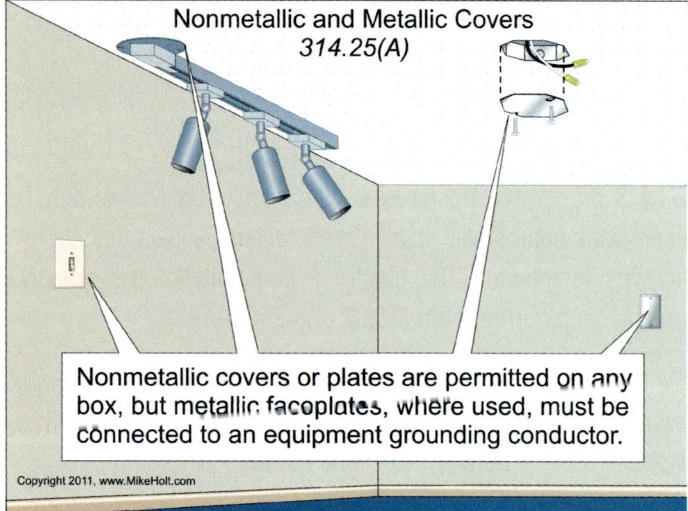

Figure 314–3

(A) Nonmetallic or Metallic. Nonmetallic covers are permitted on any box, but metal covers are only permitted if they can be connected to an equipment grounding conductor of a type recognized in 250.118, in accordance with 250.110 [250.4(A)(3)].

> **Author's Comment:** Metal switch faceplates [404.9(B)] and metal receptacle faceplates [406.6(A)] must be connected to an equipment grounding conductor.

314.28 Boxes and Conduit Bodies for Conductors 4 AWG and Larger. Boxes and conduit bodies containing conductors 4 AWG and larger that are required to be insulated must be sized so the conductor insulation won't be damaged.

Author's Comments:

- The requirements for sizing boxes and conduit bodies containing conductors 6 AWG and smaller are contained in 314.16.
- If conductors 4 AWG and larger enter a box or other enclosure, a fitting that provides a smooth, rounded, insulating surface, such as a bushing or adapter, is required to protect the conductors from abrasion during and after installation [300.4(G)].

(C) Covers. Pull boxes, junction boxes, and conduit bodies must have a cover suitable for the conditions. Nonmetallic covers are permitted on any box, but metal covers are only permitted if they can be connected to an equipment grounding conductor of a type recognized in 250.118, in accordance with 250.110 [250.4(A)(3)]. Figure 314–4

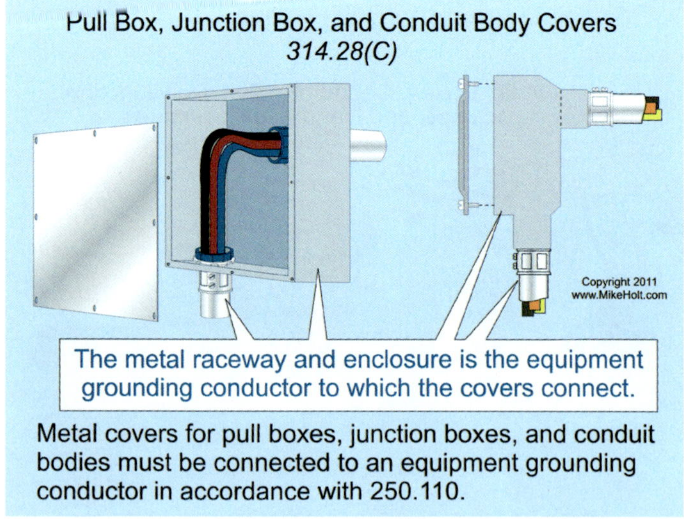

Figure 314–4

PART III. CONSTRUCTION SPECIFICATIONS

314.30 Handhole Enclosures. Handhole enclosures must be identified for underground use, and be designed and installed to withstand all loads likely to be imposed on them. Figure 314–5

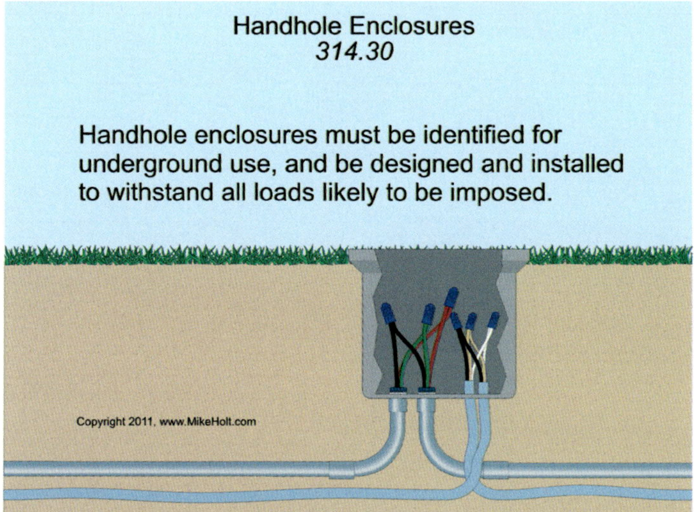

Figure 314–5

(D) Covers. Handhole enclosure covers must have an identifying mark or logo that prominently identifies the function of the enclosure, such as "electric." Handhole enclosure covers must require the use of tools to open, or they must weigh over 100 lb.

Metal covers and other exposed conductive surfaces of handhole enclosures must be connected to an equipment grounding conductor sized to the overcurrent device in accordance with 250.122. Metal covers of handhole enclosures containing service conductors must be connected to an equipment bonding jumper sized in accordance with Table 250.66 [250.92 and 250.102(C)]. Figure 314–6

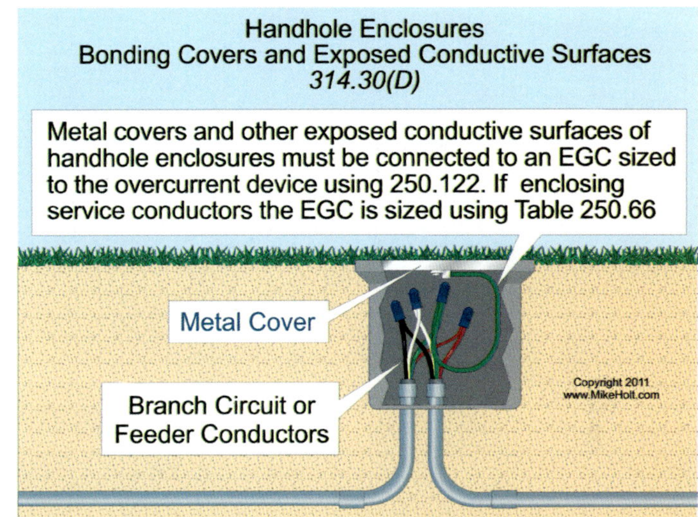

Figure 314–6

Notes

Cable Trays

INTRODUCTION TO ARTICLE 392—CABLE TRAYS

A cable tray system is a unit or an assembly of units or sections with associated fittings that forms a structural system used to securely fasten or support cables and raceways. Cable tray systems include ladder, ventilated trough, ventilated channel, solid bottom, and other similar structures. Cable trays are manufactured in many forms, from a simple hanger or wire mesh to a substantial, rigid, steel support system. Cable trays are designed and manufactured to support specific wiring methods, as identified in 392.10(A).

PART I. GENERAL

392.1 Scope. Article 392 covers cable tray systems, including ladder, ventilated trough, ventilated channel, solid bottom, and other similar structures.

392.2 Definition.

Cable Tray System. A unit or assembly of units or sections with associated fittings forming a rigid structural system used to securely fasten or support cables, raceways, and boxes.

> **Author's Comment:** Cable tray isn't a type of raceway. It's a support system for cables and raceways.

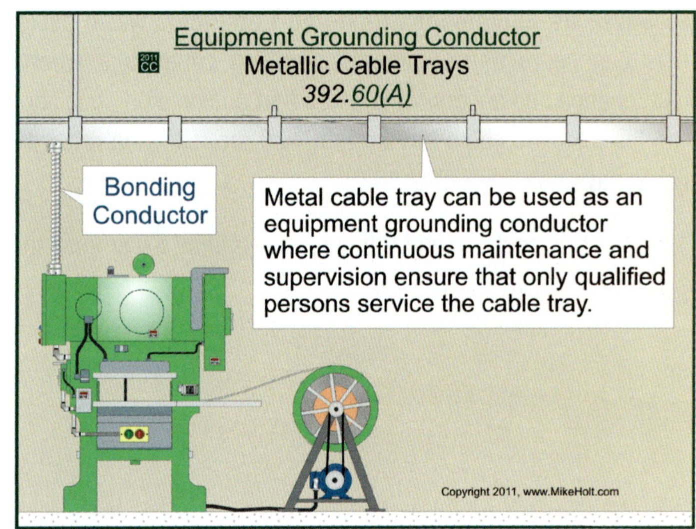

Figure 392–1.

PART II. INSTALLATION

392.60 Equipment Grounding Conductor.

(A) Metallic Cable Trays. Metallic cable trays can be used as equipment grounding conductors where continuous maintenance and supervision ensure that qualified persons service the installed cable tray system, **Figure 392–1**. The metallic cable trays that support conductors must be bonded together to ensure that they have the capacity to conduct safely any fault current likely to be imposed in accordance with 250.96(A).

Metal cable trays containing communications, data, and signaling conductors and cables must be electrically continuous through listed connections, or the use of an insulated stranded bonding jumper not smaller than 10 AWG. **Figure 392–2**

> **Author's Comment:** Nonconductive coatings such as paint, lacquer, and enamel on equipment must be removed to ensure an effective ground-fault current path, or the termination fittings must be designed so as to make such removal unnecessary [250.12].

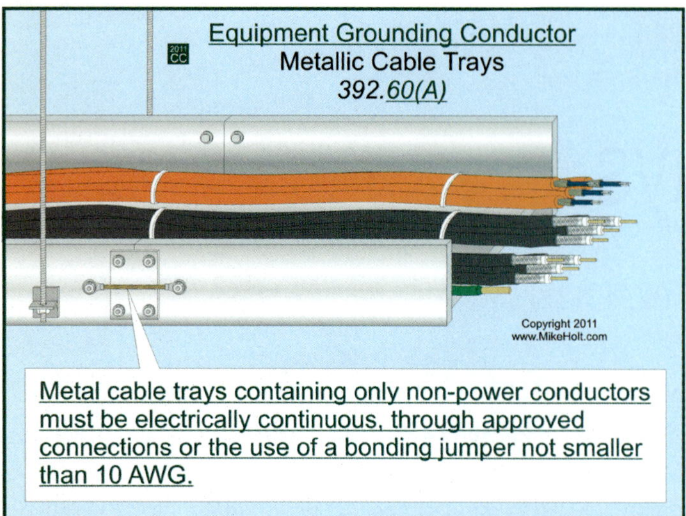

Figure 392–2

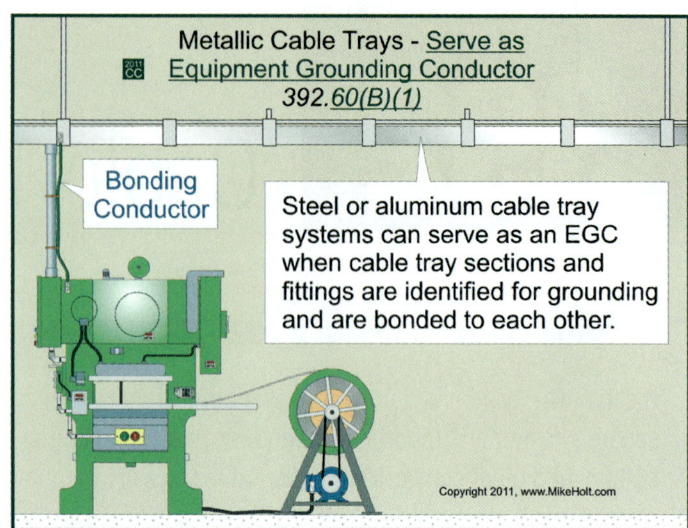

Figure 392–3

(B) Serve as Equipment Grounding Conductor. Metal cable trays can serve as equipment grounding conductors where maintenance and supervision ensure that qualified persons service the installed cable tray system, and the following requirements have been met [392.10(C)]:

(1) Cable tray sections and fittings are identified for grounding. Figure 392–3

> **Author's Comment:** Identification will be marked on each cable tray section.

(4) Cable tray sections, fittings, and connected raceways are effectively bonded to each other to ensure electrical continuity and the capacity to conduct safely any fault current likely to be imposed on them [250.96(A)]. This is accomplished by using bolted mechanical connectors or bonding jumpers sized in accordance with 250.102.

CHAPTER 3

Practice Questions

CHAPTER 3. WIRING METHODS AND MATERIALS—PRACTICE QUESTIONS

Article 300. Wiring Methods

1. All conductors of a circuit must be installed in the same raceway, cable, trench, cord, or cable tray.

   (a) True
   (b) False

2. Metal ______ for conductors must be metallically joined together to form a continuous, low-impedance fault current path capable of carrying any fault current likely to be imposed on it.

   (a) raceways and cable armor
   (b boxes and enclosures
   (c) cabinets
   (d) all of these

3. Metal raceways and cable assemblies must be mechanically secured to boxes, fittings, cabinets, and other enclosures.

   (a) raceways
   (b) cable assemblies
   (c) a or b
   (d) a and b

4. Short lengths of metal raceways used for the support or protection of cables aren't required to be electrically continuous, nor are they required to be connected to an equipment grounding conductor of a type recognized in 250.118.

   (a) True
   (b) False

Article 314. Outlet, Device, Pull and Junction Boxes; Conduit Bodies; Fittings; and Handhole Enclosures

1. Nonmetallic boxes can be used with ______.

   (a) nonmetallic cables
   (b) nonmetallic raceways
   (c) flexible cords
   (d) all of these

2. Metal boxes shall be ______ in accordance with Article 250.

   (a) grounded
   (b) bonded
   (c) a and b
   (d) none of these

3. In completed installations, each outlet box shall have a ______.

   (a) cover
   (b) faceplate
   (c) canopy
   (d) any of these

4. Handhole enclosure covers shall have an identifying ______ that prominently identifies the function of the enclosure, such as "electric."

   (a) mark
   (b) logo
   (c) a or b
   (d) manual

5. Handhole enclosure covers shall require the use of tools to open, or they shall weigh over ______.

(a) 45 lb
(b) 70 lb
(c) 100 lb
(d) 200 lb

Article 392. Cable Trays

1. A cable tray is a unit or assembly of units or sections and associated fittings forming a ______ system used to securely fasten or support cables and raceways.

(a) structural
(b) flexible
(c) movable
(d) secure

2. Cable trays can be used as a support system for ______.

(a) service conductors, feeders, and branch circuits
(b) communications circuits
(c) control and signaling circuits
(d) all of these

3. Cable trays and their associated fittings shall be ______ for the intended use.

(a) listed
(b) approved
(c) identified
(d) none of these

4. Metal cable trays containing only nonpower conductors such as communications, data, or signal conductors and cables must be electrically continuous, through listed connections or the use of an insulated stranded bonding jumper not smaller than ______.

(a) 12 AWG
(b) 10 AWG
(c) 6 AWG
(d) 4 AWG

5. Steel or aluminum cable tray systems shall be permitted to be used as an equipment grounding conductor, provided the cable tray sections and fittings are identified for ______, among other requirements

(a) equipment grounding
(b) special use
(c) industrial occupancies
(d) all of these

EQUIPMENT FOR GENERAL USE

INTRODUCTION TO CHAPTER 4—EQUIPMENT FOR GENERAL USE

With the first three chapters behind you, the final chapter in the *NEC* for building a solid foundation in general work is Chapter 4. This chapter helps you apply the first three chapters to installations involving general equipment. These first four chapters follow a natural sequential progression. Each of the next four *Code* Chapters—5, 6, 7, and 8—build upon the first four, but in no particular order. You need to understand all of the first four chapters to properly apply any of the next four.

- **Article 404—Switches.** The requirements of Article 404 apply to switches of all types. These include snap (toggle) switches, dimmer switches, fan switches, knife switches, circuit breakers used as switches, and automatic switches such as time clocks, timers, and switches and circuit breakers used for disconnecting means.
- **Article 406—Receptacles, Cord Connectors, and Attachment Plugs (Caps).** This article covers the rating, type, and installation of receptacles, cord connectors, and attachment plugs (cord caps). It also covers flanged surface inlets.
- **Article 408—Switchboards and Panelboards.** Article 408 covers specific requirements for switchboards, panelboards, and distribution boards that supply lighting and power circuits.
- **Article 410—Luminaires, Lampholders, and Lamps.** This article contains the requirements for luminaires, lampholders, and lamps. Because of the many types and applications of luminaires, manufacturer's instructions are very important and helpful for proper installation. Underwriters Laboratories produces a pamphlet called the *Luminaire Marking Guide*, which provides information for properly installing common types of incandescent, fluorescent, and high-intensity discharge (HID) luminaires.

Notes

Switches

INTRODUCTION TO ARTICLE 404—SWITCHES

The requirements of Article 404 apply to switches of all types, including snap (toggle) switches, dimmer switches, fan switches, knife switches, circuit breakers used as switches, and automatic switches, such as time clocks and timers.

404.1 Scope. The requirements of Article 404 apply to all types of switches, switching devices, and circuit breakers used as switches. Figure 404–1

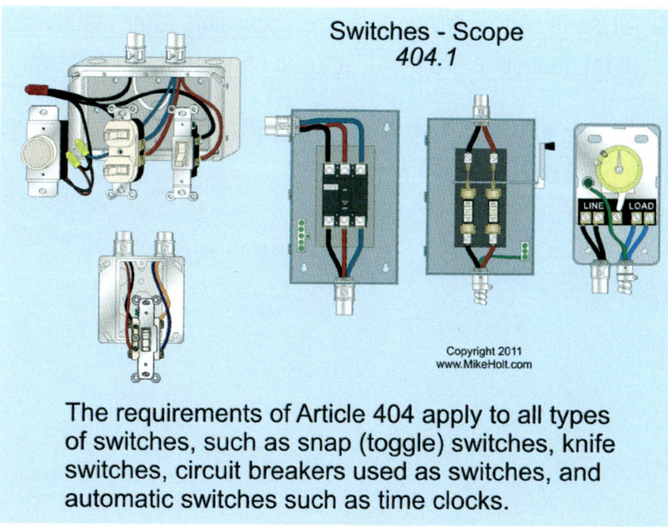

Figure 404–1

404.9 Switch Faceplates.

(A) Mounting. Faceplates for switches must be installed so they completely cover the outlet box opening and, where flush mounted, the faceplate must seat against the wall surface.

(B) Grounding. The metal mounting yokes for switches, dimmers, and similar control switches must be connected to an equipment grounding conductor of a type recognized in 250.118, whether or not a metal faceplate is installed. The metal mounting yoke is considered part of the effective ground-fault current path [250.2] by the use of one of the following means:

(1) Mounting Screw. The switch is mounted with metal screws to a metal box or a metal cover that's connected to an equipment grounding conductor of a type recognized in 250.118. Figure 404–2

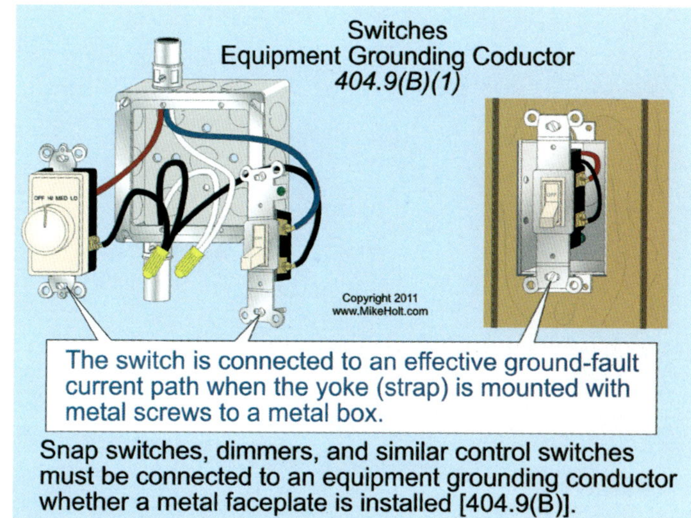

Figure 404–2

Author's Comment: Direct metal-to-metal contact between the device yoke of a switch and the box isn't required.

(2) Equipment Grounding Conductor. An equipment grounding conductor or equipment bonding jumper is connected to the grounding terminal of the metal mounting yoke. **Figure 404–3**

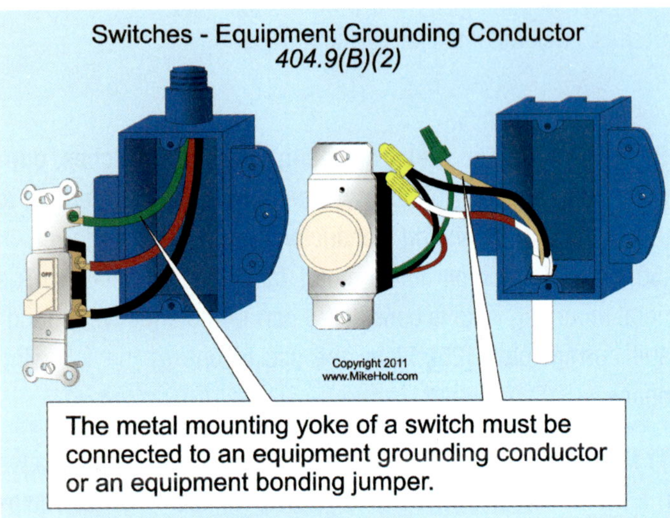

Figure 404–3

Ex 1: The metal mounting yoke of a replacement switch isn't required to be connected to an equipment grounding conductor if the wiring at the existing switch doesn't contain an equipment grounding conductor, and the switch faceplate is nonmetallic with nonmetallic screws, or the replacement switch is GFCI protected.

Ex 2: Listed assemblies aren't required to be connected to an equipment grounding conductor if all of the following conditions are met:

(1) The device is provided with a nonmetallic faceplate that can't be installed on any other type of device,

(2) The device doesn't have mounting means to accept other configurations of faceplates,

(3) The device is equipped with a nonmetallic yoke, and

(4) All parts of the device that are accessible after installation of the faceplate are manufactured of nonmetallic material.

Ex 3: A snap switch with an integral nonmetallic enclosure complying with 300.15(E).

Receptacles, Cord Connectors, and Attachment Plugs (Caps)

INTRODUCTION TO ARTICLE 406—RECEPTACLES, CORD CONNECTORS, AND ATTACHMENT PLUGS (CAPS)

This article covers the rating, type, and installation of receptacles, cord connectors, and attachment plugs (cord caps). It also addresses their grounding requirements. Some key points to remember include:

- Follow the grounding requirements of the specific type of device you're using.
- Provide GFCI protection where specified by 406.4(D)(3).
- Mount receptacles according to the requirements of 406.5 which are highly detailed.

406.1 Scope. Article 406 covers the rating, type, and installation of receptacles, cord connectors, and attachment plugs (cord caps).

Author's Comment: See 250.146 for the specific requirements on connecting the grounding terminals of receptacles to the circuit equipment grounding conductor. **Figure 406–1**

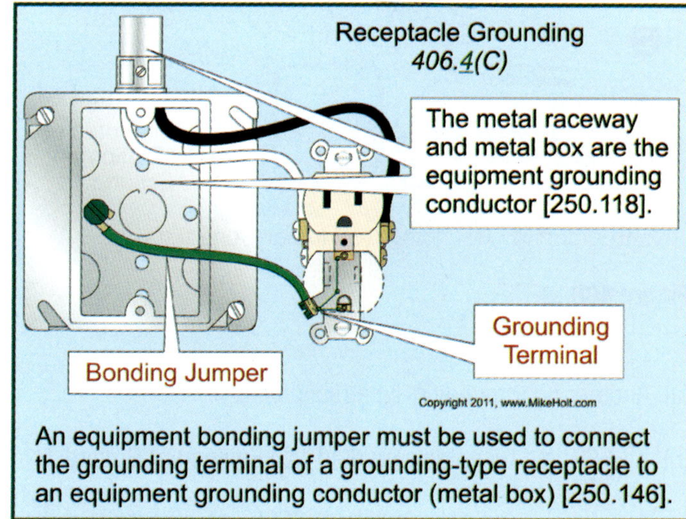

Figure 406–1

406.4 General Installation Requirements.

(A) Grounding Type. Receptacles installed on 15A and 20A branch circuits must be of the grounding type.

Ex: Nongrounding-type receptacles are permitted for replacement in an existing outlet box if no equipment grounding conductor exists in the outlet box, in accordance with 406.5(D).

(B) To be Grounded. Receptacles of the grounding type must have an equipment grounding conductor contact, and must have that contact connected to an equipment grounding conductor in accordance with 250.146 and 406.4(C).

Ex 2: Replacement receptacles aren't required to have their grounding contacts connected to an equipment grounding conductor if the receptacles are GFCI protected and installed in accordance with 406.4(D).

(C) Methods of Equipment Grounding. The grounding terminals for receptacles must be connected to an equipment grounding conductor supplied with the branch-circuit wiring.

(D) Receptacle Replacement.

(1) Grounding-Type Receptacles. If an equipment grounding conductor exists, grounding-type receptacles must replace nongrounding-type receptacles, and the receptacle's grounding terminal must be connected to an equipment grounding conductor in accordance with 406.4(C) or 250.130(C).

(2) Nongrounding-Type Receptacles. If no equipment grounding conductor exists in the outlet box for the receptacle, such as old 2-wire Type NM cable without an equipment grounding conductor, existing nongrounding-type receptacles can be replaced in accordance with (a), (b), or (c): **Figure 406–2**

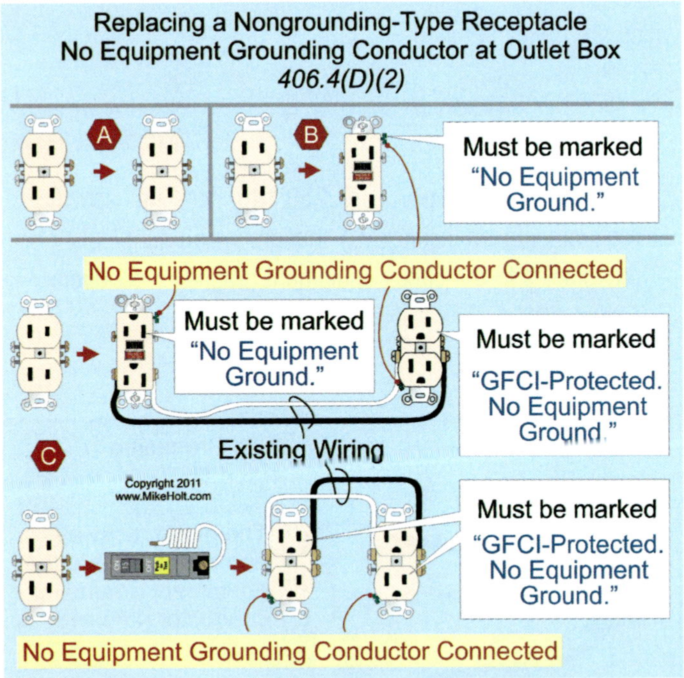

Figure 406–2

(a) Another nongrounding-type receptacle.

(b) A GFCI-type receptacle marked "No Equipment Ground."

(c) A grounding-type receptacle, if GFCI protected and marked "GFCI Protected" and "No Equipment Ground."

Author's Comment: GFCI protection functions properly on a 2-wire circuit without an equipment grounding conductor because the circuit equipment grounding conductor serves no role in the operation of the GFCI-protection device. See the definition of "Ground-Fault Circuit Interrupter" for more information. **Figure 406–3**

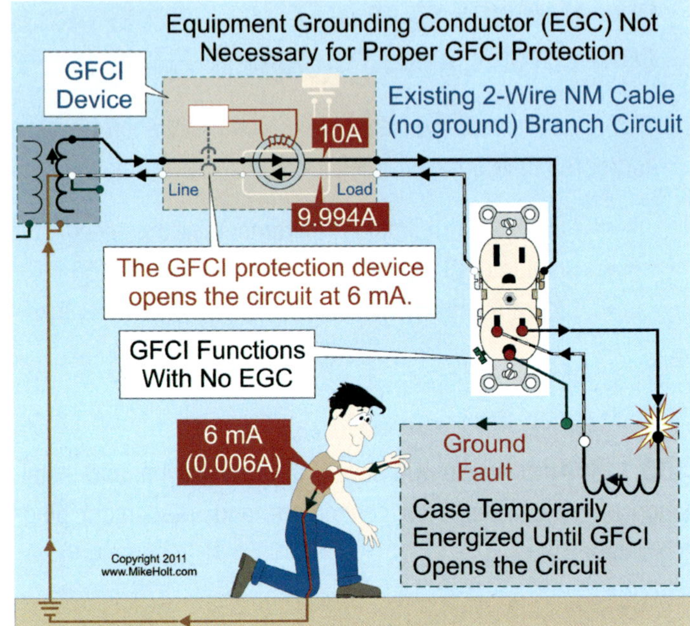

Figure 406–3

CAUTION: *The permission to replace nongrounding-type receptacles with GFCI-protected grounding-type receptacles doesn't apply to new receptacle outlets that extend from an existing outlet box that's not connected to an equipment grounding conductor. Once you add a receptacle outlet (branch-circuit extension), the receptacle must be of the grounding type and it must have its grounding terminal connected to an equipment grounding conductor of a type recognized in 250.118, in accordance with 250.130(C).* **Figure 406–4**

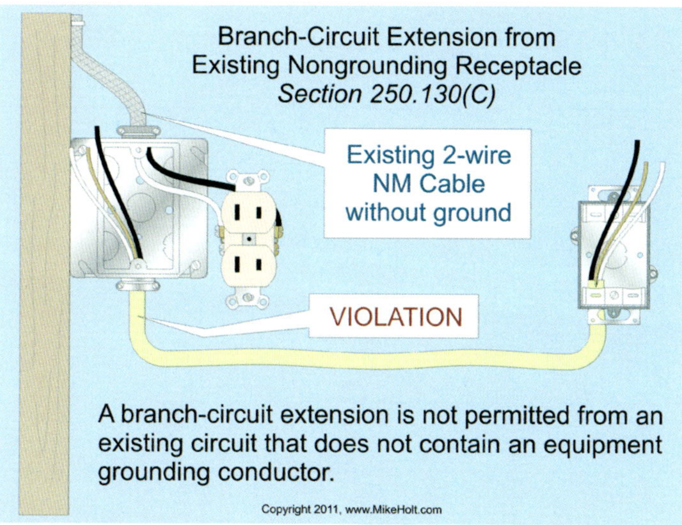

Figure 250–4

406.6 Receptacle Faceplates. Faceplates for receptacles must completely cover the outlet openings.

(B) Grounding. Metal faceplates for receptacles must be connected to the circuit equipment grounding conductor.

> **Author's Comment:** The *NEC* doesn't specify how this is accomplished, but 517.13(B) Ex 1 for health care facilities permits the metal mounting screw(s) securing the faceplate to a metal outlet box or wiring device to be suitable for this purpose. Figure 406–5

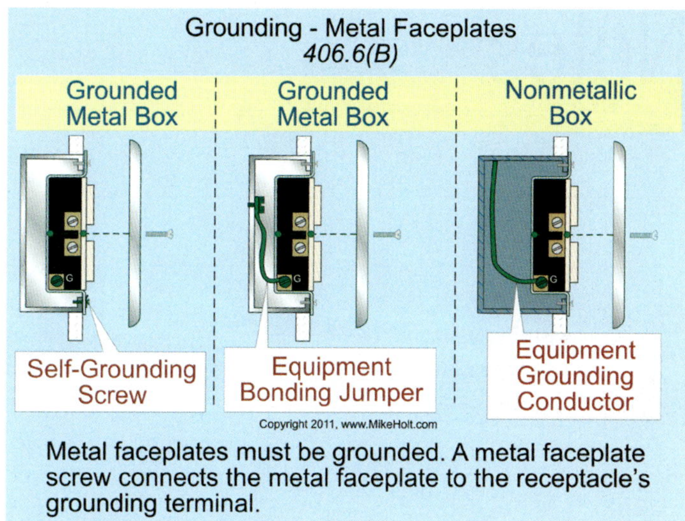

Figure 406–5

406.11 Connecting Receptacle Grounding Terminal to Equipment Grounding Conductor. The grounding terminal of receptacles must be connected to an equipment grounding conductor in accordance with 250.146.

Notes

Switchboards and Panelboards

INTRODUCTION TO ARTICLE 408—SWITCHBOARDS AND PANELBOARDS

Article 408 covers the specific requirements for switchboards and panelboards that control power and lighting circuits. Some key points to remember:

- One objective of Article 408 is that the installation prevents contact between current-carrying conductors and people or equipment.
- The circuit directory of a panelboard must clearly identify the purpose or use of each circuit that originates in the panelboard.
- You must understand the detailed grounding and overcurrent protection requirements for panelboards.

PART I. GENERAL

408.1 Scope. Article 408 covers the specific requirements for switchboards and panelboards that control power and lighting circuits. Figure 408–1

Switchboards and Panelboards
408.1

Article 408 contains the requirements for switchboards, and panelboards for light and power.

Figure 408–1

Author's Comment: For the purposes of this textbook, we'll only cover the requirements for panelboards.

PART III. PANELBOARDS

408.40 Equipment Grounding Conductor. Metal panelboard cabinets and frames must be connected to an equipment grounding conductor of a type recognized in 250.118 [215.6 and 250.4(A)(3)].

If the panelboard cabinet is used with nonmetallic raceways or cables, or where separate equipment grounding conductors are provided, a terminal bar for the circuit equipment grounding conductors must be bonded to the metal cabinet. Figure 408–2

Ex: Insulated equipment grounding conductors for receptacles having insulated grounding terminals (isolated ground receptacles) [250.146(D)] can pass through the panelboard without terminating onto the equipment grounding terminal of the panelboard cabinet. Figure 408–3

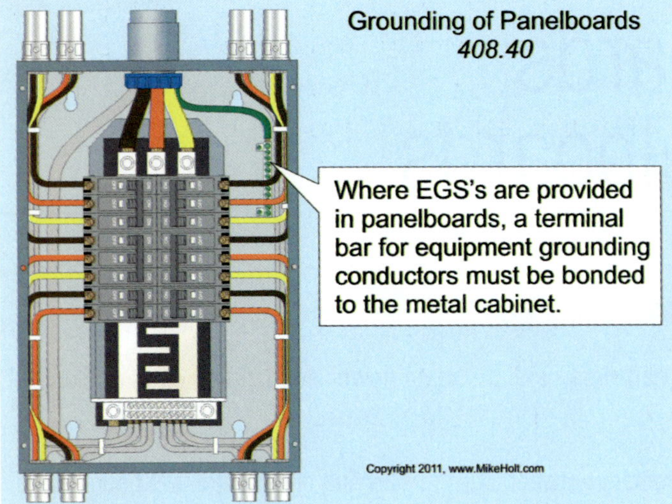

Figure 408–2

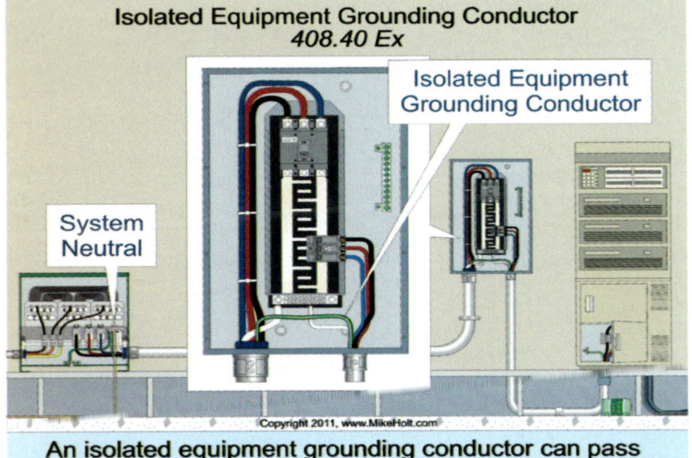

An isolated equipment grounding conductor can pass through a metal enclosure, but it must terminate to the system neutral.

Figure 408–3

Equipment grounding conductors must not terminate on the neutral terminal bar, and neutral conductors must not terminate on the equipment grounding terminal bar, except as permitted by 250.142 for services and separately derived systems. **Figure 408–4**

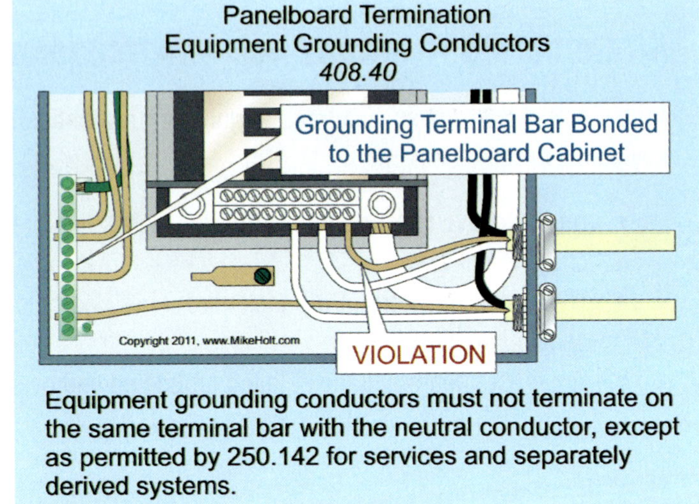

Equipment grounding conductors must not terminate on the same terminal bar with the neutral conductor, except as permitted by 250.142 for services and separately derived systems.

Figure 408–4

Author's Comment: See the definition of "Separately Derived System" in Article 100.

CAUTION: *Most panelboards are rated as suitable for use as service equipment, which means they're supplied with a main bonding jumper [250.28]. This screw or strap must not be installed except when the panelboard is used for service equipment [250.24(A)(5)] or for a separately derived system [250.30(A)(1)]. In addition, a panelboard marked "suitable only for use as service equipment" means the neutral bar or terminal of the panelboard has been bonded to the case at the factory, and this panelboard is restricted to being used only for service equipment or on separately derived systems according to 250.142(B).*

ARTICLE 410 Luminaires, Lampholders, and Lamps

INTRODUCTION TO ARTICLE 410—LUMINAIRES, LAMPHOLDERS, AND LAMPS

This article covers luminaires, lampholders, lamps, decorative lighting products, lighting accessories for temporary seasonal and holiday use, including portable flexible lighting products, and the wiring and equipment of such products and lighting installations. Even though Article 410 is highly detailed, it's broken down into 16 parts. The first five are sequential, and apply to all luminaires, lampholders, and lamps:

- General, Part I
- Location, Part II
- Boxes and Covers, Part III
- Supports, Part IV
- Equipment Grounding Conductors, Part V

This is mostly mechanical information, and it's not hard to follow or absorb. Part VI, Wiring, ends the sequence. The seventh, ninth, and tenth parts provide requirements for manufacturers to follow—use only equipment that conforms to these requirements. Part VIII provides requirements for installing lampholders. The rest of Article 410 addresses specific types of lighting.

Author's Comment: Article 411 addresses "Lighting Systems Operating at 30 Volts or Less."

PART I. GENERAL

410.1 Scope. This article covers luminaires, lampholders, lamps, decorative lighting products, lighting accessories for temporary seasonal and holiday use, portable flexible lighting products, and the wiring and equipment of such products and lighting installations. Figure 410–1

Author's Comment: Because of the many types and applications of luminaires, manufacturers' instructions are very important and helpful for proper installation. UL produces a pamphlet called the *Luminaire Marking Guide*, which provides information for properly installing common types of incandescent, fluorescent, and high-intensity discharge (HID) luminaires.

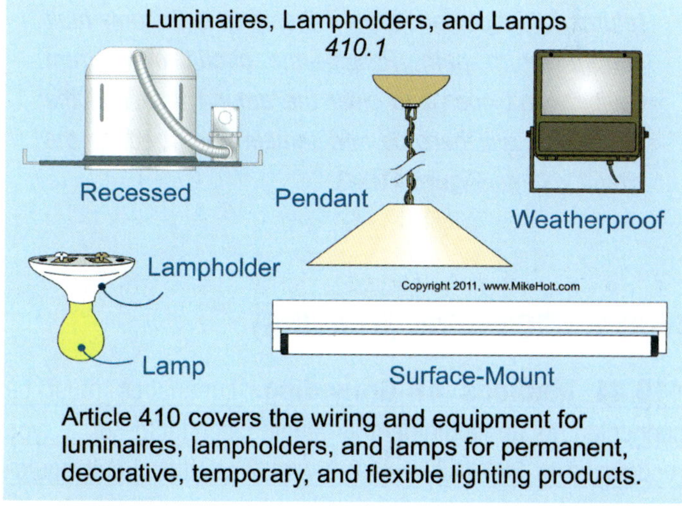

Figure 410–1

PART IV. LUMINAIRE SUPPORTS

410.30 Supports.

(B) Metallic or Nonmetallic Poles.

(5) Metal poles used for the support of luminaires must be connected to an equipment grounding conductor of a type recognized in 250.118 [250.4(A)(5)]. **Figure 410–2**

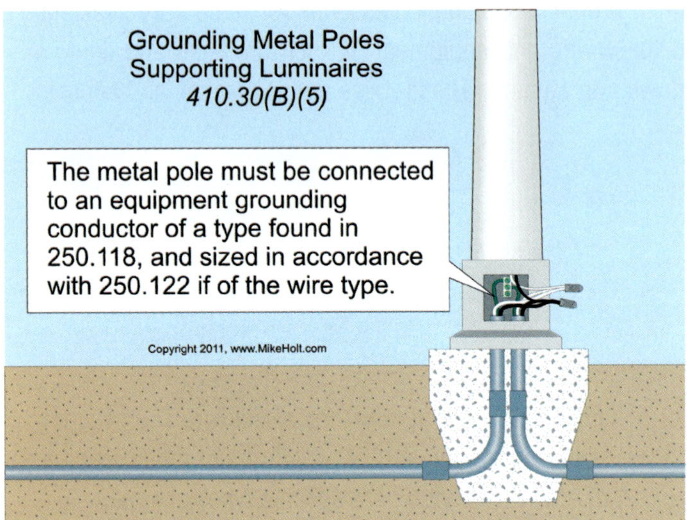

Figure 410–2

DANGER: *Because the contact resistance of an electrode to the earth is so high, very little fault current returns to the power supply if the earth is the only fault current return path. Result—the circuit overcurrent device won't open and clear the ground fault and the metal pole will become and remain energized by the circuit voltage.* **Figure 410–3**

Figure 250–3

PART V. GROUNDING (BONDING)

410.44 Methods of Grounding. Luminaires must be connected to an equipment grounding conductor of a type recognized in 250.118. If of the wire type, the circuit equipment grounding conductor must be sized in accordance with 250.122, based on the rating of the overcurrent device.

Ex 1: If an equipment grounding conductor isn't present in the outlet box for a luminaire, the luminaire must be made of insulating material and must not have any exposed conductive parts.

Ex 2: Replacement luminaires can be installed in an outlet box that doesn't contain an equipment grounding conductor if the luminaire is connected to one of the following:

(1) Grounding electrode system [250.50].

(2) Grounding electrode conductor.

(3) Panelboard equipment grounding terminal.

(4) Service neutral conductor within the service equipment enclosure.

Ex 3: GFCI-protected replacement luminaires aren't required to be connected to an equipment grounding conductor of a type recognized in 250.118 if no equipment grounding conductor exists at the outlet box.

Author's Comment: This is similar to the rule for receptacle replacements in locations where an equipment grounding conductor isn't present in the outlet box [406.4(D)(3)].

CHAPTER 4

Practice Questions

CHAPTER 4. EQUIPMENT FOR GENERAL USE—PRACTICE QUESTIONS

Article 404. Switches

1. Snap switches, including dimmer and similar control switches, shall be connected to an equipment grounding conductor and shall provide a means to connect metal faceplates to the equipment grounding conductor, whether or not a metal faceplate is installed.

   (a) True
   (b) False

2. Snap switches are considered to be part of the effective ground-fault current path when ______.

   (a) the switch is connected to the intersystem bonding termination
   (b) the switch is mounted with metal screws to a metal box or a metal cover that's connected to an equipment grounding conductor of a type recognized in 250.118.
   (c) an equipment grounding conductor or equipment bonding jumper is connected to the grounding terminal of the metal mounting yoke.
   (d) b or c

3. A snap switch that does not have means for connection to an equipment grounding conductor shall be permitted for replacement purposes only where the wiring method does not include an equipment grounding conductor and the switch is ______.

   (a) provided with a faceplate of nonconducting, noncombustible material with nonmetallic screws
   (b) GFCI protected
   (c) a or b
   (d) none of these

4. The metal mounting yoke of a replacement switch isn't required to be connected to an equipment grounding conductor if the wiring at the existing switch doesn't contain an equipment grounding conductor, and the ______

   (a) switch faceplate is nonmetallic with nonmetallic screws
   (b) replacement switch is GFCI protected
   (c) a or b
   (d) circuit is AFCI protected

5. Snap switches in listed assemblies aren't required to be connected to an equipment grounding conductor if ______.

   (a) the device is provided with a nonmetallic faceplate that cannot be installed on any other type of device and the device does not have mounting means to accept other configurations of faceplates
   (b) the device is equipped with a nonmetallic yoke
   (c) all parts of the device that are accessible after installation of the faceplate are manufactured of nonmetallic material
   (d) all of these

6. A snap switch with an integral nonmetallic enclosure complying with 300.15(E) is required to be connected to an equipment grounding conductor.

   (a) True
   (b) False

Article 406. Receptacles, Cord Connectors, and Attachment Plugs (Caps)

1. Receptacles and cord connectors having equipment grounding conductor contacts shall have those contacts connected to a(n) ______ conductor.

   (a) grounded
   (b) ungrounded
   (c) equipment grounding
   (d) neutral

2. Where a grounding means exists in the receptacle enclosure a(n) ______-type receptacle shall be used.

   (a) isolated ground
   (b) grounding
   (c) GFCI
   (d) dedicated

3. When replacing a nongrounding-type receptacle where attachment to an equipment grounding conductor does not exist in the receptacle enclosure, the receptacle can use a ______.

   (a) nongrounding-type receptacle
   (b) grounding receptacle
   (c) GFCI-type receptacle
   (d) a or c

4. Metal faceplates for receptacles shall be grounded.

   (a) True
   (b) False

Article 408. Switchboards and Panelboards

1. Conductors and busbars on a switchboard or panelboard shall be located so as to be free from ______ and shall be held firmly in place.

   (a) obstructions
   (b) physical damage
   (c) a and b
   (d) none of these

2. When equipment grounding conductors are installed in panelboards, a ______ shall be secured inside the cabinet.

   (a) grounded conductor
   (b) terminal lug
   (c) terminal bar
   (d) none of these

Article 410 Luminaires, Lampholders, and Lamps

1. Article 410 covers luminaires, portable luminaires, lampholders, pendants, incandescent filament lamps, arc lamps, electric discharge lamps and ______, and the wiring and equipment forming part of such products and lighting installations.

   (a) decorative lighting products
   (b) lighting accessories for temporary seasonal and holiday use
   (c) portable flexible lighting products
   (d) all of these

2. Metal raceways shall be bonded to the metal pole with a(n) ______.

   (a) grounding electrode
   (b) grounded conductor
   (c) equipment grounding conductor
   (d) any of these

3. Luminaires must be connected to an equipment grounding conductor of a type recognized in 250.118. If of the wire type, the circuit equipment grounding conductor must be sized in accordance with ______, based on the rating of the overcurrent device.

   (a) Table 250.66
   (b) Table 250.122
   (c) Table 310.16
   (d) a and c

4. Luminaires made of insulating material that are directly wired or attached to outlets supplied by a wiring method that does not provide a ready means for a grounding attachment to an equipment grounding conductor shall be made of insulating material and shall have no exposed conductive parts.

   (a) True
   (b) False

5. Replacement luminaires can be installed in an outlet box that doesn't contain an equipment grounding conductor if the luminaire is connected to the ______.

   (a) grounding electrode system or grounding electrode conductor
   (b) panelboard equipment grounding terminal
   (c) service neutral conductor within the service equipment enclosure
   (d) any of these

6. Replacement luminaires aren't required to be connected to an equipment grounding conductor if no equipment grounding conductor exists at the outlet box and the luminaire is ______.

   (a) more than 20 years old
   (b) mounted to the box using nonmetallic fittings and screws
   (c) mounted more than 6 ft above the floor
   (d) GFCI protected

Notes

CHAPTER 5

SPECIAL OCCUPANCIES

INTRODUCTION TO CHAPTER 5—SPECIAL OCCUPANCIES

Chapter 5, which covers special occupancies, is the first of three *NEC* chapters that deal with special topics.

Chapters 6 and 7 cover special equipment, and special conditions, respectively. Remember, the first four chapters of the *Code* are sequential and form a foundation for each of the subsequent three chapters. Chapter 8 covers communications systems and isn't subject to the requirements of Chapters 1 through 7 except where the requirements are specifically referenced in Chapter 8.

What exactly is a "Special Occupancy?" It's a location where the facility or use of the physical facility creates specific conditions that require additional measures to ensure the "practical safeguarding of people and property" purpose of the *NEC*, as put forth in Article 90.

- **Article 501—Class I Hazardous Locations.** A Class I hazardous location is an area where flammable or combustible gases or vapors of flammable liquids may present the hazard of a fire or explosion.
- **Article 502—Class II Hazardous Locations.** A Class II hazardous location is an area where the possibility of fire or explosion may exist due to combustible dust.
- **Article 503—Class III Hazardous Locations.** Class III locations are hazardous because fire or explosion risks may exist due to ignitible fibers/flyings. This includes materials such as cotton and rayon, which are found in textile mills and clothing manufacturing plants. It can also include establishments and industries such as sawmills and woodworking plants. There are no "Group" classifications for Class III locations as there are for Class I and Class II locations.
- **Article 517—Health Care Facilities.** This article applies to electrical wiring in human health care facilities such as hospitals, nursing homes, limited-care facilities, clinics, medical and dental offices, and ambulatory care, whether permanent or movable. It doesn't apply to animal veterinary facilities.
- **Article 525—Carnivals, Circuses, Fairs, and Similar Events.** This article covers the installation of portable wiring and equipment for temporary carnivals, circuses, exhibitions, fairs, traveling attractions, and similar functions, including wiring in or on structures.
- **Article 547—Agricultural Buildings.** Article 547 covers agricultural buildings or those parts of buildings or adjacent areas where excessive dust or dust with water may accumulate, or where a corrosive atmosphe

Notes

Class I (Classified) Hazardous Locations

INTRODUCTION TO ARTICLE 501—CLASS I HAZARDOUS (CLASSIFIED) LOCATIONS

If sufficient flammable or combustible gases, vapors, or liquids are or may be present to produce an explosive or ignitible mixture, you have a Class I location. Examples of such locations include fuel storage areas, certain solvent storage areas, grain processing (where hexane is used), plastic extrusion where oil removal is part of the process, refineries, and paint storage areas.

Article 501 contains Class I, Division 1 and Division 2 installation requirements, including wiring methods, seals, and specific equipment requirements.

PART I. GENERAL

501.1 Scope. Article 501 covers requirements for electrical and electronic equipment and wiring in Class I, Division 1 and 2 locations where flammable gases, flammable liquid-produced vapors, or combustible liquid-produced vapors may be present in the air in quantities sufficient to produce explosive or ignitible mixtures [500.5(B)].

PART II. WIRING

501.30 Grounding and Bonding. Because of the explosive conditions associated with electrical installations in hazardous locations [500.5], electrical continuity of metal parts of equipment and raceways must be ensured by one of the following methods whether or not an equipment grounding conductor of the wire type is installed within the metal raceway [250.100]:

- Threaded couplings or threaded entries on enclosures [250.92(B)(2)].
- Threadless raceway couplings and connectors [250.92(B)(3)].
- Bonding the raceway to an enclosure with listed devices such as a bonding-type locknut, bonding wedge, or bushing with a bonding jumper [250.92(B)(4)].

Standard locknuts alone aren't suitable for this purpose.

(B) Bonding—Flexible Raceway. Flexible metal conduit and liquidtight flexible metal conduit must have an equipment bonding jumper of the wire type installed in accordance with 250.102. **Figure 501–1**

> **Author's Comment:** Bonding jumpers are sized in accordance with Table 250.122, based on the rating of the overcurrent device [250.102(D)], and where installed outside of a raceway, the length of bonding jumpers must not exceed 6 ft and they must be routed with the raceway [250.102(E)(2)]. **Figure 501–2**

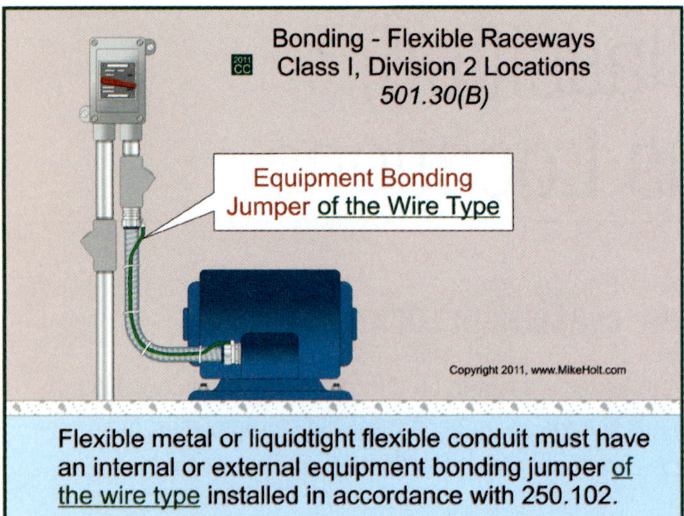

Figure 501–1

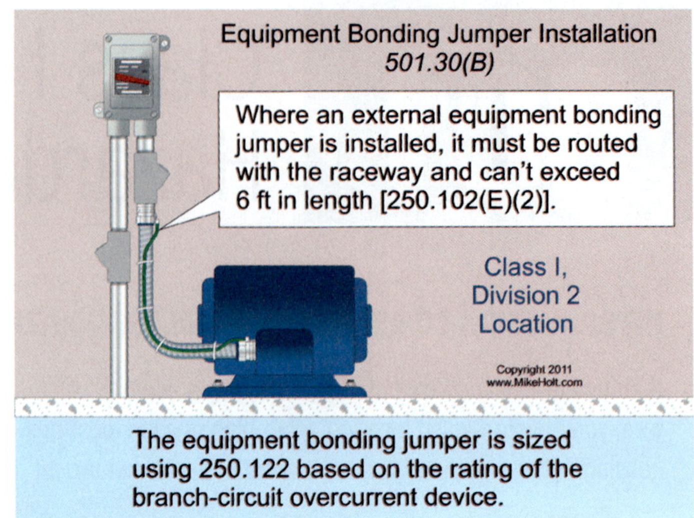

Figure 501–2

ARTICLE 502 Class II (Classified) Hazardous Locations

INTRODUCTION TO ARTICLE 502—CLASS II HAZARDOUS (CLASSIFIED) LOCATIONS

If an area has combustible dust present, it may be classified as a Class II location.

Examples of such locations include flour mills, grain silos, coal bins, wood pulp storage areas, and munitions plants.

Article 502 follows a logical arrangement similar to that of Article 501 and provides guidance in selecting equipment and wiring methods for Class II locations, including distinctions between Class II Division 1 and Class II Division 2 requirements.

PART I. GENERAL

502.1 Scope. Article 502 covers the requirements for electrical and electronic equipment and wiring in Class II, Division 1 and 2 locations where fire or explosion hazards may exist due to the presence of combustible dust, combustible metal dusts, coal, carbon black, charcoal, coke, flour, grain, wood, plastic, and chemicals in the air in quantities sufficient to produce explosive or ignitible mixtures [500.5(C) and 500.8]. **Figure 502–1**

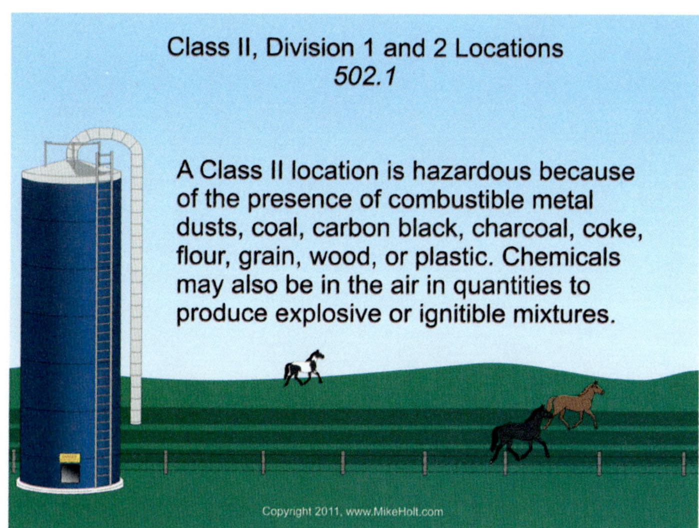

Figure 502–1

PART II. WIRING

502.30 Grounding and Bonding. Because of the explosive conditions associated with electrical installations in hazardous locations [500.5], electrical continuity of metal parts of equipment and raceways must be ensured by one of the following methods, whether or not an equipment grounding conductor of the wire type is installed within the metal raceway [250.100]:

- Threaded couplings or threaded entries on enclosures [250.92(B)(2)].
- Threadless raceway couplings and connectors [250.92(B)(3)].
- Bonding the raceway to an enclosure with listed devices such as a bonding-type locknut, bonding wedge, or bushing with a bonding jumper [250.92(B)(4)].

Standard locknuts alone aren't suitable for this purpose.

(B) Bonding—Flexible Raceway. Liquidtight flexible metal conduit must have an equipment bonding jumper of the wire type in accordance with 250.102. **Figure 502–2**

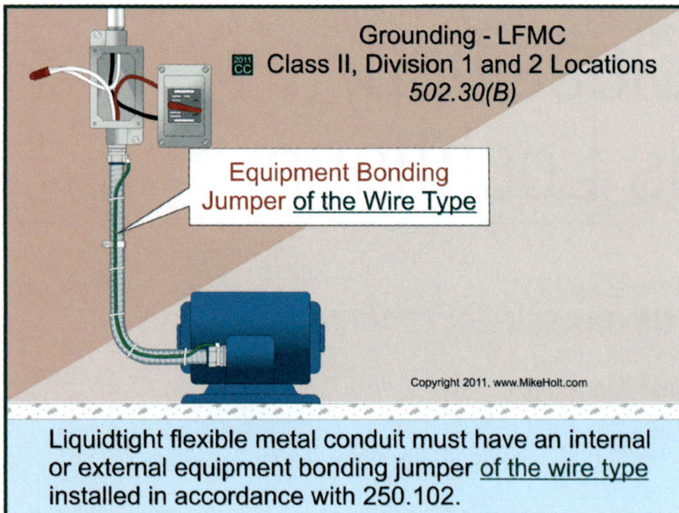

Figure 502–2

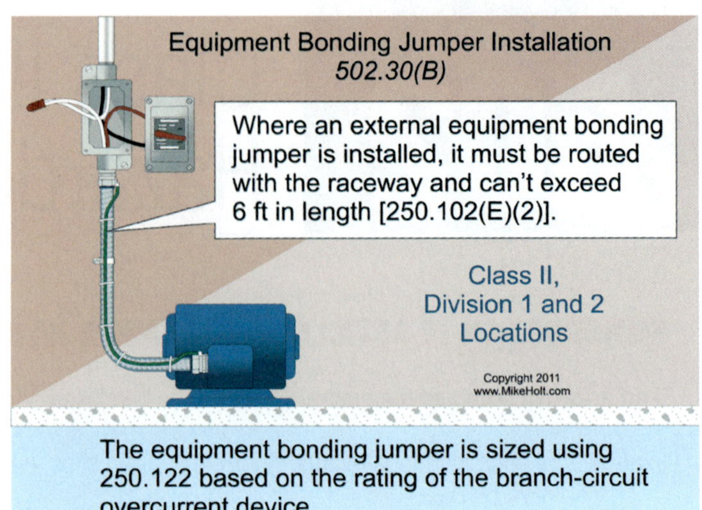

Figure 502–3

Author's Comment: Bonding jumpers are sized in accordance with Table 250.122, based on the rating of the overcurrent device [250.102(D)], and where installed outside of a raceway, the length of bonding jumpers must not exceed 6 ft and they must be routed with the raceway [250.102(E)(2)]. **Figure 502–3**

Class III (Classified) Hazardous Locations

INTRODUCTION TO ARTICLE 503—CLASS III HAZARDOUS (CLASSIFIED) LOCATIONS

The Class III location definition is cumbersome, and many people have a hard time grasping what it means. If you have easily ignitible fibers/flyings present, you may have a Class III location. Examples of such locations include sawmills, textile mills, and fiber processing plants. In many cases, the distinction between Class II and Class III locations may be simply the size of the particulate. A new definition added to Article 502 defines dust based on the size of the particles, so the same material (such as sawdust) may be subject to Article 503 if the predominant material is "larger" than the definition of dust which is covered by Article 502.

PART I. GENERAL

503.1 Scope. Article 503 covers the requirements for electrical and electronic equipment and wiring for all voltages in Class III, Division 1 and 2 locations. These are locations where fire or explosion hazards may exist because easily ignitible fibers or materials producing combustible flyings are handled, manufactured, or used but aren't likely to be suspended in the air in quantities sufficient to produce ignitible mixtures [500.5(D)].

PART II. WIRING

503.30 Grounding and Bonding. Because of the explosive conditions associated with electrical installations in hazardous locations [500.5], electrical continuity of metal parts of equipment and raceways must be ensured by one of the following methods, whether or not an equipment grounding conductor of the wire type is installed within the metal raceway [250.100]:

- Threaded couplings or threaded entries on enclosures [250.92(B)(2)].
- Threadless raceway couplings and connectors [250.92(B)(3)].
- Bonding the raceway to an enclosure with listed devices such as a bonding-type locknut, bonding wedge, or bushing with a bonding jumper [250.92(B)(4)].

Standard locknuts alone aren't suitable for this purpose.

(B) Bonding—Flexible Raceway. Liquidtight flexible metal conduit must have an equipment bonding jumper of the wire type in accordance with 250.102. Figure 503–1

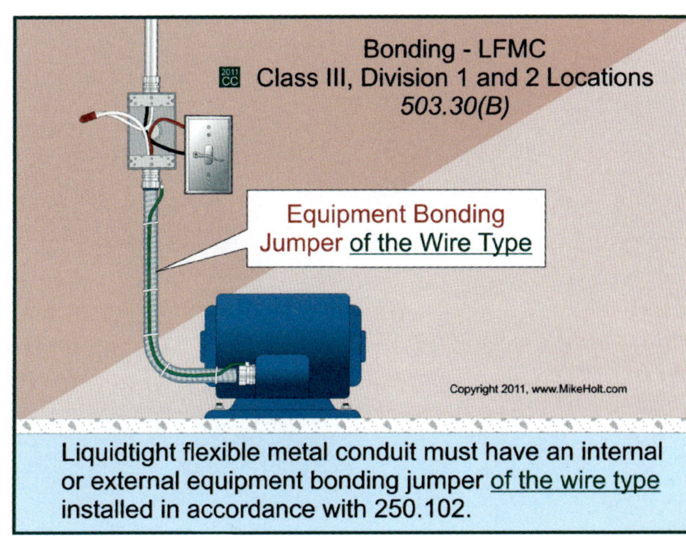

Figure 503–1

Author's Comment: Bonding jumpers are sized in accordance with Table 250.122, based on the rating of the overcurrent device [250.102(D)], and where installed outside of a raceway, the length of bonding jumpers must not exceed 6 ft and they must be routed with the raceway [250.102(E)(2)]. **Figure 503–2**

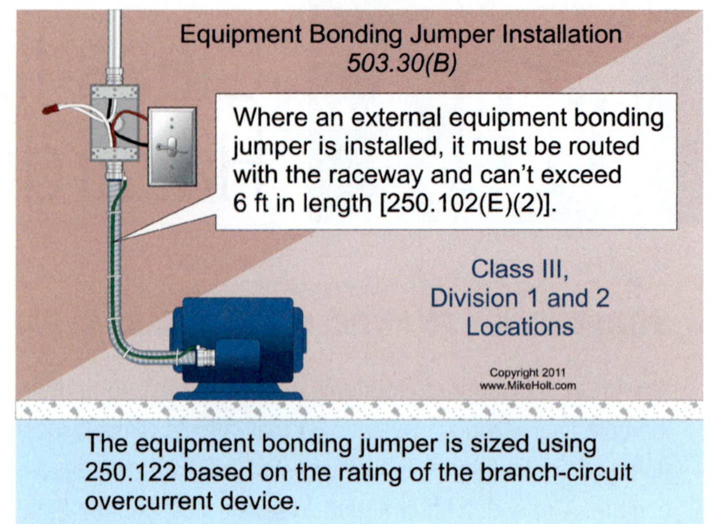

Figure 503–2

Health Care Facilities

INTRODUCTION TO ARTICLE 517—HEALTH CARE FACILITIES

Health care facilities differ from other types of buildings in many important ways. Article 517 is primarily concerned with those parts of health care facilities where patients are examined and treated. Whether those facilities are permanent or movable, they still fall under this article. However, Article 517 wiring and protection requirements don't apply to business offices, patient sleeping areas, or waiting rooms. It doesn't apply to animal veterinary facilities either.

Article 517 contains many specialized definitions that only apply to health care facilities. While you don't need to be able to quote these definitions, you should have a clear understanding of what the terms mean. As you study Parts II and III, keep in mind the special requirements of hospitals and why these requirements exist. The requirements in Parts II and III are highly detailed and not intuitively obvious. These are three of the main objectives of Article 517, Parts II and III:

- Maximize the physical and electromagnetic protection of wiring by requiring metal raceways.
- Minimize electrical hazards by keeping the voltage potential between patients' bodies and medical equipment low. This involves many specific steps, beginning with 517.11.
- Minimize the negative effects of power interruptions by establishing specific requirements for essential electrical systems.

Part IV addresses gas anesthesia stations. The main objective of Part IV is to prevent ignition. Part V addresses X-ray installations and really has two main objectives:

- Provide adequate ampacity and protection for the branch circuits.
- Address the safety issues inherent in high-voltage equipment installations.

Part VI provides requirements for low-voltage communications systems, such as fire alarms and intercoms. The main objective there is to prevent compromising those systems with inductive couplings or other sources of interference. Part VII provides requirements for isolated power systems; the main objective is to keep them actually isolated.

Be aware that the *NEC* is just one of the standards that apply to health care locations, and there may be additional requirements from other standards and special requirements for sophisticated equipment.

PART I. GENERAL

517.1 Scope. Article 517 applies to electrical wiring in health care facilities, such as hospitals, nursing homes, limited care and supervisory care facilities, clinics and medical and dental offices, and ambulatory care facilities that provide services to human beings.

> **Author's Comment:** This article doesn't apply to animal veterinary facilities.

517.2 Definitions.

Health Care Facilities. Buildings or portions of buildings in which medical, dental, psychiatric, nursing, obstetrical, or surgical care is provided. Health care facilities include, but aren't limited to, hospitals, nursing homes, limited-care facilities, supervisory care facilities, clinics, medical and dental offices, and ambulatory care facilities.

Patient Care Area. The area in a health care facility where patients are intended to be examined or treated. Rooms where patient care is administered are classified as general care areas or critical care areas. The governing body of the facility determines room usage in accordance with the type of patient care anticipated.

> **Note:** Business offices, corridors, lounges, day rooms, dining rooms, or similar areas aren't classified as patient care areas.

PART II. WIRING AND PROTECTION

517.13 Grounding of Equipment in Patient Care Areas. Wiring in patient care areas must comply with (A) and (B):

> **Author's Comment:** Patient care areas include patient rooms as well as examining rooms, therapy areas, treatment rooms, and some patient corridors. They don't include business offices, corridors, lounges, day rooms, dining rooms, or similar areas not classified as patient care areas [517.2].

(A) Wiring Methods. All branch circuits serving patient care areas must be provided with an effective ground-fault current path by installing circuits that serve patient care areas in a metal raceway or cable having a metallic armor or sheath that qualifies as an equipment grounding conductor in accordance with 250.118. **Figure 517–1**

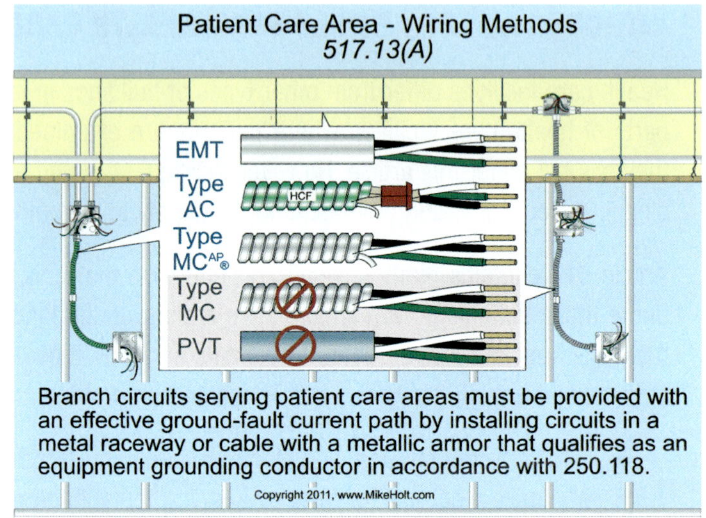

Figure 517–1

Author's Comments:

- The metal outer sheath of AC cable is listed as an equipment grounding conductor because it contains an internal bonding strip in direct contact with the metal sheath of the cable [250.118(8)]. **Figure 517–2A**
- The metal outer sheath of interlocked Type MC cable isn't listed as an equipment grounding conductor unless it contains an uninsulated equipment grounding/bonding conductor and it's listed and identified as an equipment grounding conductor. Once the bare aluminum grounding/bonding conductor exits the cable, it can be cut off because it no longer serves any purpose, **Figure 517–2B**. In addition, the effective ground-fault current path must be maintained by the use of fittings specifically listed for the cable [330.40]. See 300.12, 300.15, and 330.100.

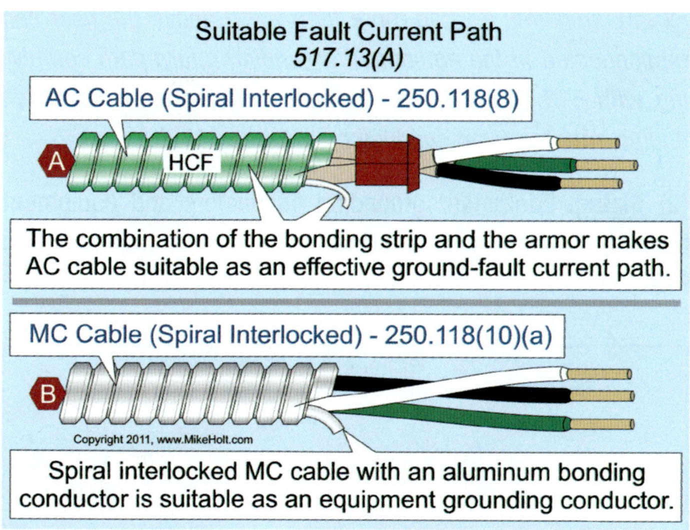

Figure 517–2

Author's Comment: The sheath of interlocked Type MC cable is not permitted for use in patient care areas because the sheath isn't listed as an equipment grounding conductor. **Figure 517–3**

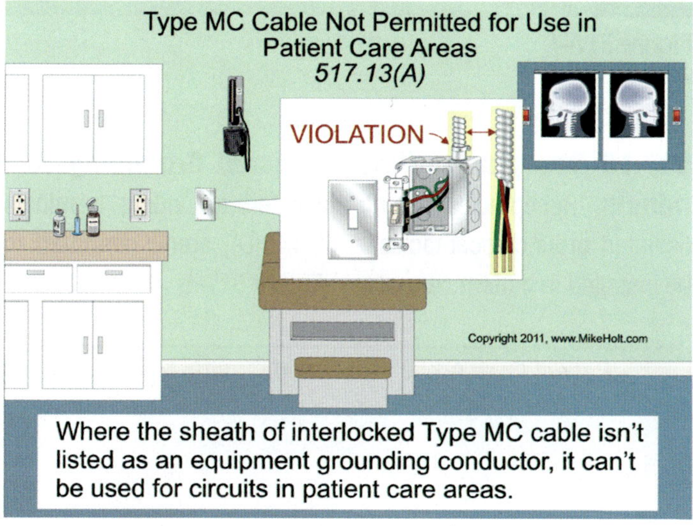

Figure 517–3

(B) Insulated Equipment Grounding Conductor.

(1) General. The following must be directly connected to an insulated copper equipment grounding conductor that's installed with the branch-circuit conductors in wiring methods required in 517.13(A).

Ex: An insulated equipment bonding jumper from a receptacle that directly connects to the equipment grounding conductor is permitted.

(1) The grounding terminals of all receptacles. **Figure 517–4**

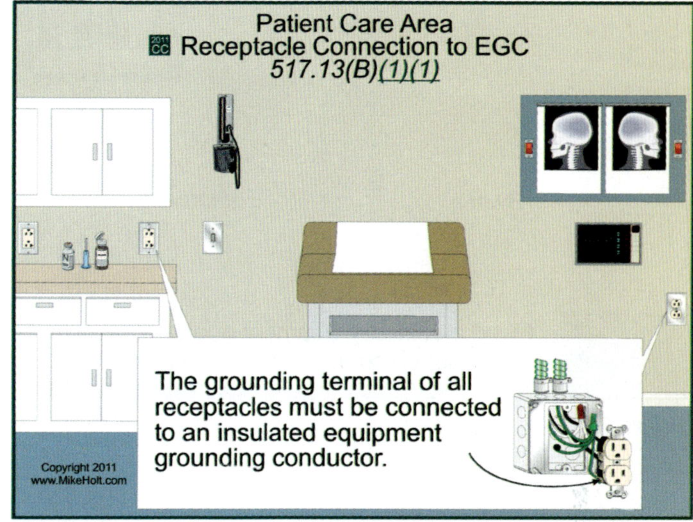

Figure 517–4

(2) Metal enclosures containing receptacles. **Figure 517–5**

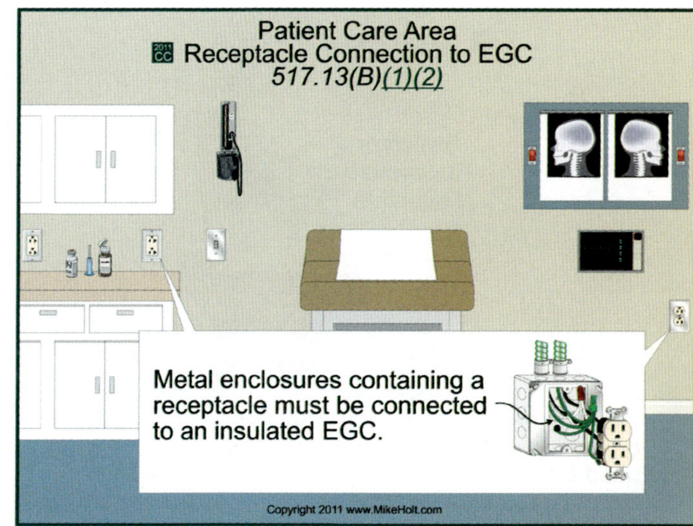

Figure 517–5

(3) Fixed electrical equipment operating at over 100V. **Figure 517-6**

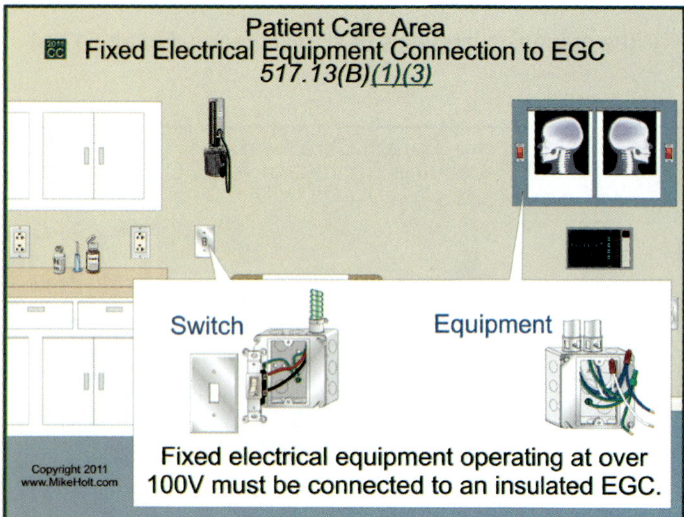

Figure 517–6

Ex 1: Metal faceplates for switches and receptacles can be connected to the equipment grounding conductor by the metal mounting screws that secure the faceplate to a metal outlet box or metal mounting yoke of switches [404.9(B)] and receptacles [406.4(C)]. **Figure 517-7**

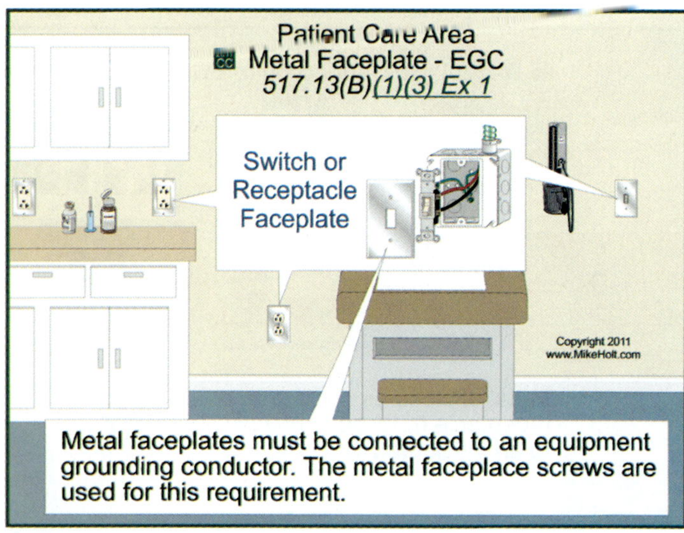

Figure 517–7

Ex 2: Luminaires located more than 7½ ft above the floor can be connected to the equipment grounding return path complying with 517.13(A), without being connected to an insulated equipment grounding conductor.

(2) Sizing. Equipment grounding conductors and equipment bonding jumpers must be sized in accordance with 250.122. **Figure 517-8**

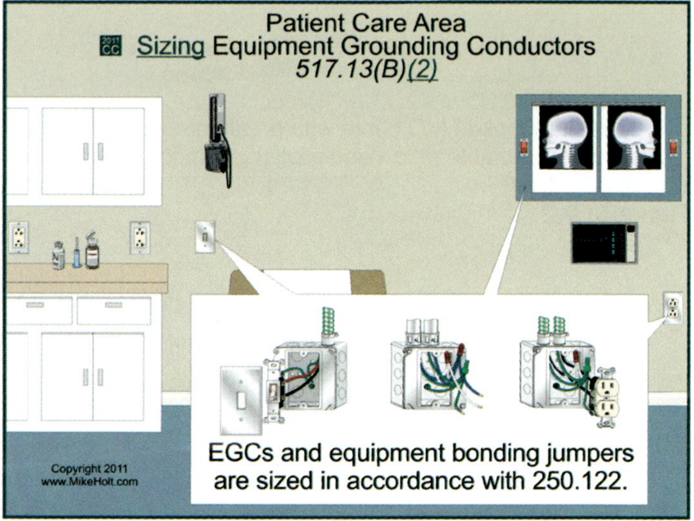

Figure 517–8

517.16 Receptacles With Insulated Grounding Terminals. Receptacles having insulated grounding terminals (isolated ground receptacles) [250.146(D)] aren't permitted to be installed in patient care areas. **Figure 517-9**

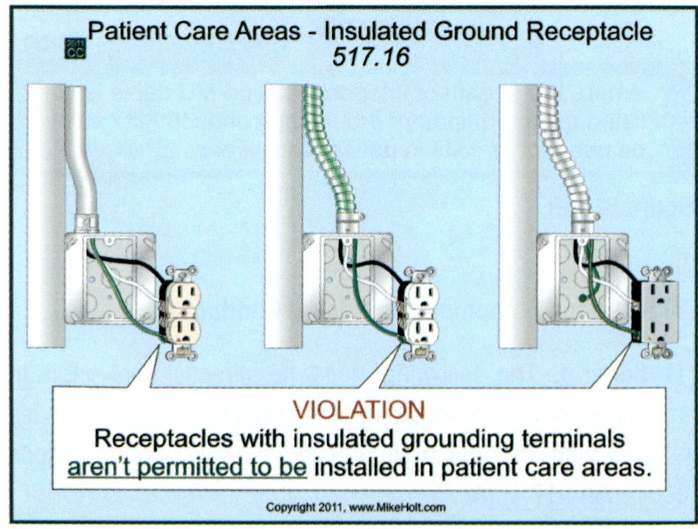

Figure 517–9

Carnivals, Circuses, Fairs, and Similar Events

INTRODUCTION TO ARTICLE 525—CARNIVALS, CIRCUSES, FAIRS, AND SIMILAR EVENTS

Article 525 covers the installation of portable wiring and equipment for carnivals, circuses, exhibitions, fairs, traveling attractions, and similar functions [525.1]. At first glance, a couple of questions arise. "Aren't these just like assembly occupancies? Why do we need Article 525 if Article 518 covers the same thing?"

Yes, these locations are similar to assembly occupancies [Article 518], but they're not the same. In fact, there are two big differences:

- Article 525 applications are temporary, while Article 518 occupancies are not.
- Article 518 doesn't cover amusement rides and attractions, while Article 525 does.

You may want to compare these two articles to see if you can spot other similarities and differences between them. Doing so will help you understand both articles better.

PART I. GENERAL REQUIREMENTS

525.1 Scope. This article covers the installation of portable wiring and equipment for carnivals, circuses, exhibitions, fairs, traveling attractions, and similar functions.

PART IV. GROUNDING AND BONDING

525.30 Equipment Bonding. The following equipment connected to the same source must be connected to an equipment grounding conductor of a type identified in 250.118:

(1) Metal raceways and metal-sheathed cable

(2) Metal enclosures

(3) Metal frames and metal parts of portable structures that contain or support electrical equipment

The circuit equipment grounding conductor of the circuit supplying the equipment in (1), (2), or (3) is permitted to serve as the bonding means.

525.31 Equipment Grounding. All equipment to be grounded must be connected to an equipment grounding conductor of a type recognized by 250.118. The circuit equipment grounding conductor must be connected to the neutral conductor at the service equipment [250.24] or source of the separately derived system [250.30] in accordance with 250.142.

The neutral circuit conductor must not be connected to the circuit equipment grounding conductor on the load side of the service disconnecting means or on the load side of a separately derived system disconnecting means.

525.32 Equipment Grounding Conductor Continuity Assurance. The continuity of the circuit equipment grounding conductor for portable electrical equipment must be verified each time the equipment is connected.

Author's Comment: Verification of the circuit equipment grounding conductor is necessary to ensure electrical safety. This rule doesn't specify how the grounding conductor is verified, what circuits are required to be verified, how the verification is recorded, or who is required or qualified to perform the verification.

Agricultural Buildings

INTRODUCTION TO ARTICLE 547—AGRICULTURAL BUILDINGS

Two factors have a tremendous influence on the lifespan of agricultural equipment: dust and moisture.

Dust gets into mechanisms and causes premature wear. But with electricity on the scene, dust adds two other dangers: fire and explosion. Dust from hay, grain, and fertilizer is highly flammable. Litter materials, such as straw, are also highly flammable. Excrement from farm animals may cause corrosive vapors that eat at mechanical equipment and wiring methods and can cause electrical equipment to fail. For these reasons, Article 547 includes requirements for dealing with dust and corrosion.

Another factor to consider in agricultural buildings is moisture, which causes corrosion. Water is present for many reasons, including wash down. Thus, this article has requirements for dealing with wet and damp environments, and also includes other requirements. For example, it requires you to install equipotential planes in all concrete floor confinement areas of livestock buildings containing metallic equipment accessible to animals and likely to become energized.

Livestock animals have a low tolerance to small levels of stray electrical current, which can cause loss of milk production and, at times, livestock fatality. As a result, the *NEC* contains specific requirements for an equipotential plane in buildings that house livestock.

547.1 Scope. Article 547 applies to agricultural buildings or to that part of a building or adjacent areas of similar nature as specified in (A) or (B).

(A) Excessive Dust and Dust with Water. Buildings or areas where excessive dust or dust with water may accumulate, such as areas of poultry, livestock, and fish confinement systems where litter or feed dust may accumulate.

(B) Corrosive Atmosphere. Buildings or areas where a corrosive atmosphere exists, and if the following conditions exist:

(1) Poultry and animal excrement.

(2) Areas where corrosive particles combine with water.

(3) Areas made damp or wet by periodic washing.

547.2 Definitions.

Equipotential Plane. An equipotential plane is an area where wire mesh or other conductive elements are embedded in or placed under concrete, and are bonded to the electrical system to prevent a voltage difference from developing within the plane [547.10(B)]. **Figure 547-1**

547.10 Equipotential Planes and Bonding of Equipotential Planes. The installation and bonding of equipotential planes must comply with (A) and (B).

(A) If an Equipotential Plane is Required. An equipotential plane must be installed in accordance with (A)(1) or (A)(2):

(1) Indoors. Indoor concrete floor confinement areas where metallic equipment is located that may become energized and is accessible to livestock. **Figure 547-2**

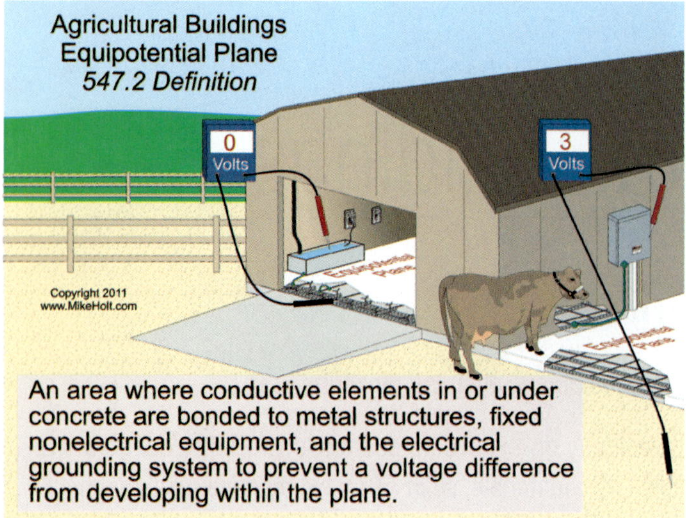

Figure 547–1

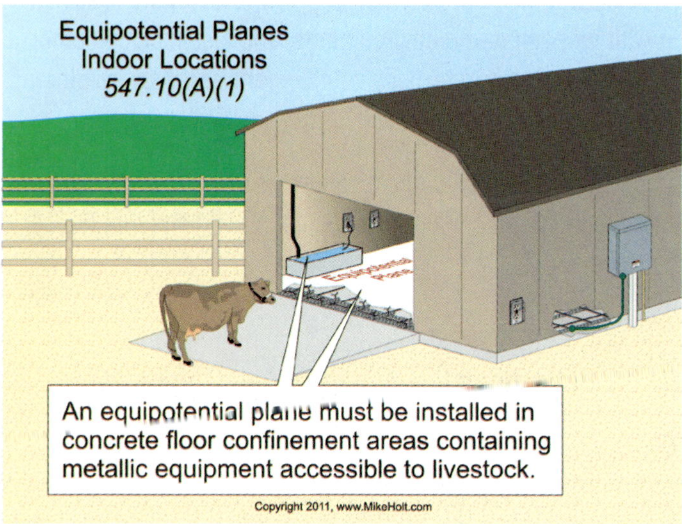

Figure 547–2

(2) Outdoors. Outdoor concrete confinement areas where metallic equipment is located that may become energized and is accessible to livestock. **Figure 547–3**

The equipotential plane must encompass the area around the equipment where the livestock stand.

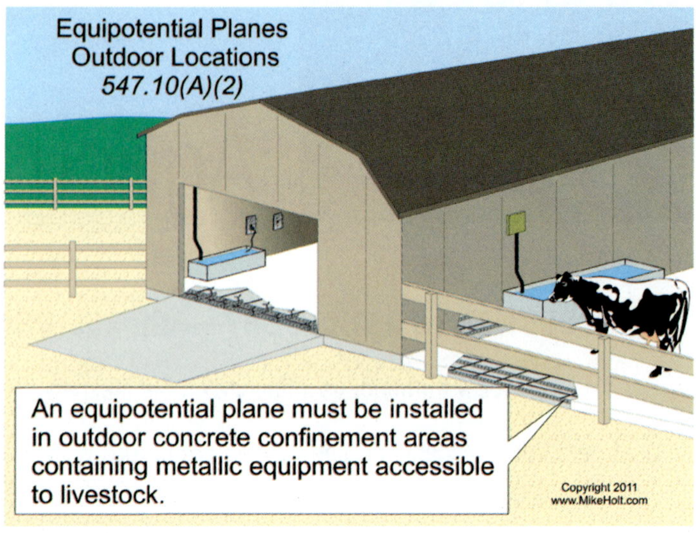

Figure 547–3

(B) Bonding of Equipotential Planes. The equipotential plane must be connected to the building/structure's electrical grounding system. The bonding conductor used for this purpose must be solid, insulated, covered, or bare copper and not smaller than 8 AWG. The bonding conductor must terminate at pressure connectors or clamps of brass, copper, copper alloy, or an equally substantial means approved by the authority having jurisdiction [250.8]. **Figure 547–4**

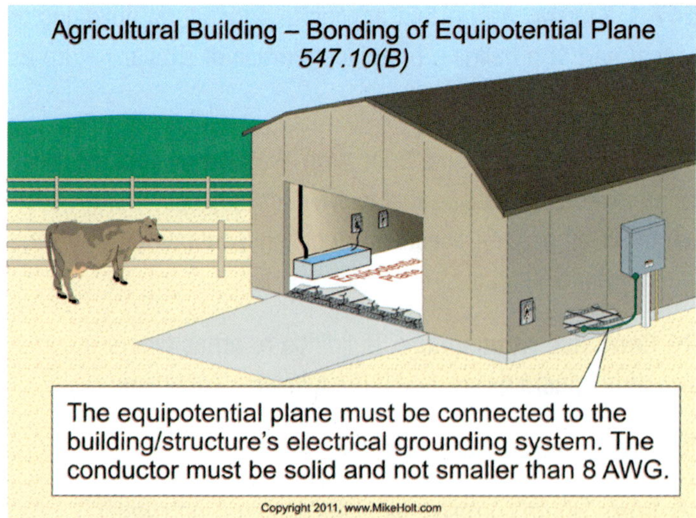

Figure 547–4

Author's Comment: See the definition of "Connector, Pressure" in Article 100.

Note 1: Methods to establish equipotential planes are described in the American Society of Agricultural and Biological Engineers Standard EP473—*Equipotential Planes in Animal Containment Areas.*

Author's Comment: This standard provides the recommendation of a voltage gradient ramp at the entrances of agricultural buildings. **Figure 547–5**

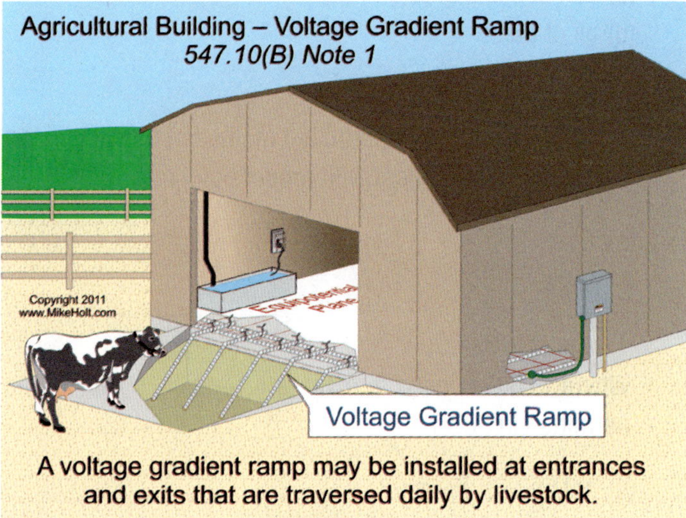

Figure 547–5

Note 2: See the American Society of Agricultural and Biological Engineers EP342.2—*Safety for Electrically Heated Livestock Waterers.*

Author's Comment: The bonding requirements contained in Article 547 are unique because of the sensitivity of livestock to stray voltage/current, especially in wet or damp concrete animal confinement areas.

In most instances the voltage difference between metal parts and the earth will be too low to present a shock hazard to persons. However, livestock might detect the voltage difference if they come in contact with the metal parts. Although potential differences may not be life threatening to the livestock, it's been reported that as little as 0.50V RMS can affect milk production.

The topic of stray voltage/current is beyond the scope of this textbook. For more information, visit www.MikeHolt.com. Click on the "Technical" link, then the "Stray Voltage" link for more details.

CHAPTER 5

Practice Questions

CHAPTER 5 SPECIAL OCCUPANCIES—PRACTICE QUESTIONS

Article 501. Class I Hazardous (Classified) Locations

1. Article 501 covers the requirements for electrical and electronic equipment and wiring for all voltages in Class I locations where fire or explosion hazards may exist due to ______.

   (a) flammable gases
   (b) flammable vapors
   (c) flammable liquids
   (d) any of these

2. In Class I locations, the locknut-bushing and double-locknut types of contacts shall not be depended on for bonding purposes.

   (a) True
   (b) False

3. When FMC or LFMC is used as permitted in Class I, Division 2 locations, it shall include an equipment bonding jumper of the wire type in compliance with 250.102.

   (a) True
   (b) False

Article 502. Class II Hazardous (Classified) Locations

1. Article 502 covers the requirements for electrical and electronic equipment and wiring in Class II, Division 1 and 2 locations where fire or explosion hazards may exist due to ______.

   (a) gases or vapors
   (b) fibers/flyings
   (c) combustible dust
   (d) all of these

2. In Class II locations, a permitted method of bonding is the use of bonding jumpers with proper fittings.

   (a) True
   (b) False

3. Where LFMC is used in a Class II Division 1 location as permitted in 502.10, it shall ______.

   (a) not be unsupported
   (b) not exceed 6 ft in length
   (c) include an equipment bonding jumper of the wire type
   (d) be listed for use in Class I locations

Article 503. Class III Hazardous (Classified) Locations

1. Article 503 covers the requirements for electrical and electronic equipment and wiring in Class III locations where fire or explosion hazards may exist due to ignitible ______.

   (a) gases or vapors
   (b) fibers/flyings
   (c) dust
   (d) all of these

2. In Class III locations, locknut-bushing and double-locknut types of fittings may be depended on for bonding purposes.

(a) True
(b) False

3. Where LFMC is used in a Class III location as permitted in 503.10, it shall ______.

(a) not be unsupported
(b) not exceed 6 ft in length
(c) include an equipment bonding jumper of the wire type
(d) be listed for use in a Class I hazardous (classified) location

Article 517. Health Care Facilities

1. Article 517 applies to electrical construction and installation criteria in health care facilities that provide services to ______.

(a) human beings
(b) animals
(c) a and b
(d) none of these

2. The requirements of Article 517 apply to buildings or portions of buildings in which medical, ______, or surgical care are provided.

(a) psychiatric
(b) nursing
(c) obstetrical
(d) all of these

3. The patient care area is any portion of a health care facility where patients are intended to be ______.

(a) examined
(b) treated
(c) registered
(d) a or b

4. All branch circuits serving patient care areas shall be provided with an effective ground-fault current path by installation in a metal raceway system, or a cable having a metallic armor or sheath assembly. The metal raceway system, or metallic cable armor, or sheath assembly shall itself qualify as an equipment grounding conductor in accordance with 250.118.

(a) True
(b) False

5. In patient care areas, the grounding terminals of all receptacles, metal boxes and enclosures containing receptacles, and all non-current-carrying conductive surfaces of fixed electrical equipment ______ shall be connected to an insulated copper equipment grounding conductor.

(a) operating at over 100V
(b) likely to become energized
(c) subject to personal contact
(d) all of these

6. Metal faceplates for switches and receptacles can be connected to the equipment grounding conductor by means of a metal mounting screw(s) securing the faceplate to a grounded outlet box or grounded wiring device in patient care areas.

(a) True
(b) False

7. Luminaires located more than 7½ ft above the floor can be connected to the equipment grounding return path complying with 517.13(A), without being connected to an insulated equipment grounding conductor.

   (a) True
   (b) False

8. In health care facilities, receptacles with insulated grounding terminals, as described in 250.146(d) shall be permitted in patient care areas.

   (a) True
   (b) False

Article 525. Carnivals, Circuses, Fairs, and Similar Events

1. Article ______ covers the installation of portable wiring and equipment for carnivals, circuses, exhibitions, fairs, traveling attractions, and similar functions.

   (a) 518
   (b) 525
   (c) 590
   (d) all of these

2. The ______ of the circuit supplying metal parts of portable structures at a carnival, circus, or fair can serve as the required bonding means.

   (a) grounded conductor
   (b) equipment grounding conductor
   (c) grounding electrode conductor
   (d) ungrounded conductor

3. At circuses and carnivals, all equipment to be grounded shall be connected to a(n) ______ conductor of a type recognized by 250.118.

   (a) equipment grounding
   (b) grounded
   (c) grounding electrode
   (d) ungrounded

4. The continuity of the grounding conductor system used to reduce electrical shock hazards at carnivals, fairs, and similar locations shall be verified each time that portable electrical equipment is connected.

   (a) True
   (b) False

547. Agricultural Buildings

1. Agricultural buildings where excessive dust and dust with water may accumulate, including all areas of ______ confinement systems where litter dust or feed dust may accumulate shall comply with Article 547

   (a) poultry
   (b) livestock
   (c) fish
   (d) all of these

2. Agricultural buildings where corrosive atmospheres exist include areas where the following exist: ______.

   (a) poultry and animal excrement
   (b) corrosive particles which may combine with water
   (c) areas of periodic washing with water and cleansing agents
   (d) all of these

3. An equipotential plane is an area where wire mesh or other conductive elements are embedded in or placed under concrete bonded to ______.

(a) all metal structures
(b) fixed nonelectrical equipment that may become energized
(c) the electrical grounding system
(d) all of these

4. The purpose of the equipotential plane is to prevent a difference in voltage from developing within the plane area.

(a) True
(b) False

5. Equipotential planes shall be installed in outdoor concrete slabs where metallic equipment is located that may be energized and is accessible to livestock, other than poultry.

(a) True
(b) False

6. The equipotential plane in an agricultural building shall be connected to the electrical grounding system with a solid copper, insulated, covered, or bare conductor and not smaller than ______.

(a) 10 AWG
(b) 8 AWG
(c) 6 AWG
(d) 4 AWG

Notes

CHAPTER

6

SPECIAL EQUIPMENT

INTRODUCTION TO CHAPTER 6—SPECIAL EQUIPMENT

Chapter 6, which covers special equipment, is the second of three *NEC* chapters that deal with special topics. Chapters 5 and 7 focus on special occupancies, and special conditions respectively. Remember, the first four chapters of the *Code* are sequential and form a foundation for each of the subsequent three. Chapter 8 covers communications systems and isn't subject to the requirements of Chapters 1 through 7 except where the requirements are specifically referenced in Chapter 8.

What exactly is "Special Equipment?" It's equipment that, by the nature of its use, construction, or by its unique nature creates a need for additional measures to ensure the "safeguarding of people and property" mission of the *NEC*, as stated in Article 90.

- **Article 600—Electric Signs and Outline Lighting.** This article covers the installation of conductors and equipment for electric signs and outline lighting as defined in Article 100. Electric signs and outline lighting include all products and installations that utilize neon tubing, such as signs, decorative elements, skeleton tubing, or art forms.
- **Article 640—Audio Signal Processing, Amplification, and Reproduction Equipment.** Article 640 covers equipment and wiring for audio signal generation, recording, processing, amplification and reproduction, distribution of sound, public address, speech input systems, temporary audio system installations, and electronic musical instruments such as electric organs, electric guitars, and electronic drums/percussion.
- **Article 645—Information Technology Equipment.** This article applies to equipment, power-supply wiring, equipment interconnecting wiring and grounding of information technology equipment and systems, including terminal units in an information technology equipment room.
- **Article 680—Swimming Pools, Spas, Hot Tubs, Fountains, and Similar Installations.** Article 680 covers the installation of electric wiring and equipment that supplies swimming, wading, therapeutic and decorative pools, fountains, hot tubs, spas, and hydromassage bathtubs, whether permanently installed or storable.
- **Article 690—Photovoltaic Systems.** Article 690 focuses on reducing the electrical hazards that may arise from installing and operating a solar photovoltaic system, to the point where it can be considered safe for property and people. The requirements of the *NEC* Chapters 1 through 4 apply to these installations, except as specifically modified by Article 690.

Notes

Electric Signs and Outline Lighting

INTRODUCTION TO ARTICLE 600—ELECTRIC SIGNS AND OUTLINE LIGHTING

One of the first things you notice when entering a strip mall is that there's a sign for every store. Every commercial occupancy needs a form of identification, and the standard method is the electric sign. Thus, 600.5 requires a sign outlet for the entrance of each tenant location. Article 600 requires a disconnecting means within sight of a sign unless the disconnecting means can be locked in the open position.

> **Author's Comment:** Article 100 defines an electric sign as any "fixed, stationary, or portable self-contained, electrically illuminated utilization equipment with words or symbols designed to convey information or attract attention."

Another requirement is height. Freestanding signs, such as those that might be erected in a parking lot, must be located at least 14 ft above vehicle areas unless they're protected from physical damage.

Neon art forms or decorative elements are subsets of electric signs and outline lighting. If installed and not attached to an enclosure or sign body, they're considered skeleton tubing for the purpose of applying the requirements of Article 600. However, if that neon tubing is attached to an enclosure or sign body, which may be a simple support frame, it's considered a sign or outline lighting subject to all of the provisions that apply to signs and outline lighting, such as 600.3, which requires the product to be listed.

> **Author's Comment:** Outline lighting is an arrangement of incandescent lamps or electric-discharge lighting to outline or call attention to certain features, such as the shape of a building or the decoration of a window [Article 100].

PART I. GENERAL

600.1 Scope. Article 600 covers the installation of conductors, equipment, and field wiring for electric signs and outline lighting, including neon tubing for signs, decorative elements, skeleton tubing, or art forms.

> **Author's Comment:** See the definition of "Outline Lighting" in Article 100.

Note: Sign and outline lighting systems can include cold cathode neon tubing, high-intensity discharge lamps (HID), fluorescent or incandescent lamps, light emitting diodes (LEDs), and electroluminescent and inductance lighting.

600.2 Definitions.

Section Sign. A sign or outline lighting system, shipped as subassemblies that require field-installed wiring between the subassemblies to complete the overall sign. The subassemblies are either physically joined to form a single sign unit or are installed as separate remote parts of an overall sign.

Skeleton Tubing. Neon tubing sign or outline lighting not attached to an enclosure.

600.7 Grounding and Bonding.

(A) Grounding.

(1) Equipment Grounding. Signs and metal equipment of outline lighting systems must be connected to the circuit equipment grounding conductor of the supply circuit using an equipment grounding conductor recognized in 250.118. **Figure 600–1**

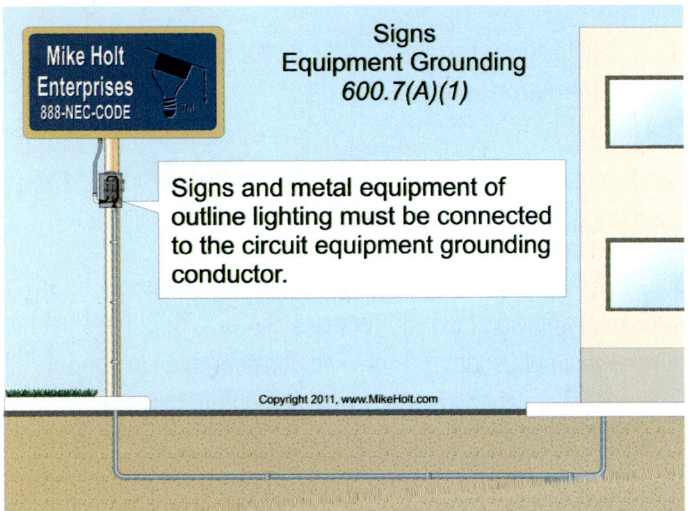

Figure 600–1

(2) Size of Equipment Grounding Conductor. The circuit equipment grounding conductor size must be in accordance with 250.122, based on the rating of the overcurrent device protecting the conductors supplying the sign.

(3) Connections. Equipment grounding conductor connections must be made in accordance with 250.8.

> **Author's Comment:** According to 250.8, equipment grounding conductors must terminate in one of the following methods:
>
> (1) Listed pressure connectors
> (2) Terminal bars
> (3) Pressure connectors listed for direct burial or concrete encasement [250.70]
> (4) Exothermic welding
> (5) Machine screws that engage at least two threads or are secured with a nut
> (6) Self-tapping machine screws that engage at least two threads
> (7) Connections that are part of a listed assembly
> (8) Other listed means

(4) Auxiliary Grounding Electrode. Auxiliary grounding electrodes aren't required for signs, but if installed, they must comply with 250.54.

> **Author's Comment:** According to 250.54, auxiliary electrodes are permitted and they need not be bonded to the building/structure grounding electrode system; the grounding conductor to the electrode need not be sized in accordance with 250.66; and the contact resistance of the electrode to the earth isn't required to comply with the 25 ohm requirement of 250.53(A)(2) Ex. **Figure 600–2**

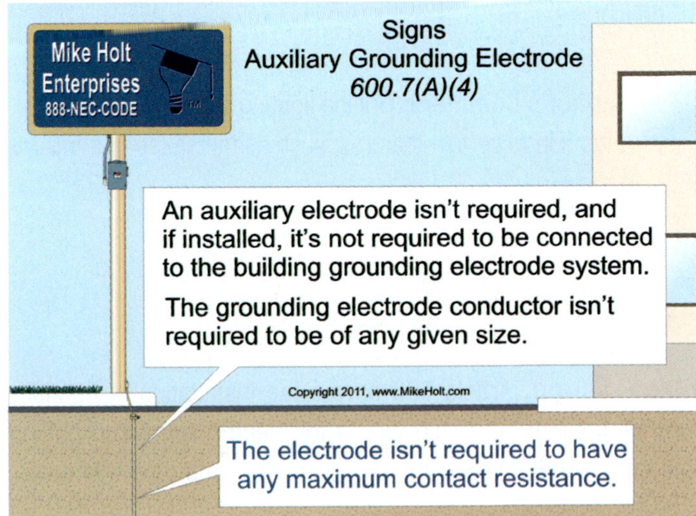

Figure 600–2

The earth must not be used as the effective ground-fault current path required by 250.4(A)(4) [250.4(A)(5)]. This is because the contact resistance of a grounding electrode to the earth is high, and very little ground-fault current returns to the electrical supply source via the earth. The result is the circuit overcurrent device won't open and clear a ground fault; therefore, metal parts will remain energized with dangerous voltage. Figure 600–3

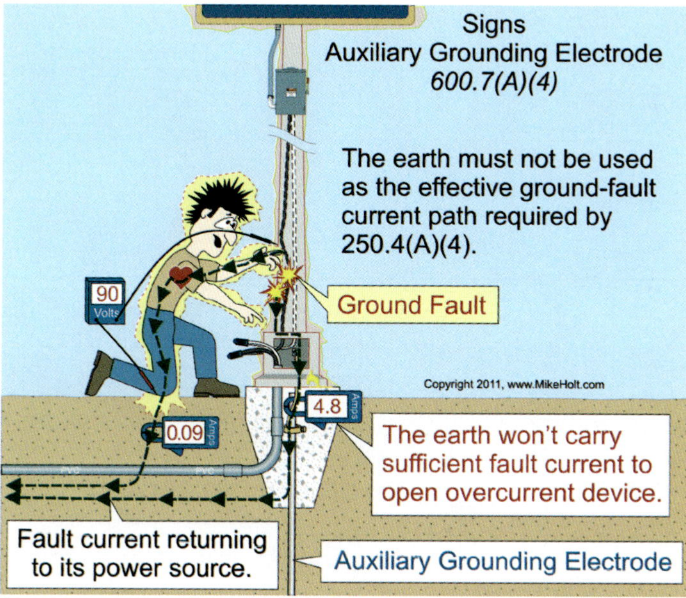

Figure 600–3

(B) Bonding.

(1) Bonding of Metal Parts. Metal parts of signs and outline lighting systems must be bonded to the transformer or power-supply equipment grounding conductor of the branch circuit or feeder supplying the sign or outline lighting system.

Ex: Remote metal parts of a section sign or outline lighting system only supplied by a remote Class 2 power supply aren't required to be connected to an equipment grounding conductor.

(2) Bonding Connections. Bonding connections must be made in accordance with 250.8.

(4) Flexible Metal Conduit Length. Listed flexible metal conduit or listed liquidtight flexible metal conduit for secondary circuit conductors for neon tubing can be used as a bonding means if the total accumulative length of the conduit doesn't exceed 100 ft.

(7) Bonding Conductors.

(1) Bonding conductors must be copper and not smaller than 14 AWG.

(2) Bonding conductors installed externally of a sign or raceway must be protected from physical damage.

600.24 Class 2 Power Sources.

(B) Bonding. Metal parts of signs and outline lighting systems must be bonded in accordance with 600.7.

600.33 LED Sign Illumination Systems, Secondary Wiring.

(D) Bonding. Metal parts of signs and outline lighting systems must be bonded in accordance with 600.7.

Notes

Audio Signal Processing, Amplification, and Reproduction Equipment

INTRODUCTION TO ARTICLE 640—AUDIO SIGNAL PROCESSING, AMPLIFICATION, AND REPRODUCTION EQUIPMENT

If you understand the three major goals of Article 640, you'll be able to better understand and apply the requirements. These three goals are:

- Reduce the spread of fire and smoke.
- Comply with other articles.
- Prevent shock.

This article includes several requirements, such as specifics in the mechanical execution of work and requirements when audio equipment is located near bodies of water, to reduce shock hazards peculiar to audio equipment installations.

In addition, Article 640 distinguishes between permanent and temporary audio installations. Part II provides requirements for permanent installations, and Part III provides requirements for temporary installations.

PART I. GENERAL

640.1 Scope. Article 640 covers equipment and wiring for audio distribution of sound and public address systems, including temporary audio system installations.

> **Note 1:** Permanently installed distributed audio system locations include, but aren't limited to, restaurants, hotels, business offices, commercial and retail sales environments, churches, and schools. Temporary installations include, but aren't limited to, auditoriums, theaters, stadiums, and outdoor events such as fairs, festivals, circuses, public events, and concerts.

640.2 Definitions.

Audio System. Within this article, the totality of all equipment and interconnecting wiring used to fabricate a fully functional audio signal processing, amplification, and reproduction system.

Loudspeaker. Equipment that converts an alternating-current electric signal into an acoustic signal.

640.7 Grounding and Bonding.

(A) General. Wireways must be connected to an equipment grounding conductor of a type recognized in 250.118 in accordance with 250.4(A)(3).

(C) Isolated Ground Receptacles. If receptacles having insulated grounding terminals (isolated ground receptacles) are installed, they must be connected to an insulated equipment grounding conductor in accordance with 250.146(D) [406.3(D)]. **Figure 640–1**

> **Note:** See 406.3(D) for the identification requirements for isolated ground receptacles.

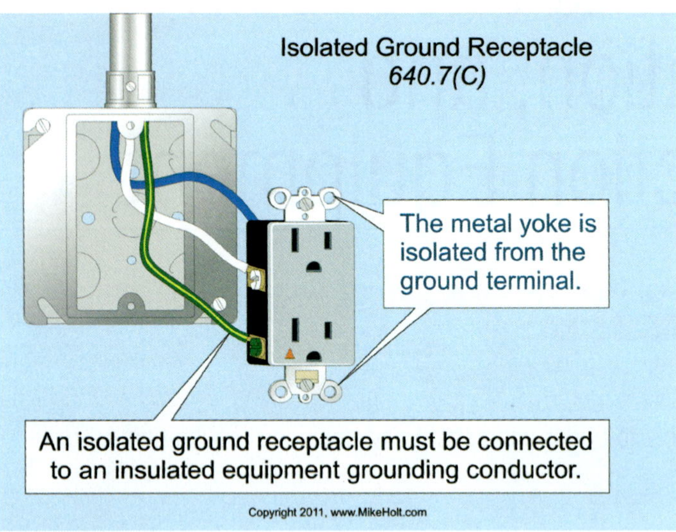
Isolated Ground Receptacle
640.7(C)
The metal yoke is isolated from the ground terminal.
An isolated ground receptacle must be connected to an insulated equipment grounding conductor.
Copyright 2011, www.MikeHolt.com

Figure 640–1

Information Technology Equipment

INTRODUCTION TO ARTICLE 645—INFORMATION TECHNOLOGY EQUIPMENT

One of the unique things about Article 645 is the requirement for a shutoff switch readily accessible from the exit doors of information technology equipment rooms [645.10]. This requirement seems to be wrong on its face because it allows someone to shut off the IT room from a single point. So despite having a UPS and taking every precaution against a power outage, the IT system is still vulnerable to a shutdown from a readily accessible switch at the principal exit doors. What was the *Code*-Making Panel thinking of when they added this requirement?

They were thinking of fire and rescue teams. Having a means to shut down the power and disconnect the batteries before entering the IT room during a fire allows the rescue team to use fire hoses and other equipment without risking contact with energized equipment. Yes, there's loss of IT function during the shutdown, but if the room needs fire and rescue teams, loss of the IT function is the least of its problems at that time. The shutdown allows the rescue of people and property. A breakaway lock can protect the IT room from inadvertent shutdown via this switch.

What about the rest of Article 645? The major goal is to reduce the spread of fire and smoke. The raised floors common in IT rooms pose additional challenges to achieving this goal, so this article devotes a fair percentage of its text to raised floor requirements. Fire-resistant walls, separate HVAC systems, and other requirements further help to achieve this goal.

645.1 Scope. Article 645 covers equipment, power-supply wiring, and interconnecting wiring of information technology equipment and systems in an information technology equipment room that meets all of the requirements of 645.4.

> **Note:** For information on the requirements for the protection of IT equipment and IT areas, see NFPA 75, *Standard for the Protection of Information Technology Equipment.*

645.2 Definitions.

Information Technology Equipment (ITE). Equipment used for creation and manipulation of data, voice, and video, but not communications equipment.

Information Technology Equipment Room. A room that contains the information technology equipment.

645.15 Equipment Grounding Conductor. Signal reference structures must be bonded to the circuit equipment grounding conductor for the information technology equipment. **Figure 645–1**

> **Note 2:** If isolated ground receptacles are installed, they must be connected to an insulated equipment grounding conductor in accordance with 250.146(D) and 406.3(D).

Signal Reference Grounding
645.15
Grounding Electrode
Power Center with Circuit Breakers and Isolating Transformer
Signal Reference Grid
Copyright 2011 www.MikeHolt.com
Signal reference structures must be bonded to the equipment grounding conductor of the system that provides power for the IT equipment.

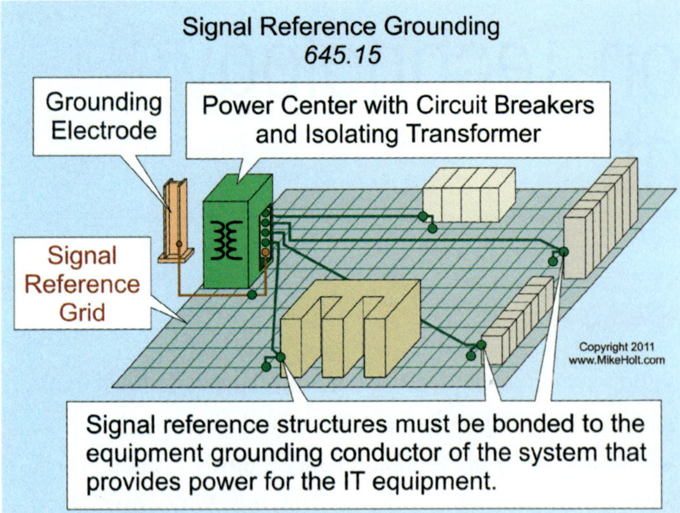

Figure 645–1

Swimming Pools, Spas, Hot Tubs, Fountains, and Similar Installations

INTRODUCTION TO ARTICLE 680—SWIMMING POOLS, SPAS, HOT TUBS, FOUNTAINS, AND SIMILAR INSTALLATIONS

The requirements contained in Article 680 apply to the installation of electrical wiring and equipment for swimming pools, hot tubs, spas, fountains, and hydromassage bathtubs. The overriding concern of Article 680 is to keep people and electricity separated.

This article is divided into seven parts. The various parts apply to certain types of installations, so be careful to determine which parts of this article apply to what and where. For instance, Part I and Part II apply to spas and hot tubs installed outdoors, except as modified in Part IV. In contrast, hydromassage bathtubs are only covered by Part VII. Read the details of this article carefully so you'll be able to provide a safe installation.

- **Part I—General.**
- **Part II—Permanently Installed Pools.** Installations at permanently installed pools must comply with both Parts I and II of this article.
- **Part III—Storable Pools.** Installations of storable pools must comply with Parts I and III of Article 680.
- **Part IV—Spas and Hot Tubs.** Spas and hot tubs must comply with Parts I and IV of this article; outdoor spas and hot tubs must also comply with Part II in accordance with 680.42.
- **Part V—Fountains.** Parts I and II apply to permanently installed fountains. If they have water in common with a pool, Part II also applies. Self-contained, portable fountains are covered by Article 422, Parts II and III.
- **Part VI—Pools and Tubs for Therapeutic Use.** Parts I and VI apply to pools and tubs for therapeutic use in health care facilities, gymnasiums, athletic training rooms, and similar installations. If they're portable appliances then Article 422, Parts II and III apply.
- **Part VII—Hydromassage Bathtubs.** Part VI applies to hydromassage bathtubs, but no other parts of Article 680 do.

PART I. GENERAL

Author's Comment: The requirements contained in Part I of Article 680 apply to permanently installed pools [680.20], storable pools [680.30], outdoor spas and hot tubs [680.42], and fountains [680.50].

680.1 Scope. The requirements contained in Article 680 apply to the installation of electric wiring and equipment for swimming pools, hot tubs, spas, fountains, and hydromassage bathtubs.

680.2 Definitions.

Forming Shell. A structure mounted in the wall of permanently installed pools, storable pools, outdoor spas, outdoor hot tubs, or fountains designed to support a wet-niche luminaire.

Hydromassage Bathtub. A permanently installed bathtub with a recirculating piping system designed to accept, circulate, and discharge water after each use.

Permanently Installed Swimming, Wading, Immersion, and Therapeutic Pools. Those constructed in the ground or partially in the ground, and all others capable of holding water in a depth greater than 42 in., and pools installed inside of a building, regardless of water depth, whether or not served by electrical circuits of any nature.

> **Author's Comment:** The definition of a pool includes Baptisteries (immersion pools), which must comply with the requirements of Article 680.

Pool. Manufactured or field-constructed equipment designed to contain water on a permanent or semipermanent basis and used for swimming, wading, immersion, or other purposes.

Spa or Hot Tub. A hydromassage pool or tub designed for recreational use typically not drained after each use.

Wet-Niche Luminaire. A luminaire intended to be installed in a forming shell where the luminaire will be completely surrounded by water.

PART II. PERMANENTLY INSTALLED POOLS

680.21 Motors.

(A) Wiring Methods. The wiring to a motor must comply with (A)(1) unless modified by (A)(2), (A)(3), (A)(4), or (A)(5). Figure 680–1

(1) General. Branch-circuit conductors for permanently installed pool, outdoor spa, and outdoor hot tub motors must be installed in rigid metal conduit, intermediate metal conduit, PVC conduit, or Type MC cable listed for the location (sunlight-resistant or for direct burial). The wiring methods must contain an insulated copper equipment grounding conductor sized in accordance with 250.122, but in no case can it be smaller than 12 AWG.

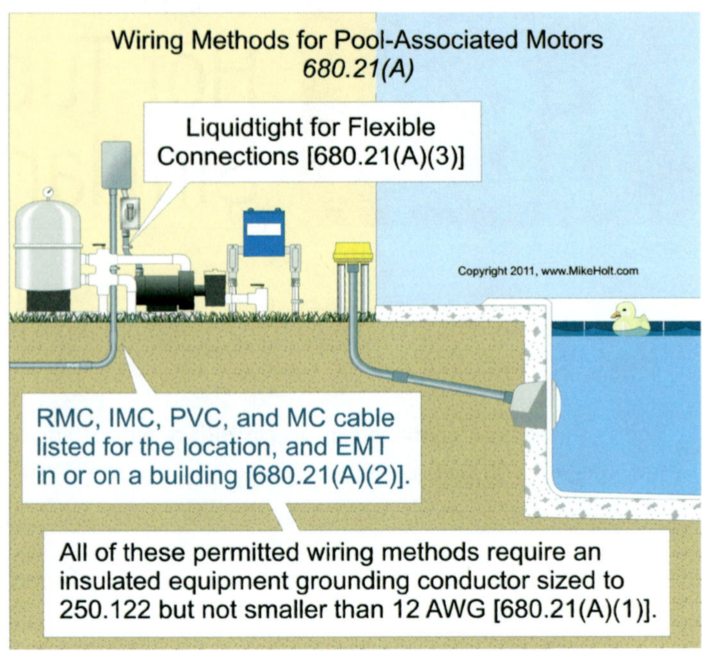

Figure 680–1

(2) On or Within Buildings. If installed on or within buildings, electrical metallic tubing is permitted to supply permanently installed pool, outdoor spa, and outdoor hot tub motors.

> **Author's Comment:** If electrical metallic tubing is used, it must contain an insulated copper equipment grounding conductor as required by 680.21(A)(1).

(3) Flexible Connections. Liquidtight flexible metal or liquidtight flexible nonmetallic conduit is permitted for permanently installed pool, outdoor spa, and outdoor hot tub motors.

> **Author's Comment:** If liquidtight flexible metal or liquidtight flexible nonmetallic conduit is used, it must contain an insulated copper equipment grounding conductor as required by 680.21(A)(1).

(4) One-Family Dwelling. In the interior of a dwelling unit or accessory building associated with a dwelling unit, any Chapter 3 wiring method is permitted. If branch-circuit conductors are installed in a raceway, the wiring method must contain an insulated copper equipment grounding conductor as required by 680.21(A)(1). If a cable assembly is used, the circuit equipment grounding conductor can be uninsulated. Figure 680–2

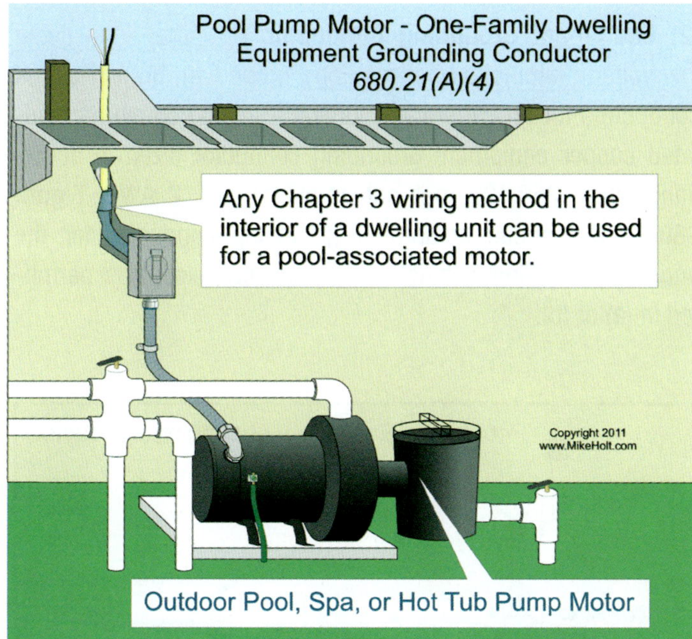

Figure 680–2

(5) Cord-and-Plug Connections. A cord no longer than 3 ft, with an attachment plug and containing a copper equipment grounding conductor, sized in accordance with 250.122, but not smaller than 12 AWG is permitted for pool associated motors. Figure 680–3

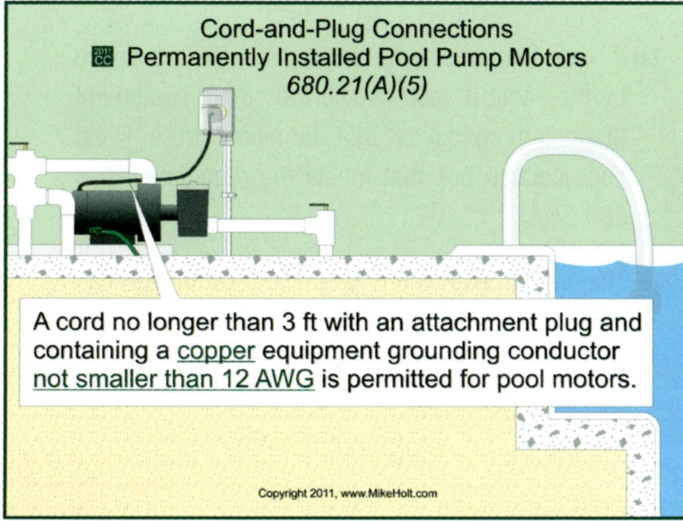

Figure 680–3

Author's Comment: For outdoor spas and hot tubs, the cord must be GFCI protected and it can be up to 15 ft long [680.42(A)(2)].

680.23 Underwater Luminaires.

(B) Wet-Niche Underwater Luminaires.

(1) Forming Shells. Forming shells for wet-niche underwater luminaires must be equipped with provisions for raceway entries. All forming shells used with PVC conduit systems must include provisions for terminating an 8 AWG copper conductor.

(2) Wiring to the Forming Shell. The raceway that extends directly to the underwater pool wet-niche forming shell must comply with (a) or (b).

(a) Metal Raceway. Brass or corrosion-resistant rigid metal conduit approved by the authority having jurisdiction.

(b) Nonmetallic Raceway. A nonmetallic raceway containing an 8 AWG insulated (solid or stranded) copper bonding jumper must terminate in the forming shell and junction box, unless a listed low-voltage lighting system not requiring grounding is used. Figures 680–4 and 680–5

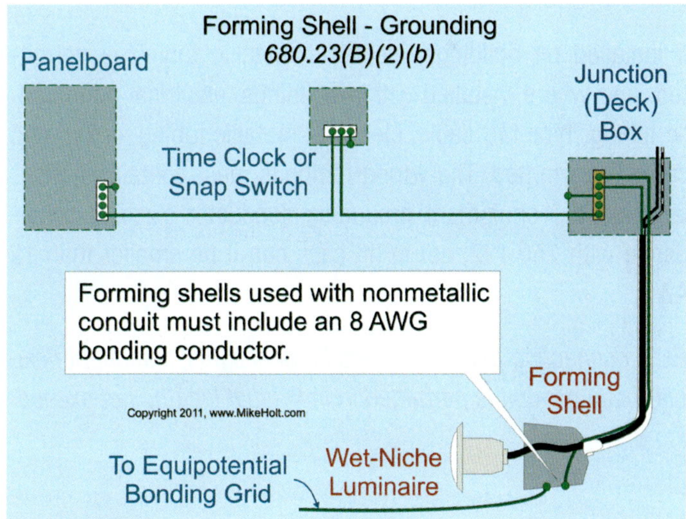

Figure 680–4

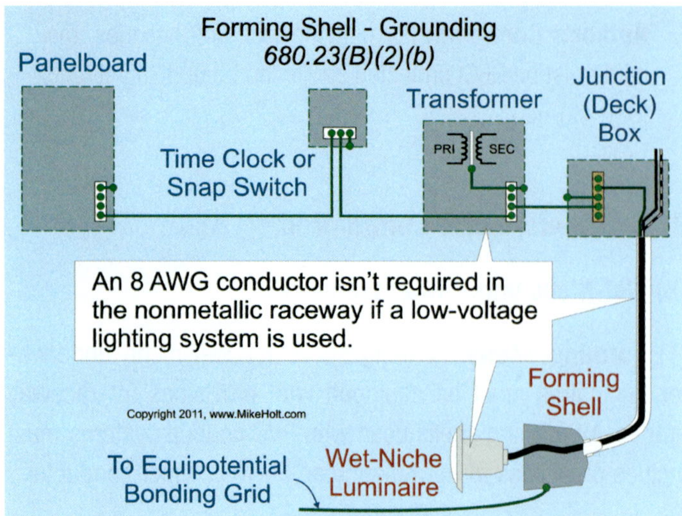

Figure 680–5

The termination of the 8 AWG bonding jumper in the forming shell must be covered with a listed potting compound to protect the connection from the possible deteriorating effect of pool water.

(F) Branch-Circuit Wiring.

(1) Wiring Methods. Branch-circuit wiring for underwater luminaires must be rigid metal conduit, intermediate metal conduit, liquidtight flexible nonmetallic conduit, or PVC conduit [680.23(B)(2)].

If installed on buildings, electrical metallic tubing is permitted, and where installed within buildings, electrical nonmetallic tubing, Type MC cable, electrical metallic tubing, or Type AC cable is permitted. The wiring methods must contain an insulated copper equipment grounding conductor sized in accordance with 250.122, but in no case can it be smaller than 12 AWG.

Ex: If connecting to transformers for pool lights, liquidtight flexible metal conduit is permitted in individual lengths not exceeding 6 ft.

(2) Equipment Grounding Conductor. For other than listed low-voltage luminaires not requiring grounding, branch-circuit conductors for an underwater luminaire must contain an insulated copper equipment grounding conductor sized in accordance with 250.122, but not smaller than 12 AWG, **Figure 680–6**. The circuit equipment grounding conductor for the underwater luminaire must not be spliced, except as permitted in (a) or (b).

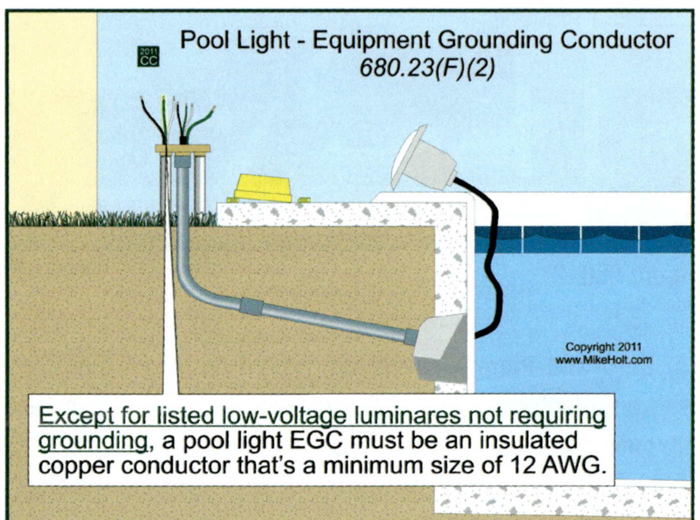

Figure 680–6

(a) If more than one underwater luminaire is supplied by the same branch circuit, the circuit equipment grounding conductor can terminate at a listed pool junction box that meets the requirements of 680.24(A).

(b) The circuit equipment grounding conductor can terminate at the grounding terminal of a listed pool transformer that meets the requirements of 680.23(A)(2).

680.24 Junction Box, Transformer, or GFCI Enclosure.

(F) Grounding. The metal parts and/or the circuit equipment grounding conductor terminals of a junction box, transformer enclosure, or other enclosure in the supply circuit to a wet-niche luminaire must be connected to the equipment grounding terminal of the supplied circuit panelboard. **Figure 680–7**

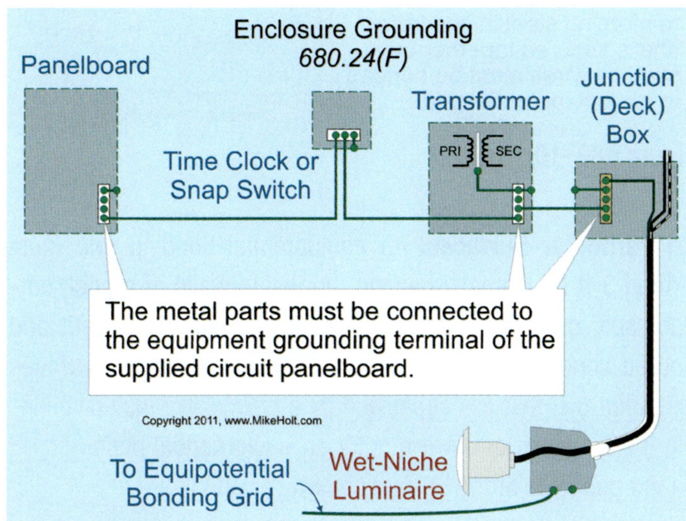

Figure 680–7

680.25 Feeders.

(A) Wiring Methods.

(1) Feeder conductors to panelboards containing permanently installed pool, outdoor spa, or outdoor hot tub equipment circuits must be installed in rigid metal conduit or intermediate metal conduit. If not subject to physical damage, the following wiring methods are permitted: **Figure 680–8**

(a) Liquidtight flexible nonmetallic conduit

(b) PVC conduit

(d) Electrical metallic tubing is permitted where installed on or within a building

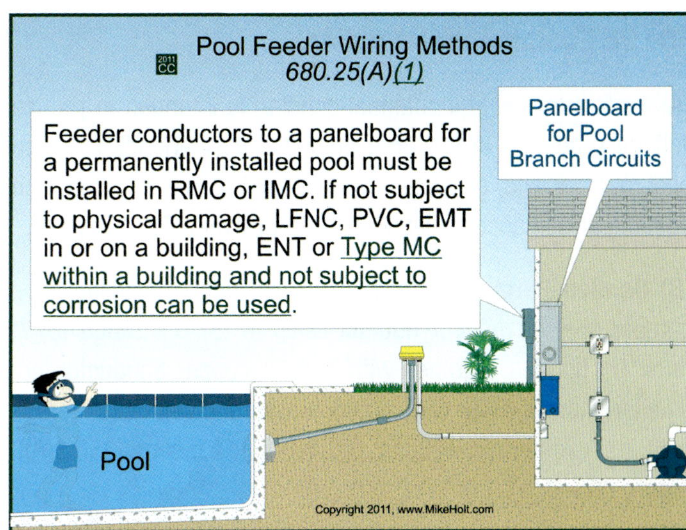

Figure 680–8

(e) Electrical nonmetallic tubing is permitted where installed within a building

(f) Type MC cable installed within a building and if not subject to a corrosive environment

Ex: Branch circuits for permanently installed pool, outdoor spa, or outdoor hot tub equipment can originate from an existing panelboard if the existing feeder contains an equipment grounding conductor within the outer sheath of a cable.

(B) Equipment Grounding Conductor. An insulated copper or aluminum equipment grounding conductor must be installed with the feeder conductors between the grounding terminal of the pool, outdoor spa, or outdoor hot tub equipment panelboard and the grounding terminal of the applicable service equipment.

(1) Size. This feeder equipment grounding conductor must be sized in accordance with 250.122, but not smaller than 12 AWG.

(2) Separate Buildings. If a feeder is run to a separate building/structure to supply permanently installed swimming pool, outdoor spa, or outdoor hot tub equipment, an insulated equipment grounding conductor must be installed with the feeder conductors to the disconnecting means at the separate building/structure [250.32(B)].

680.26 Equipotential Bonding.

(A) Performance. Equipotential bonding is intended to reduce voltage gradients in the area around a permanently installed pool, outdoor spa, or outdoor hot tub by the use of a common bonding grid in accordance with 680.26(B) and (C).

(B) Bonded Parts. The parts of a permanently installed pool, outdoor spa, or outdoor hot tub listed in (B)(1) through (B)(7) must be bonded together with a solid copper conductor not smaller than 8 AWG with listed pressure connectors, terminal bars, exothermic welding, or other listed means [250.8(A)]. **Figure 680–9**

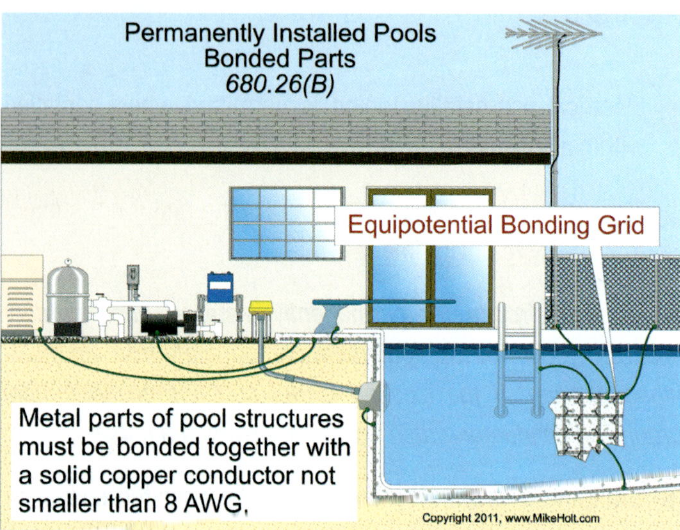

Figure 680–9

Equipotential bonding isn't required to extend to or be attached to any panelboard, service equipment, or grounding electrode.

(1) Concrete Pool, Outdoor Spa, and Outdoor Hot Tub Shells.

(a) Structural Reinforcing Steel. Unencapsulated structural reinforcing steel in concrete shells secured together by steel tie wires. **Figure 680–10**

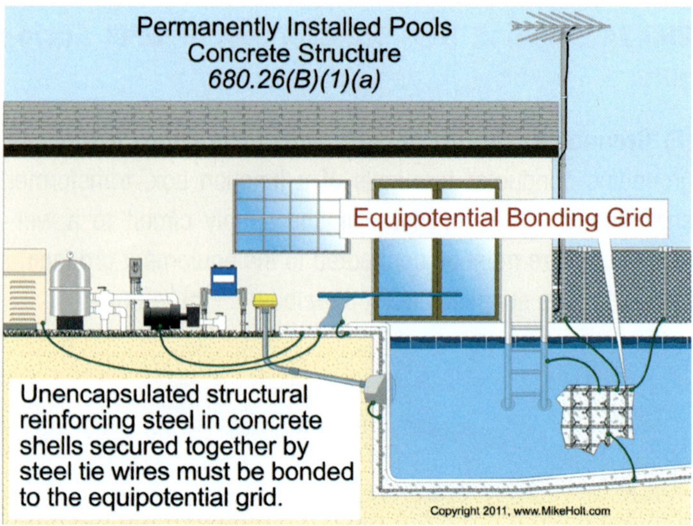

Figure 680–10

(2) Perimeter Surfaces. An equipotential bonding grid must extend 3 ft horizontally beyond the inside walls of a pool, outdoor spa, or outdoor hot tub, including unpaved, paved, and poured concrete surfaces, **Figure 680–11**. Perimeter surfaces less than 3 ft that are separated by a permanent wall or building 5 ft in height or more require an equipotential bonding grid on the pool side of the permanent wall or building.

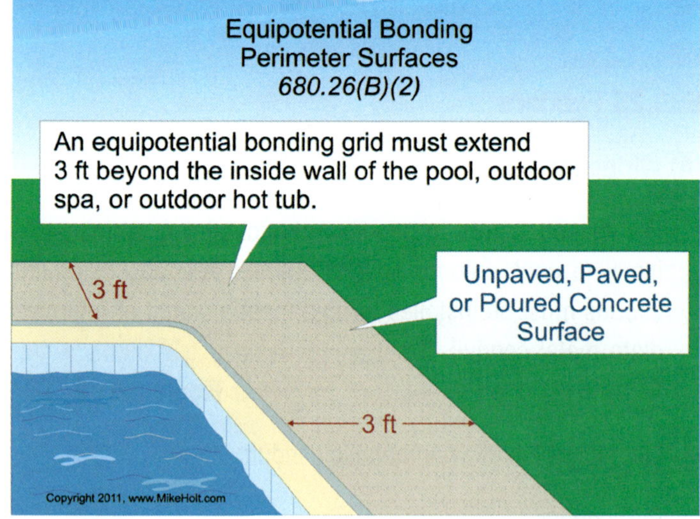

Figure 680–11

The bonding grid must comply with (a) or (b) and be attached to the conductive pool reinforcing steel at a minimum of four points uniformly spaced around the perimeter of the walls of a pool, outdoor spa, or outdoor hot tub.

(a) Structural Reinforcing Steel. Unencapsulated structural reinforcing steel in concrete shells secured together by steel tie wires [680.26(B)(1)(a)]. **Figure 680–12**

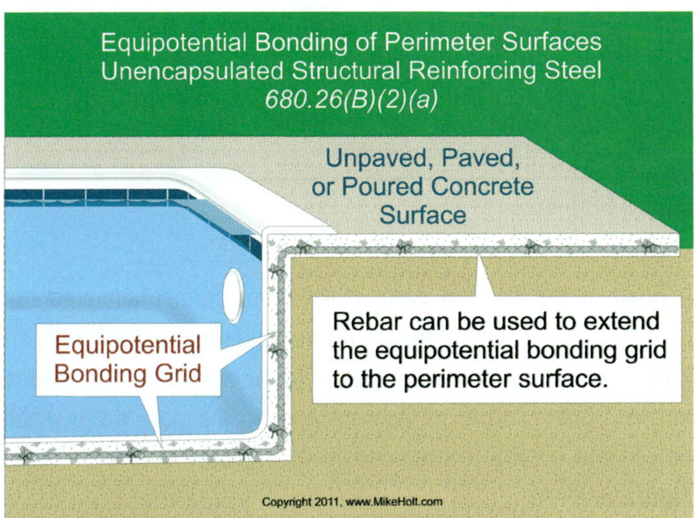

Figure 680–12

> **Author's Comment:** The *NEC* doesn't provide any guidance on the installation requirements for structural reinforcing steel when used as a perimeter equipotential bonding grid.

(b) Alternative Means. Where the structural reinforcing steel isn't available (or is encapsulated in a nonconductive compound, such as epoxy), an equipotential bonding grid meeting all of the following requirements must be installed: **Figure 680–13**

(1) The bonding conductor must be 8 AWG bare solid copper.

(2) The bonding grid must follow the contour of the perimeter surface.

(3) Listed splicing devices must be used.

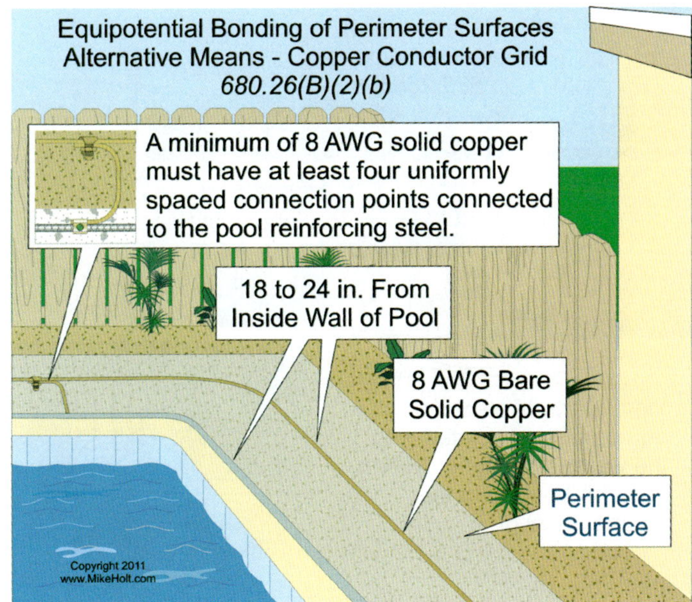

Figure 680–13

(4) The bonding conductor must be 18 to 24 in. from the inside walls of the pool.

(5) The bonding conductor must be secured in or under the deck or unpaved surface within 4 to 6 in. of the underside of the deck.

(3) Metallic Components. Metallic parts of the pool, outdoor spa, or outdoor hot tub structure must be bonded to the equipotential grid.

(4) Underwater Metal Forming Shells. Metal forming shells and mounting brackets for luminaires and speakers must be bonded to the equipotential grid.

(5) Metal Fittings. Metal fittings sized 4 in. and larger that penetrate into the pool, outdoor spa, or outdoor hot tub structure, such as ladders and handrails must be bonded to the equipotential grid.

(6) Electrical Equipment. Metal parts of electrical equipment associated with the pool, outdoor spa, or outdoor hot tub water circulating system, such as water heaters and pump motors, and metal parts of pool covers must be bonded to the equipotential grid. **Figure 680–14**

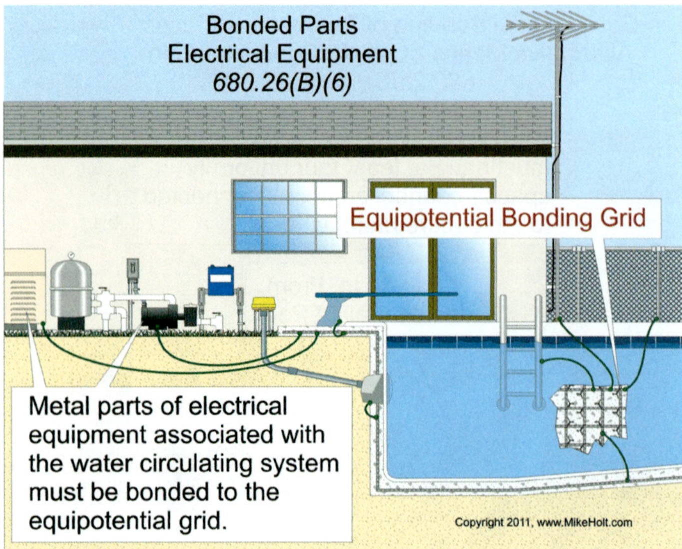

Figure 680–14

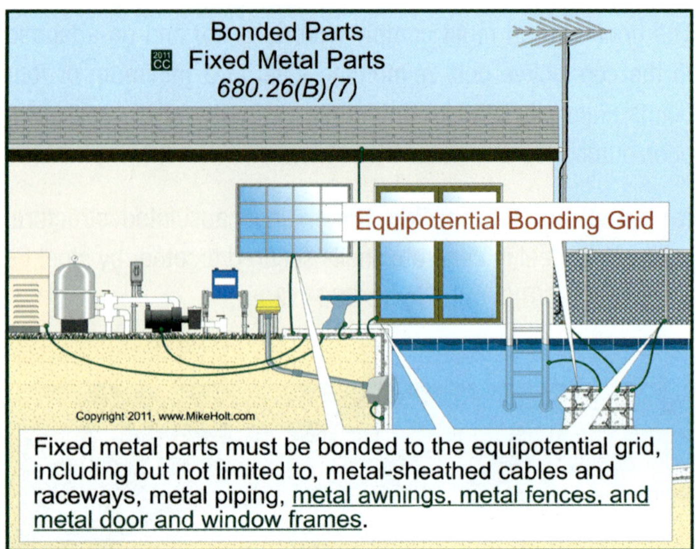

Figure 680–15

Ex: Metal parts of listed double-insulation equipment isn't required to be bonded to the equipotential grid.

(a) Double-Insulated Water-Pump Motors. If a double-insulated water-pump motor is installed, a solid 8 AWG copper conductor from the bonding grid must be provided for a replacement motor.

(b) Pool Water Heaters. Pool water heaters must be grounded and bonded in accordance with equipment instructions.

(7) Fixed Metal Parts. All fixed metal parts must be bonded to the equipotential grid, including but not limited to, metal-sheathed cables and raceways, metal piping, metal awnings, metal fences, and metal door and window frames. **Figure 680–15**

Ex 1: If separated from the pool, outdoor spa, or outdoor hot tub structure by a permanent barrier that prevents contact by a person.

Ex 2: If located more than 5 ft horizontally of the inside walls of the pool, outdoor spa, or outdoor hot tub structure.

Ex 3: If located more than 12 ft measured vertically above the maximum water level.

(C) Pool Water. Pool water must have an electrical connection to one or more of the bonded parts described in 680.26(B). If none of the bonded parts is in direct connection with the pool water, the pool water must be in direct contact with an approved corrosion-resistant conductive surface that exposes not less than 9 sq in. of surface area to the pool water at all times, and it must be bonded in accordance with 680.26(B). **Figure 680–16**

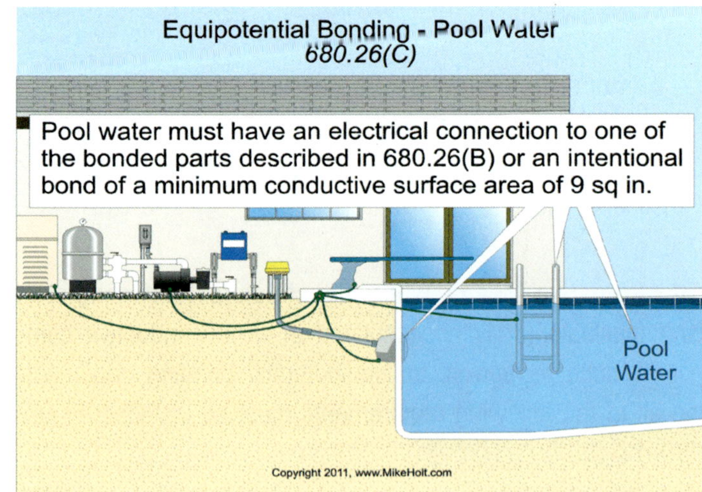

Figure 680–16

Author's Comment: The conductive surface should be located where it's not exposed to physical damage or dislodgement during usual pool activities.

PART IV. SPAS AND HOT TUBS

680.43 Indoor Installations. Electrical installations for an indoor spa or hot tub must comply with Parts I and II of Article 680, except as modified by this section. Indoor installations of spas or hot tubs can be connected by any of the wiring methods contained in Chapter 3.

Ex 2: The equipotential bonding requirements for perimeter surfaces contained in 680.26(B)(2) don't apply to a listed self-contained spa or hot tub installed above a finished floor.

(D) Bonding. The following parts of an indoor spa or hot tub must be bonded together:

(1) Metal fittings within or attached to the indoor spa or hot tub structure.

(2) Metal parts of electrical equipment associated with the indoor spa or hot tub water circulating system unless part of a listed self-contained spa or hot tub.

(3) Metal raceways and metal piping within 5 ft of the inside walls of the indoor spa or hot tub, and not separated from the indoor spa or hot tub by a permanent barrier.

(4) Metal surfaces within 5 ft of the inside walls of an indoor spa or hot tub not separated from the indoor spa or hot tub area by a permanent barrier.

Ex 1: Nonelectrical equipment, such as towel bars or mirror frames, which aren't connected to metallic piping, aren't required to be bonded.

(E) Methods of Bonding. Metal parts associated with the spa or hot tub as described in 680.43(D) must be bonded by any of the following methods:

(1) Threaded metal piping and fittings

(2) Metal-to-metal mounting to a common frame or base

(3) A solid copper conductor not smaller than 8 AWG

PART V. FOUNTAINS

680.55 Methods of Equipment Grounding.

(B) Supplied by a Flexible Cord. Equipment supplied by a flexible cord must have exposed metal parts connected to an insulated copper equipment grounding conductor that's an integral part of the cord.

PART VII. HYDROMASSAGE BATHTUBS

680.70 General. A hydromassage bathtub is only required to comply with the requirements of Part VII; it's not required to comply with the other parts of this article.

> **Author's Comment:** A "Hydromassage Bathtub" is defined as a permanently installed bathtub with a recirculating piping system designed to accept, circulate, and discharge water after each use [680.2].

680.74 Equipotential Bonding. Metal piping systems and grounded metal parts in contact with the circulating water must be bonded to the hydromassage circulating pump motor that's not double insulated with an 8 AWG or larger bare copper conductor. Figure 680–17

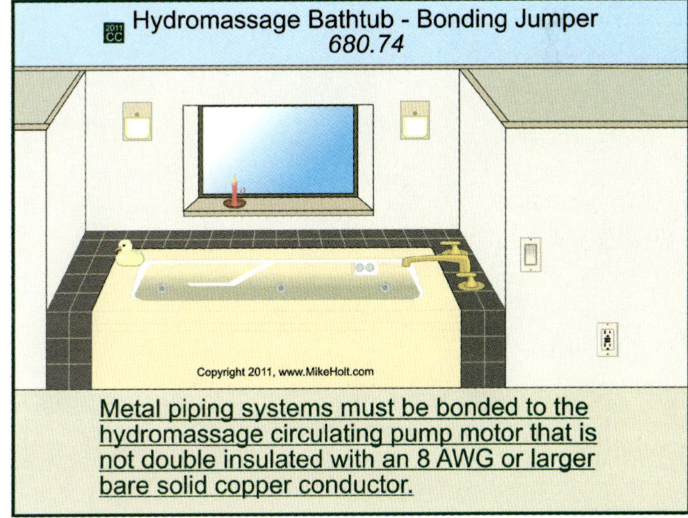

Figure 680–17

Where the metal piping systems or grounded metal parts in contact with the circulating water isare present with a double insulated motor, an 8 AWG or larger bare copper conductor must be provided at the hydromassage circulating motor with sufficient length to terminate on a replacement non-double insulated pump motor. **Figure 680–18**

The metal piping to motor bonding jumper is not be required to be attached to any panelboard, service equipment, or electrode.

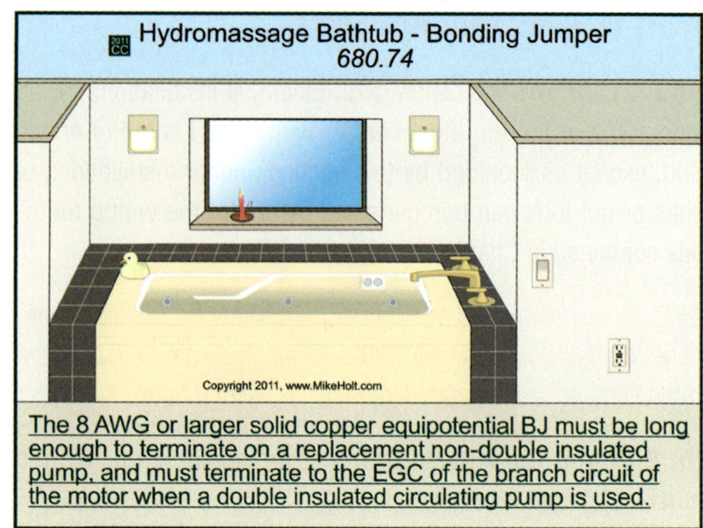

Figure 680–18

ARTICLE 690 Photovoltaic Power Systems

INTRODUCTION TO ARTICLE 690—PHOTOVOLTAIC POWER SYSTEMS

You've seen, or maybe own, photocell-powered devices such as night lights, car coolers, and toys. These generally consist of a small solar panel and a small light or motor. Typically, these run on less than 10V dc and draw only a fraction of an ampere. These kinds of devices are very different from a system that can power a house or small commercial building.

Consider the sheer size and weight of solar panels for providing electrical power to a building. You're looking at mechanical and site selection issues that may require specialized expertise. The value of these panels also means there are security issues to consider, which may require more than just installing locks. There are also civil and architectural issues to address.

In summary, these installations are complicated and require expertise in several non-electrical areas, which the *NEC* doesn't address.

Article 690 focuses on reducing the electrical hazards that may arise from installing and operating a solar photovoltaic system, to the point where it can be considered safe for property and people.

This article consists of nine Parts, the last of which applies only to systems over 600V. The requirements of Chapters 1 through 4 apply to these installations, except as specifically modified by Article 690.

PART I. GENERAL

690.1 Scope.

Article 690 applies to photovoltaic (PV) electrical energy systems, array circuit(s), inverter(s), and charge controller(s) for such systems which may be interactive with other electrical power sources or stand-alone, with or without energy storage (batteries). **Figures 690–1 and 690–2**

690.2 Definitions.

Array. An electrical assembly of PV modules that convert sunlight to direct current (dc), components with a support structure and foundation, tracker, and other components that form a direct-current power-producing unit. **Figure 690–3**

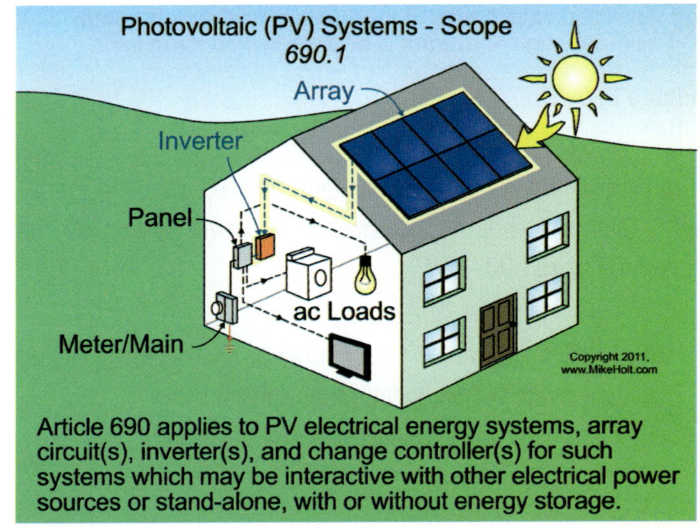

Figure 690–1

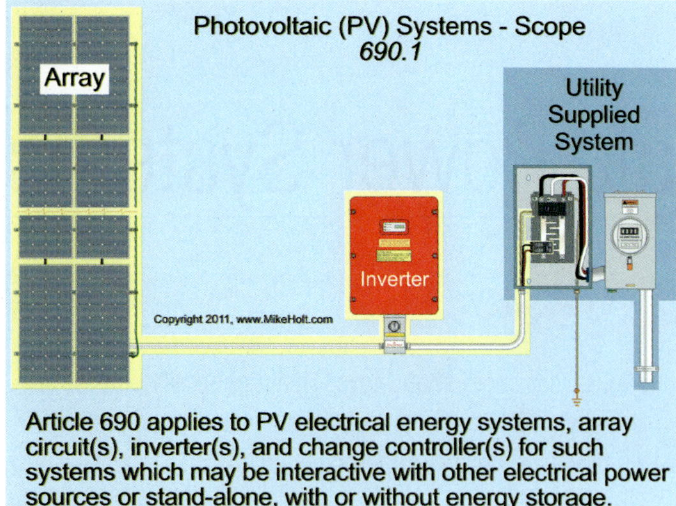

Figure 690–2

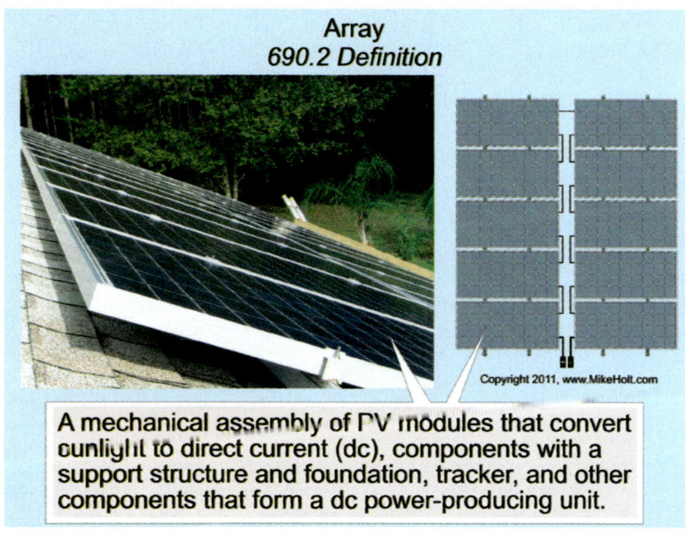

Figure 690– 3

Interactive System. A PV system that operates in parallel (interactive) with the electrical utility power system via the inverter. **Figure 690–4**

> **Author's Comment:** The PV array is connected to the inverter direct-current input; the inverter outputs alternating current (ac) to the premises load or utility grid.

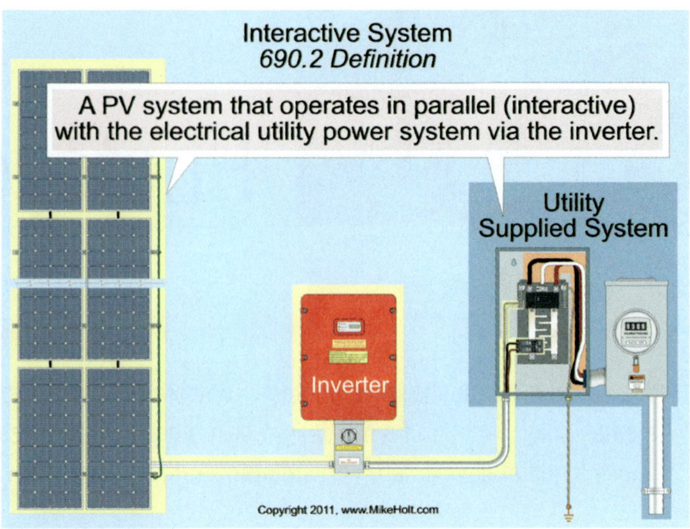

Figure 690–4

Inverter. Electrical equipment that changes direct current from the PV system to utility-grade alternating current. **Figure 690–5**

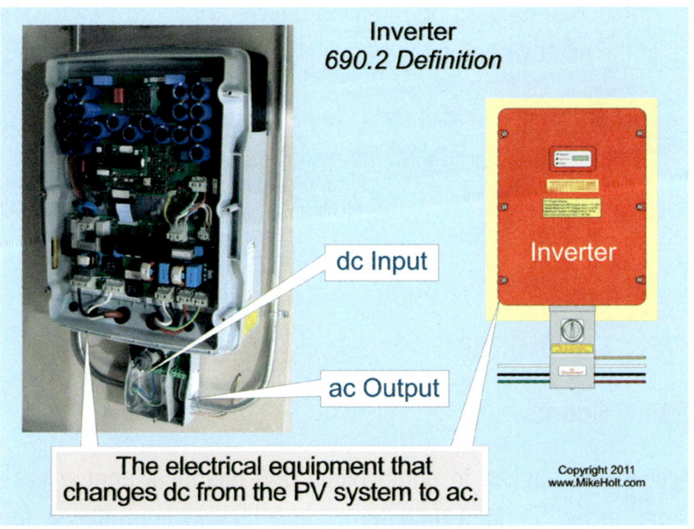

Figure 690–5

Module. A PV unit designed to generate direct-current power when exposed to sunlight. **Figure 690–6**

Stand-Alone System. A PV system that supplies power without an interconnection to another electric power source. **Figure 690–7**

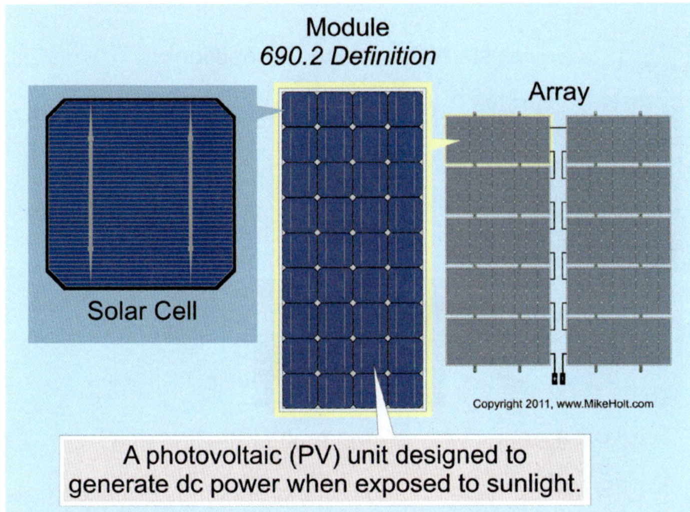

Figure 690–6

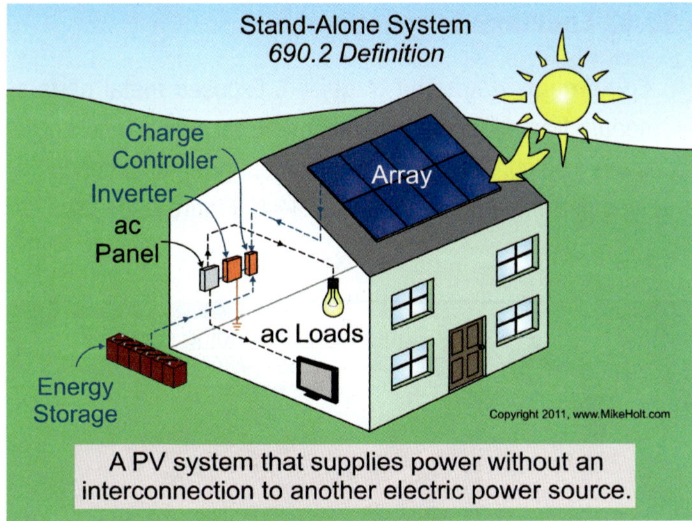

Figure 690–7

Author's Comment: Stand-alone systems below 50V must be installed in accordance with Article 720 in addition to Article 690.

PART V. GROUNDING

690.41 System Grounding.

To limit the voltage induced by lightning, one conductor of a 2-wire PV system operating at over 50V must be solidly grounded (connected to the earth) in accordance with 250.4(A)(1). **Figure 690–8**

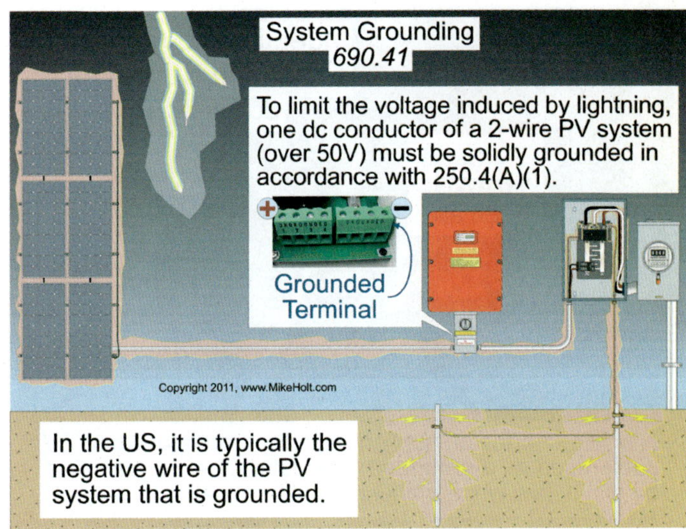

Figure 690–8

Author's Comment: Most PV systems in the U.S. have the negative conductor of the PV system grounded to the earth (typically at the inverter); therefore this conductor is called the "grounded conductor." According to 200.6, the insulation of the grounded conductor of a circuit must be white or gray, but 200.6(A)(2) allows single-conductor, sunlight-resistant, outdoor-rated cable to be identified by a distinctive white marking at all terminations. **Figures 690–9 and 690–10**

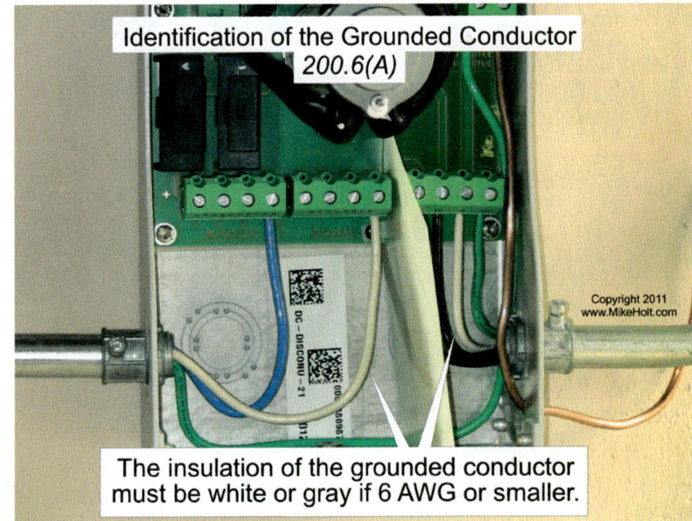

Figure 690–9

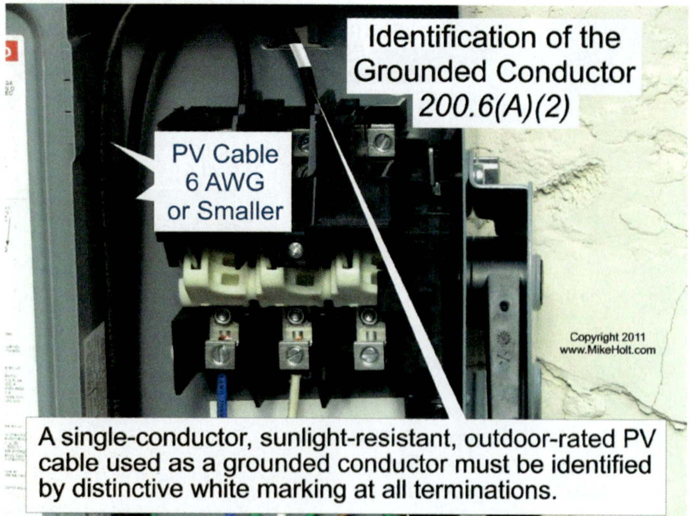

Figure 690–10

690.42 Point of System Grounding Connection.

For grounded PV systems, the grounding connection can be at any "single" point on the grounded conductor of the PV direct-current output circuit. **Figure 690–11**

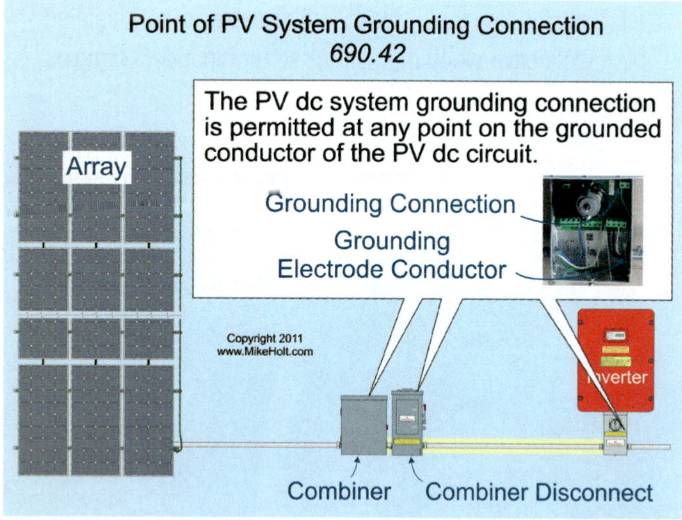

Figure 690–11

Ex: PV systems with ground-fault protection that incorporates the system grounding connection must not have an additional grounding connection. **Figure 690–12**

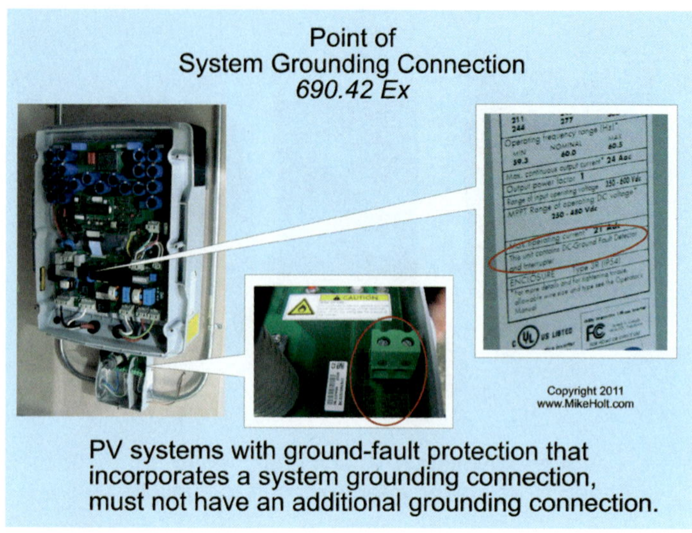

Figure 690–12

690.43 Equipment Grounding.

(A) Equipment Grounding Required. Exposed metal parts of PV module frames, electrical equipment, raceways, and enclosures must be connected to an equipment grounding conductor of a type permitted in 250.118 [250.134]. **Figure 690–13**

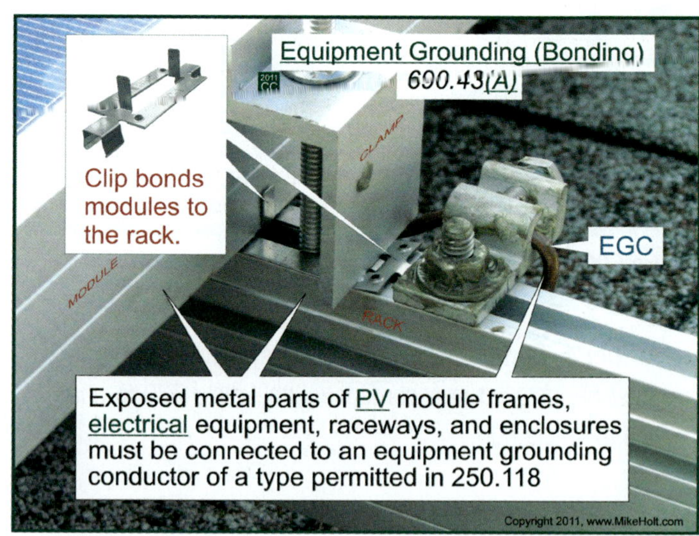

Figure 690–13

(B) Equipment Grounding Conductor Required. An equipment grounding conductor must be installed between the PV array and associated equipment.

(C) Structure as Equipment Grounding Conductor. Devices listed and identified for grounding the metallic frames of PV modules and associated equipment can be used to bond the exposed metal surfaces of the modules and equipment to the metal racks.

Metallic mounting racks used as an equipment grounding conductor must be identified as an equipment grounding conductor or have identified bonding jumpers/devices connected between the separate metallic racks and be connected to an equipment grounding conductor as required by 690.43(A).

(D) Securing Devices and Systems. Devices and systems used for securing PV modules to metal mounting racks that serve as an equipment grounding conductor must be identified for such purposes. **Figure 690–14**

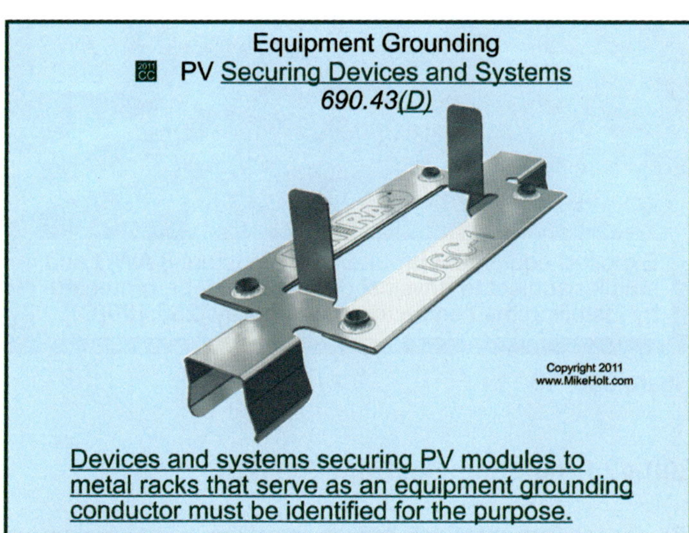

Figure 690–14

(E) Adjacent Modules. Devices identified and listed for bonding the metallic frames of PV modules can be used to bond the metallic frames of PV modules to the metallic frames of adjacent PV modules. **Figure 690–15**

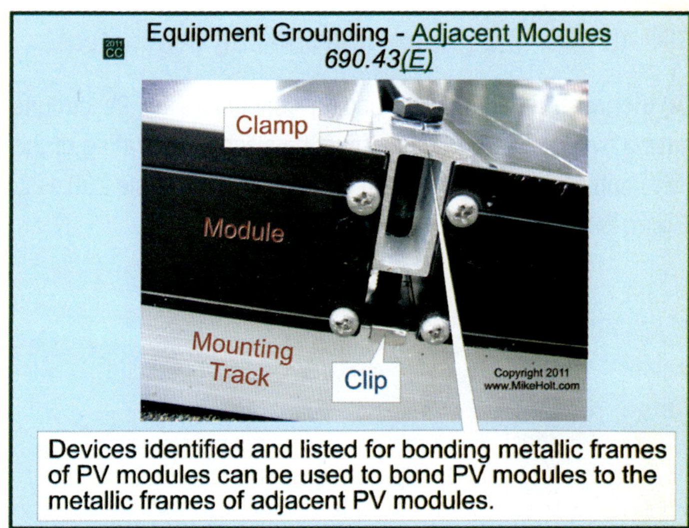

Figure 690–15

(F) Run Together. All conductors of a circuit, including the equipment grounding conductor, must be installed in the same raceway or cable, or otherwise run with the PV array circuit conductors when they leave the vicinity of the PV array [300.3(B)]. **Figure 690–16**

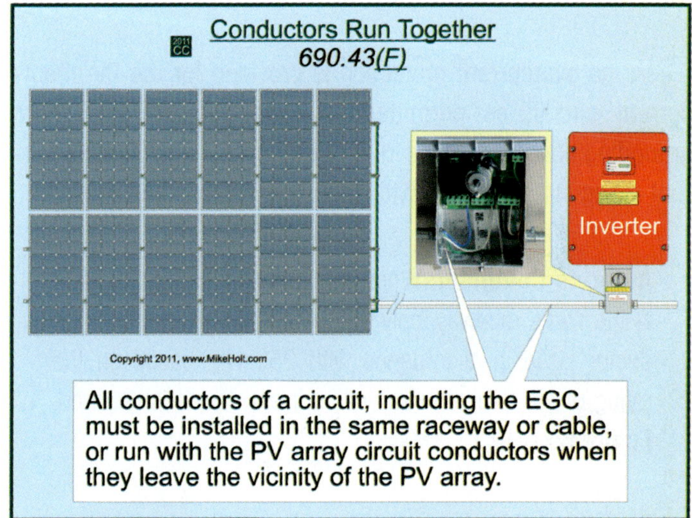

Figure 690–16

690.45 Size of Equipment Grounding Conductors.

(A) General. Equipment grounding conductors for PV circuits having overcurrent protection must be sized to the rating of the PV circuit overcurrent device in accordance with Table 250.122. **Figure 690–17**

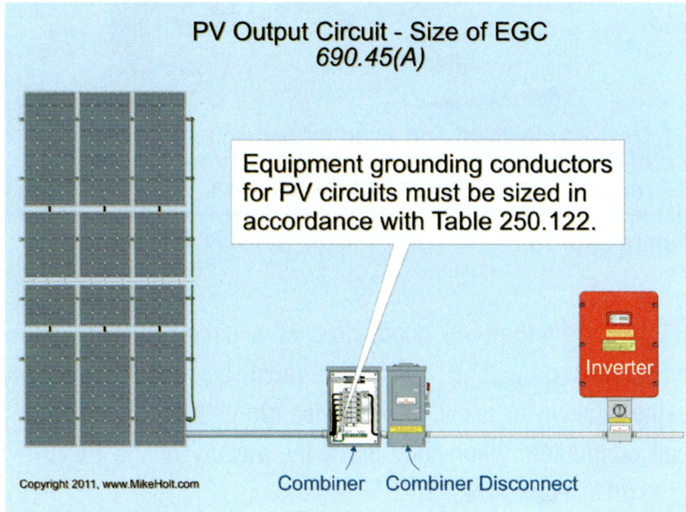

Figure 690–17

Where no overcurrent protection is provided for the PV direct-current circuit, as permitted in 690.9 Ex, the equipment grounding conductor is sized to the PV circuit short-circuit current rating in accordance with Table 250.122.

> **Author's Comment:** When multiple circuits are installed in the same raceway, only one equipment grounding conductor sized in accordance with 250.122 based on the rating of the largest circuit overcurrent device is required. **Figure 690–18**

690.46 Array Equipment Grounding Conductors.

Exposed equipment grounding conductors 8 AWG and smaller subject to physical damage must be protected by installing the conductor in a raceway [250.120(C)]. **Figure 690–19**

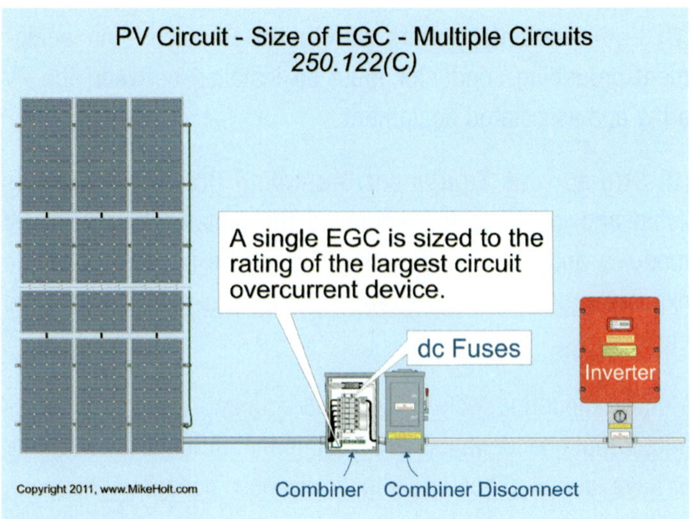

Figure 690–18

Figure 690–19

690.47 Grounding Electrode System.

(B) Direct-Current Systems. If installing a dc system, a grounding electrode system must be provided in accordance with 250.166 with a grounding electrode conductor in accordance with 250.64.

A common dc grounding electrode conductor is permitted to serve multiple inverters with the size of the common grounding electrode and the tap conductors in accordance with 250.166. The tap conductors must be connected to the common grounding electrode conductor in such a manner that the common grounding electrode conductor remains without a splice or joint.

(C) Alternating- and Direct-Current Grounding Requirements. PV systems with direct-current modules having no direct connection between the direct-current grounded conductor and alternating-current grounded conductor must be bonded to the alternating-current grounding system by one of the methods listed in (1), (2), or (3).

> **Note 1:** ANSI/UL 1741—*Standard for Inverters, Converters, and Controllers for Use in Independent Power Systems* has the grounding electrode conductor (GEC) connection point identified. In PV inverters, the terminals for the direct-current and alternating-current equipment grounding conductors common with each other are marked "direct-current GEC terminal."

> **Note 2:** For utility-interactive systems, the existing premises grounding system serves as the alternating-current grounding system.

(1) Separate Direct-Current Grounding Electrode System Bonded to the Alternating-Current Grounding Electrode System. A separate direct-current grounding electrode bonded to the alternating-current grounding electrode system with a bonding jumper sized to the larger of the existing alternating-current grounding electrode conductor or direct-current grounding electrode conductor specified by 250.166. **Figure 690–20**

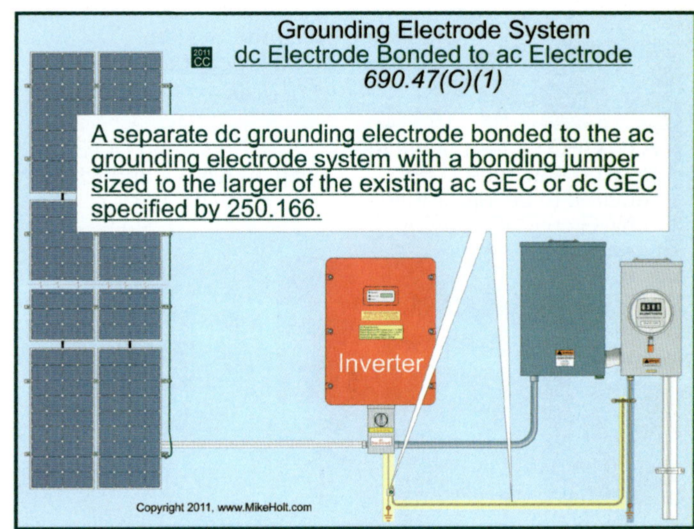

Figure 690–20

The direct-current grounding electrode conductor or bonding jumper to the alternating-current grounding electrode system can't be used as the required alternating-current equipment grounding conductor.

(2) Common Direct-Current and Alternating-Current Grounding Electrode. A direct-current grounding electrode conductor sized in accordance with 250.166 run from the marked direct-current grounding electrode connection point to the alternating-current grounding electrode. **Figures 690–21, 690–22, and 690–23**

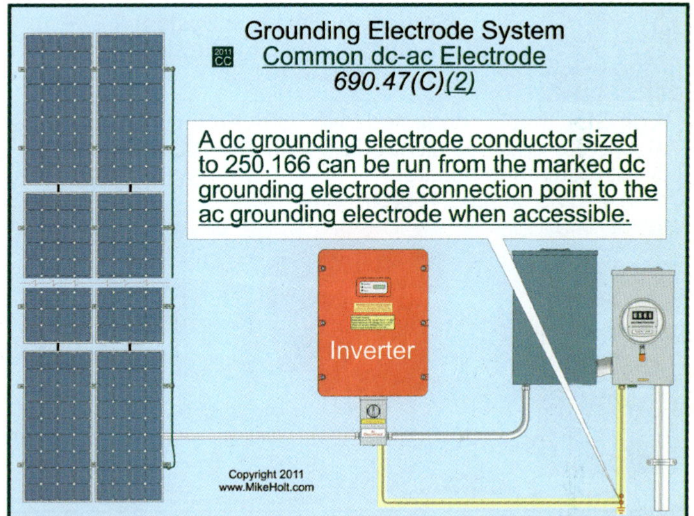

Figure 690–21

Where an alternating-current grounding electrode isn't accessible, the direct-current grounding electrode conductor is permitted to terminate to the alternating-current grounding electrode conductor by irreversible compression-type connectors listed as grounding and bonding equipment or by the exothermic welding process [250.64(C)(1)]. See **Figure 690–22**

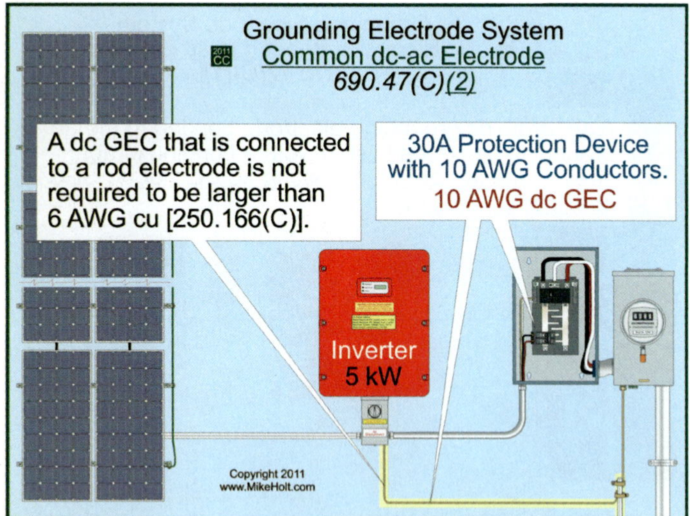

Figure 690–22

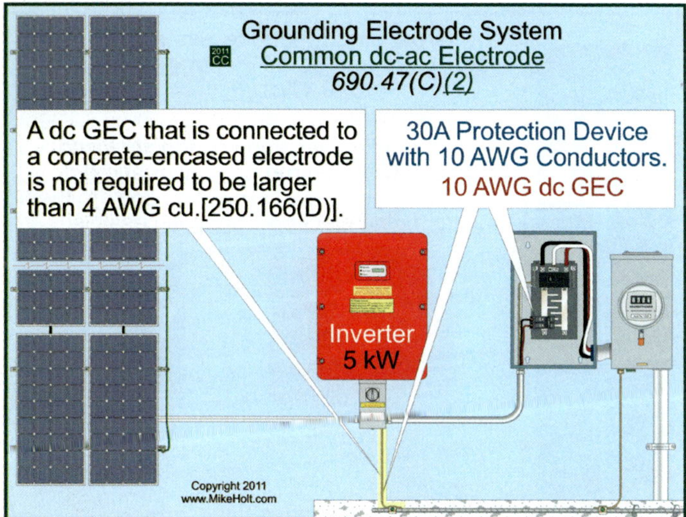

Figure 690–23

The direct-current grounding electrode conductor or bonding jumper to the alternating-current grounding electrode system can't be used as the required alternating-current equipment grounding conductor.

(3) Combined Direct-Current Grounding Electrode Conductor and Alternating-Current Equipment Grounding Conductor. An unspliced, or irreversibly spliced, combined equipment grounding/grounding electrode conductor run from the marked direct-current grounding electrode connection point along with the alternating-current circuit conductors to the grounding busbar in the associated alternating-current equipment. **Figure 690–24**

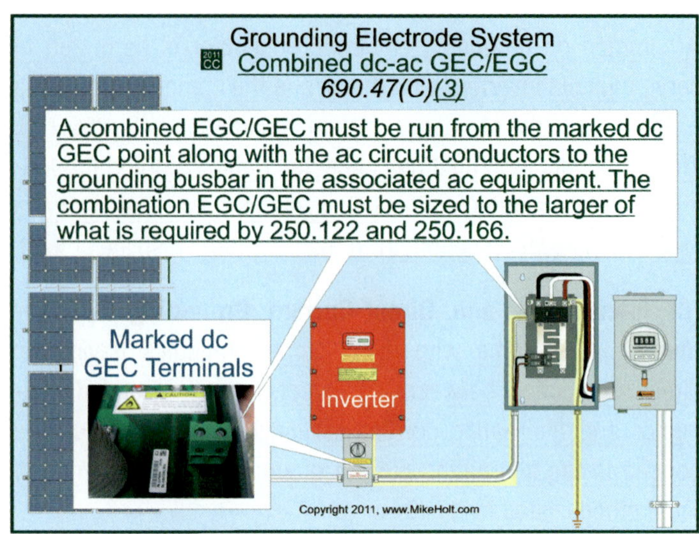

Figure 690–24

The combined equipment grounding/grounding electrode conductor must be sized to the larger of 250.122 or 250.166 and be installed in accordance with 250.64(E).

Example: *What size equipment grounding/grounding electrode conductor is required for a 5 kW inverter where the output circuit conductors, 10 AWG, are protected by a 30A protection device?* **Figure 690–25**

Answer: *Section 250.122 requires the equipment grounding conductor to be sized no smaller than 10 AWG, and 250.166(B) requires the grounding electrode conductor to be sized no smaller than the system circuit conductors, but no small than 8 AWG. In this case, the combined equipment grounding/grounding electrode conductor must be a minimum 8 AWG.*

Author's Comment: To prevent inductive choking of grounding electrode conductors, ferrous raceways and enclosures containing grounding electrode conductors must have each end of the raceway or enclosure bonded to the grounding electrode conductor in accordance with 250.92(B) [250.64(E)]. Nonferrous metal raceways, such as aluminum rigid metal conduit, enclosing the grounding electrode conductor aren't required to meet the "bonding each end of the raceway to the grounding electrode conductor" provisions of this section.

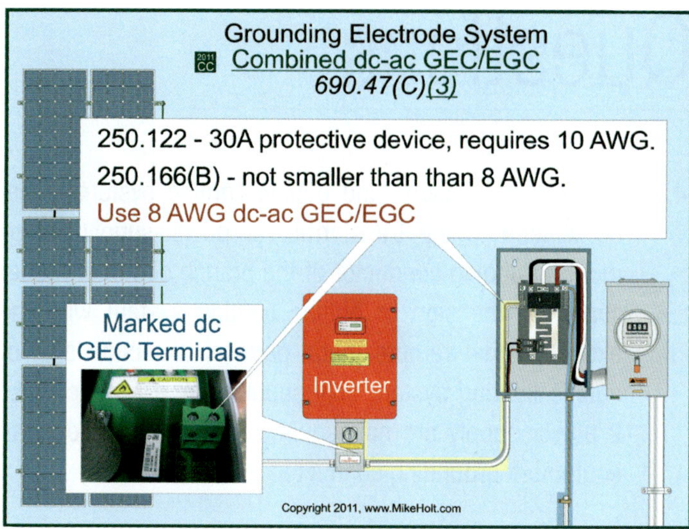

Figure 690–25

CAUTION: *The effectiveness of a grounding electrode is significantly reduced if a ferrous metal raceway containing a grounding electrode conductor isn't bonded to the ferrous metal raceway at both ends. This is because a single conductor carrying high-frequency induced lightning current in a ferrous raceway causes the raceway to act as an inductor, which severely limits (chokes) the current flow through the grounding electrode conductor. ANSI/IEEE 142—Recommended Practice for Grounding of Industrial and Commercial Power Systems (Green Book) states: "An inductive choke can reduce the current flow by 97 percent."*

Author's Comment: To save a lot of time and effort, install the grounding electrode conductor in PVC conduit suitable for the application [352.10(F)].

690.48 Continuity of Equipment Grounding Systems. Where the removal of equipment opens the bonding connection between the grounding electrode conductor and exposed conducting surfaces of PV equipment, a bonding jumper is required while the equipment is removed.

690.49 Continuity of PV Source and Output Circuit Grounded Conductors. Where the removal of equipment opens the connection between the grounding electrode conductor and PV system grounded conductor, a bonding jumper must be installed to maintain system grounding while equipment is removed.

690.50 Equipment Bonding Jumpers. Equipment bonding jumpers 8 AWG and smaller subject to physical damage must be protected from physical damage by installing the conductor in a raceway in accordance with 250.120(C).

CHAPTER 6

Practice Questions

CHAPTER 6. SPECIAL EQUIPMENT—PRACTICE QUESTIONS

Article 600. Electric Signs and Outline Lighting

1. Article 600 covers the installation of conductors and equipment for ______.

    (a) electric signs
    (b) outline lighting
    (c) neon tubing
    (d) all of these

2. A section sign is a sign or ______, shipped as subassemblies that require field-installed wiring between the subassemblies to complete the overall sign.

    (a) outline lighting system
    (b) skeleton tubing system
    (c) neon system
    (d) sign body

3. For an outline lighting system, the equipment grounding conductor size shall be in accordance with ______ based on the rating of the overcurrent device protecting the conductors supplying the sign.

    (a) 250.66
    (b) 250.122
    (c) 310.13
    (d) 310.16

4. Metal parts of signs and outline lighting systems must be bonded to the transformer or power-supply equipment grounding conductor of the branch circuit or feeder supplying the sign or outline lighting system with the exception that remote metal parts of a section sign or outline lighting system only supplied by a remote Class 2 power supply are not required to be connected to an equipment grounding conductor.

    (a) True
    (b) False

5. Listed flexible metal conduit or listed liquidtight flexible metal conduit for secondary circuit conductors for neon tubing can be used as a bonding means if the total accumulative length of the conduit does not exceed ______.

    (a) 3 ft
    (b) 10 ft
    (c) 50 ft
    (d) 100 ft

Article 640. Audio Signal Processing, Amplification, and Reproduction Equipment

1. Electronic organs or other electronic musical instruments are included in the scope of Article 640.

    (a) True
    (b) False

Article 645. Information Technology Equipment

1. Article 645 covers the ______ of information technology equipment and systems in an information technology equipment room that meets the requirements of 645.4.

   (a) equipment
   (b) power-supply wiring
   (c) interconnecting wiring
   (d) all of these

2. Exposed non-current-carrying metal parts of an information technology system shall be ______.

   (a) bonded to an equipment grounding conductor
   (b) double insulated
   (c) GFCI protected
   (d) a or b

Article 680. Swimming Pools, Fountains, and Similar Installations

1. Permanently installed swimming pools include those constructed in the ground or partially in the ground, and capable of holding water in a depth greater than ______ in.

   (a) 36
   (b) 42
   (c) 48
   (d) 54

2. A spa or hot tub is a hydromassage pool or tub and is not designed to have the contents drained or discharged after each use.

   (a) True
   (b) False

3. A wet-niche luminaire is intended to be installed in a ______.

   (a) transformer
   (b) forming shell
   (c) hydromassage bathtub
   (d) all of these

4. For other than dwelling units, the branch circuits for pool-associated motors shall be installed in wiring methods including ______. Any wiring method employed shall include an insulated copper equipment grounding conductor sized in accordance with 250.122, but not smaller than 12 AWG.

   (a) PVC conduit
   (b) electrical metallic tubing where installed on or within buildings
   (c) flexible metal conduit
   (d) a or b

5. When PVC conduit extends from the pool light forming shell to a pool junction box, an 8 AWG ______ conductor shall be installed in the raceway.

   (a) solid bare
   (b) solid insulated
   (c) stranded insulated
   (d) b or c

6. Wet-niche luminaires installed in swimming pools shall be removable from the water for inspection, relamping or other maintenance. The luminaire maintenance location shall be accessible ______.

   (a) while the pool is drained
   (b) without entering the pool water
   (c) during construction
   (d) all of these

7. Branch-circuit wiring on the supply side of enclosures and junction boxes for underwater luminaires shall be installed in ______.

(a) RMC or IMC
(b) LFNC and PVC conduit
(c) any wiring method
(d) a or b

8. EMT where installed on buildings, is permitted to contain branch-circuit wiring for underwater pool luminaires.

(a) True
(b) False

9. Wet-niche luminaires shall be connected to an equipment grounding conductor not smaller than ______ AWG.

(a) 12
(b) 10
(c) 8
(d) 6

10. The ______ conductor terminals of a junction box (pool deck box), transformer enclosure, or other enclosure in the supply circuit to a wet niche luminaire shall be connected to the equipment grounding terminal of the panelboard.

(a) equipment grounding
(b) grounded
(c) grounding electrode
(d) ungrounded

11. An 8 AWG or larger solid copper equipotential bonding conductor shall be extended to service equipment to eliminate voltage gradients in the pool area.

(a) True
(b) False

12. For equipotential bonding of pool and spa equipment, a solid 8 AWG copper conductor shall be run back to the service equipment. This conductor shall be unbroken.

(a) True
(b) False

13. The ______ pool bonding conductor shall be connected to the equipotential bonding grid either by exothermic welding or by pressure connectors in accordance with 250.8.

(a) 8 AWG
(b) insulated or bare
(c) copper
(d) all of these

14. The swimming pool structure, including the structural reinforcing steel of the pool shell and deck, except reinforcing steel encapsulated with a nonconductive compound shall be bonded.

(a) True
(b) False

15. Which of the following shall be bonded?

(a) Metal parts of electrical equipment associated with the pool water circulating system.
(b) Pool structural metal.
(c) Metal fittings within or attached to the pool.
(d) all of these

16. Metal conduit and metal piping within ______ horizontally of the inside walls of the pool shall be bonded unless separated by a permanent barrier.

(a) 4 ft
(b) 5 ft
(c) 8 ft
(d) 10 ft

17. The equipotential bonding requirements for perimeter surfaces contained in 680.26(B)(2) don't apply to a listed self-contained spa or hot tub installed above a finished floor.

    (a) True
    (b) False

18. Metal parts of electric equipment associated with an indoor spa or hot tub water circulating system shall be bonded.

    (a) True
    (b) False

19. Metal raceways and metal piping within ______ of the inside walls of an indoor spa or hot tub, and not separated from the indoor spa or hot tub by a permanent barrier, shall be bonded.

    (a) 4 ft
    (b) 5 ft
    (c) 7 ft
    (d) 12 ft

20. Metal parts associated with an indoor spa or hot tub shall be bonded by ______.

    (a) the interconnection of threaded metal piping and fittings
    (b) metal-to-metal mounting on a common frame or base
    (c) a solid copper bonding jumper not smaller than 8 AWG solid
    (d) any of these

21. Fountain equipment supplied by a flexible cord shall have all exposed non-current-carrying metal parts grounded by an insulated copper equipment grounding conductor that is an integral part of the cord.

    (a) True
    (b) False

22. Metal piping systems and all grounded metal parts in contact with the circulating water of a hydromassage bathtub shall be bonded together using a(n) ______ solid copper bonding jumper not smaller than 8 AWG.

    (a) insulated
    (b) covered
    (c) bare
    (d) any of these

23. The 8 AWG solid bonding jumper required for hydromassage bathtubs shall not be required to be extended to any ______.

    (a) remote panelboard
    (b) service equipment
    (c) electrode
    (d) all of these

24. Metal piping systems and metal parts in contact with the circulating water must be bonded together and to the circulating pump motor with an 8 AWG bare solid copper conductor if it's not double-insulated. The solid bare 8 AWG copper conductor isn't required to be bonded to any remote panelboard, service equipment, or electrode. The solid bare 8 AWG copper conductor used for bonding hydromassage bath tubs must have sufficient length to terminate on a ______, and must terminate to the equipment grounding conductor of the motor circuit when a double-insulated circulating pump motor is used.

    (a) replacement non-double-insulated pump motor
    (b) replacement double-insulated pump motor
    (c) grounding electrode
    (d) b or c

Article 690 Solar Photovoltaic (PV) Systems

1. The provisions of Article 690 apply to ______ systems, including inverter(s), array circuit(s), and controller(s) for such systems.

   (a) photoconductive
   (b) photovoltaic
   (c) photogenic
   (d) photosynthesis

2. An alternating-current photovoltaic module is designed to generate ac power when exposed to______.

   (a) electromagnetic induction
   (b) heat
   (c) sunlight
   (d) hysteresis

3. A direct-current power-producing unit, mechanically integrated with modules or panels, a support structure and foundation, tracker, and other components as required, is known as a(n) "______."

   (a) pulse width modulator
   (b) array
   (c) capacitive supply bank
   (d) alternating-current photovoltaic module

4. ______ include photovoltaic cells, devices, modules, or modular materials that are integrated into the outer surface or structure of a building and serve as the outer protective surface of that building.

   (a) Protective photovoltaics
   (b) Building integrated photovoltaics
   (c) Bipolar photovoltaic arrays
   (d) Bipolar photoconductive arrays

5. A ______ controller controls dc voltage, dc current, or both, and is used to charge a battery.

   (a) charge
   (b) power
   (c) photovoltaic
   (d) b and c

6. A(n) ______ is a device that changes direct-current input to an alternating-current output.

   (a) diode
   (b) rectifier
   (c) transistor
   (d) inverter

7. A(n) ______ is a complete, environmentally protected unit consisting of solar cells, and other components, exclusive of tracker, designed to generate direct-current power when exposed to sunlight.

   (a) interface
   (b) battery
   (c) module
   (d) cell bank

8. The circuit conductors between the inverter or direct-current utilization equipment and the photovoltaic source circuit(s) are part of the ______.

   (a) photovoltaic output circuit
   (b) photovoltaic input circuit
   (c) inverter input circuit
   (d) inverter output circuit

9. A single array or aggregate of arrays that generates direct-current power at system voltage and current is the photovoltaic ______.

   (a) output source
   (b) source circuit
   (c) power source
   (d) array source

10. The circuit(s) between modules and from modules to the common connection point(s), of the direct-current system is known as the "______."

(a) photovoltaic source circuit
(b) photovoltaic array circuit
(c) photovoltaic input circuit
(d) photovoltaic output circuit

11. The photovoltaic system voltage is the direct-current voltage of any photovoltaic source or photovoltaic output circuit.

(a) True
(b) False

12. The solar ______ is the basic photovoltaic device that generates electricity when exposed to light.

(a) battery
(b) cell
(c) atom
(d) ray

13. The ______ is the total components and subsystems that, in combination, convert solar energy into electric energy suitable for connection to a utilization load.

(a) solar photovoltaic system
(b) solar array
(c) a and b
(d) neither a or b

14. A stand-alone system supplies power with an electrical production and distribution network.

(a) True
(b) False

15. A ______ is an electrical subset of a photovoltaic array.

(a) panel
(b) module
(c) circuit
(d) subarray

16. To limit the voltage induced by lightning, one conductor of a 2-wire PV system operating at over ______ must be solidly grounded (connected to the earth) in accordance with 250.4(A)(1).

(a) 15V
(b) 30V
(c) 50V
(d) none of these

17. The direct-current system grounding connection must be made at any ______ point(s) on the photovoltaic output circuit.

(a) one
(b) two
(c) three
(d) four

18. A(n) ______ between a photovoltaic array and other equipment must be installed.

(a) grounded conductor
(b) main bonding jumper
(c) equipment grounding conductor
(d) system bonding jumper

19. Devices ______ for grounding the metallic frames of PV modules and associated equipment can be used to bond the exposed metal surfaces of the modules and equipment to the metal racks.

(a) identified as equipment grounding conductors
(b) approved as equipment grounding conductors
(c) listed as equipment grounding conductors
(d) a and c

20. Metallic mounting racks used as an equipment grounding conductor must be ______ as an equipment grounding conductors or have ______ bonding jumpers/devices connected between the separate metallic racks and be bonded to the grounding system.

(a) listed
(b) labeled
(c) identified
(d) a and b

21. Devices and systems used for securing PV modules to metal mounting racks that serve as an equipment grounding conductor must be ______ for the purpose of grounding PV modules.

(a) listed
(b) labeled
(c) identified
(d) a and b

22. Devices ______ for bonding the metallic frames of PV modules shall be permitted to bond the metallic frames of PV modules to the metallic frames of adjacent PV modules.

(a) listed
(b) labeled
(c) identified
(d) a and c

23. All conductors of a circuit, including the equipment grounding conductor must be installed in the same raceway or cable, or otherwise run with the PV array circuit conductors when they leave the vicinity of the PV array.

(a) True
(b) False

24. Equipment grounding conductors for PV circuits having overcurrent protection must be sized to the rating of the PV circuit overcurrent device in accordance with ______.

(a) 250.122
(b) 250.66
(c) Table 250.122
(d) Table 250.66

25. Where no overcurrent protection is provided for the PV dc circuit, as permitted in 690.9 Ex, the equipment grounding conductor is sized to the PV circuit short-circuit current rating in accordance with ______.

(a) 250.122
(b) 250.66
(c) Table 250.122
(d) Table 250.66

26. Where exposed and subject to physical damage, array equipment grounding conductors smaller than 4 AWG must be protected by a raceway or cable armor.

(a) True
(b) False

27. A common dc grounding electrode conductor of a PV system is permitted to serve multiple inverters with the size of the common grounding electrode and the tap conductors in accordance with 250.166. The tap conductors must be connected to the common grounding electrode conductor in such a manner that the common grounding electrode conductor remains ______.

(a) without a splice or joint
(b) inside inverter enclosures
(c) inside a raceway
(d) supported on insulators

28. PV systems having no direct connection between the dc grounded conductor and the ac grounded conductor shall have a(n) ______ which shall be bonded to the ac grounding system.

    (a) alternating-current grounding system
    (b) direct-current grounding system
    (c) separately derived grounding system
    (d) none of these

29. PV systems with direct-current modules having no direct connection between the direct-current grounded conductor and alternating-current grounded conductor must be bonded to the alternating-current grounding system by a(n)______.

    (a) separate direct-current grounding electrode bonded to the alternating-current grounding electrode system with a bonding jumper
    (b) direct-current grounding electrode conductor sized to 250.166 run from the marked direct-current grounding electrode connection point to the alternating-current grounding electrode
    (c) unspliced, or irreversibly spliced, combined equipment grounding/grounding electrode conductor run from the marked direct-current grounding electrode connection point along with the alternating-current circuit conductors to the grounding busbar in the associated alternating-current equipment
    (d) all of these

30. Where the removal of equipment opens the bonding connection between the ______ and exposed conducting surfaces of PV equipment, a bonding jumper is required while the equipment is removed.

    (a) equipment grounding conductor
    (b) grounded conductor
    (c) grounding electrode conductor
    (d) ungrounded conductor

31. Where the removal of the utility-interactive inverter or other equipment disconnects the bonding connection between the grounding electrode conductor and the photovoltaic source and/or photovoltaic output circuit grounded conductor, a(n) ______ shall be installed to maintain the system grounding while the inverter or other equipment is removed.

    (a) grounding electrode conductor
    (b) fuse
    (c) bonding jumper
    (d) overcurrent device

Notes

CHAPTER

8 COMMUNICATIONS SYSTEMS

INTRODUCTION TO CHAPTER 8—COMMUNICATIONS SYSTEMS

Chapter 8 of the *National Electrical Code* covers the wiring requirements for communications systems such as telephones, radio and TV antennas, satellite dishes, closed-circuit television (CCTV), and cable TV (CATV) systems, as well as network-powered and broadband-powered communications systems. **Figure 1**

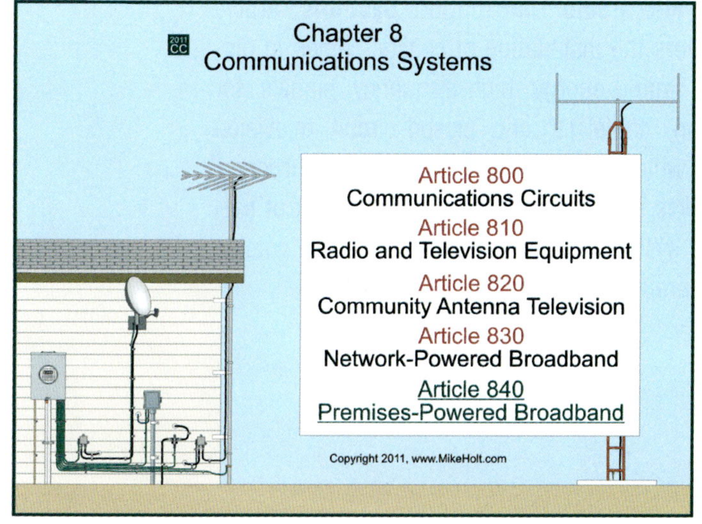

Figure 1

Communications systems aren't subject to the general requirements contained in Chapters 1 through 4 or the special requirements of Chapters 5 through 7, except where a Chapter 8 rule specifically refers to one of those chapters [90.3]. Also, installations of communications equipment under the exclusive control of communications utilities located outdoors, or in building spaces used exclusively for such installations, are exempt from the *NEC* [90.2(B)(4)]. **Figure 2**

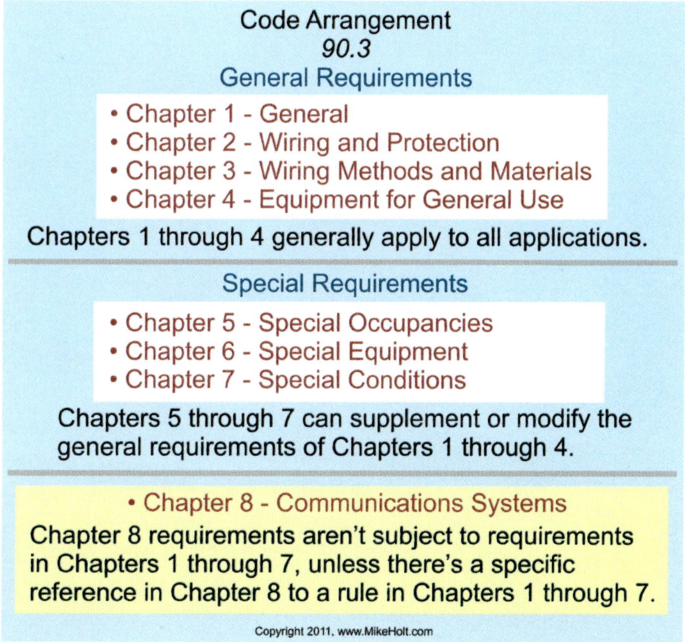

Code Arrangement
90.3
General Requirements

- Chapter 1 - General
- Chapter 2 - Wiring and Protection
- Chapter 3 - Wiring Methods and Materials
- Chapter 4 - Equipment for General Use

Chapters 1 through 4 generally apply to all applications.

Special Requirements

- Chapter 5 - Special Occupancies
- Chapter 6 - Special Equipment
- Chapter 7 - Special Conditions

Chapters 5 through 7 can supplement or modify the general requirements of Chapters 1 through 4.

- Chapter 8 - Communications Systems

Chapter 8 requirements aren't subject to requirements in Chapters 1 through 7, unless there's a specific reference in Chapter 8 to a rule in Chapters 1 through 7.

Copyright 2011, www.MikeHolt.com

Figure 2

- **Article 800—Communications Circuits.** Article 800 covers the installation requirements for telephone wiring and for other related telecommunications purposes such as computer local area networks (LANs), and outside wiring for fire and burglar alarm systems connected to central stations.

- **Article 810—Radio and Television Equipment.** This article covers antenna systems for radio and television receiving equipment, amateur radio transmitting and receiving equipment, and certain features of transmitter safety. It also includes antennas such as multi-element, vertical rod and dish, and the wiring and cabling that connects them to the equipment.

- **Article 820—Community Antenna Television (CATV) and Radio Distribution Systems.** Article 820 covers the installation of coaxial cables to distribute limited-energy high-frequency signals for television, cable TV, and closed-circuit television (CCTV), which is often used for security purposes. This article also covers the premises wiring of satellite TV systems where the dish antenna is outside and covered by Article 810.

- **Article 840—Premises-Powered Broadband Communications Systems.** Article 840 covers premises-powered optical fiber-based broadband communications systems. The systems use optical fiber cable to the premises supplying a broadband signal to an optical network terminal that converts the broadband signal into traditional telephone, video, high-speed internet, and interactive services.

Communications Circuits

INTRODUCTION TO ARTICLE 800—COMMUNICATIONS CIRCUITS

This article has its roots in telephone technology. Consequently, it addresses telephone and related systems that use twisted-pair wiring. Here are a few key points to remember about Article 800:

- Don't attach incoming communications cables to the service-entrance power mast.
- It's critical to determine the "point of entrance" for these circuits.
- Ground the primary protector as close as practicable to the point of entrance.
- Keep the grounding electrode conductor for the primary protector as straight and as short as possible.
- If you locate communications cables above a suspended ceiling, route and support them to allow access via ceiling panel removal.
- Keep these cables separated from lightning protection circuits.
- If you install communications cables in a Chapter 3 raceway, you must do so in conformance with the *NEC* requirements for the raceway system.
- Special labeling and marking provisions apply—follow them carefully.

Note: The term "Grounding Conductor" previously used in this article has been replaced by either "Bonding Conductor" or "Grounding Electrode Conductor (GEC)" where applicable to more accurately reflect the application and function of the conductor. **Figures 800–1 and 800–2**

Author's Comment: For Articles 800, 810, and 820, the difference between a "bonding conductor" and a "grounding electrode conductor" is where they terminate. The bonding conductor terminates at the intersystem bonding termination; the grounding electrode connects to the power grounding electrode system [250.50].

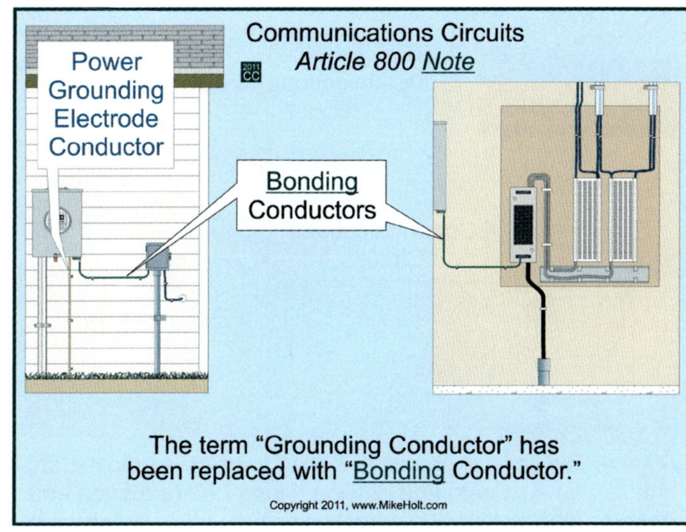

Figure 800–1

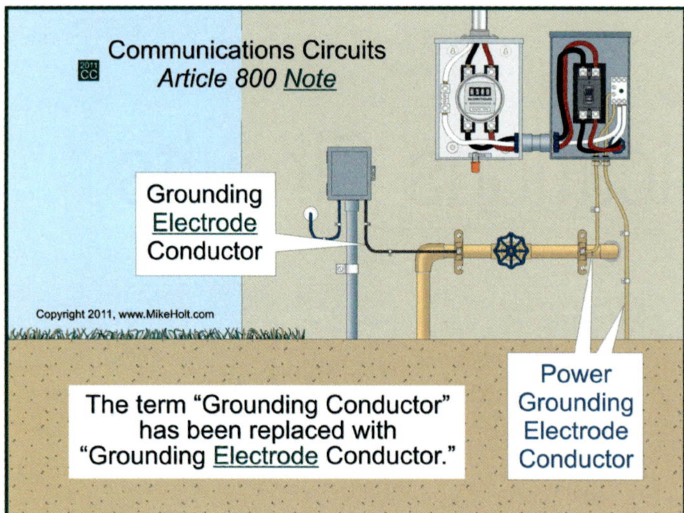

Figure 800–2

PART I. GENERAL

800.1 Scope. This article covers circuits that extend voice, audio, video, interactive services, and outside wiring for fire alarms and burglar alarms from the communications utility to the customer's communications equipment up to and including equipment such as a telephone, fax machine, or answering machine [800.2] and communications equipment. **Figure 800–3**

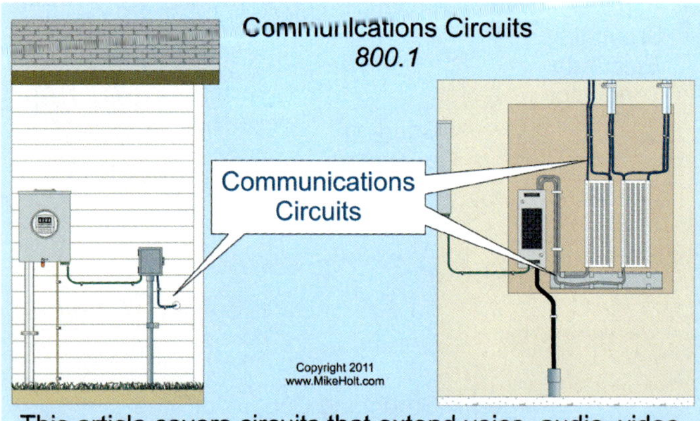

Figure 800–3

Note: The *NEC* installation requirements don't apply to communications utility equipment located outdoors or in building spaces where under the exclusive control of the communications utility [90.2(B)(4)]. **Figure 800–4**

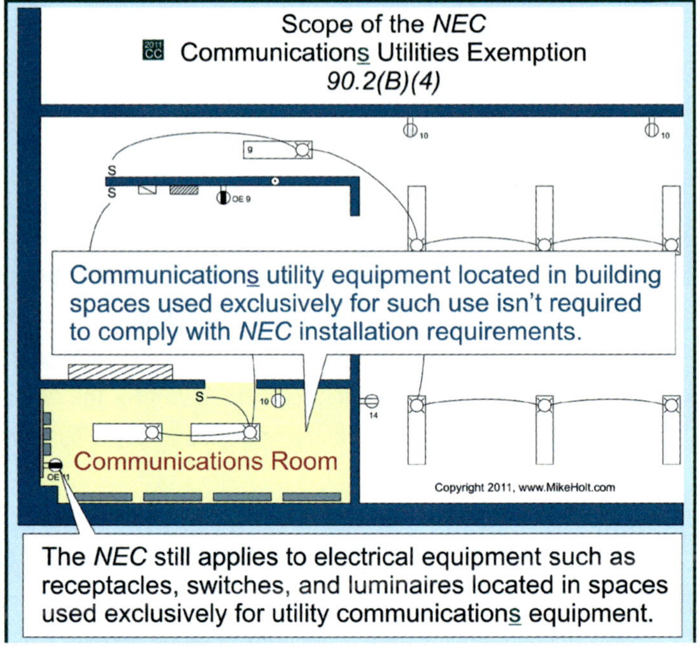

Figure 800–4

PART III. PROTECTION

800.90 Primary Protection.

(A) Application. A listed primary protector is required for each communications circuit.

(B) Location. The primary protector must be located as close as practicable to the point of entrance.

Note: The point of entrance is defined as the point within the building where the communications cable emerges from an external wall, from a concrete floor slab, or from a rigid metal conduit or an intermediate metal conduit connected to an electrode by a grounding electrode conductor in accordance with 800.100 [800.2].

Author's Comment: Selecting a primary protector location to achieve the shortest practicable primary protector bonding conductor or grounding electrode conductor [800.100(A)(4)] helps reduce differences in potential between communications circuits and other metallic systems during lightning events.

800.93 Grounding or Interruption of Metallic Sheath Members of Communications Cables.

(A) Entering Buildings. In installations where the communications cable enters a building, the metallic sheath members of the cable shall be either grounded as specified in 800.100 or interrupted by an insulating joint or equivalent device. The grounding or interruption shall be as close as practicable to the point of entrance. Figure 800–5

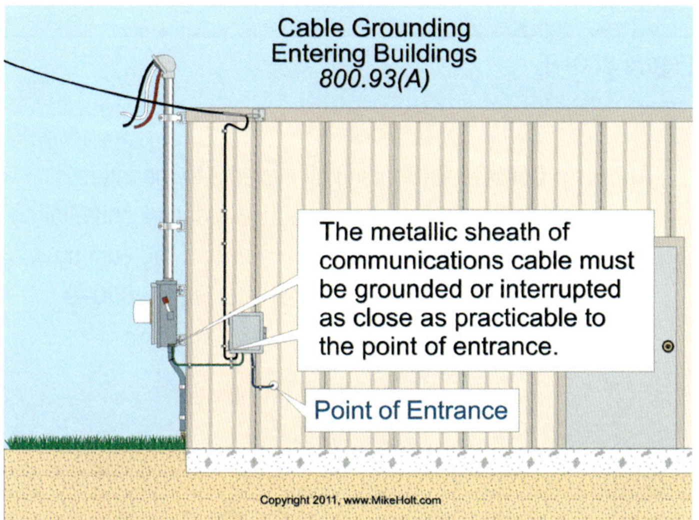

Figure 800–5

PART IV. GROUNDING METHODS

800.100 Cable and Primary Protector Bonding and Grounding. The primary protector and the metallic member of cable sheaths must be bonded or grounded in accordance with (A) through (D).

(A) Bonding Conductor or Grounding Electrode Conductor.

(1) Insulation. Listed and be insulated, covered, or bare.

(2) Material. Copper or other corrosion-resistant conductive material, stranded or solid.

(3) Size. Not be smaller than 14 AWG with a current-carrying capacity of not less than the grounded metallic sheath member or protected conductor of the communications cable, but not required to be larger than 6 AWG.

(4) Length. As short as practicable and for one- and two-family dwellings, the bonding conductor or grounding electrode conductor must not exceed 20 ft in length. Figure 800–6

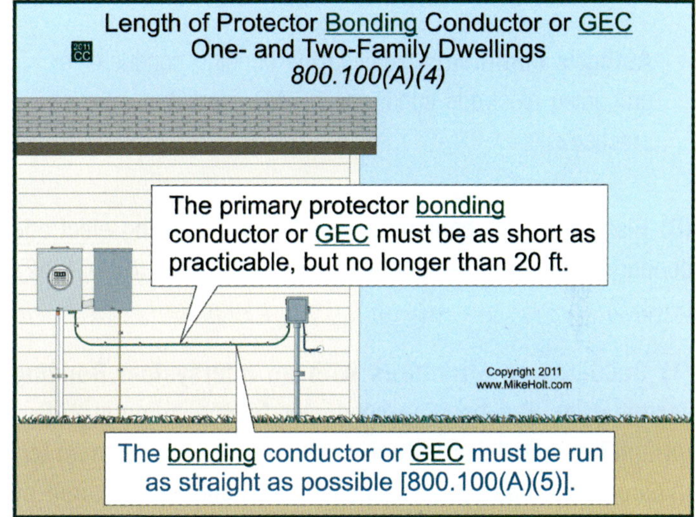

Figure 800–6

Note: Limiting the length of the bonding conductor or grounding electrode conductor helps limit induced potential (voltage) differences between the building's power and communications systems during lightning events.

Ex: If the bonding conductor or grounding electrode conductor is over 20 ft in length for one- and two-family dwellings, a separate ground rod not less than 5 ft long [800.100(B)(3)(2)] with fittings suitable for the application [800.100(C)] must be installed. The additional ground rod must be bonded to the power grounding electrode system with a minimum 6 AWG conductor [800.100(D)].

(5) Run in Straight Line. Run in as straight a line as practicable.

Author's Comment: Lightning doesn't like to travel around corners or through loops, which is why the grounding electrode conductor or bonding jumper must be run as straight as practicable.

(6) Physical Protection. The bonding conductor and grounding electrode conductor must not be subject to physical damage. If installed in a metal raceway, both ends of the raceway must be bonded to the contained conductor or connected to the same terminal or electrode to which the bonding conductor or grounding electrode conductor is connected.

Author's Comment: Installing the bonding conductor or grounding electrode conductor in PVC conduit is a better practice.

(B) Electrode. The bonding conductor or grounding electrode conductor must be connected in accordance with (B)(1), (B)(2), or (B)(3):

(1) Buildings or Structures with an Intersystem Bonding Termination. The bonding conductor for the primary protector and the metallic sheath of communications cable must terminate to the intersystem bonding termination as required by 250.94. **Figure 800–7**

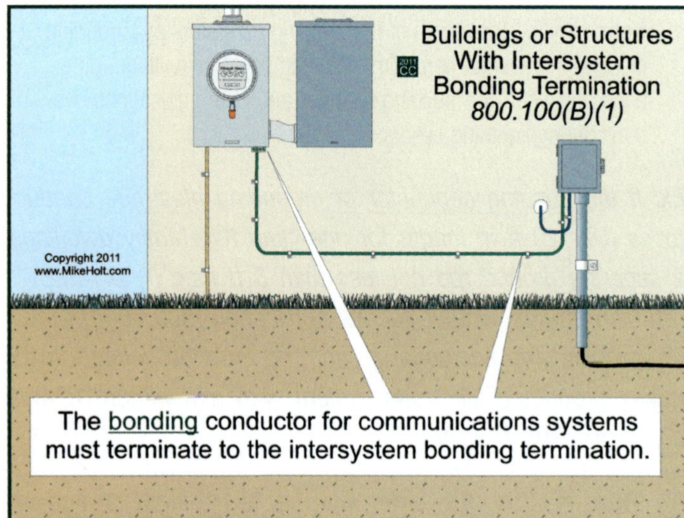

Figure 800–7

Note: According to the Article 100 definition, an "Intersystem Bonding Termination" is a device that provides a means to connect bonding conductors for communications systems to the grounding electrode system, in accordance with 250.94. **Figure 800–8**

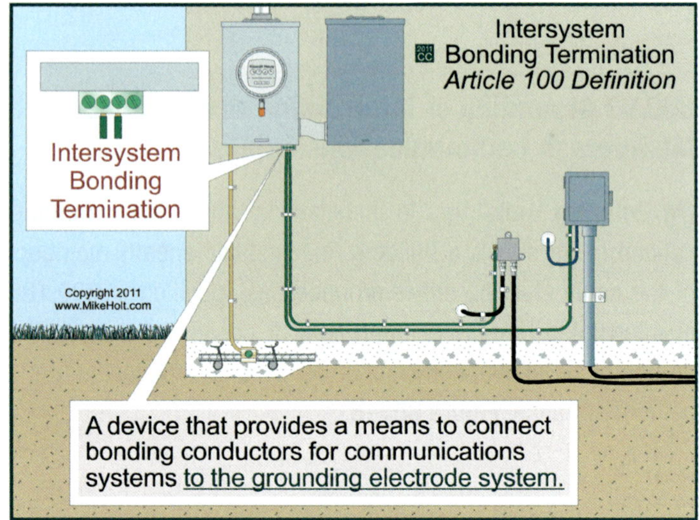

Figure 800–8

Author's Comment: Bonding all systems to the intersystem bonding termination helps reduce induced potential (voltage) differences between the power and the communications systems during lightning events. **Figure 800–9**

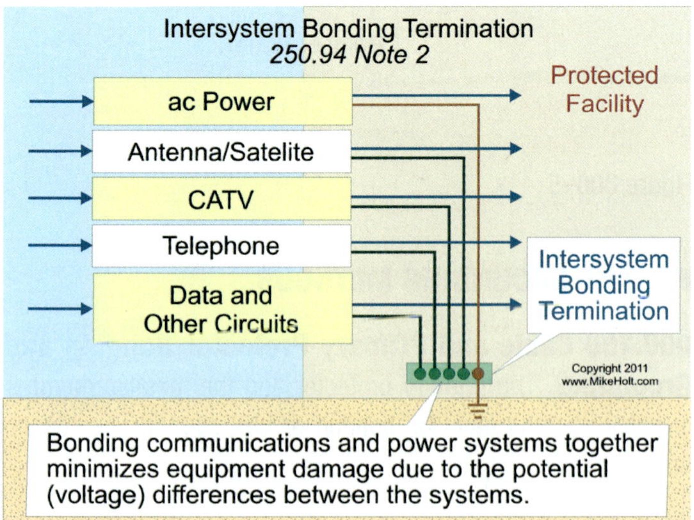

Figure 800–9

(2) Building/Structure Without Intersystem Bonding Termination. The bonding conductor or grounding electrode conductor must terminate to the nearest accessible: **Figure 800–10**

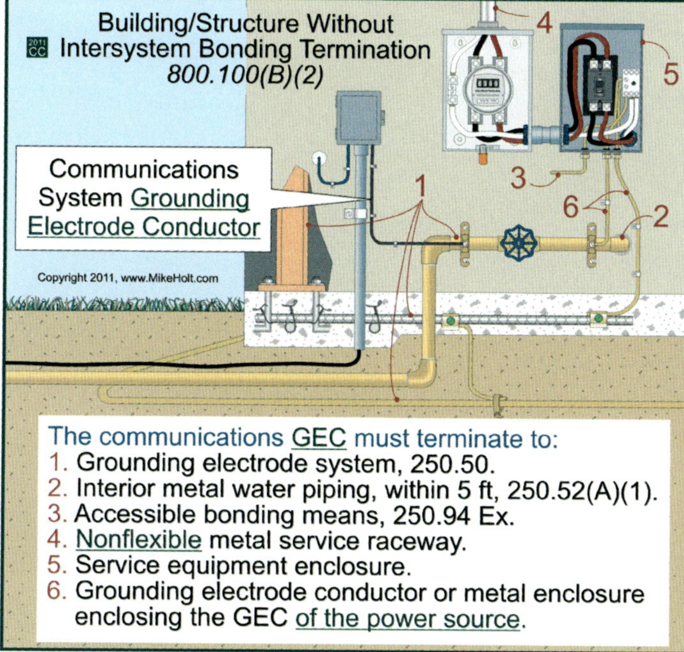

Figure 800–10

(1) Building/structure grounding electrode system [250.50].

(2) Interior metal water piping system, within 5 ft from its point of entrance [250.52(A)(1)].

(3) Accessible means external to the building, as covered in 250.94 Ex.

(4) Nonflexible metallic service raceway.

(5) Service equipment enclosure.

(6) Grounding electrode conductor or the grounding electrode conductor metal enclosure of the power service.

(7) Grounding electrode conductor or the grounding electrode of a remote building/structure disconnecting means [250.32].

The intersystem bonding termination must be mounted on the fixed part of an enclosure so that it won't interfere with the opening of an enclosure door. A bonding device must not be mounted on a door or cover even if the door or cover is nonremovable.

(3) In Buildings or Structures Without Intersystem Bonding Termination or Grounding Means. The grounding electrode conductor must connect to:

(1) Any individual grounding electrode described in 250.52(A)(1), (A)(2), (A)(3), or (A)(4).

(2) Any individual grounding electrode described in 250.52(A)(6) and (A)(7), or to a ground rod not less than 5 ft long and ½ in. in diameter located not less than 6 ft from electrodes of other systems. **Figure 800–11**

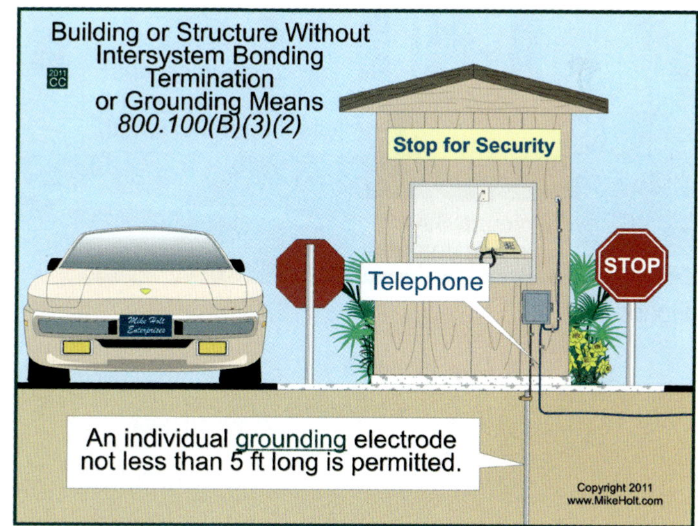

Figure 800–11

Author's Comment: The reason communications ground rods only need to be 5 ft long is because that's the length the telephone company used before the *NEC* contained requirements for communications systems. Telephone company ground rods were only 5 ft long because that's the length that would fit in their equipment trailers.

(C) Electrode Connection. Terminations at the grounding electrode must be by exothermic welding, listed lugs, listed pressure connectors, or listed clamps. Grounding fittings that are concrete-encased or buried in the earth must be listed for direct burial [250.70].

(D) Bonding of Electrodes. If a separate grounding electrode, such as a ground rod, is installed for a communications system, it must be bonded to the building's power grounding electrode system with a minimum 6 AWG conductor. **Figure 800–12**

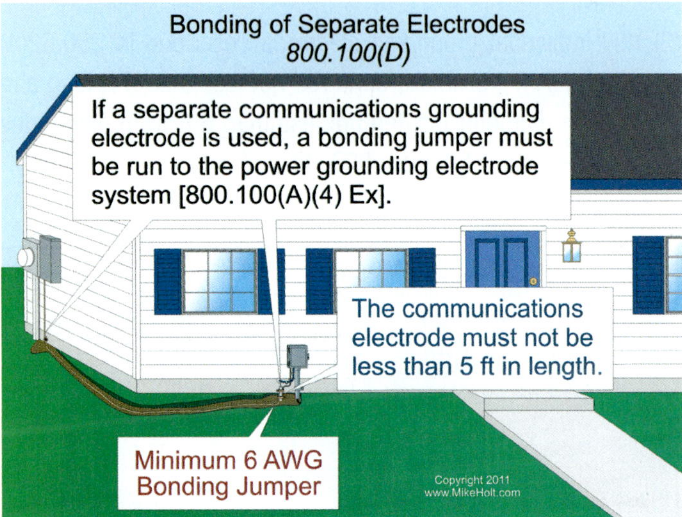

Figure 800–12

Note 2: Bonding helps reduce induced potential (voltage) between the power and communications systems during lightning events.

Radio and Television Equipment

INTRODUCTION TO ARTICLE 810—RADIO AND TELEVISION EQUIPMENT

This article covers transmitter and receiver equipment—and the wiring and cabling associated with that equipment. Here are a few key points to remember about Article 810:

- Avoid contact with conductors of other systems.
- Don't attach antennas or other equipment to the service-entrance power mast.
- If the mast isn't grounded properly, voltage surges caused by nearby lightning strikes can destroy it.
- Keep the bonding conductor or grounding electrode conductor as straight as practicable, and protect it from physical damage.
- If the mast isn't bonded properly, you risk flashovers and possible electrocution.
- Keep in mind that the purpose of bonding is to prevent a difference of potential between metallic objects and other conductive items, such as swimming pools.
- Clearances are critical, and Article 810 contains detailed clearance requirements. For example, it provides separate clearance requirements for indoor and outdoor locations.

Note: The term "Grounding Conductor" previously used in this article has been replaced by either "Bonding Conductor" or "Grounding Electrode Conductor (GEC)" where applicable to more accurately reflect the application and function of the conductor. **Figures 810–1 and 810–2**

PART I. GENERAL

810.1 Scope. Article 810 contains the installation requirements for the wiring of television and radio receiving equipment, such as digital satellite receiving equipment for television signals and amateur/citizen band radio equipment antennas. **Figure 810–3**

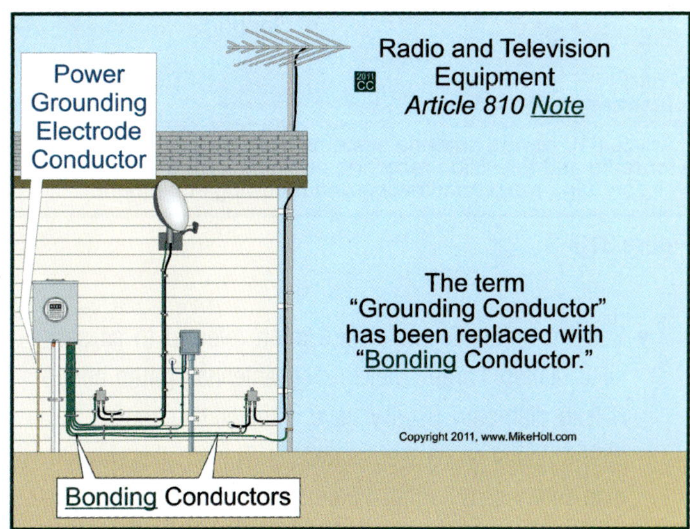

Figure 810–1

Author's Comment: Article 810 covers:

- VHF/UHF antennas, which receive local television signals.
- Amateur radio transmitting and receiving equipment, including HAM radio equipment (a noncommercial [amateur] communications system).

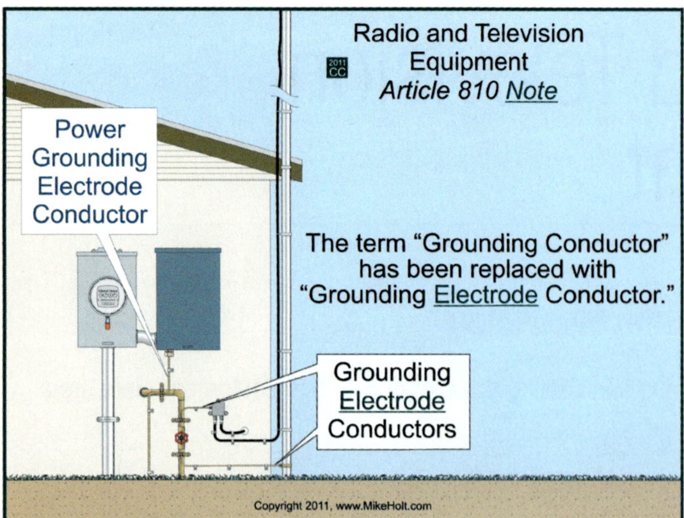

Figure 810–2

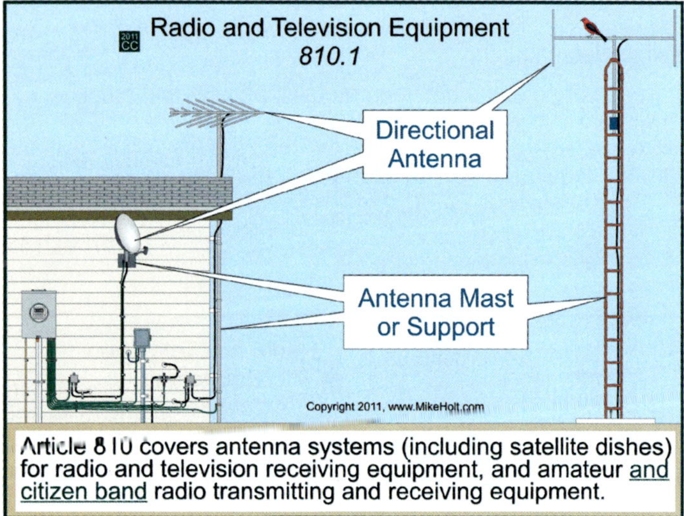

Figure 810–3

- Satellite antennas, which are often referred to as satellite dishes. Large satellite dish antennas (often about 6 ft in diameter) usually have a motor that moves the dish to focus on different satellites. The smaller satellite dish antennas (18 in. in diameter) are usually aimed at a single satellite.
- Roof-mounted antennas for AM/FM/XM radio reception.

PART II. RECEIVING EQUIPMENT—ANTENNA SYSTEMS

810.15 Metal Antenna Supports—Grounding. Outdoor masts and metal structures that support antennas must be grounded in accordance with 810.21. **Figure 810–4**

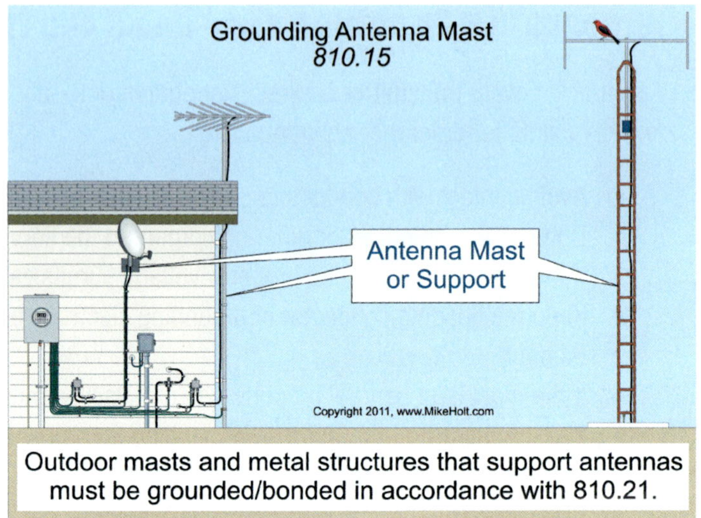

Figure 810–4

810.20 Antenna Discharge Unit.

(A) Required. Each lead-in conductor from an outdoor antenna must be provided with a listed antenna discharge unit. **Figure 810–5**

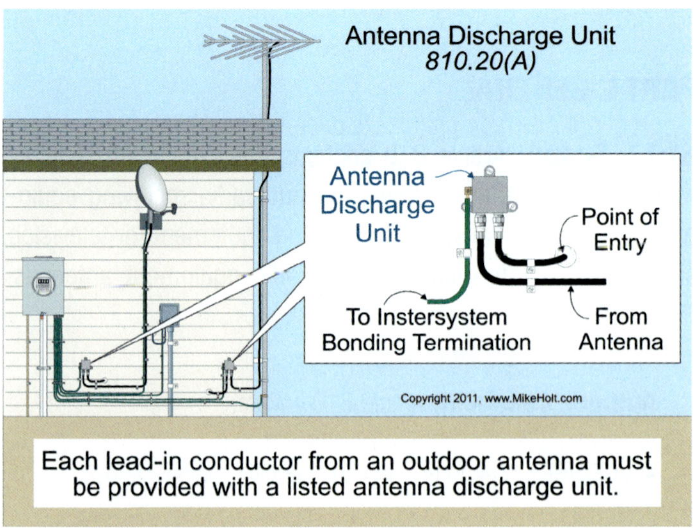

Figure 810–5

(B) Location. The antenna discharge unit must be located outside or inside the building, nearest the point of entrance, but not near combustible material.

(C) Grounding. The antenna discharge unit must be grounded in accordance with 810.21.

810.21 Bonding Conductor or Grounding Electrode Conductors.

The antenna mast [810.15] and antenna discharge unit [810.20(C)] must be grounded as follows. Figure 810–6

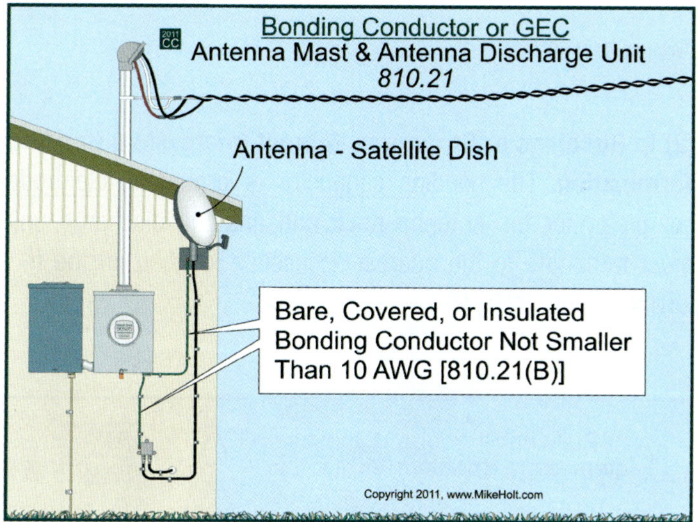

Figure 810–6

Author's Comment: Grounding the lead-in antenna cables and the mast helps prevent voltage surges caused by static discharge or nearby lightning strikes from reaching the center conductor of the lead-in coaxial cable. Because the satellite dish sits outdoors, wind creates a static charge on the antenna as well as on the cable attached to it. This charge can build up on both the antenna and the cable until it jumps across an air space, often passing through the electronics inside the low noise block down converter feedhorn (LNBF) or receiver. Connecting the coaxial cable and dish to the building grounding electrode system (grounding) helps to dissipate this static charge.

Nothing can prevent damage from a direct lightning strike, but grounding with proper surge protection can help reduce damage to the satellite dish and other equipment from nearby lightning strikes.

(A) Material. The bonding conductor or grounding electrode conductor to the electrode [810.21(F)] must be copper or other corrosion-resistant conductive material, stranded or solid.

(B) Insulation. Insulated, covered, or bare.

(C) Supports. The bonding conductor or grounding electrode conductor must be securely fastened in place.

(D) Mechanical Protection. The bonding conductor or grounding electrode conductor must be mechanically protected where subject to physical damage, and where installed in a metal raceway both ends of the raceway must be bonded to the bonding conductor or grounding electrode conductor.

Author's Comment: Installing the bonding conductor or grounding electrode conductor in PVC conduit is a better practice.

(E) Run in Straight Line. The bonding conductor or grounding electrode conductor must be run in as straight a line as practicable.

Author's Comment: Lightning doesn't like to travel around corners or through loops, which is why the bonding conductor or grounding electrode conductor must be run as straight as practicable.

(F) Electrode. The bonding conductor or grounding electrode conductor must terminate in accordance with (1), (2), or (3).

(1) Buildings or Structures With an Intersystem Bonding Termination. The bonding conductor for the antenna mast and antenna discharge unit must terminate to the intersystem bonding termination as required by 250.94 [Article 100 and 250.94]. Figure 810–7

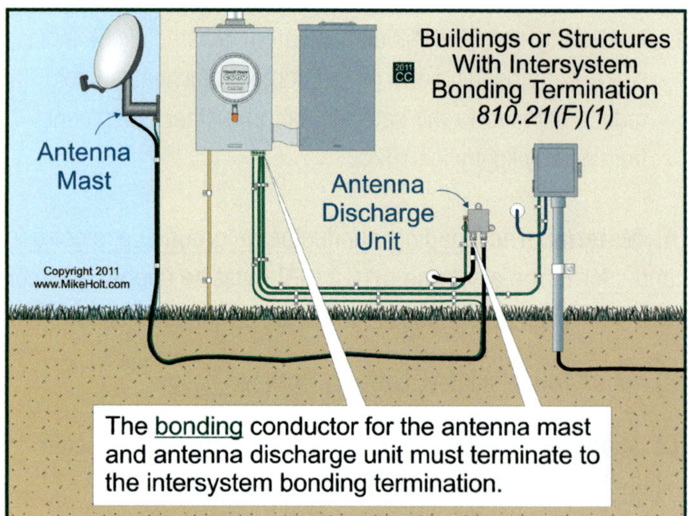

Figure 810–7

Note: According to the Article 100 definition, an Intersystem Bonding Termination is a device that provides a means to connect bonding conductors for communications systems to the grounding electrode system, in accordance with 250.94. **Figure 810–8**

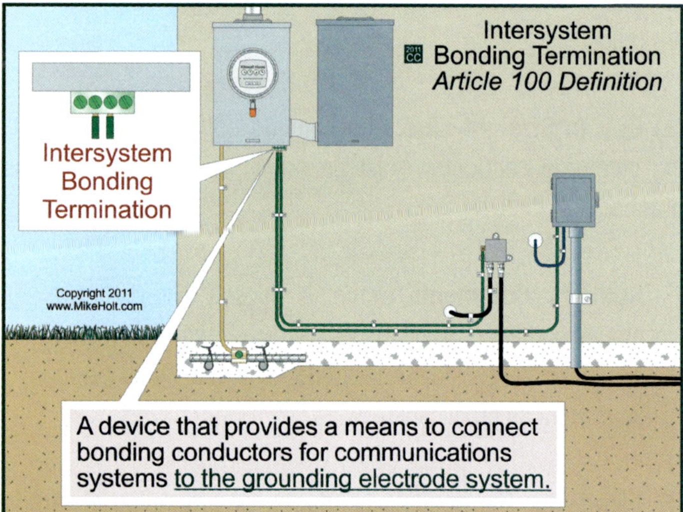

Figure 810–8

Author's Comment: Bonding all systems to the intersystem bonding termination helps reduce induced potential (voltage) differences between the power and the radio and television systems during lightning events. **Figure 810–9**

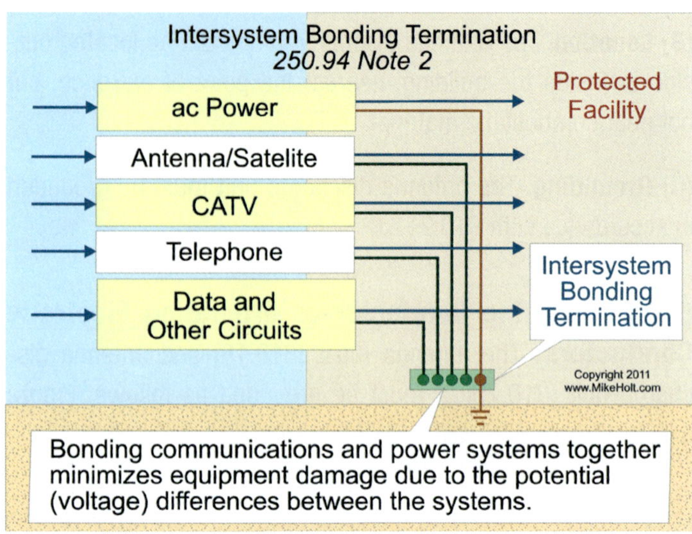

Figure 810–9

(2) In Buildings or Structures Without Intersystem Bonding Termination. The bonding conductor or grounding electrode conductor for the antenna mast and antenna discharge unit must terminate to the nearest accessible location on the following: **Figure 810–10**

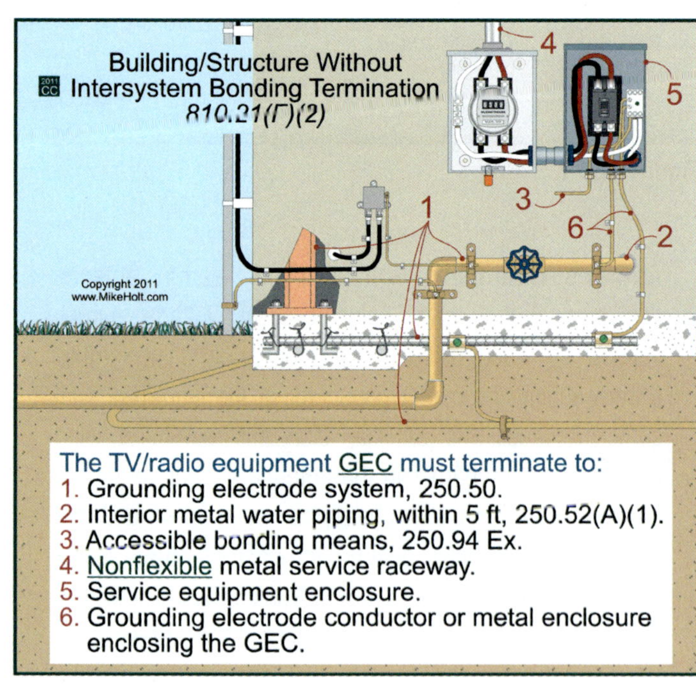

Figure 810–10

(1) Building/structure grounding electrode system [250.50].

(2) Interior metal water piping system, within 5 ft from its point of entrance [250.52(A)(1)]. **Figure 810–11**

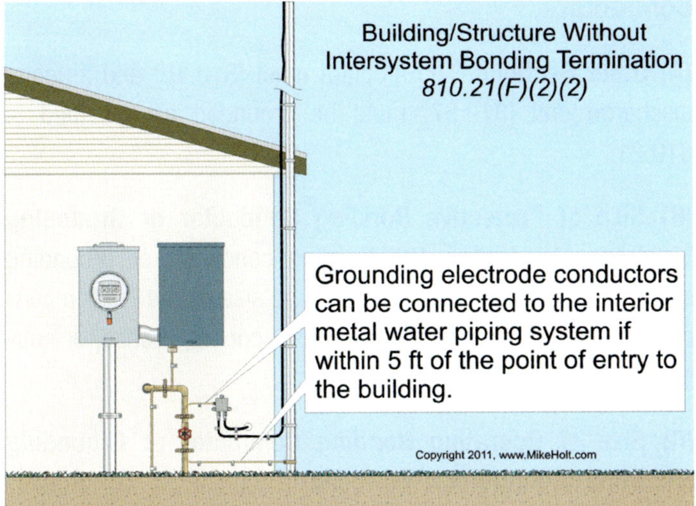

Figure 810–11

(3) Accessible means external to the building, as covered in 250.94.

(4) Nonflexible metallic service raceway.

(5) Service equipment enclosure.

(6) Grounding electrode conductor or the grounding electrode conductor metal enclosure.

(3) In Buildings or Structures Without a Grounding Means. The grounding electrode conductor for the antenna mast and antenna discharge unit must be connected to any grounding electrode as described in 250.52.

(G) Inside or Outside Building. The bonding conductor or grounding electrode conductor can be installed either inside or outside the building.

(H) Size. The bonding conductor or grounding electrode conductor must not be smaller than 10 AWG copper or 17 AWG copper-clad steel or bronze.

Author's Comment: Copper-clad steel or bronze wire (17 AWG) is often molded into the jacket of the coaxial cable to simplify the grounding of the lead-in conductor from an outdoor antenna to the discharge unit [810.21(F)].

(J) Bonding of Electrodes. If a ground rod is installed to serve as the grounding electrode for the radio and television equipment, it must be connected to the building's power grounding electrode system with a minimum 6 AWG conductor. **Figure 810–12**

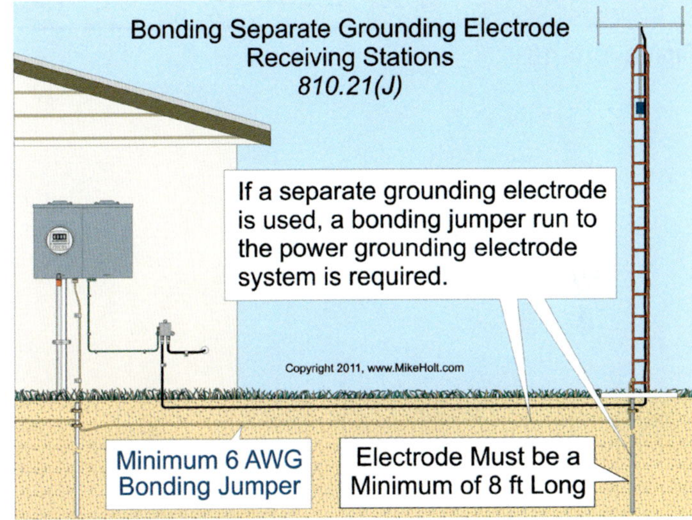

Figure 810–12

(K) Electrode Connection. Termination of the bonding conductor or grounding electrode conductor must be by exothermic welding, listed lugs, listed pressure connectors, or listed clamps. Grounding fittings that are concrete-encased or buried in the earth must be listed for direct burial [250.70]. **Figure 810–13**

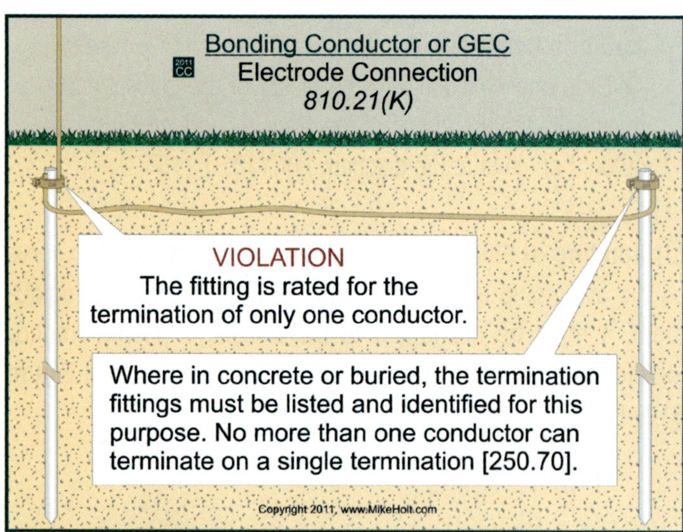

Figure 810–13

PART III. AMATEUR AND CITIZEN BAND TRANSMITTING AND RECEIVING ANTENNA SYSTEMS

810.58 Bonding Conductor or Grounding Electrode Conductors.

(A) Other Sections. The antenna mast [810.15] and antenna discharge unit [810.57] must be grounded as specified in 810.21.

(B) Size of Protective Bonding Conductor or Grounding Electrode Conductor. The bonding conductor or grounding electrode conductor must be the same size as the lead-in conductors, but not smaller than 10 AWG copper, bronze, or copper-clad steel.

(C) Size of Operating Bonding Conductor or Grounding Electrode Conductor. The bonding conductor or grounding electrode conductor for transmitting stations must not be smaller than 14 AWG copper or its equivalent.

Community Antenna Television (CATV) and Radio Distribution Systems

INTRODUCTION TO ARTICLE 820—COMMUNITY ANTENNA TELEVISION (CATV) AND RADIO DISTRIBUTION SYSTEMS

This article focuses on the distribution of television and radio signals within a facility or on a property via cable, rather than their transmission or reception via antenna. These signals are limited energy, but they're high frequency.

- As with Article 800, you must determine the "point of entrance" for these circuits.
- Ground the incoming coaxial cable as close as practicable to the point of entrance.
- If coaxial cables are located above a suspended ceiling, route and support them to allow access via ceiling panel removal.
- Clearances are critical, and Article 820 contains detailed clearance requirements. For example, it requires at least 6 ft of clearance between coaxial cable and lightning conductors.
- If the building or structure has an intersystem bonding termination, the bonding conductor must be connected to it.
- If you use a separate grounding electrode, you must run a bonding jumper to the power grounding system.

Note: The term "Grounding Conductor" previously used in this article has been replaced by either "Bonding Conductor" or "Grounding Electrode Conductor (GEC)" where applicable to more accurately reflect the application and function of the conductor. **Figures 820–1 and 820–2**

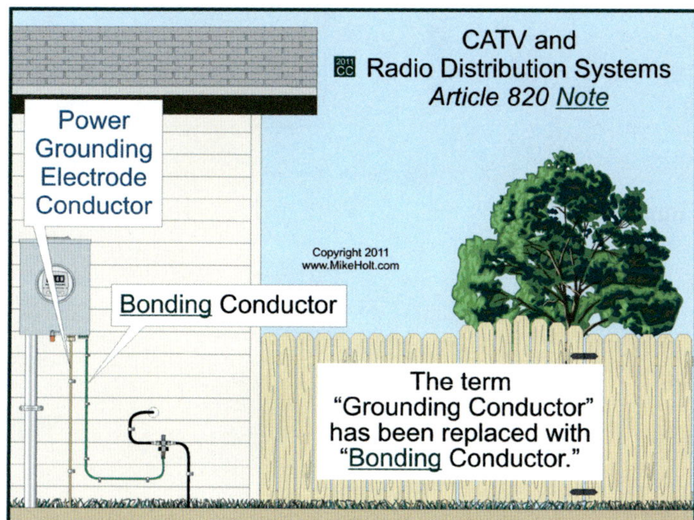

Figure 820–1

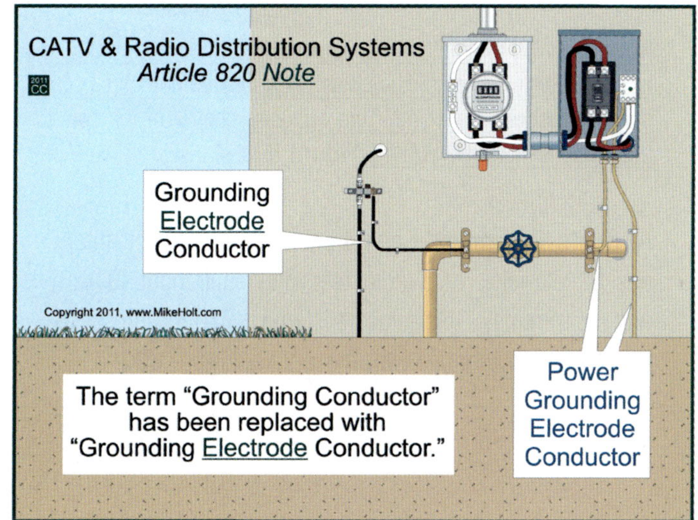

Figure 820–2

Author's Comment: For Articles 800, 810, and 820, the difference between a "bonding conductor" and a "grounding electrode conductor" is where they terminate. The bonding conductor terminates at the intersystem bonding termination; the grounding electrode connects to the power grounding electrode system [250.50].

PART I. GENERAL

820.1 Scope. Article 820 covers the installation of coaxial cables for distributing high-frequency signals typically employed in community antenna television (CATV) systems. **Figure 820–3**

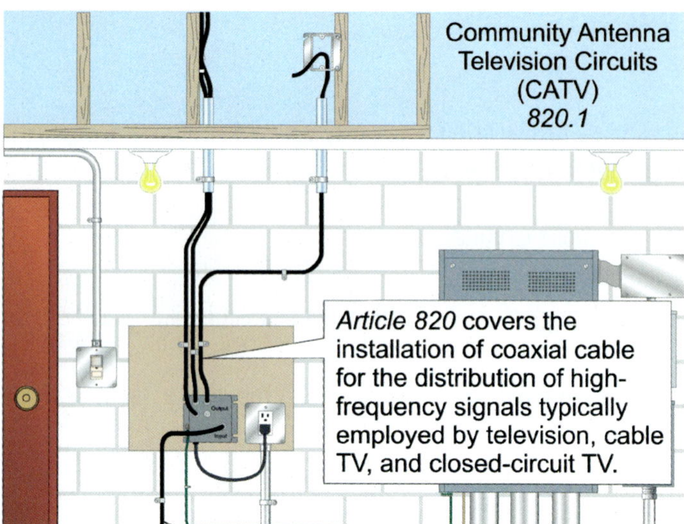

Figure 820–3

Note: The *NEC* installation requirements don't apply to communications utility equipment, such as CATV located outdoors or in building spaces where under the exclusive control of the communications utility [90.2(B)(4)]. **Figure 820–4**

Author's Comment: Coaxial cables that connect antennas to television and radio receiving equipment [810.3] and community television systems [810.4] must be installed in accordance with this article. **Figure 820–5**

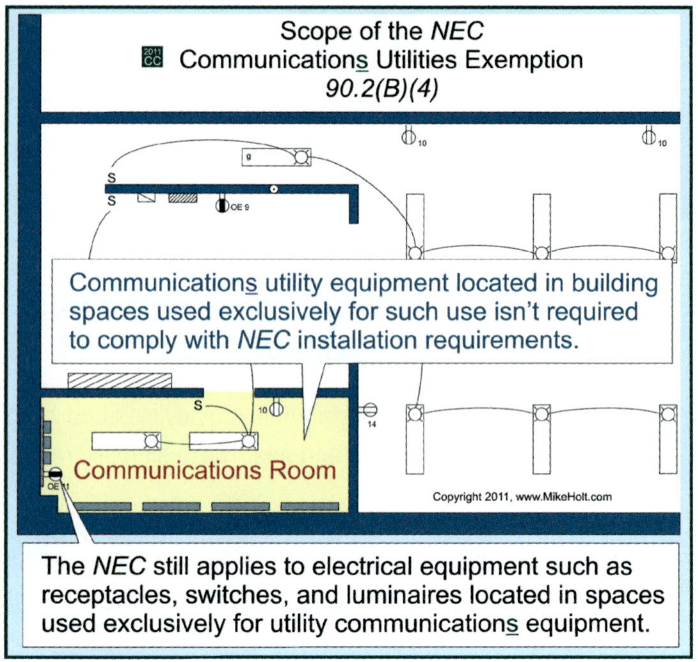

Figure 090–4

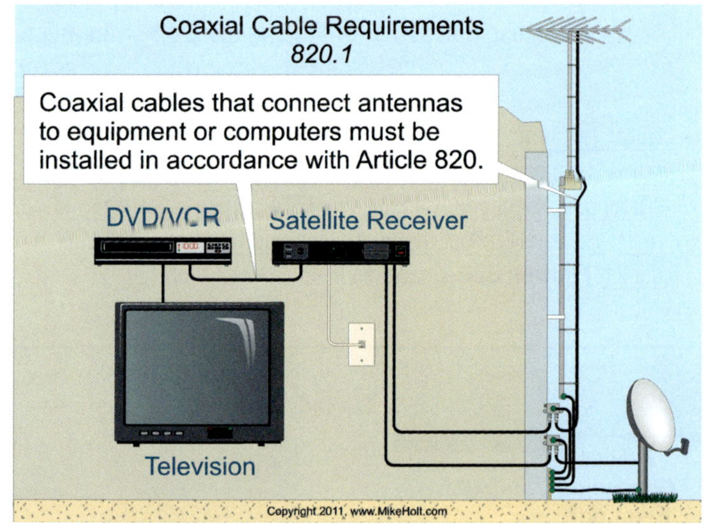

Figure 820–5

PART III. PROTECTION

820.93 Grounding of the Outer Conductive Shield of Coaxial Cables.

(A) Coaxial CATV Cables Entering Building. Coaxial CATV cables entering the building or terminating on the outside of the building must have the metallic sheath members grounded as specified in 820.100. Figure 820–6

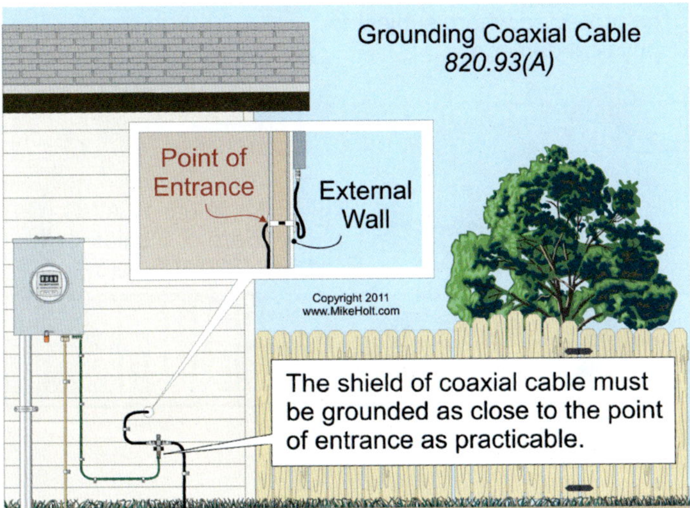

Figure 820–6

Note: Limiting the length of the bonding conductor or grounding electrode conductor helps limit damage to equipment because of a potential (voltage) difference between communications equipment and other systems during lightning events.

PART IV. GROUNDING METHODS

820.100 Cable Bonding and Grounding. The outer conductive shield of a coaxial cable must be bonded or grounded in accordance with the following:

Ex: Coaxial cable confined within the premises and isolated from the outside cable plant can be grounded by a connection to an equipment grounding conductor. Connecting to an equipment grounding conductor through a grounded receptacle using a dedicated grounding conductor and permanently connected listed device is permitted. Use of a cord and plug for the connection to an equipment grounding conductor isn't permitted.

(A) Bonding Conductor or Grounding Electrode Conductor.

(1) Insulation. The bonding conductor or grounding electrode conductor must be listed and be insulated, covered, or bare.

(2) Material. The bonding conductor or grounding electrode conductor must be copper or other corrosion-resistant conductive material, stranded or solid.

(3) Size. The bonding conductor or grounding electrode conductor must not be smaller than 14 AWG with a current-carrying capacity of not less than the grounded metallic sheath member or protected conductor of the communications cable, but not required to be larger than 6 AWG.

(4) Length. The bonding conductor or grounding electrode conductor for CATV systems must be as short as practicable. For one- and two-family dwellings, the bonding conductor or grounding electrode conductor must not exceed 20 ft. Figure 820–7

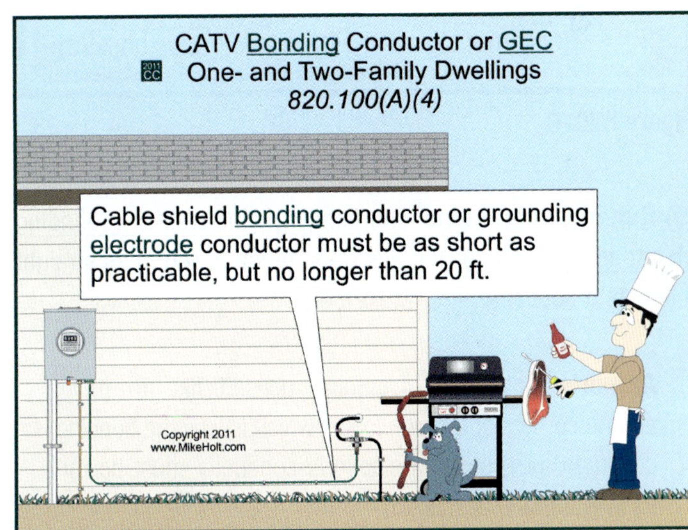

Figure 820–7

Note: Limiting the length of the bonding conductor or grounding electrode conductor will help to reduce potential (voltage) differences between the building's power and CATV systems during lightning events.

Ex: If it's not practicable to limit the coaxial bonding conductor or grounding electrode conductor to 20 ft in length for one- and two-family dwellings, a separate ground rod not less than 8 ft long, with fittings suitable for the application [250.70 and 820.100(C)] must be installed. The additional ground rod must be bonded to the power grounding electrode system with a minimum 6 AWG conductor [820.100(D)]. **Figure 820–8**

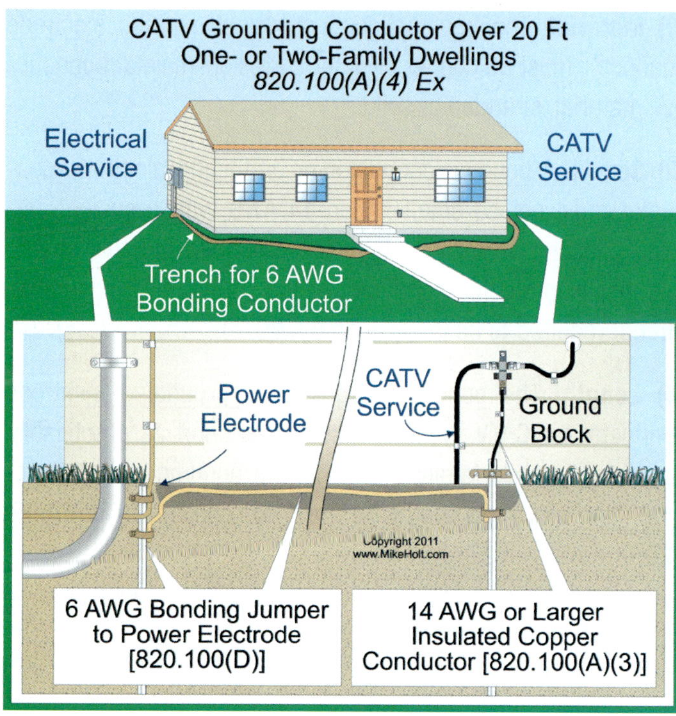

Figure 820–8

(5) Run in Straight Line. The bonding conductor or grounding electrode conductor to the electrode must be run in as straight a line as practicable.

Author's Comment: Lightning doesn't like to travel around corners or through loops, which is why the bonding conductor or grounding electrode conductor must be run as straight as practicable.

(6) Physical Protection. The bonding conductor or grounding electrode conductor must be mechanically protected where subject to physical damage, and where installed in a metal raceway both ends of the raceway must be bonded to the bonding conductor or grounding electrode conductor. **Figure 820–9**

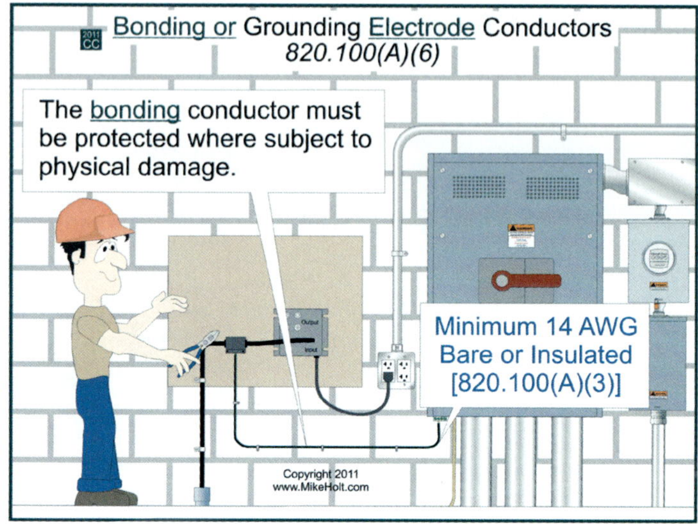

Figure 820–9

Author's Comment: Installing the bonding conductor in PVC conduit is a better practice.

(B) Electrode. The bonding conductor or grounding electrode conductor must be connected in accordance with (B)(1), (B)(2), or (B)(3).

(1) Buildings or Structures with an Intersystem Bonding Termination. The bonding conductor or grounding electrode conductor for the CATV system must terminate to the intersystem bonding termination as required by 250.94. **Figure 820–10**

Note: According to the Article 100 definition, an "Intersystem Bonding Termination" is a device that provides a means to connect bonding conductors for communications systems to the grounding electrode system, in accordance with 250.94. **Figure 820–11**

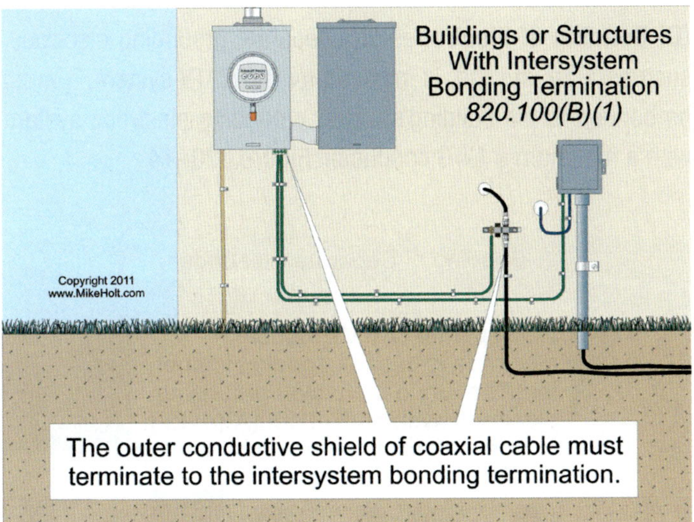

Figure 820–10

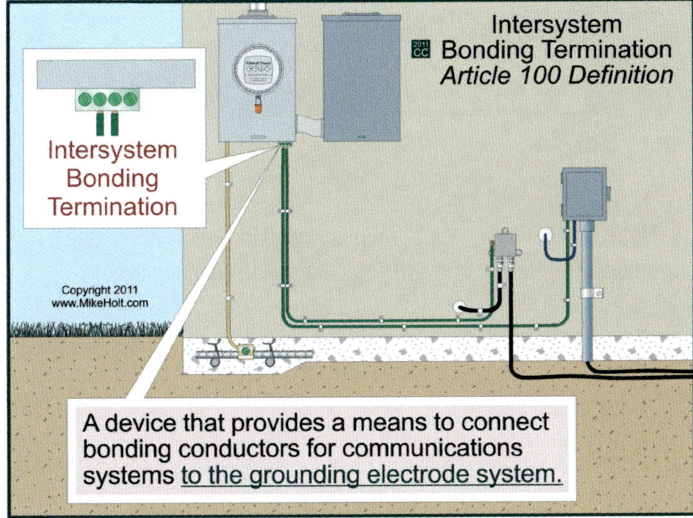

Figure 820–11

Author's Comment: Bonding all systems to the intersystem bonding termination helps reduce induced potential (voltage) differences between the power and the radio and television systems during lightning events.

(2) In Buildings or Structures With a Grounding Means. At existing structures, the bonding conductor or grounding electrode conductor must terminate to the nearest accessible: Figure 820–12

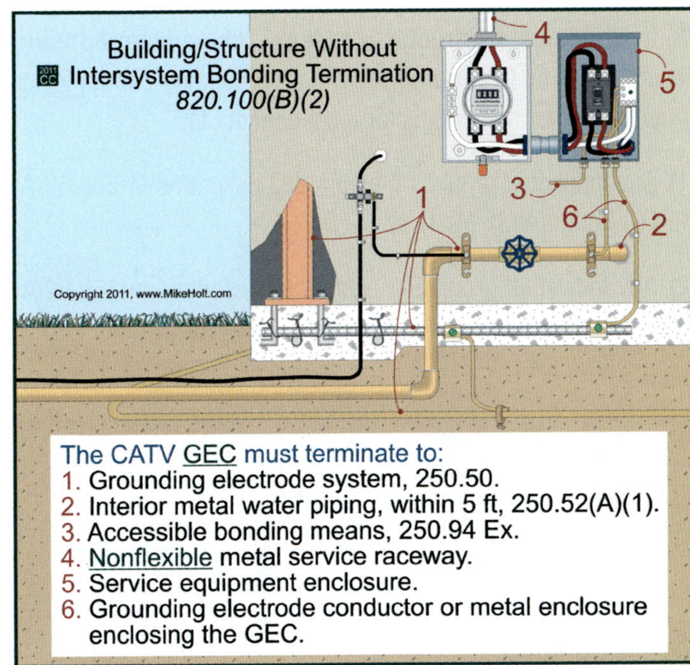

Figure 820–12

(1) Building/structure grounding electrode system [250.50].

(2) Interior metal water piping system, within 5 ft from its point of entrance [250.52(A)(1)].

(3) Accessible means external to the building, as covered in 250.94 Ex.

(4) Nonflexible metallic service raceway of the power service.

(5) Service equipment enclosure.

(6) Grounding electrode conductor or the grounding electrode conductor metal enclosure.

(7) The bonding conductor or grounding electrode conductor or the grounding electrode of a remote building/structure disconnecting means [250.32].

The intersystem bonding termination must be mounted on the fixed part of an enclosure so that it won't interfere with the opening of an enclosure door. A bonding device must not be mounted on a door or cover even if the door or cover is nonremovable.

(3) In Buildings or Structures Without Intersystem Bonding Termination or Grounding Means. The bonding conductor or grounding electrode conductor must connect to:

(1) Any individual grounding electrodes described in 250.52(A)(1), (A)(2), (A)(3), (A)(4), or

(2) Any individual grounding electrodes described in 250.52(A)(5), 250.52(A)(6), and (A)(7). Figure 820–13

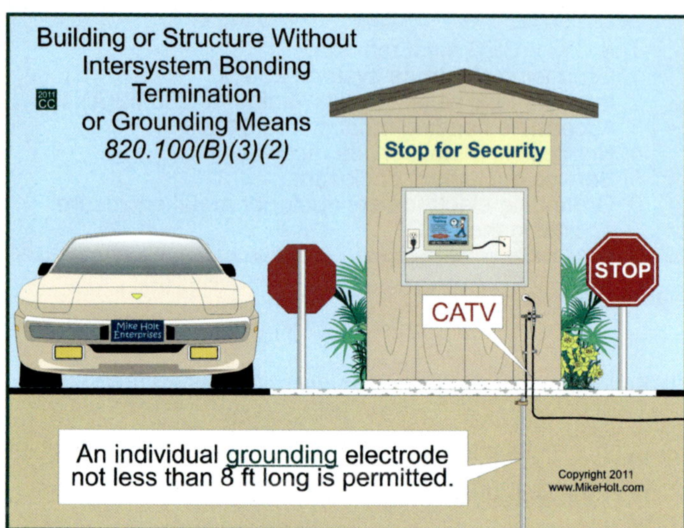

Figure 820–13

(C) Electrode Connection. Terminations to the grounding electrode must be by exothermic welding, listed lugs, listed pressure connectors, or clamps. Grounding fittings that are concrete-encased or buried in the earth must be listed for direct burial [250.70].

(D) Bonding of Electrodes. If a separate grounding electrode, such as a ground rod, is installed for the CATV system, it must be bonded to the building's power grounding electrode system with a minimum 6 AWG conductor. Figure 820–14

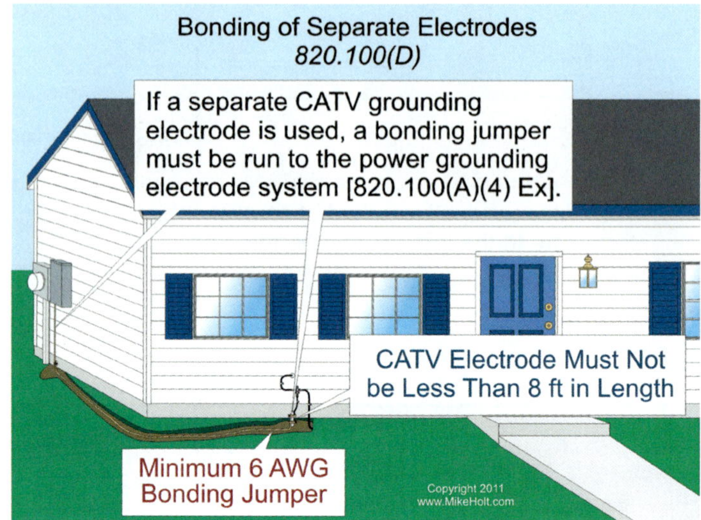

Figure 820–14

Note 2: Bonding helps reduce induced potential (voltage) between the power and CATV system during lightning events.

CHAPTER

8

Practice Questions

CHAPTER 8. COMMUNICATIONS SYSTEMS—PRACTICE QUESTIONS

Article 800. Communications Circuits

1. In one- and two-family dwellings where it is not practicable to achieve an overall maximum primary protector grounding conductor length of 20 ft, a separate ground rod not less than ______ shall be driven and it shall be connected to the power grounding electrode system with a 6 AWG conductor.

   (a) 5 ft
   (b) 8 ft
   (c) 10 ft
   (d) 20 ft

2. Limiting the length of the primary protector grounding conductors for communications circuits helps to reduce voltage between the building's ______ and communications systems during lightning events.

   (a) power
   (b) fire alarm
   (c) lighting
   (d) lightning protection

3. For buildings with grounding means but without an intersystem bonding termination, the grounding conductor for communications circuits shall terminate to the nearest ______.

   (a) building or structure grounding electrode system
   (b) interior metal water piping system, within 5 ft from its point of entrance
   (c) service equipment enclosure
   (d) any of these

4. Communications electrodes must be bonded to the power grounding electrode system using a minimum ______ copper bonding jumper.

   (a) 10 AWG
   (b) 8 AWG
   (c) 6 AWG
   (d) 4 AWG

Article 810. Radio and Television Equipment

1. Article ______ contains the installation requirements for the wiring of television and radio receiving equipment, such as digital satellite receiving equipment for television signals and amateur/citizen band radio equipment antennas.

   (a) 680
   (b) 700
   (c) 810
   (d) 840

2. Each lead-in conductor from an outdoor antenna shall be provided with a listed antenna discharge unit, unless enclosed in a grounded metallic shield.

   (a) True
   (b) False

3. Antenna discharge units shall be located outside the building only.

   (a) True
   (b) False

4. The grounding conductor for an antenna mast shall be ______ protected where subject to physical damage.

   (a) electrically
   (b) mechanically
   (c) arc-fault
   (d) none of these

5. Radio and television receiving antenna systems must have bonding or grounding electrode conductors that are ______.

   (a) copper or other corrosion-resistant conductive material
   (b) insulated, covered, or bare
   (c) securely fastened in place and mechanically protected where subject to physical damage
   (d) all of these

6. The bonding conductor or grounding electrode conductor for a radio/television antenna system must be mechanically protected where subject to physical damage, and where installed in a metal raceway both ends of the raceway must be bonded to the ______ conductor.

   (a) contained
   (b) grounded
   (c) ungrounded
   (d) b or c

7. The grounding conductor for an antenna mast or antenna discharge unit shall be run to the grounding electrode in as straight a line as practicable.

   (a) True
   (b) False

8. If the building or structure served has an intersystem bonding termination, the grounding conductor for an antenna mast shall be connected to the intersystem bonding termination.

   (a) True
   (b) False

9. The grounding conductor for an antenna mast or antenna discharge unit, if copper, shall not be smaller than 10 AWG.

   (a) True
   (b) False

10. If a separate grounding electrode is installed for the radio and television equipment, it shall be bonded to the building's electrical power grounding electrode system with a bonding jumper not smaller than ______ AWG.

   (a) 10
   (b) 8
   (c) 6
   (d) 1/0

Article 820. Community Antenna Television and Radio Distribution Systems

1. Article ______ covers the installation of coaxial cables for distributing high-frequency signals typically employed in community antenna television (CATV) systems.

   (a) 300
   (b) 430
   (c) 800
   (d) 820

2. The outer conductive shield of a CATV coaxial cable entering a building shall be grounded as close to the point of entrance as practicable.

(a) True
(b) False

3. The conductor used to ground the outer cover of a CATV coaxial cable shall be permitted to be ______.

(a) insulated
(b) 14 AWG minimum
(c) bare
(d) all of these

4. In one- and two-family dwellings, the grounding conductor for CATV shall be as short as practicable, not to exceed ______ in length.

(a) 5 ft
(b) 8 ft
(c) 10 ft
(d) 20 ft

5. In one- and two-family dwellings where it is not practicable to achieve an overall maximum grounding conductor length of ______ for CATV, a separate grounding electrode as specified in 250.52(A)(5), (6), or (7) shall be used.

(a) 5 ft
(b) 8 ft
(c) 10 ft
(d) 20 ft

6. Limiting the length of the primary protector grounding conductors for community antenna television and radio systems reduces voltages that may develop between the building's ______ and communications systems during lightning events.

(a) power
(b) fire alarm
(c) lighting
(d) lightning protection

7. The grounding conductor for CATV coaxial cable shall be ______ protected where subject to physical damage.

(a) electrically
(b) arc-fault
(c) physically
(d) none of these

8. A bonding jumper not smaller than ______ copper or equivalent shall be connected between the CATV system's grounding electrode and the power grounding electrode system at the building or structure served where separate electrodes are used.

(a) 12 AWG
(b) 8 AWG
(c) 6 AWG
(d) 4 AWG

Notes

Index

Notes

Save 25% On These Great NEC Programs

when you use discount code DCGB25

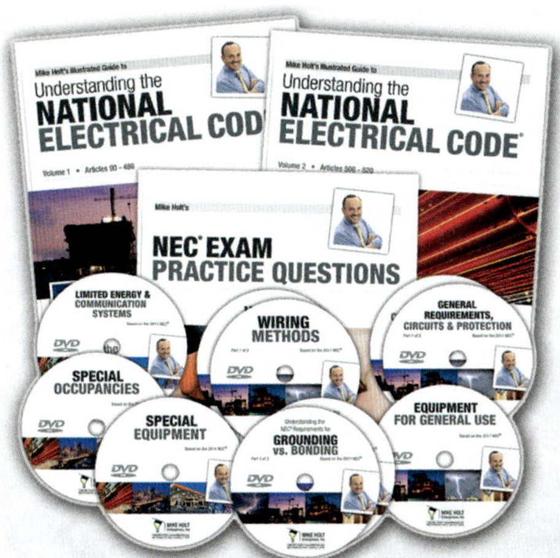

2011 Detailed Code **Library**

The Detailed Code Library includes three textbooks and 10 DVDs
Understanding the NEC Volume 1
Understanding the NEC Volume 2
Practice Questions Book
General Requirements DVD Pt. 1 and Pt. 2
Grounding vs. Bonding DVD
Wiring Methods DVD Pt. 1 and Pt. 2
Equipment for General Use DVD
Special Occupancies DVD
Special Equipment DVD
Limited Energy and Communication Systems DVD
List Price- ~~$569.00~~ $426.75

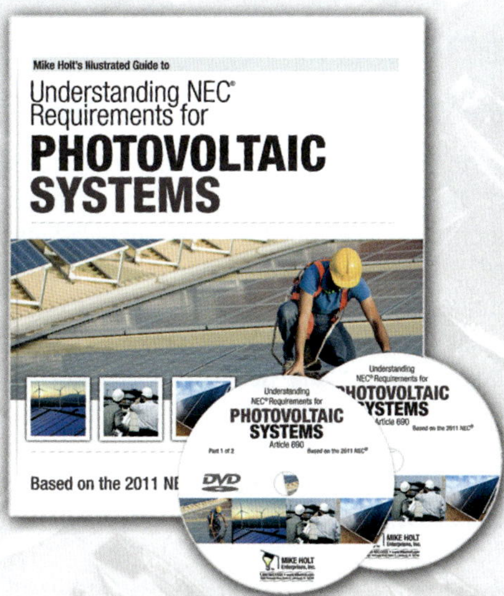

2011 NEC Requirements for **Photovoltaic Systems DVD Program**

Looking for a great way to really understand what the NEC says about Photovoltaic Systems? This DVD program gives you a great overview on the NEC requirements that govern solar installations. You will learn the principles of circuit requirements, disconnecting means, wiring methods, grounding, marking and connection to other sources as they relate to solar power. Mike's dynamic teaching style will help clarify the code rules and the detailed illustrations in the books will make it easy for you to apply what you are learning.

This program includes:
NEC Requirements for Photovoltaic Systems Textbook
NEC Requirements for Photovoltaic Systems DVD Pt. 1 and Pt. 2
List Price- ~~$198.00~~ $148.50

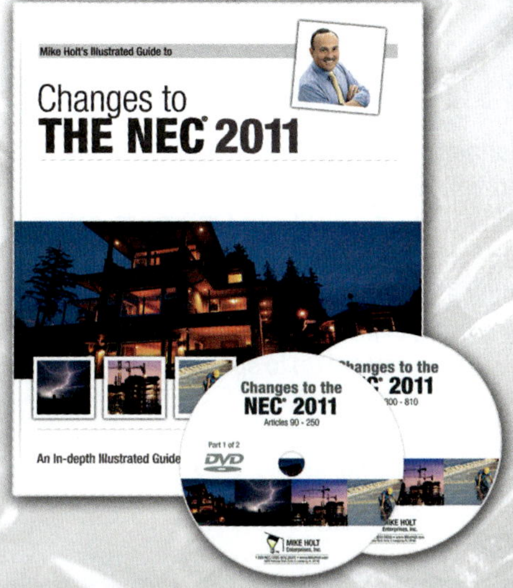

Changes to the **NEC 2011 DVD Program**

Don't let the scale of the changes to the Code intimidate you, this full-color guide and DVD program will walk you through the most essential code changes in an organized and beautifully illustrated format. Author's comments and analysis of the changes help you understand the reason for the change and the proper application of the rule. Mike's team of experts help bring the material to life and really explain the change and how to apply it. This is an excellent package to help you get up to speed on the changes.

This program includes:
Changes to the NEC 2011 Textbook
Changes to the NEC 2011 DVD Part 1 [Articles 90 - 250]
Changes to the NEC 2011 DVD Part 2 [Articles 300 - 840]
List Price- ~~$198.00~~ $148.50

Order Now - Call 888.NEC.CODE (632.2633)